Geographies of Tourism and Gl

C000002320

Series Editors

Dieter K. Müller, Department of Geography, Umeå University, Umeå, Sweden
Jarkko Saarinen, Geography Research Unit, University of Oulu, Oulu, Finland
Carolin Funck, Graduate School of Integrated Arts and Sciences, Higashi-
Hiroshima City, Hiroshima, Japan

In a geographical tradition and using an integrated approach this book series addresses these issues by acknowledging the interrelationship of tourism to wider processes within society and environment. This is done at local, regional, national, and global scales demonstrating links between these scales as well as outcomes of global change for individuals, communities, and societies. Local and regional factors will also be considered as mediators of global change in tourism geographies affecting communities and environments. Thus *Geographies of Tourism and Global Change* applies a truly global perspective highlighting development in different parts of the world and acknowledges tourism as a formative cause for societal and environmental change in an increasingly interconnected world.

The scope of the series is broad and preference will be given to crisp and highly impactful work. Authors and Editors of monographs and edited volumes, from across the globe are welcome to submit proposals. The series insists on a thorough and scholarly perspective, in addition authors are encouraged to consider practical relevance and matters of subject specific importance. All titles are thoroughly reviewed prior to acceptance and publication, ensuring a respectable and high quality collection of publications.

More information about this series at http://www.springer.com/series/15123

Mathis Stock

Editor

Progress in French Tourism Geographies

Inhabiting Touristic Worlds

 Springer

Editor
Mathis Stock
Institute of Geography and Sustainability
University of Lausanne
Lausanne, Switzerland

ISSN 2366-5610   ISSN 2366-5629   (electronic)
Geographies of Tourism and Global Change
ISBN 978-3-030-52138-7   ISBN 978-3-030-52136-3   (eBook)
https://doi.org/10.1007/978-3-030-52136-3

This Springer imprint is published by the registered company Springer Nature Switzerland AG
The registered company address is: Gewerbestrasse 11, 6330 Cham, Switzerland

Contents

List of Figures

List of Tables

Chapter 1
Introduction: A 'French Touch' to Tourism Geography

Mathis Stock

1.1 Introduction

The francophone tourism research community is a lively one, characterised by key concepts, research agendas and research questions, which differ from anglophone research. Nevertheless, language barriers mean this research is not readily available to the general anglophone public. The aim of this collection of essays is therefore to present recent developments in francophone tourism geography. In doing so, we endeavour not only to present specific French tourism geography, but to include more general francophone geographies. In addition to France, francophone research on tourism in Canada, Belgium, Switzerland, the Maghreb and Africa contributes to the growing interest in tourism as a major social phenomenon. Francophone research communities exchange their knowledge on the basis of a specific epistemological culture. They recognise that science is "produced by people with bodies, situated in time, space, culture, and society, and struggling for credibility and authority" (Shapin 2010). Tourism research is therefore organised according to different scientific cultures, which are not only differentiated according to business-orientated and fundamental research or disciplinary boundaries and post-disciplinary processes (Tribe 2010), but also according to language communities with specific scientific cultures that produce specific theoretical worlds. The last point is language-related: French language allows one to play differently with spatial metaphors and connotations.

This specific organisation of knowledge is apparent in francophone tourism geography, in which knowledge circulations are organised according to more heavily guarded disciplinary boundaries than in anglophone geography. Although recently there has been a convergence of sociology, anthropology and geography in respect of tourism, economics is relatively less integrated into geographical analyses of

M. Stock (✉)
Institute of Geography and Sustainability, University of Lausanne, Lausanne, Switzerland
e-mail: mathis.stock@unil.ch

© The Editor(s) (if applicable) and The Author(s), under exclusive license to
Springer Nature Switzerland AG 2021
M. Stock (ed.), *Progress in French Tourism Geographies*, Geographies of
Tourism and Global Change, https://doi.org/10.1007/978-3-030-52136-3_1

tourism (Stock 2020). This relates to francophone geography's specific trajectory, whose problematisations move in different directions than anglophone geography.[1] Specifically, the corollary of the double emergence of a renewed social and cultural geography over the last 20 years and an *économie territoriale* – which can be translated as "place economy" or "territorial economy", close to "regional science" – has been the relative weakening of economic geography.[2] This is apparent in tourism geography, where economical dimensions were strongly in focus throughout the 1970s and 1990s, but from the 2000s onward, the social and cultural dimensions of tourism have been relatively more explored.

Overall, the last 30 years have been the theatre of "turns" and "rethinkings" in social sciences in general and in geography in particular. A long list of turns has gradually been added to the original "linguistic turn" (Rorty) and affect geography: the "interpretive turn" in humanistic geography (Ley 1985), a "spatial turn" (Soja 1989) as a call for a renewed social theory *cum* space; a "cultural turn" (Jameson 1998) for a renewed understanding of symbolic dimensions, a "practice turn" (Schatzki et al. 2001) for insistence on "doing" rather than "representing", a "mobilities turn" (Sheller and Urry 2006) for the understanding of societies as being mobile, and an "emotional turn" (Bondi et al. 2005) as a call for the studies of emotions. Although there is no need to take these rhetoric and performative labels too seriously, the appropriation of these perspectives has been effective in francophone geography. Tourism is currently approached as system with embodied mobile practices, existential and symbolic dimensions, and with specific political and economic dimensions. In francophone geography, the interpretive turn and the cultural turn specifically focussed the problematisation on the sense and signification of tourist practices and places, which are critical for one-dimensional rejections as being *per se* alienating or less legitimate than other forms of travel. Research has heavily invested tourism's symbolic dimensions and imaginations as well as the territorial dimensions in accounts of the touristification of resorts, cities, and regions.[3]

Moreover, what is called "French theory" in anglophone readings, i.e. a post-positivist and post-structuralist position with post-modern stances towards a situated knowledge, also has effects on geography. Yet, this postmodern philosophy and sociology were integrated into geography and tourism geography by means of different routes: on the one hand, "French theory" does not seem "French" to the francophone public. Therefore, relational thinking about place, mobility, tourism, culture, and society has played a key role in recent developments without always explicitly referring to an exotic Other called "French theory". On the other hand, original developments have relied on these theories. For instance, Lévy (1994,

---

[1] See the remarkable volume by Benko and Strohmayer (2004) on commonalities and divergences – available both in English and French – and Clément, Stock and Volvey (2020) for an account of the last 20 years of French geography.

[2] See Colletis-Wahl et al. (2006) for a general account of "territorial economy" and Peyrache-Gadeau (2017) and Talandier (2013) for an approach to tourism economics.

[3] See the French national platform *theses.fr* at http://theses.fr/en/accueil.jsp that lists all French PhD dissertations for the last 30 years. To date there are 280 dissertations on tourism geography.

1999) developed Lefebvre's analysis towards a renewed theory of the urban; Lussault (2007) developed Certeau's analysis towards a practice theory *cum* space; and Foucault's power and discourse analysis was developed towards a relational territoriality (Raffestin 1980). These developments within francophone theoretical geography have been mobilised in francophone tourism geography for the last twenty years.

A very specific aspect points towards tourism as part of a "civilisation process" in the sense of Norbert Elias (2012), *i.e.* a non-random, long-term process towards a relatively more precise control of the environment, the body, and emotions. This historical social science focuses on the embeddedness of individuals in figurations of various shapes and allows for a reconstruction of political organisations' emergence at larger scale levels, whose corollary is the relatively greater individualisation and differentiation of human societies. In this civilisation process, there are moments and places of normalised relaxation in relation to social norms, called "controlled relaxation of self-control" (Elias and Dunning 1986). Tourism has been interpreted as one of the means – together with leisure – that makes this loosening of control over affects and the quest for excitement possible in contemporary societies (Equipe MIT 2002; Stock et al. 2017). In Eliasian terms, tourism can be seen as a "quest for excitement" and "decontrolled controlling of self-control", therefore creating a situation in which specific norms, which differ from everyday life, refer to the tourist body. But tourism is also the "control of violence": as a controlled and pacified confrontation with the Other, tourism can be regarded as a situation and a specific way of producing culture. This has also led to investigations into tourists' learning processes as an apprenticeship of the (self-)control of the tourist body (Coeffé et al. 2019). Tourism as a learning and socialisation process – following Simone de Beauvoir's famous sentence on femininity (*"on ne naît pas femme, on le devient"*), "one is not born but becomes a tourist" – points towards a process-orientated understanding of tourism, which also echoes Löfgren's (1999) point of "learning how to be a tourist". A number of studies adopted this point in order to understand different aspects of these learning and socialisation processes in tourism geography by focussing on a specific aspect of tourism's role in the constitution of an individual in late-modern societies (Equipe MIT 2002; Brougère and Fabbiano 2014; Peyvel 2019).

To sum up, francophone tourism geography benefitted largely from the theoretical advances in social and cultural geography as well as from the social sciences in general, whereas economic geographical approaches to tourism remain scarce. One the one hand, research on consumption patterns, business models, and political economies of place has lost its appeal, which is related to an overall process of the loss of competence in francophone academia's economic geography. On the other, tourism's symbolic dimensions have led to a relational definition of tourism: tourism as a specific relationship to the world, where the combination of recreation and otherness are essential.

1.2 "Touristic Worlds"

The subtitle of this collection of essays contains the expression "touristic worlds". This reflects the eponymic francophone scientific journal *Mondes du tourisme*, set up as an interdisciplinary agenda for tourism based on the idea of articulating the different worlds tourism creates through very different political, economic and cultural actors. This subtitle also mobilises the rarely used adjective "touristic", which, according to the Oxford English Dictionary, has been found in the English language since the 1840s. Dean MacCannell (1999) uses it throughout his book *The tourist*, for instance, in "touristic space" and "touristic desire", perhaps following the French adjective "*touristique*". MacCannell (1999) also explains: "The term touristic names the line dividing the exchange of human notice, on the one side, and commercial exchange on the other. 'Touristic' is the place where those kinds of exchanges meet" (p. 193).

We could theoretically connect this idea of touristic worlds with at least two social sciences and humanities concepts. First, the notion "lifeworld" (*Lebenswelt*) stems from phenomenology and points to the individual worlds that humans inhabit. The philosopher Husserl (1936) developed this notion as a taken-for-granted world and the basis for the relationship with the world. The notion refers to the obvious and the unquestioned foundation of all types of everyday acting and thinking. It constitutes each individual person's only real world (Waldenfels 1984). Defined by Schütz (1973) as the subjective formation of meaning, it focuses on the interpretations and knowledge that people develop of the world. In geography, it has been key in analyses of spatialities, i.e. the subjective significations of places, distances, and limits, used, for instance, in phenomenological geography. In tourism analysis, attention is paid to individual interpretations of otherness, activities, sights, attractions, etc. It provides an understanding of which activities are interpreted as "touristic", and which are interpreted as "everyday" life, and how tourist activities and places make sense for specific practice communities, cultures, and social classes. Imaginations are key to understand the highly differentiated worldmakings and ideologies (*Weltanschauung*) that people enact in their daily life. In a broader sense, there is a connexion to the idea of "being-in-the-world" (Heidegger), with *Dasein* constituting subjectivities as individual worlds: inhabiting therefore denotes the control of the sense of the individual place in, and connecting, to the world. In geography, the different significations of inhabiting these subjective worlds connect concrete spatialities to imaginations and emotions.

Nevertheless, the worlds that humans create are not only based on subjectivities, but also on commonalities. These are related, and there is a strong argument to regard the individual and the social as two sides of the same coin and not to approach them as two separate universes (Elias 2012). They are just two different ways of approaching human societies, two different dimensions, differentiated for the sake of scientific analysis. Related to the lifeworld's subjectivities, the "social worlds" notion translates different organisations and orders of significations as well as the symbolic systems and practices that make sense for specific communities (Strauss

1978). Social worlds are universes of discourse (Mead 1938) and generate shared perspectives, which also inform collective identities. Place-based communities create numerous worlds, but practice communities on various scales also do so: worlds of music, art, sports, work, leisure, and religion point towards a very differentiated engagement with the world that humans develop. Some worlds imply very strongly shared commitments to certain activities and the sharing of resources and ideologies (Strauss 1978; Becker 1982). Each of these various worlds develop different relations with tourism, therefore allowing for an understanding of why different destinations, attractions or experiences are meaningful to them, but also of why the same destinations and attractions are assigned different meanings and experienced differently. For instance, in the world of kayaking, paragliding and rock climbing, specific destinations are selected as emblematic places, which would have no meaning for other worlds (see Chap. 4 by Valérian Geffroy in this book). Moreover, specific cultural worlds interpret destinations in specific ways. Interestingly, specific destinations are meaningful for several worlds, which therefore develop global centralities (see Chap. 13 by Philippe Violier in this book).

Moreover, Schütz (1973) distinguished between four different types of worlds with which humans are confronted: (1) the world of the immediate environment (*Umwelt*) designated as immediate temporal and spatial coexistence, (2) the world of contemporaries (*Mitwelt*), as humans coexisting without immediate contact, (3) the world of predecessors (*Vorwelt*) as the bygone world, only reachable as memory and (4) the world of successors (*Nachwelt*) as the one that comes after us, only representable as the future. He also distinguished between the subjective, the social and the physical worlds that humans make sense of. In geography, Werlen (1993, 1996) examined the implications of this approach in detail, developing it in the direction of the "practice of worlding" (*Praxis der Welt-Bindung*) as geographical relations with, and appropriations of, different worlds. This approach went beyond mere symbolic elements, also investigating how, in different situations, people are related *practically* to the world by mobilising space. It is interesting to observe that contemporary worlds are constructed via social media, allowing a geographical approach to tourism worlds, because they are constituted via technologies (see Chap. 5 by Morgane Müller-Roux in this book). Moreover, since each social world constructs its specific social space, emblematic places and the production of spatial differentiation refer to specific geographical imaginations. Individuals potentially change position and status when moving from one social world (family, work, tourism, etc.) to another. Mobility can therefore be understood as a change of both geographical *and* social place, and as movement between places seen as adequate and meaningful by individual actors.

Hollinshead's (2009) notion of "worldmaking", which constructs dominant imaginaries of a place, mirrors the above idea. With this ability to produce realities, tourism has a worldmaking power, an ability to produce realities (Hollinshead et al. 2009). Hollinshead bases his work on Nelson Goodman's concept of the world as different symbolic systems, allowing us to understand the multiplicity of social and individual worlds that humans inhabit. Similar to the phenomenological philosophy discussed above, this idea regards humans as constituting sets of activities that make sense in a specific world, but would be strange in a different world. As such, tourism seems to be one of the most powerful forms of contemporary worldmaking, as specific interpretations of the world where common worlds are produced. Moreover, as urbanising force, they create also "urban touristic worlds" (Duhamel and Knafou 2007).

Tourism constructs indeed specific worlds that differ from other forms of worldmaking. Tourism is seen as a specific contrasting world, contrary to the ordinary everyday world. Several attributes have been used to designate this specific tourism world: a "concrete utopia" or "heterotopia" (Foucault 1984), an "anti-world" (*Gegenwelt*) (Hennig 1999), a "liminal space" (Shields 1991) or an "elsewhereland" (Löfgren 1999). All refer to a specific space-time where interpretations follow the logics of recreation associated with otherness as enchantment. Although these imagined places as "other" by tourists can also be approached as "common" places for geographers and residents, imaginations of enchantment are key when analysing these tourism worlds. Specifically, geographical imaginations are relatively more mobilised than in other social worlds: places constructed as paradise, wilderness, romantic, traditional, modern, magic, mythical, etc. constitute the basis of tourism worlds. Imaginations and imaginaries have long been a specific interest in francophone geography, with specific theoretical borrowings (Amirou 2012; Graburn and Gravari-Barbas 2012). Especially, the distinction of "imaginary" (*imaginaire*) and "imagination", a distinction proposed by Jean-Paul Sartre in order to distinguish the content from the process of symbolisations, has been useful. Materialities also contribute to the constitution of specific worlds, allowing for a material and immaterial assemblage. The processes of tourism worlds' constitution seem to be key for understanding the variety of contemporary tourisms. Indeed, there is no tourism world as such, but a highly differentiated plurality of tourism worlds based on imaginations and practices, where the quest for "enchantment" is essential (Winkin 2001).

These worlds are inhabited by humans who move between places, cross borders and practice places. Consequently, there is a strong link between the concept of dwelling and the concept of worlding (see Chap. 2 by Mathis Stock in this book). In line with phenomenological geography, the "existential" nature of tourism practice has been recognised as a source of individual transformation and tourism practice involves the individual, particularly through confrontation with otherness (Equipe MIT 2002; Ceriani et al. 2005). Rather than a futile and trivial, or even alienating, practice, tourism can be assigned an existential dimension when coupling with the idea of inhabiting. Following norms or engaging resistance against norms, using technological systems, taking advantage of the status as tourist and engaging their social, economic, cultural and spatial capital, individuals inhabit movement and places. The distinctive element is the change of place, through which tourists transform temporarily into a Other and change their spatial and social position. Since it is an embodied practice, bodily engagement and adaptation modify with the change of social and spatial contexts. The desire of identification with the locals – exploited by AirBnb through the marketing slogan "living like a local" – leads to a mimicking of cultural practices and practices of appropriating place. Since tourists are practically related to these worlds, they develop skills and knowledge about tourist spaces in order to cope with the specific issues that the tourism worlds requires from its practitioners (see Chap. 3 by Léopold Lucas in this book).

These worlds are peopled with myths. Tourism is one of the essential systems that develop contemporary myths. Since the interpretive turn (Ley 1985), geography has understood that it is not geographical places as such, but the meaning of geographical places that is central to understanding the constitution of the World and the different social worlds. Geographical myths are therefore studied throughout geography, and a geographical approach to tourism captures one of the fundamental myths – tourist places as "other" places (*heterotopias*). The investigation of these geographical myths of tourism is now well established, and current work emphasises the plurality of the meanings assigned to tourist places according to different interests and relationships to them (Pott 2007; Coëffé 2010). Research on tourism imaginations and mythologies (Chadefaud 1988) as well as on placemaking seen as the "invention" of tourist places (Knafou 1991) has been key in this endeavour. In francophone geography, the term "*haut-lieu*" is used to highlight a place's specific symbolic importance, which could be translated into English as a symbolic or an emblematic place. Mont-Blanc and Chamonix as emblematic places for alpinism (Debarbieux 1993; Mao 2007); the Nepalese Himalaya as an emblematic place for trekking (Sacareau 2009), and the hiking itineraries of Ile de la Réunion (Germanaz 2013) all exemplify a specific way of the spatializing of tourism worlds. In this book, the two chapters on heritage (Chaps. 6 and 7) can be read as an analysis of a specific myth-making, i.e. specific materialities interpreted as heritage and therefore relate to the tourism world.

In the contemporary context, the tourism world has been subjected to globalisation in the sense of the emergence of shared place imaginaries. Some of the most visited attractions are truly global in the sense that people from all over the world come to visit them (see Chap. 13). Moreover, some of tourism's stereotypes have also been globalised, which Löfgren (1999) points out for the example of the beach, using the term "global beach". Within this global tourism field, stakeholders construct different tourism worlds by means of market segmentations. Is the tourism world congruent with the ecumene, the Earth's inhabited space? If we adopt the tourism perspective as a code, as a means of interpreting the world, it is astonishing to observe this tourism code's generalisation over the last 200 years by means of globalisation (Equipe MIT 2011). An extension of the touristic code to potentially every single geographical place and practice – a "touristic ecumene" (Equipe MIT 2011) – has occurred. This occurrence mirrors MacCannell's (1999) saying that "anything is potentially an attraction". When the tourism code is activated, elements are seen as attractions, thus constructing a tourism world, a symbolic and material scene that recognises the powers and constraints of such a world. Tourism seems to be a particularly powerful code and world today, especially regarding its power to transform people and places.

We could add another dimension with epistemological implications: science creates theoretical worlds by imagining metaphors, narratives and concepts in a scientific situation. Geographical imaginations differ from sociological imaginations or economical imaginations. In geography, narratives on "placemaking", "ecumene", "spatial restructuring", "time-space compression", "location", "bordering", "regionalisation", "territory", "spatial organisation", "spatiality", etc. have shaped these theoretical worlds. They do not form a uniform or universal knowledge, but are differentiated by their cultural and language communities. This differentiation is, for instance, apparent through the differentiated use of "place" and "territory" in francophone and anglophone geography, but also through their different ways of structuring thought process and academic publications. The latter is probably one of the reasons – besides the foreign language issue, which could be seen as nearly solved due to computer-assisted translator tools such as *Google translate* or *DeepL* – why we have difficulties with integrating different epistemic cultures into our work. Different scientific cultures have been developing within geography, each with its own codes. Moreover, individuals develop specific "epistemological styles", each with their own theoretical worlds, which are often incommensurable with other theoretical worlds. In this perspective, "tourism worlds" could also refer to the different worlds geographers create in their theorisations of tourism. This book could also be read as a specific theoretical worldmaking that francophone geographers propose in respect of tourism.

1.3 Geohistorical Approaches to Tourism

The historical contextualisation of tourism has been a significant element within francophone geography. A *geohistory* of tourism, which allows a more adequate understanding of the tourism's restructuring since the beginning of the nineteenth century, has been systematically suggested. "Geohistory" is a term historian Fernand Braudel popularised and which French geography is increasingly utilising. While classical "historical geography" is preoccupied with geographical problems of the past, "geohistory" is more concerned with the spatial dimensions of long-term social and spatial processes (Grataloup 2013). Such an approach has been used as a joint analysis of temporal and spatial dimensions of tourism at local and global scales (Equipe MIT 2005, 2011). These contributions systematically identify the historical moments and geographical places of tourism innovations, such as the invention of British seaside resorts as an assemblage of various traditions around the 1780s, the emergence of the summer season of a traditional winter destination (the Mediterranean Sea) in the 1920s by Americans residing in Paris, the invention of winter sports in the Swiss Alps in the 1870s. This approach focusses the investigation on a cultural geohistory of tourism by tying the spatial and temporal elements together in order to understand the moments when the practices of place change irremediably, thus affecting the economic system and the very place identity. Since other actors and places mimicked these emblematic places, the emergence of multiple similar types of tourist places can be reconstructed. A geohistory of tourism allows therefore for an understanding of the dynamic emerging of new tourist practices and their imitations.

A geohistorical approach to tourism has also been applied to the analysis of historically existent tourism systems: the emergence of modern tourism around 1800 and the invention of the first tourism system around the 1830s, which was industrialised from the 1870s to 1914; the mass tourism system in the USA from the 1920s onward, in Europe from the 1950s and the contemporary mass tourism (Equipe MIT 2011). This can be tied to globalisation, which has, more recently, interested historians as a "global history" approach. Although tourism has been neglected in the analysis of the globalisation processes of the social, cultural, political and economic realms, it can be understood as a geohistorical process of expanding culture and capitalism (Gay and Decroly 2018). Tourism globalisation is regarded as a historical process with several accelerations and decelerations (Antonescu and Stock 2014), leading to ongoing forms of circulations (Sacareau et al. 2015). The reconstruction of tourism globalisation therefore begins at the end of eighteenth century as a geohistorical process centred on the UK and Continental Europe's seaside resorts, cities and mountains, before expanding to the rest of Europe and the USA. Tourism to South America spas already developed in the 1850s, as it did to Californian seaside resorts. Britain and France's colonial systems rapidly expanded tourism to their respective spheres of domination: the Indian and the Indochina *hill stations* being cases in point. Between the 1870s and 1914, a globalisation wave intensifies this movement, which was halted between 1914 and 1945, a period that favoured national tourism practices. From the 1950s onwards, tourism's globalisation resumed at an unprecedented scale (see Chap. 13 by Philippe Violier in this book).

This geohistorical approach is also used in what is classically labelled "regional geography", also called "*géographie des territoires*" (the geography of "places") in contemporary francophone geography. "Regional geography" refers to the analysis of *singular* places with respect to their spatial structures and representations. Historical processes and territorial dynamics are therefore important (see Chap. 6 by Dominic Lapointe in this book). Geographical research has concentrated so strongly on the French Alps that it is impossible to give an account of the sheer mass of contributions here.[4] For instance, the national parks movement is regarded as a tourism development in the Alps with conflicts between preservation and development. Regional development in the Alpine regions has also attracted attention (Dissart et al. 2015). A tourism transition has been observed, interpreted as a "post-tourism" movement, with seasonalities between the mountains and seaside reversed since 1860 (Bourdeau 2009; Vlès 2014). Research on the historical development of the beach as a tourist destination (Duhamel and Talandier 2015) and the reworking of centralities and peripheries of destinations (Bernard et al. 2017) has been undertaken, for instance, in Tahiti through the development of tourism (Blondy 2016). The emergence of domestic tourism in Vietnam and its link with colonialism (Peyvel 2011) as well as the development of tourist practices in China (Taunay (2019) have also been in the geohistorical approach's focus.

---

[4] The *Journal of Alpine Geography* (https://journals.openedition.org/rga/index.html) is now a bilingual journal with many publications relating to tourism issues.

More specifically, resort development is approached as a historically significant process, with tourism only being one of the issues. Resort development has been interpreted as a change of place qualities, with *variable trajectories* over time (Equipe MIT 2002, 2011). This means that resorts should not be identified as resorts once and for ever, but that they change their geographical qualities over time. They evolve, for instance, into cities or into other territorial forms, such as residential suburbs of urban agglomerations or second home communities. This attention to a place's changing qualities over time is an answer to the limitations of traditional models of resort development: the latter imply resorts can decline or redevelop or undergo restructuring, but underestimate the possibility of changing towards something else than a resort (see Chap. 12 in this book). One of the achievements of geohistorical resort analyses is to analyse their changing place qualities and a whole body of literature has been developing on this issue (Equipe MIT 2011; Vlès 2014; Vlès and Bouneau 2016). For instance, Brighton & Hove provides an interesting case study of the specific ways a resort transforms itself into a city (Stock 2001). Another possibility is the transformation of resorts into "leisure communities" where properties are exchanged without any market coordination (Equipe MIT 2002). Whole urban agglomerations, such as the Côte d'Azur or South California, but also cities, such as Brighton, Atlantic City, etc., rely on their early tourism urbanisations as resorts. Mullins (1991) and Soane (1993) already provided cases in point, although tourism today is just one, sometimes minor, element of these agglomerations. The key to this understanding is to see tourism as one activity of a given place and not to identify the geographical place as only a tourist *destination*. Although resorts can decline from a tourism point of view and exit the general tourism field, they can reconnect with other activity fields (see Chap. 12).

Over the last 150 years, there have certainly been examples of relatively stable resorts, and this remarkable stability needs to be explained, given that tourism is a highly volatile activity dependent on fast-changing fashions, preferences and innovations: new attractions (skiing, snowboarding, heritage, etc.) challenge nineteenth century attractions and sights (cascades, glaciers, caves, etc.) (Bourdeau 2009). The tourism worlds change over time and resorts dependent on one series of worldmakings and interpretations can decline rather quickly and need to reinvent themselves. Despite this flow of emerging and declining resorts, destinations' stability over a long period of time also needs to be questioned and to be approached from a geohistorical perspective.

Finally, the quest to find answers to questions on why certain resorts experience relatively more intense urbanisation processes than others has resulted in ongoing research since the 2000s. Similarly, the problem of the linkage of urbanisation and touristification has been a constant issue in French tourism geographies during this time (see Chap. 11 in this book). Historically, tourist resorts can be regarded as emerging urban nodes transforming rural places into places of touristic urbanity, which is interpreted as a "transfer of urbanity" or a "transfer of centrality" (Equipe MIT 2002) from metropolises to seaside and mountain resorts. This interpretation could be connected to Lefebvre's (1970) urban theory, which states the city's explosion leads to an urbanisation of the mountains and seaside via the leisure industry.

This tourism-led urbanisation can be interpreted as an element of planetary urbanisation, as discussed in Lefebvre (1970) and, more recently, in Brenner and Schmid (2011). The reconstruction of the linkage or synergies between touristification and urbanisation processes since the 1800's are therefore at stake (Stock and Lucas 2012).

1.4   To Which Extent Tourism could change Theoretical Geography?

How tourism as a scientific object and a perspective relates to general or theoretical geography? This question would necessitate a reconstruction of the history of francophone tourism geography, which is not the purpose here.[5] Several indications of a distinct relationship between tourism and the discipline of geography have become apparent over the last 20 years. Despite the adoption of a post-modern stance of situated knowledge, the link with conceptualisation has not weakened. There has been an ongoing reflection on the positioning of the research object "tourism" within geography. We compare two statements in order to understand the change in French tourism geography over the last 70 years. According to Guichonnet (1951, p. 359), "through the multiplicity of phenomena that it combines, tourism geography appears to be one of the newest and most suggestive *branches* of human geography" (my translation and emphasis). At that time, the invention of a specific "tourism geography" was at stake just as a distinctive "industrial geography", "rural geography" and "urban geography", in order to create legitimate sub-disciplines, each with their own commissions and theories, and relatively independent and closed to one another. In contrast, Knafou et al. (1997) state: "Today, this 'geographical approach to tourism' aims to use the concepts and methods of geography to study tourism and, at the same time, to use a better knowledge of the functioning of tourism activity and tourist places to advance geography in general and the analysis of the transformation of places in particular". This means a geographical approach to tourism is open to other disciplines and to the different branches of geography. Moreover, tourism is no longer a self-contained object, but also a *perspective* that other cognitive projects can use: it means thinking of social problems *through* tourism, not only just thinking of tourism. Tourism geography is therefore seen as contributing to general or theoretical geography, and not only as an application of general geographical models. For instance, a theory of place transformation or a theory of spatiality could make use of concepts generated around tourism issues.

Furthermore, tourism includes original phenomena that challenge or pose problems for traditional geographical models and forms of theorising. For instance, from the viewpoint of a sedentarist geographical tradition, which emphasises on work

---

[5]The first accounts of tourism in francophone geography go back to the 1930s just as we find in British, US-American and German geography. See Lazzarotti (2003), Ceriani et al. (2008), Morisset, Sarrasin and Ethier (2012) and Stock et al. (2017) for historical contextualisations.

and routines, tourism is about mobility, play, deroutinising activities, etc. We could therefore ask the following question: "Can geography be integrated into such a phenomenon, erect it as its own object and treat it *without calling itself into question* (…)?" (Lazzarotti 2003, p. 262, my translation and emphasis). This question forces us to reflect on how the analysis of the tourism phenomenon can affect geography's classical conceptual frameworks. The challenge is therefore not to apply classical geographical concepts to tourism problems, but to critically assess their limitations. Consequently, there is a dialogue between theoretical geography and tourism-related analyses, which implies also thinking about models, concepts and theories in geography. Since geography means analysing the "geographicity" or "geographicality" (*géographicité*) of human societies, the question is raised how one can think *geographically* about human societies *through* tourism.

Several examples of this dialogue between theoretical geography and tourism as scientific problem can be put forward. First, centrality is one of the essential concepts in geography, because it refers to a place's polarisation processes in relation to other geographical places. It expresses the capture of resources, capital and relatively more important population than in peripheral areas. Classically, tourist sites are considered peripheral places (Christaller 1964). However, tourist places can also be developing centralities, because tourists choose, within a global tourism field, certain resorts with relatively more symbolic capital than others. As a relational concept, centrality might allow for a renewed understanding of tourist places' power. Tourism therefore addresses new questions to the theory of central places about what centrality means (Bernard et al. 2017). Specifically, global centralities – classically restricted to "global cities" – are also emerging outside cities, such as globally renowned surf spots (Tehahoupoo, Biarritz, Hawaii, etc.) and seaside and mountain resorts (St. Tropez, Zermatt, St. Moritz, etc.), which is incompatible with classical theory. An alternative theory of centrality could build on globally renowned tourist places, temporarily inhabited by tourists and therefore corresponding to a specific tourism world.

Secondly, mobility is part of the originality of tourism in relation to other geographical problems. As Cazes (1992, p. 127) points out from the point of view of economic geography, "it has been noted on several occasions that the profound originality of the tourism phenomenon lies in the movement of consumers towards the product to be consumed, i.e. in a completely reversed trade flow compared to other economic sectors" (my translation). Tourist mobility therefore poses problems for traditional geographical models, because the economies of place are so-called "visitor economies", where temporarily present consumers are the key element (*économies présentielles*). Moreover, the tourist is considered to be a fundamentally mobile person, exemplifying individuals in mobile societies practicing places considered as out of the ordinary. This vision of mobility as practice contrasts with the idea of tourism as a "flow", which has been central to the spatial analysis paradigm since the 1960s. This renewed consideration of mobility is the element that has most transformed geographers' study of tourism over the past 20 years. This shift is in fact accompanied by a profound change in the social sciences since the 1990s, which have become relatively more aware of the significance of spatial mobility issues in all societal phenomena. This "mobilities turn" in the social sciences or the "new mobilities paradigm" (Urry and Sheller 2006) go hand in hand with the creation of new scientific journals, manuals and scientific events on this issue. Nevertheless, tourism is not seen as mere mobility, but also a practice of tourist places. The "mooring" metaphor (Berthelot and Hirschhorn 1996; Hannam et al. 2006; Debarbieux 2014) represents these moments of sojourn in an otherwise mobile world. For theoretical geography, there is the chance to address the inhabitant not only as immobile, but as strategically coping with mobility and immobility. The recently developed research on multilocality is one of developments that captures the dialectics of movement and stillness.

Tourism can also be connected to *urban theory*. Urban theory traditionally emphasises the quality and evolution of cities, as distinguished from rural places. Urban geography has left urban forms and processes other than that of the city relatively untouched, although there has recently been a discussion on "planetary urbanisation" (Schmid and Brenner 2011). Through tourism, we can challenge some of urban geography's classic models and conceptualisations. Firstly, there is the recognition that the city is not the only type of urban place: through the transfer of urbanity, tourist resorts are constituted as specific urban places, created for urbanites who inhabit touristically. Their urbanity differs from that of cities in the sense that it is a mono-functional instead of a poly-functional and seasonal urbanity. It is possible to reconstruct the specific "touristic urbanity" of such places (Coëffé 2010). Secondly, tourism also allows for a reflection on the urbanisation processes of geographical places. The concept "urbanisation" is traditionally used to frame the accumulation and concentration of population and activities in cities. From the tourism perspective, this concept designates the emergence and development of urbanity. Lefebvre (1970) already mentioned the urbanisation of the mountains and the seaside through what he called the "leisure industry". Moreover, a relational and process-orientated thinking allows for an approach of progressive urbanisation of resorts: urban issues such as densification, diversification, emergence of centrality can be observed. This can radically transform a former "touristic urbanity". Finally, the city itself has been the place of a "recreational turn" (Stock 2007), with touristification processes taking place (Gravari-Barbas 1998; Gravari-Barbas and Guinand 2017). Thinking of urbanity through tourism has therefore become an important issue that francophone tourism geography has been pursuing.

Finally, otherness is traditionally associated with issues of exclusion and racism, since a relationship with otherness is perceived as intolerable and politically problematic. Otherness perceived as problematic is found in classic models of residential choice, particularly in the (US-)American context, with the emergence of gated communities or, at least, relatively homogeneous residential neighbourhoods from a cultural, economic or social point of view. The exclusion of the Other as an interpretative device has been key in theoretical geography, and the tension between identity and otherness is important in social science at least since the reflections on the "Stranger" by Simmel, Schütz, Levinas etc.. In contrast, tourism involves a *desire* of otherness in all its forms, albeit in a controlled manner, which challenges traditional geographic models. As discussions on "orientalism" (Saïd 1978) and "staged authenticity" (MacCannell 1999) show, otherness is a specific construction both embodied by "tourates" and imagined by "tourists", with specific imaginaries constructing the difference between an "us" and a "them". Sexual otherness, landscape otherness, food otherness, cultural otherness, etc. contribute to this geography of otherness within a tourism world. Heavily criticized within a post-colonial geography because of persisting power relations, otherness is nevertheless constructed as a desire and enchantment in the tourism world. A controlled yet desired otherness challenges the classic question of the Other, for it transforms the Stranger into a legitimate temporary inhabitant of given places.

To sum up, tourism geography plays a specific role in theoretical geography by suggesting the figure of the tourist, conceived as a mobile, situated, skilled, and reflexive inhabitant. The question of inhabiting tourism worlds seems to be a timely approach to the late-modern individual in its geographic dimensions, and fosters research in many different domains. The key concept of inhabiting allows the question of mobility and the question of the appropriation of places to be combined. Hence, the subtitle of this book is: "inhabiting touristic worlds".

1.5 Problematizing Tourism with a 'French Touch'

This collection of essays problematizes tourism in a specific way. The first four chapters deal with questions of tourist practices and mobility. Chapter 2 (Mathis Stock) makes the notion of inhabiting explicit as an important current francophone geography and positions it as central element for studying tourism. The term "inhabiting" has been developed as a key concept in francophone tourism geography and is currently pervasively used in French theoretical geography. It is utilised to interpret the mobile tourist not as a mere stranger, but as a person who engages with the tourist place, albeit temporarily, in order to uncover symbolic and material appropriation processes. Different issues, such as over-tourism, and the difference between leisure, tourism and mobility, can be interpreted through this lens. Chapter 3 (Léopold Lucas) emphasises the different ways tourists inhabit the city by engaging certain competences and knowledge in order to cope with unfamiliar spaces. He studies the different ways tourists depend on knowledge in a case study of Los Angeles by observing tourists' mobilities in the city. Chapter 4 (Valérian Geffroy) deals with tourist practices based on sports activities and mediated by digital technologies. The technologically mediated worldmakings are apparent in a specific practice, outdoor sports. Chapter 5 (Morgane Roux) focuses on the technological dimensions of tourist practices as "equipped" practice: digital technologies raise the issue of disconnection and the distinction between home and away – seen as the very foundation of tourism theory –, as well as the use of social media to create touristic worlds of nature. The study of Banff National Park allows a highly differentiated understanding of social media's effects on performing tourist practices as well as the issues of a tourism world's disconnection from a connected everyday world.

The next four chapters deal with questions of tourist places, especially under the heading of the French expression "*territoire*". Dominic Lapointe (Chap. 6) develops the notion of "touristic territory" in order to analyse tourism development's contemporary processes. Framed differently in francophone geography, "territory" is a key concept in tourism geography, but there is a translation issue between the French and the English word. "*Territoire*" does not correspond exactly to the English "territory", due to its different connotations and conceptual developments. It is used for denoting appropriated space within social geography, but also controlled space in political geography (Lévy 2013). It is used very often in local development projects and can also be epistemologically regarded as replacing the former "regional geography". These elements are exemplified in the account Saïd Boujrouf, Ayoub El Ouarti, Fatima El Khadali, Saïd Abbanay, Nada Baki, Carmen Romera and Veronica Blanco provide (Chap. 7) of heritage processes and touristification processes in the High Atlas, in Morocco, which lead to conflicts about resources. The notion of the "commons" allows for a reflection on tourist resources and the role of tourism in territorial projects. Chapter 8 (Maria Gravari-Barbas and Sébastien Jacquot) examines heritage and tourism from the viewpoints of different forms of engagement and in order to demonstrate heritage's relational character. Tourism contributes to the multiple definitions and redefinitions of heritage through various narratives and forms of actions, which the authors term "concernment". Chapter 9 (Mosè Cometta) mobilises discourse methodology to raise the question of over-tourism in Ticino, where institutions change their management of tourism in a specific Swiss canton over time. This chapter therefore provides a critical appraisal of neoliberalism in the tourism sector. Chapter 10 (Clément Marie dit Chirot) presents an argument in favour of materialist approaches to tourism, and proposes a political economy of place through a Lefebvrian approach. Tourist space is regarded as contradictory, but integrated into the capitalist production of space, especially through the production of scarcity, and the main characteristics. This approach allows for the understanding of power asymmetries and conflicts in the production of tourist space.

The three last chapters deal with urbanisation processes embedded in globalisation by means of a geohistorical approach. Chapter 11 (Vincent Coëffé and Mathis Stock) examines the issue of "urban tourism" as not solely related to cities. In order to show that tourism is genuinely an urban question, it insists on tourism's very urban dimension, because tourism transfers urban values to each location and practice. The chapter differentiates between the touristification of cities and the urbanisation of resorts as two distinct processes of tourism's "double urban revolution". Approaching tourists as urbanites and tourism as part of the urban revolution allow a rethink of tourism's urban issues. Chapter 12 (Mathis Stock, Olivier Crevoisier, Christophe Clivaz, and Leïla Kebir) take on the classic question of resort development and question their uneven development. In the course of the last 200 years, specific types of resorts have experienced constant innovation and tourism over time, whereas others have only experienced this for short periods. In order to understand these differences, the chapter develops the concept of a "touristic capital" of resorts, which act with differentiated power in the global tourism field. Philippe Violier reconstructs this ever-changing global field in Chap. 13. He approaches the economic and cultural change in tourism as several "revolutions" stretching from the beginning of the nineteenth century to the beginning of the twenty-first century. One of the dynamics is the never-ending conception and implementation of new tourist attractions, which lie at the heart of this history of tourism globalisation. Capitalist development fostered a gradual diffusion of tourist places over time and space to form a current global field of tourist places. The contemporary period is seen as the "third" tourism revolution, after the two previous revolutions: the invention of tourism around 1800 and the emerging of mass tourism from the 1920s onward.

All in all, these chapters present a "French touch" to tourism geography; I hope this volume will be a stepping stone that will allow for new articulations between different scientific cultures in the future.

References

Amirou, R. (2012). *L'imaginaire touristique*. Paris: CNRS Editions.

Antonescu, A., & Stock, M. (2014). Reconstruction of the globalisation of tourism. *Annals of Tourism Research, 45*(1), 77–88. https://doi.org/10.1016/j.annals.2013.12.001.

Becker, H. (1982). *Art worlds*. Berkeley: University of California Press.

Benko, G., & Strohmayer, U. (2004). *Horizons géographiques*. Paris: Bréal.

Bernard, N., Blondy, C., & Duhamel, P. (Eds.). (2017). *Tourisme entre marginalité et périphéries*. Rennes: PUR.

Berthelot, J.-M., & Hirschhorn, M. (Eds.). (1996). *Mobilités et Ancrages. Vers un nouveau mode de spatialisation*. Paris: L'Harmattan.

Blondy, C. (2016). Le tourisme, un facteur de développement durable des territoires insulaires tropicaux ? Tourisme, aménagement, environnement et société locale à Bora Bora (Polynésie française). *Mondes du Tourisme* (online) https://doi.org/10.4000/tourisme.1283.

Bondi, L., Davidson, J., & Smith, M. (2005). Introduction: Geography's emotional turn. In L. Bondi, J. Davidson, & M. Smith (Eds.), *Emotional geographies* (pp. 1–16). London: Ashgate.

Bourdeau, Ph. (2009). From après-ski to après-tourism: The Alps in transition? *Journal of Alpine Research* [online], 97(3), https://doi.org/10.4000/rga.1054.

Brougère, G. & Fabbiano, G. (ed.). (2014). Apprentissages en situation touristique, Villeneuve-d'Ascq: Presses universitaires du Septentrion.

Cazes, G. (1992). *Fondements pour une géographie du tourisme et des loisirs*. Paris: Bréal.

Ceriani, G., Duhamel, P., Knafou, R., & Stock, M. (2005). Le tourisme et la rencontre de l'autre, L'Autre. *Cliniques, cultures et sociétés*, 63–71.

Ceriani-Sebregondi, G., Chapuis, A., Gay, J. C., Knafou, R., Stock, M., & Violier, P. (2008). Quel serait l'objet d'une science du tourisme? *Téoros*, 27(1), 7–13. http://journals.openedition.org/teoros/1629.

Chadefaud, M. (1988). *Aux origines du tourisme dans les pays de l'Adour : du mythe à l'espace : un essai de géographie historique*. University of Pau: University Press.

Christaller, W. (1964). Some considerations of tourism location in Europe: The peripheral regions underdevelopped countries recreation areas. *Papers of the Regional Science Association, 12*, 95–105. https://doi.org/10.1007/BF01941243.

Clément, V., Stock, M., & Volvey, A. (Eds.). (2020). *Mouvements de géographie*. Rennes: PUR. in press.

Coëffé, V. (2010). Le tourisme, fabrique d'urbanité. Matériaux pour une théorie de l'urbain, *Mondes du Tourisme* n°2, p. 57–69.

Coëffé, V., Guibert, Ch. & Taunay, B. (2019). Usages sociaux et spatialités du bronzage en Chine, *EspacesTemps.net* [online] https://www.espacestemps.net/articles/usages-sociaux-et-spatial-ites-du-bronzage-en-chine/; https://doi.org/10.26151/espacestemps.net-9468-vg57

Colletis-Wahl, K., Corpataux, J., Crevoisier, O., Kebir, L., Pecqueur, B, & Peyrache-Gadeau, V. (2006). The *territorial economy*: A general approach in order to understand and deal with globalization. *Networks, Governance and Economic Development*. Edward Elgar Publishing, 21–29.

Debarbieux, B. (1993). Du haut lieu en général et du mont Blanc en particulier. *Espace géographique, 22*(1), 5–13. https://doi.org/10.3406/spgeo.1993.3123.

Debarbieux, B. (2014). Enracinement – Ancrage – Amarrage: raviver les métaphores. *L'Espace géographique* 2014/1 (Tome 43), p. 68–80.

Dissart, J.C., Dehez, J., Marsat, J.B. (ed.) (2015). *Tourism, recreation and regional development*. London: Routledge https://doi.org/10.4324/9781315550695.

Duhamel, P., & Knafou, R. (Eds.). (2007). *Mondes urbains du tourisme*. Paris: Belin.

Duhamel, P., Talandier, M., & Toulier, B. (Eds.). (2015). *Le balnéaire. De la Manche au monde*. Rennes: PUR.

Elias, N. (2012). *What is sociology?* Dublin, University College Dublin Press (1st ed. 1970).

Elias, N., & Dunning, E. (1986). *Quest for excitement. Sport and leisure in the civilising process*. Oxford: Blackwell.

Équipe, M. I. T. (2002). *Tourismes 1. Lieux communs*. Paris: Belin.

Équipe, M. I. T. (2005). *Tourismes 2. Moments de lieux*. Paris: Belin.

Équipe, M. I. T. (2011). *Tourismes 3. La révolution durable*. Paris: Belin.

Foucault, M. (1984). *Dits et écrits*. Paris: Gallimard.

Gay, J.-C., & Decroly, J.-M. (2018). Les logiques de la diffusion du tourisme dans le Monde: une approche géohistorique. *L'Espace géographique, 47*(2), 102–120.

Germanaz, C. (2013). Le haut lieu touristique comme objet spatial linéaire: le somin Volcan (île de La Réunion). Fabrication, banalisation et patrimonialisation. *Cahiers de géographie du Québec, 57*(162), 379–405. https://doi.org/10.7202/1026525ar.

Grataloup, C. (2013). Géohistoire. In J. Lévy & M. Lussault (Eds.), *Dictionnaire de la géographie et de l'espace des sociétés*. Paris: Belin.

Gravari-Barbas, M. (1998). Belle, propre, festive et sécurisante: l'esthétique de la ville touristique. *Norois, 178*, 175–193. https://doi.org/10.3406/noroi.1998.6863.

Gravari-Barbas, M. & Graburn, N. (2012). Tourist imaginaries, *Via* [online], http://journals.openedition.org/viatourism/1180

Gravari-Barbas, M. & Guinand, S. (éd.). (2017). Tourism and gentrification in contemporary metropolises. International perspectives. London: Taylor and Francis.

Guichonnet, P. (1951). The tourist season of summer 1950 in the Mont Blanc Massif. *Revue de géographie alpine, 39*(2), 357–380.

Hannam, K., Sheller, M., & Urry, J. (2006). Editorial. Mobilities, immobilities and moorings. *Mobilities, 1*, 1–22.

Hennig, C. (1999). *Reiselust*. Frankfurt: Suhrkamp.

Hollinshead, K. (2009). The "Worldmaking" prodigy of tourism: The reach and power of tourism in the dynamics of change and transformation. *Tourism Analysis, 14*(1), 139–152.

Hollinshead, K., Ateljevic, I., & Ali, N. (2009). Worldmaking agency–Worldmaking authority: The sovereign constitutive role of tourism. *Tourism Geographies, 11*(4), 427–443.

Husserl, E. (1976). *Die Krisis der europäischen Wissenschaften*, Den Haag [1st edition 1936].

Jameson, F. (1998). *The cultural turn. Selected writings on the postmodern. 1983–1998*. London: Verso.

Knafou, R. (1991). L'invention du lieu touristique: la passation d'un contrat et le surgissement simultané d'un nouveau territoire. *Revue de géographie alpine, 79*(4), 11–19.

Knafou, R., Bruston, M., Deprest, F., Duhamel, P., Gay, J.-C., & Sacareau, I. (1997). Une approche géographique du tourisme. *L'Espace géographique, 26*(3), 193–204.

Lazzarotti, O. (2003). Tourisme et géographie: le grand dérangement. In M. Stock (Ed.), *Le tourisme: acteurs, lieux et enjeux* (pp. 255–277). Paris: Belin.

Lefebvre, H. (1970). *La révolution urbaine*. Paris: Anthropos.

Lévy, J. (1994). *L'espace légitime*. Paris: Presses de Sciences Po.

Lévy, J. (1999). *Le tournant géographique. Penser l'espace pour lire le monde*. Paris: Belin.

Lévy, J. (2013). Territoire. In J. Lévy & M. Lussault (Eds.), *Dictionnaire de la géographie et de l'espace des sociétés*. Paris: Belin.

Ley, D. (1985). Cultural/humanistic geography. *Progress in Human Geography, 9*, 415–423.

Löfgren, O. (1999). On holiday. In *A history of vacationing*. Berkeley: University of California Press.

Lussault, M. (2007). *L'Homme spatial*. Paris: Seuil.

MacCannell, D. (1999). *The tourist: A new theory of the leisure class*. New York: Schocken Books (1st edition 1976).

Mao, P. (2007). La ressource territoriale d'un haut-lieu touristique, l'exemple de Chamonix Mont-Blanc. In H. Gumuchian & B. Pecqueur (Eds.), *La Ressource territoriale* (pp. 66–77). Paris: Economica.

Mead, G. H. (1972). *The philosophy of the Act*. Chicago: University of Chicago Press (1st ed. 1938).

Morisset, L., Sarrasin, B., & Ethier, S. (Eds.). (2012). *Épistémologie des études touristiques*. PUQ: Québec.

Mullins, P. (1991). Tourism urbanization. *International Journal of urban and regional reasearch, 15*(3), 326–342.

Peyrache-Gadeau, V. (2017). Innovation in sustainable tourism projects in Alpine resorts. In L. Kebir, O. Crevoisier, P. Costa, & V. Peyrache-Gadeau (Eds.), *Sustainable innovation and regional development: Rethinking innovative milieus*. Northampton: Edward Elgar Publishing.

Peyvel, E. (2011). Visiting Indochina, the imaginary of the French colonial period in today's touristic Việt Nam. *Journal of Tourism and Cultural Change, 9*(3), 226–236. https://doi.org/10.108 0/14766825.2011.620121.

Peyvel, E. (éd.) (2019). L'éducation au voyage : pratiques touristiques et circulations des savoirs, Rennes: Presses universitaires de Rennes.

Pott, A. (2007). Orte des Tourismus. In *Eine raum- und gesellschaftstheoretische Untersuchung*. Bielefeld: Transcript.

Raffestin, C. (2019). *Pour une géographie du pouvoir* (1st edition 1980.). Lyon: ENS Éditions https://books.openedition.org/enseditions/7627; https://doi.org/10.4000/books.enseditions.7627.

Sacareau, I. (2009). Évolution des politiques environnementales et tourisme de montagne au Népal. *Journal of Alpine Research* [online], 97, 3, URL: http://journals.openedition.org/rga/1018; https://doi.org/10.4000/rga.1018.

Sacareau, I., Taunay, B., & Peyvel, E. (Eds.). (2015). *La mondialisation du tourisme. Les nouvelles frontières d'une pratique*. Rennes: Presses Universitaires de Rennes.

Said, W. E. (1978). *Orientalism*. New York: Pantheon Books.

Schatzki, T. R., Knorr-Cetina, K., & Von Savigny, E. (2001). *The practice turn in contemporary theory*. London/New York: Routledge.

Schmid, C. & Brenner, N. (2011). Planetary urbanization, M. GANDY (dir.), *Urban constellations* (pp. 10–13). Berlin: Jovis Verlag.

Schütz, A. (1973). *Der sinnhafte Aufbau der sozialen Welt*. Frankfurt: Suhrkamp.

Shapin, S. (2010). *Never pure: Historical studies of science as if it was produced by people with bodies, situated in time, space, culture, and society, and struggling for credibility and authority*. Baltimore: Johns Hopkins University Press.

Sheller, M., & Urry, J. (2006). The new mobilities paradigm. *Environment and Planning A, 38*(2), 207–226.

Shields, R. (1991). *Places on the margin. Alternative geographies of modernity*. London: Routledge.

Soane, J. (1993). *Fashionable resort regions. Their evolution and transformation with particular reference to Bournemouth, Nice, Los Angeles and Wiesbaden*. Wallingford: CABI.

Soja, E. (1989). *Postmodern geographies: The reassertion of space in social theory*. London: Verso.

Stock, M. (2001). Brighton and Hove, station touristique ou ville touristique? *Géocarrefour-Revue Géographique de Lyon, 76*(2), 127–131.

Stock, M. (2007). European cities: Towards a recreational turn?, *Hagar. Studies in Culture, Polity and Identities, 7*(1), 115–134.

Stock, M. (2020). Penser géographiquement avec et par le tourisme. In V. Clément, M. Stock, & A. Volvey (Eds.), *Mouvements de géographie*. PUR: Rennes. in press.

Stock, M., & Lucas, L. (2012). La double révolution urbaine du tourisme. *Espaces & Sociétés, 151*, 15–30.

Stock, M., Coëffé, V., & Violier, P. (2017). *Les enjeux contemporains du tourisme : une approche géographique*. Rennes: Presses Universitaires de Rennes.

Strauss, A. (1978). A social world perspective. In N. Denzin (Ed.), *Studies in symbolic interaction* (pp. 119–128). Greenwich: JAI Press.

Talandier, M. (2013). Redéfinir l'enjeu de l'économie présentielle et le rôle des femmes dans les économies locales. *Journal of Alpine Research* [online], *101*, 1. https://doi.org/10.4000/rga.2028

Taunay, B. (2019). Geohistorical analysis of coastal tourism in China (1841–2017). In I. Yeoman & U. McMahon-Beattie (Eds.), *The future past of tourism: Historical perspectives and future evolutions* (pp. 78–90). Bristol: Blue Ridge Summit. https://doi.org/10.21832/9781845417086-010.

Tribe, J. (2010). Tribes, territories and networks in the tourism academy. *Annals of Tourism Research, 37*(1), 7–33.

Vlès, V. (2014). *Metastations, mutations urbaines des stations de montagne*. Bordeaux: Presses Universitaires de Bordeaux.

Vlès, V., & Bouneau, C. (Eds.). (2016). *Stations en tension*. Bruxelles: Peter Lang.

Waldenfels, B. (1984). *In den Netzen der Lebenswelt*. Frankfurt: Suhrkamp.

Werlen, B. (1993). *Society, action and space: An alternative human geography*. London: Routledge.

Werlen, B. (1996). Geographie globalisierter Lebenswelten. *Österreichische Zeitschrift für Soziologie, 21*(2), 97–128.

Winkin Y. (2001), Le touriste et son double, in Yves Winkin, *Anthropologie de la communication*, Paris/Bruxelles: De Boeck Université, pp. 206–224.

Mathis Stock is a professor with the Institute of Geography and Sustainability at Lausanne University (Switzerland), where he leads the research group "Cultures and Natures of Tourism". His research deals with the urbanising force of tourism, the controversies around tourism in cities, and mobility and multilocality approached from the perspective of practice theory. He dialogues with social theory and develops a theory of dwelling, posited at the heart of theoretical geography. He is editor-in-chief of the scientific journal *Mondes du tourisme*.

Chapter 2
Inhabiting as Key Concept for a Theory of Tourism?

Mathis Stock

2.1 Introduction

In French theoretical geography, there has recently been a movement towards the engagement with, and the definition of, the very classic geographical concept of "inhabiting" or "dwelling" (*habiter*). These notions began a trajectory that broadened their meaning and, instead of focusing on the immobile, the sedentary, the attachment to one place in terms of belonging and proximity, now puts the relationship to multiple places into the focus. This also includes mobile lifestyles to be understood as specific forms of inhabiting the world. A very sustained editorial activity can be noted: several books (Berque 1996; Lévy 2004; Paquot et al. 2007; Frelat-Kahn and Lazzarotti 2012; Morel-Brochet and Ortar 2012), thematic journal issues (Travaux de l'Institut de Géographie de Reims 2004; Annales de Géographie 2015; Mondes du tourisme 2018), monographs (Lazzarotti 2006; Besse 2013), articles (Hoyaux 2002; Hoyaux 2015), dissertations.[1] The term has even found a place in the dictionary of geography as "spatiality of individual actors" (Lévy and Lussault 2003, my translation), and later, "process of reciprocal adjustment between spaces and spatialities" (Lévy and Lussault 2013a, b, my translation) as well as in the *Sage Handbook of Human Geography* (Lévy 2014).

The notion has therefore gained in significance and constitutes a specific development of French-speaking geography whereas in English-speaking scientific culture the term "dwelling" remains confined to humanistic geography, more precisely a phenomenological geography (see Seamon and Mugerauer 1985). As Seamon (1980,

---

[1] See the national platform for doctoral dissertations http://theses.fr/en/accueil.jsp for contributions on "habiter" in French social science.

M. Stock (✉)
Institute of Geography and Sustainability, University of Lausanne, Lausanne, Switzerland
e-mail: mathis.stock@unil.ch

© The Editor(s) (if applicable) and The Author(s), under exclusive license to
Springer Nature Switzerland AG 2021
M. Stock (ed.), *Progress in French Tourism Geographies*, Geographies of
Tourism and Global Change, https://doi.org/10.1007/978-3-030-52136-3_2

148) points out, "A phenomenological geography [...] directs its attention to the essential nature of man's dwelling on earth. [...] A phenomenological geography asks the significance of people's inescapable immersion in a geographical world". In French-speaking geography, "dwelling" and inhabiting designates not only dwelling on Earth as phenomenological problem of familiar place-making and proximity, but is more and more used as a concept framing practices as problem of norms, capital, capacities, inequalities, technological equipment, where distance, location, limits, places and networks are seen as problems to solve, constraints to overcome or resources to use in the daily life (Stock 2015). The concept "inhabiting" thus aims at unpacking the "everyday geographies" – what Werlen (1996) terms "practice of worlding" (*Praxis der Weltbindung*) –, the multiple spatial dimensions of the life-world, including tourism.

It is interesting to acknowledge that part of this development has its roots in tourism geography – with Knafou et al. (1997) defining tourism as "mode of inhabiting" (*mode d'habiter*) –, allowing for the quite rare moment in the history of geography where tourism geography has something to offer to theoretical geography. This very traditional concept has also been mobilised in order to approach mobility. In sociology and anthropology, the attempt of the association between dwelling and mobility can be acknowledged: through the idea of "Dwelling-in-traveling" (Clifford 1992), inhabiting of movement is considered, yet the multi-locality of contemporary social life is not problematized. When Urry (2000) states, "contemporary form of dwelling almost always involve diverse forms of mobility" (Urry 2000, 133), the link between mobility and issues of dwelling is established. The expressions "inhabiting the car" and "inhabiting the road" (Urry 2006), "dwelling-in-motion" (Hannam et al. 2006) go in the same direction and search for a renewed understanding of the way mobile societies inhabit places and movements. The relationship between mobility and inhabiting is therefore posited as issue for social sciences. Three elements seem at stake: a thorough critique of traditional theories of dwelling, the development of a theory of mobility as problem of dwelling and, finally, an understanding of contemporary forms of dwelling as dependent of mobility (Stock 2007).

This chapter aims at evaluating to which extent the notion of inhabiting could be a key element of a theory of tourism. A first issue seems to be the conceptualisation of inhabiting, because it has been applied to immobile beings-in-the-world. Therefore, it has to be evaluated to which extent it makes sense to transfer it to tourist practices. In this text, the concept of 'dwelling' is used as overall category, related to phenomenological theory, whereas the concepts of inhabiting and inhabitants will allow for the description of various forms of engaging with spatiality.[2] It extends the notion of dwelling to all kinds of meaningful relationships to place and pleads for a differentiated vocabulary. A second point will delve into the idea of tourism as a specific "mode of inhabiting": it unpacks both the implications of practising place as a tourist and develops the idea of the tourist as temporary inhabitant.

---

[2] This corresponds to the distinction in French between the verb "*habiter*" and the noun "*l'habiter*". The latter could be translated as "dwelling" and the former as "to inhabit".

A third point will contextualise the tourist practices within overall mobilities as "dwelling styles". The final will address some of the issues the mobilisation of the term inhabiting can tackle.

2.2 Issues of Traditional Theories of Dwelling from the Point of View of Mobility and Multi-locality

There is still a need for critically assess traditional theories of dwelling, a task which has not been conducted yet in geography or in the other social sciences. The latter rely still without much criticism on Heidegger's phenomenological philosophy who brought the concept of dwelling into the discussion. Heidegger develops a critique of functional thinking and a means of putting spatiality in the centre of thought. He defines it as "the ways the mortals are on the Earth" (2004a, 142), as "fundamental trait of the human Dasein" (2004b, 183): "The relation of man to places and through places to spaces is based on dwelling. The relationship between man and space is nothing other than dwelling conceived as essential" (Heidegger 2004a, 152) (my translation).[3] Dwelling means therefore a relational spatiality. The question of the spatiality of the inhabited world is clarified by Heidegger as the problem of "proximity" and "de-distanciation" (*Ent-fernung*). In doing so, he modifies the functionalist assumption of a crisis of dwellings – we need housing in order to inhabit – into an existentialist reading: we dwell on Earth by creating places and therefore the issue of housing, planning and construction arises. In geography, this led to questions of "geographicality" or "geographicity" ("*géographicité*") (Dardel 1952), authenticity and insideness (Relph 1976) as well as familiarity of places, belonging and attachment (Tuan 1977). There have been attempts to approach tourism as dwelling within a narrow Heideggerian conception, for instance as creating proximity (Pons-Obrador 2003). It acknowledges the symbolic appropriation of place by tourists, the constitution of familiarity and insideness by tourists and the inclusion of place as meaningful for tourists.

Another tradition in phenomenological philosophy can be noted. Merleau-Ponty's (1945, 162) development of the bodily engagement makes the connection with inhabiting: "We should not say that our body is *in* space, nor, for that matter, that it is *in* time. It *inhabits* space and time" (my translation).[4] This formulation allows for an understanding of a relational space, where the body's spatiality rather than an absolute space, separated from the body, is imagined. Recently, this specific idea of dwelling as bodily engagement with the environment is developed by Ingold (2000), and as a description of inhabiting as a tourist by Palme (2018) and Prince

---

[3] "*die Weise, wie die Sterblichen auf der Erde sind*" (2004a, 142); "*Grundzug des menschlichen Daseins*" (2004b, 183); "*Bezug der Menschen zu Orten und durch Orte zu Räumen*" (2004a, 152). „*Der Bezug des Menschen zu Orten und durch Orte zu Räumen beruht im Wohnen. Das Verhältnis von Mensch und Raum ist nichts anderes als das wesentlich gedachte Wohnen*"(ibid., 152).

[4] "Il ne faut donc pas dire que notre corps est *dans* l'espace ni d'ailleurs qu'il est dans le temps. Il *habite* l'espace et le temps".

(2018). It allows for an approach, where inhabiting is not only seen as a problem of imagining specific worlds, but also the bodily engagement and the sensations and emotions attached to practices. When describing surfing, philosopher Gilles Deleuze once coined it as "inhabiting the waves".

However, these approaches are called into question by the increased spatial mobility and multilocality as central characteristics of late modern societies. For urban, mobile and digital societies develop specific forms of dwelling, there is a need to submit to thorough criticism the classic work on dwelling, and not to take it for granted. Conceptualising "dwelling" only as proximity and familiarity leads to the exclusion of mobile lifestyles where routinized confrontation with otherness is key. Mobile social life necessitates a renewed understanding of dwelling under late-modern conditions. For humans inhabit not only one place, which determines their spatiality, but many different places are inhabited by "geographically plural individuals" (Stock 2006). As Rolshoven (2007, 181) puts it: "Multilocality means *vita activa* in several places: the active everyday life in its entirety is distributed over different places that are visited for longer or shorter periods of time and used for smaller or greater functional division" (my translation).[5] As Stock (2006, 10) puts it: "what we can call 'poly-topic dwelling' as opposed to 'mono-topic dwelling' is characterized by the search for adequacy between places and practices. This means that for each project, for each stage of life, individuals tend to choose the appropriate place by adopting migratory or circulatory strategies" (my translation).[6] Therefore, there is a need to develop a concept of "dwelling" that is not only based on inhabiting *one* place, but is able to represent all the places and mobilities practiced by mobile individuals. That is why I suggest the use of the concept of inhabiting as individuals' spatiality, i.e. the ensemble of places and movements organised strategically by individuals. It allows for unpacking the different forms of inhabiting where mobility is key and could be expanded to all forms of individuals' spatiality. It would allow for the recognition of individual dwelling styles, which are more or less informed by mobility. It would include all the places and movements that make sense for the individuals in certain contexts, be it familiar places or places of the Other, onetime or routine mobilities or the most complex spatiotemporal coordination of activities.

For this is what the term "dwelling" seems to be all about: investigating multiple practices in terms of their manifold spatial dimensions (Lussault and Stock 2010). This step could be decisive for the understanding of mobile lifestyles, because multiple geographical references to identity, multiple forms of mobility and the differentiated practices of proper places (*Eigenort*) and places of otherness (*Fremdort*)

---

[5] „Multilokalität bedeutet *Vita activa* an mehreren Orten: Der tätige Lebensalltag in seiner Gesamtheit verteilt sich auf verschiedene Orte, die in mehr oder weniger grossen Zeiträumen aufgesucht und mit einer mehr oder weniger grossen Funktionsteiligkeit genutzt werden".

[6] "ce que l'on peut nommer 'l'habiter poly-topique' par rapport à 'l'habiter mono-topique' se caractérise par la recherche d'*adéquation* entre lieux et pratiques. Cela signifie que pour chaque projet, pour chaque tranche de vie, les individus tendent à choisir le lieu *adéquat* par l'adoption de stratégies migratoires ou circulatoires".

can facilitate the understanding of late modern societies.[7] For tourism studies, it means a very specific situation the tourist is placed in, a "touristic situation", where the very sense of place as distant, non-familiar, strange is significant and where mobility is key. The tourist inhabits a place as a *place of otherness* in contrast to the familiar places of everyday life, and this very break with routines and familiarity. The use of the term "inhabiting" allows then for the addressing the *existential* nature of embodied touristic practices. As a source of individual transformation, tourism involves the individual and his or her subjectivity, particularly through the confrontation with otherness and the emotions and sensitivities attached to it (Equipe MIT 2002). Instead of being understood as an alienating practice, tourism can be understood as a practice that makes sense for individuals and citizens, where recreation as "controlled de-controlling of emotions" (Elias 1986) disrupts a specific regime of routinized habitus inscribed in the body. "Inhabiting touristically" can then be investigated as relationship of tourist practices with place as a decontrolling of emotions and decentring of bodily routines within a specific "process of civilisation" (Elias 1986).

2.3 Addressing Different Dimensions of Inhabiting

We can differentiate between several categories and concepts, which could allow for an analysis of different issues of tourism. "Dwelling" can be used as overall category, related to phenomenological theory as encompassing problematisation, without prejudice of various forms of engaging with spatiality. Then, we might want to differentiate between "inhabiting" as practice, "co-inhabiting" as co-presence with human and non-human actants, "inhabitant" as specific person, "mode of inhabiting" as the specific relationship to place within a specific activity, "dwelling style" the places and movements developed by individuals and "dwelling regime" as the dominant regulation of societal spatiality.

Inhabiting Refers to practice and connotes the spatial dimensions of human practice as "make do with space" where the accomplishment of the action of confronting with space that is important. The expression "inhabiting touristically" refers to the way in which re-creation is articulated with mobility and otherness and thus becomes a specific way of apprehending how humans make do with space. The term inhabiting thus problematizes the appropriation, corporeality, and meaning of human practice with space. Referring to the theory of practice in the broadest sense (Stock 2015), norms, habitus, technical instruments, meanings, inequalities, imaginary, etc. are mobilized with the notion of inhabiting. "Inhabiting" is to be understood as *ensemble* of practices bound to norms, technologies, resources: inhabiting can be defined as a practice in which spatial references in all their dimensions (localisation

---

[7]The distinction between proper place (*Eigenort*) and other place (*Fremdort*) stems from Waldenfels (1984).

and orientation, landscape, distance, border, place, location, scale, etc.) are mobilised as a problem or resource.

Inhabitant Refers to the person, with his or her corporeality and rights and duties: inhabitants are mobile, geographically plural and temporary in the sense that they are only present part-time in different geographical locations and are not "permanent inhabitants". However, their status varies according to their mobility and differs in a given place, for example between residents and tourists. Understanding all the humans present in a place as "inhabitants" allows us to go beyond the tourist/ habitant dichotomy traditionally implemented. They are all temporary inhabitants of the geographical place in question, in a wide variety of capacities and projects, each with their own mode of inhabiting. "Inhabitants" are designated as humans co-present with a place, with whatever intentionality it may be.

Mode of Inhabiting Refers to the practice of engagement in a specific place and the way in which the tourist's intention makes sense for the tourist. By associating otherness and re-creation, the touristic mode of inhabiting mobilises a specific relationship to space. This makes it possible to understand, for example, how a Parisian's mode of inhabiting Paris differs from a Chinese's mode of inhabiting Paris, even though they may visit the same places in modes of re-creation. Otherness and the meaning assigned to place are not the same. The term therefore refers to the way in which tourist places are invested with sense according to different projects and intentionalities.

Dwelling Style Refers to the spatial dimension of lifestyle, i.e. the practical articulation between places and mobility. The notion of inhabiting allows for focussing on individual systems of mobility and place, articulating the practice of movement to the practice of places. Hypothetically, a continuum exists between relatively more polytopic and relatively more monotopic styles of dwelling (Stock 2006). It is indeed essential, if we are to understand the meaning of touristic practices, to insert individual tourism practice into a wider network of mobilities and geographical locations. Dwelling styles are largely dependent on the incommensurable social worlds in which humans move.

Dwelling Regime Synonymous with "regime of geographicity", it designates the geographical conditions in which the tourist is placed: it can be characterised by three elements today: mobility, urbanity, digitality, all of which are hyper-segregated and hyper-inegalitarian. (1) There are "mobility regimes" that promote and support some travel (including tourism and business travel) and control and criminalize others (including migration). Increased accessibility – both in terms of time and cost – has led to a transformation in the practice of tourism, for instance short stays in cities as a new way of inhabiting. (2) Tourists inhabit urban places, including tourist sites and resorts as well as national parks, created by city dwellers for city dwellers and carrying an urban imagination. Ongoing global urbanization is largely informed by tourism. (3) Tourists inhabit digitally informed spaces and are assisted by digital systems: booking, orientation, communication etc. are done with the help of digital instruments. The social media potentially suspend the classic distinction, constitutive of tourism, between home/away and thus raise new questions for tourism studies.

Co-inhabiting Humans do not inhabit alone, but are in a relationship of proximity and co-presence with other humans and other non-humans. The term "co-inhabiting" refers to the bodily co-presence *in situ* between human and non-human actants. Tourists co-inhabit with other tourists and thus form a 'tourist society', which is an important element in tourism practice (a tourist alone in an empty tourist place would be out of the ordinary), but can lead to conflicts of use between tourists in busy tourist places. Tourists also co-inhabit with residents, which is one of the central elements of the desire of tourists: to do as the locals do and identify with the locals by practising the same places as the locals. However, this co-inhabitating also generates conflicts of use: the controversies surrounding "overtourism" in European cities between 2016 and 2020 can be interpreted as problems of co-inhabiting and conflicts over the right to the city (Stock 2019). Tourists also cohabit with animals in specific tourist situations such as ecotourism or animal watching, requiring a specific regulation of the distances between human and non-human bodies.

These several interrelated concepts make it possible not to limit inhabiting to the only spaces of daily life, to the only spaces practiced "usually" in the everyday life. If we are to capture all the places involved in the contemporary life of individuals, then we must go beyond the usual and routinized places and focus also on the unusual places people inhabit. Thus, inhabiting is not reduced to the activities of residency, but multiple mobilities and places come into focus. Moreover, seen as inhabiting, the spatial dimensions of practice come into focus and thus a decisive contribution of geography to the social sciences is to be made by incorporating spatial dimensions into social theory.

2.4 Tourist Practices as "Mode of Inhabiting" and the Tourist as Temporary Inhabitant

Touristic practice can be interpreted as a specific mode of inhabiting, where place is practiced through a recreational intentionality, and where place is interpreted as place of otherness (Stock 2014). Tourists inhabit places not as ordinary inhabitants but informed by a touristic interpretation of the world. By defining inhabiting as developing a sense of place and a meaningful practice of place, tourist mobilities are one of the essential elements. The use of the term "inhabiting" means refusing the sole point of view of tourism as "usage" or "consumption". Indeed, practices are understood as "tactical" (Certeau 1990, pp. 64–65). The practices are then seen not as alienating routines, but as "inventions of daily life" (Certeau 1990). They are conceived as a way of ruse towards the expectations of state power and industry (including tourism). The analysis of touristic practice as a political act and not as an act of consumption would thus enrich the study of the inhabitant. The practice of tourism as a ruse, not as a mere follow up of prescriptions, makes it possible to insist on the possible autonomy of the tourist who diverts tourist offers. Besides standardized "fordist tourism", there is a movement towards "post-Fordist tourism" (Cuvelier 1998), which is a flexible way of arranging tourist practice and in which individual autonomy plays an important role. Thus, "inhabiting touristically" also means the reconstruction of inventing one's own tourism practices as a practice of resistance to social norms or to the proposals of the tourism industry. I will unpack this in two steps: First, tourism can be framed as a mode of inhabiting in the form of "displacement" where a change of place is associated with the practice of a "other" place, fundamentally different of a regime of familiarity, yet the term of inhabiting is useful. Second, the tourist as temporary inhabitant of place would allow to tear down the dichotomy between tourist and the resident or host and guest by stating everybody is a temporary inhabitant of all the places he/she inhabits.

2.4.1 Playful Inhabiting and Quest for Excitement

"Tourism is a *dis-placement*, i.e. a change of place, a change of 'inhabiting': the tourist temporarily leaves his place of residence for one or more places located outside the sphere of his daily life. The displacement operates a discontinuity that allows another mode of inhabiting dedicated to the sole *recreation*" (Knafou et al. 1997, 194, my translation and emphasis). A change of place – both in the social and geographical sense – is the essential element in order to inhabit places differently from the everyday life. This mode of inhabiting is a playful one, centred on practices of "recreation". This playful inhabiting of place contrasts with mode of inhabiting centred on work, routines, "everyday life". Tourist practices are understood as a specific spatial problem of dis-placement, because it is about mobility competences and competences of dealing with "otherness". Yet, how people practice places as a tourist? How do they *inhabit* places *touristically*? Which mode of engagement is in effect when a geographical place is practiced by mobile persons? But also, how, *theoretically*, can we set up an analytical framework to detect in an empirical work the variations between different forms of inhabiting (or dwelling modes)?

One way to affront this question is to refer to *modes of engagement* as defined in Schützian phenomenological sociology: "Modes of engagement (…) mean the attitude of the I-consciousness to the world" (Schütz 1973).[8] It is defined here as the coupling between intentionality and the relationship to the world engaged in practice. For example, practicing a place of Otherness for recreation purposes deploys a different mode of engagement than practicing a other place for work purposes; it also different from practicing a familiar place for recreation purposes. Hence the

---

[8] "Unter Lebensform ist […] die Einstellung des Ich-Bewusstseins zur Welt gemeint" (Schütz 1973).

relevance of distinguishing between different ways of inhabiting geographical places. Applied in tourism, persons inhabit places temporarily *as* tourists, i.e. they "inhabit touristically". An interesting shift in the understanding of current tourist practices occurred if tourists could be framed as "inhabitants", that is, as humans developing a specific touristic relationship to places they practice.

In order to unpack tourism as a *playful* practice of places, we refer to Caillois' (1958) theory of play. He distinguishes four categories of play as *illynx, mimesis, agon, alea,* which can be mobilised within tourism theory as examples of deroutinizing activities. As Elias (1986) formulates in his "spectre of leisure", there is a continuum between routinized activities and deroutinizing activities as self-determined leisure. Tourism means inhabiting places for deroutinizing activities. Moreover, we could argue every single element – even eating, sleeping, etc. – is assigned a new "touristified" sense because of the specific context and situation. Pott (2007) makes this clear with his claim of a "code" within tourist practices, that sees elements as "exciting" in a tourist situation where it would be boring in an everyday situation. For instance, the traffic, noise or hustle of the metropolis is coded as exciting within a touristic situation whereas it is coded as problematic in everyday situation. A playful mode of inhabiting places is therefore apparent. This transition from one set of standards to another is decisive for understanding the effects of this way of inhabiting. "Inhabiting touristically" is therefore a specific, temporary mode of inhabiting place where the enchantment comes from a relatively greater autonomy compared to the norms of daily life.

Second, the tourism mode of inhabiting can be framed as a mode of engagement of "legitimate outsiders". This refers to the distinction of two different inhabiting modes as *insiders* or *outsiders* of geographical places, which mobilises both Relph's (1976) geographical idea of "insideness" versus "outsideness" to a place and the sociological insider/outsider distinction Elias and Scotson (1994) make for communities. Insiders are those who have a relationship of familiarity with place, outsiders are those who have a distant relationship to the place. In order to approach the relationship to place, we can distinguish at a first level the "residents" from the "visitors". However, as outsiders, they are considered as legitimate outsiders, not to be confused with the illegitimate outsider as the "Stranger" classical sociological literature talks about. Since tourist places are organized as a form of hospitality, tourists are certainly temporary inhabitants of a place, yet a distanciated practice of place since the latter is a place of otherness.

The specific mode of inhabiting is based on the apprehension of the inhabited place as place of otherness, coupled with a project of recreation, *i.e.* practices of rupture with everyday life and a "controlled decontrolling of self-control", as expresses Elias (1986). It is an "explosive cocktail", because a specific balance between self-control and relaxation is set up by the tourist as well as the confrontation with the norms of the temporarily inhabited place. This legitimacy of the tourist has recently been called into question by various forms of resistance from residents, especially in European cities such as Barcelona, Venice, Berlin (Colomb and Novy 2017) and raises the question of co-inhabiting.

2.4.2 *"Inhabiting Touristically": Tourists as Temporary Inhabitants of Places*

There would be a need to delve deeper into the specific ways people engage a touristic mode of inhabiting. Inhabiting involves tracing the practices and their constitution in situations with competences, techniques, corporeality, interpretations and interpretations of meaning as well as stagings *in actu*. However, dispositions, capacities, possibilities are unequally distributed, i.e. different degrees of ability to control one's own actions and spatialities have to be acknowledged. If an analytical framework for the spatiality of practices were to be developed, the following elements could be emphasized: (I) spacing skills, (II) techniques and instruments, (III) spatial capital, (IV) formal and informal norms.

1. *Spacing skills.* Geographical skills are deployed by individuals. A know-how concerning all forms of spatiality – here, elsewhere, location, limits, distances, landscape, etc. – is thus mobilized during the execution of the action. Spatial skills (knowledge and know-how), body techniques, instruments, tricks that are mobilized to pass the test of space for different actions. Here, we would like to distinguish cognitive skills from behavioural skills: knowing how to behave correctly in a Palace hotel or on the train, for example. A reflection can then be engaged on the competencies of the contemporary subject for whom the hypothesis of the individual as "geographically plural" can be put forward (Stock 2006). As temporary inhabitants of multiple places, several new capacities have emerged: the ability to manage several geographical referents of identity, the ability to distance oneself from the local scale, the ability to transform other places into familiar places, the ability to precise spatio-temporal coordination, the ability to manage presences/absences (see Lucas in this book for an insight in this topic).

   In short, individuals develop spatial management skills, which can be used in multiple situations. Lussault (2007) develops the idea of "elementary forms of spatial competences" in order to systematise these spatial competences: (1) competence of placing and arrangement as the capacity of the adequate place for oneself in relation with others, (2) competence of scaling as the capacity of discrimination of the size of spatial units, (3) competence of metrics as discrimination propinquity and distance and ways of measuring them, (4) competence of delimitation as capacity of regionalisation and assigning limits to spatial units, (5) competence of transgressing limits as techniques and habits of passing over all sorts of limits, (6) competence of wayfinding as the capacity of composing and controlling itineraries. They are not given features, but capacities or competences unequally distributed, i.e. acquired and learned differently by people. From the point of view of the tourist, these competences are key when coping with spaces of otherness (see chapter 3 by Léopold Lucas in this book).

2. *Equipped practices.* These skills are applied through techniques and instruments. Tourist pratices can be framed as practices equipped with technical instruments, technical objects: the human being is not naked, but equips himself

with increasingly sophisticated technical instruments that accompany him in his dwelling. And it is not only his shelter, but all the technical instruments including clothing, shoes, backpack, smartphone, credit card, badge, metro pass, water bottle, etc. that allow him to inhabit touristically. It is therefore the question of the interrelationship between techniques, technology and technical object that is raised and which aims to solve spatial problems, whether it is a question of distance, access, otherness or others. To this end, "technique" can be defined from a Platonian point of view as "mediation between intention and action, whether it concerns the ideal or the material world" (Lévy 2003, p. 893, my translation). We can thus focus on "spatial technologies", i.e. the spatial dimensions these technical objects make possible to solve: standardized hotels or holiday clubs whose access is controlled, passports that make it possible to cross borders, means of payment (currency or electronic). Beyond technical objects, it is also important to take "techniques" seriously, i.e. the way of coupling intention and action, in particular through the engagement of the body (see the chapter by Valérian Geffroy in this book).

3. *Spatial capital.* Inhabiting touristically relies on resources, such as economic, social and cultural resources. Bourdieu (1994) coined it as social, economic, cultural and symbolic *capital* that allow agents to take advantages within in a specific social field. From a geographic point of view, we could add the spatial dimensions of capital used by individuals. Geographer Jacques Lévy coined the term "spatial capital" and defined it as "the benefits of mastering a set of geographical arrangements. It is based on scale and metrics. (Lévy 2013a, b, 147). This goes beyond skills, the know-how concerning space as we have seen above, to integrate other elements. The experience of places of otherness, a specific residential biography, but also the control of mobility or "mobility capital" (Kaufmann et al. 2004; Ceriani-Sebregondi 2004) where mobility potentials in the form of available means of transport as well as the skills necessary to mobilise them contribute to the highly differentiated spatial capital among individuals. Research has shown how a specific spatial capital helps tourists to navigate in an unknown environment (Lucas 2018; Violier 2018), yet more research on spatial capital is needed.

4. *Norms.* Formal and informal norms are key when analysing the question of inhabiting since "mobility itself as a rights-based activity" (Prytherch 2012, p. 301). Indeed, mobility is a practice governed by law (Blomley 1994; Cresswell 2010; Prytherch 2012), particularly in terms of means of transport (horses and pedestrians banned on the streets since 1920, diesel-powered cars banned in some German cities in 2019). As a consumer, commercial law applies, as a migrant, nationality law and international law applies, etc. Mobility regimes produce unequal rights. The value of mobility as a positive value of freedom of movement (Cresswell 2006) has to be examined, because it legitimises the presence of mobile individuals as tourists in cities. Freedom of movement is recognized by national and international law. This allows for individual rights of nationals – when traveling

abroad – to be able to return to their home country (and to be sequestered at the border), and also the right to visit or migrate and locate a residency within the country, without being constrained through legal aspects. Inhabiting specific tourism worlds depend heavily on legal norms, and can be analysed within "regimes of mobility" (Glick Schiller and Salazar 2013) as legal framework of mobilities.

2.5   Towards the Study of "Dwelling Styles"

A limitation of many studies on mobility is that they confine their object of study to only one form of movements, for example international migration, tourism, commuting, leisure, consumption mobilities, daily movements, residential mobility, which give then birth to specific subfields, without connecting the different social contexts. For each form of mobility, we can certainly highlight the specific rationality and intentionality. Nevertheless, these mobilities, social contexts and rationalities are interdependent. It is therefore not enough to work for instance on so-called "daily" mobilities without linking them to other forms of mobility. Moreover, tourist mobilities are linked to other forms of mobilities, be it migration, leisure, work, etc. mobilities and to flows of information, money, materiality, commodities, etc.. There is much to gain if systems of mobility (Urry 2000) rather than only individual movements were approached. Indeed, mobility can also be a way of life, discussed as "lifestyle mobilities" (McIntyre et al. 2006) and as a transnational way of life (Pries 2008). Finally, these social contexts are spatially differentiated, located in multiple places separated from each other, and linked together by movements. They do not exist independently of each other, and the individual systems of mobility are dependent on the adequacy between social context and place quality.

If we are to understand tourist mobilities, we have to embed them within a broader system of mobilities. That implies for the researcher to reconstruct "dwelling styles", i.e. mobile lifestyles, based on more or less movements and places. The concept of "inhabiting" allows for grasping in an alternative way the problem of mobility. It is acknowledged individuals in contemporary societies develop a mobile social life (Larsen et al. 2007) or mobile lifestyle, addressed by Thrift (1996) as "structure of feeling (…) termed mobility". Addressing the question of dwelling implies taking seriously the "mobilities turn" in social sciences in order to understand how people inhabit places and movements. In turn, mobilities studies can learn from the notion of dwelling because it can add an alternative interpretation: current mobility requires an understanding not only of "movements from A to B", but must include the practice of places – addressed through the metaphor of "mooring" in the literature (Hannam et al. 2006) – and the multiple forms of appropriating mobilities. The relationship between different social contexts is ensured by a physical movement of the individual and physical co-presence implies an *in situ* practice. It is this articulation between the practice of places and multiple forms of movements that can be framed as "inhabiting", focusing the research on individual systems of mobility and places. This shall be called here "dwelling styles" as spatial translation of the notion of "lifestyles".

Figure 2.1 shows a study where people were asked about the places and movements throughout a year (Lévy 2004). It represents the dwelling style of an individual from Tours/France and its multiple mobilities and place practices. It also represents the activities during the movements as mobility is not a void time, but a time used for multiple activities.

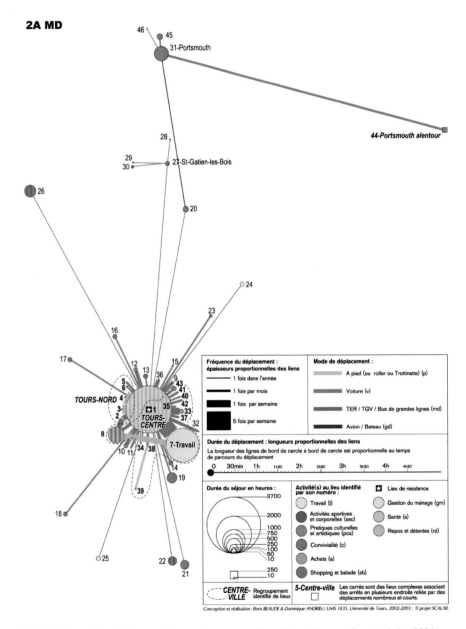

Fig. 2.1 Annual mobilities and places of one person from Tours, France. (Source: Lévy 2004)

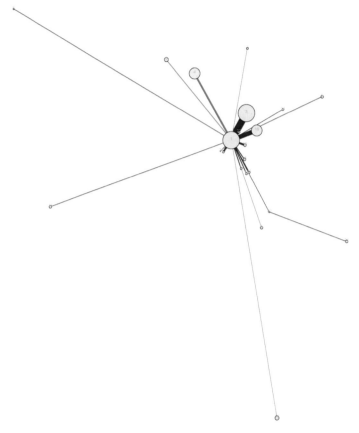

Fig. 2.2 Annual mobilities and places of one person from Bussigny, Switzerland. (Source: Stock et al. 2009)

In a following study (Stock et al. 2009), we investigated similar patterns, but taking also into account migration biographies in order to understand the accumulation of a "spatial capital" of individuals. I focus on three cases in order to make understand the advantages in contextualising tourist practices in an ensemble of mobilities, including migration biographies. It relies on visualisation techniques, where the size of the circles indicates the time spent in each place throughout the year and the length of lines the time spent in transport. Three examples can be developed. A female professional, 39 years old, living in Bussigny (suburb of Lausanne, Switzerland) has developed a quadri-centric way of inhabiting: (1) her place of residence, (2) her partner's place of residence, (3) her place of work where she has her office and (4) her place of work in London where she frequently goes for meetings. She uses two almost exclusive modes of transport, airplane and automobile. She always combines other activities with its primary purpose of travel: its business trips give rise to weekend extensions for skiing (Denver-Vail), shopping (London, Paris, Hamburg, Rome) or bringing her companion for the weekend (Vienna). (Fig. 2.2).

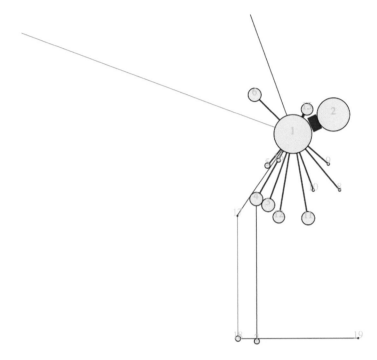

Fig. 2.3 Annual mobilities and places of one person from Lausanne, Switzerland. (Source: Stock et al. 2009)

The second case is about a young employee (male, 27 years old, Bussigny, suburb of Lausanne, Switzerland): poly-centric system due to a dispersion of its life in multiple places. Its presence in the residential area is mainly used for overnight stays. The workplace is certainly located near the car, but its leisure time has systematically passed "outside": every weekend, places other than Bussigny benefit from its presence whether for skiing (Verbier, Chamonix, Portes du Soleil) or rock climbing (Jura, Viuz-en-Sallaz, Gap) or for friends (Chamonix, Annemasse, Geneva, Annecy) or for parents (Thonon, Calgary) or for windsurfing (Essaouira). All these destinations are reached by car or, less frequently, by plane (Essaouira, Calgary). (Fig. 2.3).

The third case is about an employee (female, 50 years old, Geneva) who develops a duo-centric dwelling system, centred on the Vernier district in Geneva and Crans-Montana where she occupies a *chalet* for week-end and holidays. Crans-Montana plays such an important role that the children play trumpet in the local brass band and she spends two months in the summer and almost every weekend of the year. The family does not own a car and travels mainly by public transport: a profound knowledge has been developed over the years where they know all the relevant public transport timetables by heart. This allows to understand how to inhabit a place challenges the very notion of "second home", since the administrative notion is not adequate to the ways Crans-Montana is inhabited. The emotional engagement clashes with the administrative framing. (Fig. 2.4).

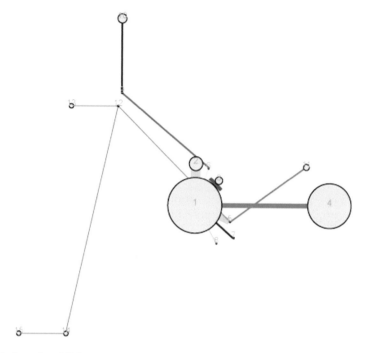

Fig. 2.4 Annual mobilities and places of one person from Geneva, Switzerland. (Source: Stock et al. 2009)

All movements and place practices can be subsumed by the notion of "dwelling styles". These include the practices as well as the different meanings attached to mobility and places. The variability of individual systems of places and movements comes therefore into light. Through this operation, we no longer understand only one single mobility carried out, but all mobility at the individual level. As a "style", it points towards the *individualization* of the spatial dimension of lifestyles, which are more or less infused with mobilities.

2.6 The Notion of Inhabiting as an Answer to Current Issues?

Overall, the perspective of dwelling suggests to ask the question how places are *inhabited* by individuals in order to understand their signification within a larger set of places and mobilities. There are several issues the perspective of dwelling could help addressing. The first involves the classical distinction between hosts and guests. Contemporary mobile lifestyles express multiple mobilities from one social and spatial context to another. The perspective of temporary inhabitants allows both for the understanding residents are temporary inhabitants in their own city, which is inhabited temporarily by tourists and other mobile persons. The usual distinction is only a situational one: the Berliner resident facing the Barcelona tourist today is the tourist tomorrow facing the Barcelonito resident. This suggests to question the whole continuum of *temporary inhabitants* in a given place, which could be a fruitful research perspective.

This is also related to the second home discussion. On the one hand, in contrast to a very narrow definition of tourism as recreational practice of places of otherness, second homes develop a different relationship to place: that of attachment and familiarity. One the other hand, multilocality studies, by focussing on forms of multiple residency, report routinized second home practices with civic engagement (Hilti 2016), but also a subtler understanding of what "second home" means for different people: for professional, leisure, study or family purposes, as an investment vehicle, as social distinction, as appropriation of otherness. Therefore, I suggest to ask the question how places are *inhabited* by individuals in order to understand their signification within a larger set of places and mobilities. The question of the various ways those residences are inhabited and make sense in a strategically organized lifestyle based on mobility is therefore raised. It also could help address the issue of short-term rentals (such as AirBnB): inhabiting an authentic local apartment and neighbourhood – "belong anywhere" reads one of the slogans – as powerful imaginary could help interpret the contemporary appropriation of these forms of inhabiting.

Moreover, the contemporary problem of overtourism and the challenge these short-term rentals poses to cities can be seen as an issue of "co-inhabiting" of multiple projects of inhabiting cities: although often framed as opposition between tourists and residents, there is in fact an array of conflicting copresence in cities. As Eggli and Stock (2020) show for the example in Luzern, residents, tourists, leisure, shopping, commuting, second homes, working, etc. contribute to congestion, and partially the touristification of everyday life. The right to the city for all people raised the issue of the tension between the freedom of movement of tourists and other mobile people and the interests of mobile residents (Stock 2019).

Finally, new (leisure) mobilities challenge traditional forms of tourism and ideal-typical definitions of social science because of the capacity of practising destinations in a new way or embedding recreational practices within a lifestyle dedicated to leisure, for instance via "city breaks". In the last twenty years, several forms of mobility practices have been accounted for, such as lifestyles based on leisure and "lifestyle mobilities" (McIntyre et al. 2006). Especially, it raises the question if this "commuting" between cities on a European level for leisure activities such as visiting museums or exhibits, sports events, shopping etc. is to be interpreted as tourism – even as "new urban tourism" (Frisch et al. 2019) – or as new kinds of leisure mobilities. Practices such as following as fan the favourite sports club around Europe, attending music and theatre performances, shopping, but also clubbing, drinking beer, meeting peers are contemporary mobility practices labelled as "tourism", yet at odds with a "mode of inhabiting" traditionally called tourism. With the renewed accessibilities of places within the everyday life, there is therefore the issue of distinguishing leisure and tourism as two different modes of inhabiting places and mobilities. It calls for a need to reassess the relationship between leisure theory and tourism theory in a context of changing accessibilities and changing work and residency contexts.

The interpretation through the lens of dwelling would insist on the necessity to distinguish different forms of presence, i.e. *inhabiting* the different places and emphasize the network of places people inhabit in order to weigh the significance of each place to another. A "mode of inhabiting" called tourism is not only based on a specific practice such as going to a museum, but engaging with a place as "other" place within a realm of recreation. As such, it would differ from modes of engaging with places as familiar places. Therefore, the current discussion about "tourism at home" or "proximity tourism" could also be tackled (Jeuring and Haartsen 2016). If tourism is about a specific way of inhabiting, the practice of a familiar place does not correspond to a touristic activity although the distanciation and a specific gaze can be recognized.

2.7   Conclusion

A theory of dwelling that frames tourism in a specific way would thus rely on the following interrelated concepts: inhabiting, modes of inhabiting, dwelling styles, co-inhabiting. Especially, the perspective of dwelling asks how places within a larger set of places and mobilities are *inhabited* by individuals. Tourist practices are therefore approached as one way of inhabiting places and can therefore be framed as specific spatial practices where different spatial issues in comparison with other kinds of practices are at stake. Especially, place seen as "other" place and "dis-placement" as specific form of mobility seems characteristic to this understanding. Two arguments have been made: first, an argument towards tourists as temporary inhabitants of tourist places, where mobility is essential. Tourists as temporary inhabitants of places can be integrated in a larger framework of contemporary geographical conditions: the relatively higher degree of mobility expresses a "post-sedentary" world where inhabitants are mobile individuals and not immobile individuals. That leads to a theoretical perspective of dwelling in which the practices of residing or sheltering do not summarize the question of dwelling, but are rather one aspect of it. For example, touristic practices contribute also to the lifestyles, and thus, dwelling styles, of individuals through the creation of place-relations, an experience of places and movements, the coping with specific places.

Second, the notion of "inhabiting" is extended to all kinds of meaningful relationship to place. This allows for considering the contemporary human beings as temporary inhabitants, thus integrating the presence/absence patterns and the mobility component in the analysis. That means individuals practice places temporarily, even the residence is not a permanent home despite the legal claims. Moreover, individuals develop specific dwelling modes (*modes d'habiter*), i.e. specific relationship to place according to the intentionality with which they practice space. Touristic practice can be interpreted as a specific mode of dwelling, where place is practiced through a recreational intentionality, and where place is interpreted as place of otherness. If inhabiting means developing a sense of place and a meaningful practice of place, then we can contend late-modern societies develop specific meaningful practices of place where mobilities, and specifically, tourist mobilities are the essential elements. Therefore, a "mode of inhabiting", *i.e.* a relationship to place maintained for the duration of the touristic situation, in which otherness is key. Inhabiting the place is therefore at stake in the definition of tourism, not a specific practice like going to a museum or visiting a formerly unknown or less known neighbourhood during a guided tour. Two aspects are particularly interesting. First, lifestyles in contemporary societies are highly differentiated, thus corresponding to the process of individualization on the one hand, and on the other hand, the process of increased differentiation of societies. This has as a spatial corollary the differentiation of dwelling styles, understood as the emergence of differences and distinctions between individuals and others through coherent systems of mobility and places.

Yet, the question of inhabiting also opens up the question of co-inhabiting (*cohabitation*). Jean-Marc Besse expresses this as follows: "To exist, for the human being, is always living 'with', always co-inhabitating, however little it may be. This observation must form the basis of any reflection on dwelling" (Besse 2015, 388, own translation).[9] This collective dimension is important in the current discussion about "overtourism": it resorts in fact to the capacity to co-exist, i.e. inhabiting together the same place and to multiple conflictual projects for, and co-presence in the same place between multiple temporary inhabitants, among them residents and tourists. But, it also refers to the problem in second home communities, where identity and sociality are negotiated by more or less mobile people. Rather than an administrative problem of "second" home, it points towards the problem of co-inhabiting. *Via* the term "inhabitance", Butler (2007) – probably the translation proposed from the French "*l'habiter*" – aims at the reconstruction of the multiple forms of inhabiting occurring *with* and *in* a place. In an era where mobility is a key element of so-called "late-modern" societies, places are precisely characterised by the various and conflicting projects people engage, be it on a temporary or a more or less permanent basis. The inhabiting of cities and resorts in a period of massive, yet individualized tourism, might be a key for further investigation of the conflictual and political dimensions of tourism.

These mobile dwelling styles express the advent of "temporary inhabitants" and questions the very notion of "permanent inhabitants" – seen by some as a juridical "fiction" (Ford 1999) because of the assignment to one address and citizenship while being a mobile traveller –, as well as the advent of individuals who are geographically plural (Stock 2006). It would help to go beyond the often-criticized

---

[9] *"Exister, pour l'être humain, c'est toujours vivre avec, toujours cohabiter, aussi peu que ce soit. Cette constatation doit former la base de toute réflexion sur l'habiter"*

dichotomy between "host" and "guest" or "resident" versus "tourist". A renewed figure of the inhabitant could emerge, where instead of defining and assigning values of sedentarism or stillness, a more fluid and mobile quality of being mobile could be used to define contemporary inhabitants. Inhabiting is both creating identifications with places and relating these significant places through movement. It also allows for a renewed reflection upon the inhabitants' right to the city. The tourist as temporary inhabitant of places would allow conflicting issues of contemporary tourism to be seen as co-inhabiting: the desire of otherness, yet the harnessing and control of otherness through commodifying mediations; the practice of unfamiliar places, yet the technological equipment in order to deal with it and the appropriation of space by the tourist; the desire of authenticity, yet the encounter with a commodified reality; the desire of identification, yet the resistance of the visited.

References

Annales de Géographie (2015). Thematic Issue "Habiter: mots et regards croisés", n°704. (https://www.cairn.info/revue-annales-de-geographie-2015-4.htm).

Berque, A. (1996). *Être humains sur la Terre*. Paris: Gallimard.

Besse, J.-M. (2013). *Habiter. Un monde à mon image*. Paris: Flammarion.

Besse, J.-M. (2015). Voisinages. *Annales de Géographie, 704*, 385–390.

Blomley, N. (1994). *Law, space, and the geographies of power*. New York: Guildford.

Bourdieu, P. (1994). Raisons pratiques. In *Sur la théorie de l'action*. Paris: Seuil.

Butler, C. (2007). Sydney: Aspiration, asylum and the denial of the right to the city. In A. Philippopoulos-Mihalopoulos (Ed.), *Law and the city* (pp. 205–220). Abingdon: Routledge-Cavendish.

Caillois, R. (1958). *Les Jeux et les hommes: le masque et le vertige*, Paris, Gallimard. (transl. as *Man, play, and games*. University of Illinois Press, 2001).

Ceriani, G. (2004). Migrations internationales: vers un nouvel habiter ? In *Travaux de l'Institut de Géographie de Reims* (Vol. 115–118, pp. 59–74).

Clifford, J. (1992). Traveling cultures. In L. Grossberg, C. Nelson, & P. A. Treichler (Eds.), *Cultural studies* (pp. 96–116). London: Routledge.

Colomb, C., & Novy, J. (Eds.). (2017). *Protest and resistance in the tourist city*. London: Routledge.

Cresswell, T. (2006). *On the move. Mobility in the modern Western world*. London: Routledge.

Cresswell, T. (2010). Towards a Politics of Mobility, Environment and Planning Part D: Society and Space, n°1, p. 17–31.

Cuvelier, P. (1998). *Anciennes et nouvelles formes de tourisme : une approche socio-économique*. Paris: L'Harmattan.

Dardel, E. (1952). *L'homme et la Terre. Nature de la réalité géographique*. Paris: CTHS (edition 1990).

De Certeau, M. (1990). *L'invention du quotidien, I: Arts de faire,* Paris, Gallimard (1st ed. 1980) (transl. as *The practice of everyday life*, University of California Press, 1984).

Eggli, F. & Stock, M. (2020). Leben mit Tourismus in Luzern, Schweiz. *Berichte. Geographie und Landeskunde*, 93(3).

Elias, N. (1986). Introduction. In N. Elias & E. Dunning (Eds.), *Quest for excitement. Sport and leisure in the civilising process*. Oxford: Blackwell.

Elias, N., & Scotson, J. (1994). *The established and the outsiders*. London: Sage.

Equipe M. I. T. (2002). *Tourismes 1. Lieux communs.* Paris: Belin.

Ford, R. (1999). Law's territory (a history of jurisdiction). *Michigan Law Review, 97*(4), 843–930.

Frelat-Kahn, B., & Lazzarotti, O. (Eds.). (2012). *Habiter. Vers un nouveau concept?* Paris: Armand Colin.

Frisch, T., Sommer, C., Stoltenberg, L. & Stors L. (Eds.) (2019). *Tourism and everyday life in the contemporary city.* London: Routledge.

Glick Schiller, N. & Salazar, N. (2013). Regimes of mobility across the globe, Journal of Ethnic and Migration, vol. 39, n° 2, 2013.

Hannam, K., Sheller, M., & Urry, J. (2006). Editorial. Mobilities, Immobilities and moorings. *Mobilities, 1*(1), 1–22.

Heidegger, M. (2004a). ... dichterisch wohnet der Mensch..., in Heidegger M., *Vorträge und Aufsätze*, Stuttgart: Klett, 181–198 (trans. as ...Poetically Man Dwells..., in *Poetry, Language, Thought*, New York: Harper & Row Publishers, 1971).

Heidegger, M. (2004b). Bauen, Wohnen, Denken, in Heidegger M., *Vorträge und Aufsätze*, Stuttgart: Klett, 139–156 (transl. as Building, Dwelling, Thinking, in *Basic Writings*, San Francisco: Harper Collins Publishers, 1977).

Hilti, N. (2016). Multi-local lifeworlds: Between movement and mooring. *Cultural Studies, 30*(3), 467–482.

Hoyaux, A.-F. (2002). Entre construction territoriale et constitution ontologique de l'habitant. Introduction épistémologique aux apports de la phénoménologie au concept d'habiter, *Cybergeo – European Journal of Geography*, n° 102. http://cybergeo.revues.org/1824

Hoyaux, A.-F. (2015). Habiter: Se plaçer plaçant et se penser pensant. *Annales de Géographie, 704*, 366–384.

Ingold, T. (2000). *The perception of the environment. Essays on livelihood, dwelling and skill.* London: Routledge.

Jeuring, J., & Haartsen, T. (2016). The challenge of proximity: The (un)attractiveness of near-home tourism destinations. *Tourism Geographies, 16*(1), 118–141.

Kaufmann, V., Bergman, M., & Joye, D. (2004). Motility: Mobility as capital. *International Journal of Urban and Regional Research, 28*(4), 745–756.

Knafou, R., Bruston, M., Deprest, F., Duhamel, P., Gay, J.-C., & Sacareau, I. (1997). Une approche géographique du tourisme. *L'Espace géographique, 26*(3), 193–204.

Larsen, J., Urry, J., & Axhausen, K. (2007). Networks and tourism. Mobile social life. *Annals of Tourism Research, 34*(1), 244–262.

Lazzarotti, O. (2006). *Habiter. La condition géographique.* Paris: Belin.

Lévy, J. (Ed.). (2004). *Scalab. Les échelles de l'habiter.* Paris: PUCA.

Lévy, J. (2013a). Capital spatial. In J. Lévy & M. Lussault (Eds.), *Dictionnaire de la géographie et de l'espace des sociétés* (pp. 147–149). Paris: Belin.

Lévy, J. (2013b). Habiter. In J. Lévy & M. Lussault (Eds.), *Dictionnaire de la géographie et de l'espace des sociétés* (pp. 480–482). Paris: Belin.

Lévy, J. (2014). Inhabiting. In R. Lee et al. (Eds.), *The sage handbook of human geography* (pp. 45–68). London: Sage Handbooks.

Lévy, J., & Lussault, M. (2003). Habiter. In J. Lévy & M. Lussault (Eds.), *Dictionnaire de la géographie et de l'espace des sociétés* (pp. 440–442). Paris: Belin.

Lucas, L. (2018). Les bus touristiques, une technologie spatiale pour habiter les métropoles. Le cas de Los Angeles. *Mondes du Tourisme, 14*: http://journals.openedition.org/tourisme/1671

Lussault, M. (2007). *L'Homme spatial.* Paris: Seuil.

Lussault, M., & Stock, M. (2010). 'Doing with space'. Towards a pragmatics of space. *Social Geography, 5*(1), 1–8. http://www.soc-geogr.net/5/11/2010/sg-5-11-2010.pdf.

McIntyre, N., Williams, D., & McHugh, K. (2006). *Multiple dwelling and tourism. Negotiating place, home and identity.* Wallingford: CABI.

Merleau-Ponty, M. (1945). *Phénoménologie de la perception.* Paris: Gallimard.

Morel-Brochet, A., & Ortar, N. (Eds.). (2012). *La fabrique des modes d'habiter. Homme, lieux et milieux de vie.* Paris: L'Harmattan.

Mondes du tourisme. (2018). Thematic Issue "Habiter le Monde en touriste"., 14. https://journals. openedition.org/tourisme/1437.

Palmer, C. (2018). *Being and dwelling through tourism: An anthropological perspective.* Abingdon: Routledge.

Paquot, T., Lussault, M., & Younès, C. (Eds.). (2007). *Habiter, le propre de l'humain.* Paris: La Découverte.

Pons-Obrador, P. (2003). Being-on-holiday: Tourist dwelling, bodies and place. *Tourist Studies, 3*(1), 47–66.

Pott, A. (2007). *Tourismusorte. Eine gesellschafts- und raumtheoretische Untersuchung am Beispiel des Städtetourismus.* Bielefeld: Transcript.

Pries, L. (2008). *Die Transnationalisierung der sozialen Welt: Sozialräume jenseits von Nationalgesellschaften.* Frankfurt am Main: Suhrkamp.

Prince, S. (2018). Dwelling in the tourist landscape: Embodiment and everyday life among the craft-artists of Bornholm. *Tourist Studies, 18*(1), 63–82.

Prytherch, D. (2012). Legal geographies. Codifying the right-of-way: Statutory geographies of urban mobility and the street. *Urban Geography, 33*(2), 295–314.

Relph, E. (1976). *Place and placelessness.* London: Pion.

Rolshoven, J. (2007). Multilokalität als Lebensweise in der Spätmoderne. *Schweizerisches Archiv für Volkskunde, 103*, 157–179.

Schütz, A. (1973). *Der sinnhafte Aufbau der sozialen Welt.* Frankfurt: Suhrkamp. (1st ed. 1932).

Seamon, D. (1980). Body-subject, time-space routines, and place-ballets. In A. Buttimer & D. Seamon (Eds.), *The human experience of space and place* (pp. 148–165). London: Croom Helm.

Seamon, D., Mugerauer, R. (1985). *Dwelling, place and environment. Towards a Phenomenology of Person and World.* Dordrecht: Martinus Nijhoff.

Stock, M. (2006). L'hypothèse de l'habiter polytopique, *Espacestemps.net.* https://www.espaces-temps.net/articles/hypothese-habiter-polytopique/

Stock, M. (2007). Théorie de l'habiter. Questionnements. In T. Paquot, M. Lussault, & C. Younès (Eds.), *Habiter, le propre de l'humain* (pp. 103–125). Paris: La Découverte.

Stock, M. (2014). 'Touristisch wohnet der Mensch'. Zu einer kulturwissenschaftlichen Theorie mobiler Lebensweisen. *Voyage, 16*, 54–68.

Stock, M. (2015). Habiter comme 'faire avec l'espace'. Réflexions à partir des théories de la pratique. *Annales de Géographie, 704*, 424–441.

Stock, M. (2019). Inhabiting the city as tourists. Issues for urban and tourism theory. In T. Frisch, C. Sommer, L. Stoltenberg, & N. Stors (Eds.), *Tourism and everyday life in the contemporary city* (pp. 42–66). London: Routledge.

Stock, M., Letissier, F., Ruzicka-Rossier, M., Lévy, J. (2009). *Mobilité individuelle et espace urbain. Une recherche transculturelle (Los Angeles, Tokyo, Genève).* Final report for FNRS, 197p.

Thrift, N. (1996). *Spatial formations.* Londres: Sage.

Travaux de l'Institut de Géographie de Reims. (2003). *Thematic Issue "Habiter"* (pp. 115–118) https://www.persee.fr/issue/tigr_0048-7163_2003_num_29_115.

Tuan, Y.-F. (1977). *Space and place. The perspective of experience.* Minneapolis: University of Minnesota Press.

Urry, J. (2000). *Sociology beyond societies.* London: Routledge.

Urry, J. (2006). Inhabiting the car. In S. Böhm, C. Jones, C. Land, & M. Paterson (Eds.), *Against automobility* (pp. 17–31). Oxford: Blackwell.

Violier, P. (2018). Mobilité des individus et familiarité construite: des arrangements qui offrent aux touristes des prises pour parcourir le monde. *Mondes du tourisme, 12.* http://journals.openedition.org/tourisme/1365.

Waldenfels, B. (1984). *In den Netzen der Lebenswelt.* Frankfurt: Suhrkamp.

Werlen, B. (1996). Geographie globalisierter Lebenswelten. *Österreichische Zeitschrift für Soziologie, 21*(2), 97–128.

Mathis Stock is a professor with the Institute of Geography and Sustainability at Lausanne University (Switzerland), where he leads the research group "Cultures and Natures of Tourism". His research deals with the urbanising force of tourism, the controversies around tourism in cities, and mobility and multilocality approached from the perspective of practice theory. He dialogues with social theory and develops a theory of dwelling, posited at the heart of theoretical geography. He is editor-in-chief of the scientific journal *Mondes du tourisme*.

Chapter 3
Tourists and the City: Knowledge as a Challenge for Inhabiting

Léopold Lucas

3.1   Introduction

This chapter emphasizes the fact that inhabiting a city must not be taken for granted for tourists: coping with an unusual urban space is a challenge, and knowledge is at the heart of this problem. Our starting point is to consider tourism as a way of inhabiting places (Stock 2007a, 2019). This is the meaning of *"and"* in the phrase "tourists and the city" reflecting the idea that "tourists are not only in place, but also involved with the place, although not in the same manner that non-tourists are" (Pons-Obrador 2003: 51). Thus, we must consider tourists not *on* or *in* a city but rather as dealing *with* an urban space. This expression, 'dealing with' (see Lussault and Stock 2010), raises the idea of a co-production between tourists and a city: a city imposes a specific urban configuration (through buildings, urbanism, planning, transportation, local law and regulation, etc.) that tourists have to cope with, while on the other hand, tourism creates new urban agencies, new spatial dynamics, new places and neighbourhoods. Our purpose is to examine the following question: how are tourists *able* to inhabit cities?

Investigated by some now-classic works (Ashworth and Tunbridge 1990; Hoffman 2003; Judd 2003; Judd and Fainstein 1999; Law 2002; Maitland and Newman 2009; Page and Hall 2003; Selby 2004a), the concept of the 'tourist city' recently underwent a true renewal thanks to a range of very inspiring studies (Bellini and Pasquinelli 2016; Maciocco and Serreli 2012). As world tourism cities face new challenges (Maxim 2019), crucial issues such as protests against tourism (Colomb

The original version of this chapter was inadvertently published with incorrect affiliation. The correction to this chapter is available at https://doi.org/10.1007/978-3-030-52136-3_14

L. Lucas (✉)
Univ. Littoral Côte d'Opale, Univ. Lille, ULR 4477 - TVES - Territoires Villes
Environnement & Société, Dunkerque, France

and Novy 2016), gentrification (Gravari-Barbas and Guinand 2017), the complexity of conflicts resulting from tourism (Sommer and Helbrecht 2017), the sharing culture (Stors and Baltes 2018), the experience economy (Lorentzen and Hansen 2015), social media branding (Kolb 2017; Vanolo 2017), interpretation of the urban landscape (Metro-Roland 2016), and the use of public space for recreational events (Smith 2017) have been investigated. Many works in the urban tourism[1] field focus on new urban tourist places (Füller and Michel 2014; Gravari-Barbas and Delaplace 2015; Novy and Huning 2008), leading to the hypothesis that the 'post-world tourist cities' are metropolitan laboratories for urban futures (Simpson 2016). The city as a place for tourists raises many issues for urban and tourism theory (Stock 2019) and we definitely must accept that tourism is shaping a new order in the urban world (Duhamel and Knafou 2007a, b). The city has become an 'entertainment machine' (Clark 2004) as recreation is not only a major economic but also a social, cultural, and spatial component of these urban systems. Tourism is now entirely infused into the everyday lives of cities (Frisch et al. 2019).

Tourism is an now obvious part of every city, but for each tourist, the practices of a city are not obvious. However, despite growing efforts targeting visitors' experiences and practices in cities (Bauder and Freytag 2015; Freytag 2008, 2010; Lucas 2018, 2019a, b; Maitland 2013; Rossetto 2012; Salas-Olmedo et al. 2018), the tourist practices of cities are not central to research (Wearing and Foley 2017). This paper contributes to developing a theoretical framework for spatial practices. The proposition argues that to cope with space, individuals mobilize (i) a stock of knowledge, (ii) skills/competences, and (iii) spatial capital. We will focus particularly on the knowledge aspect.

Little attention has been explicitly paid to 'urban tourist knowledge' (Selby 2004b), and research has been mostly conducted in a quantitative way (Tsaur et al. 2010) to analyse 'prior knowledge' (Gursoy 2003; Kerstetter and Cho 2004), information search behaviour (Fodness and Murray 1999; Lu and Chen 2014) or knowledge sharing via social media (Okazaki et al. 2017). This interest in spatial knowledge has been a central topic for behavioural geography – especially during the nineties, with Reginald Golledge as the leading figure (Golledge et al. 1995; Hirtle and Hudson 1991; Thorndyke and Goldin 1983) – and has also been a more recent interest of cognitive and psychological approaches to sense of direction and mobility (Manley 2016; Moores 2015; Stern and Leiser 1988; Tversky 2000; Wen et al. 2011), sometimes within virtual environments (Gillner and Mallot 1998; Jansen et al. 2010; Richardson et al. 1999; Tlaukaa et al. 2005). These works focus on how individuals (humans but also animals) learn a route by heart, memorize a specific path, and build a 'cognitive map' and 'mental representation'. Through a behavioural perspective, these studies emphasize routines and habits within a usual environment. However, what do humans do when they face an unknown situation? Some research attempts to explain the process of spatial knowledge acquisition in new environments (Ishikawa and Montello 2006). However, ultimately, the idea is the same: all of this research looks at spatial knowledge as a *result* of one's behaviour. By contrast, our argument is to focus on knowledge as a *prerequisite* for spatial

---

[1] See Coeffe and Stock (Chap. 11 in this book) for an in-depth analysis about the difference between 'urban tourism' and 'tourist city'.

practices.[2] We argue that knowledges[3] are crucial elements for understanding spatial practices or, more precisely, how individuals cope with space. The goal of this paper is thus not to understand what individuals learn from spatial experimentation but rather what they need to cope with a new place. Indeed, tourist practice is a situation of discovery and innovation, where individuals need to produce something new while they are inhabiting a city. In that sense, it is an illustrative expression of the 'creativity of the action' as expressed by Hans Joas (1997). This paper examines how knowledge participates effectively in the ways tourists inhabit a metropolis.

To that end, the first part exposes how tourism, through tourist practices, designs a new urbanness for cities. In the second part, we highlight how knowledge is essential to the way tourists inhabit a city. We adopt a phenomenological frame, drawing on Alfred Schutz' theory of what he calls the individual's 'stock of knowledge'. Schutz distinguishes three main components of this stock: basic elements, routine knowledge and specific components (Schutz 1971; Schutz and Luckmann 1973).[4] We express a fundamental point: to "know" (something) is not enough, it is also necessary to be capable of using it. We need to make a clear distinction between knowledge and skills, seen as mastery of techniques. The argumentation will be empirically based on interviews conducted during a survey about tourist practices in Los Angeles (Lucas 2014).

3.2 The "Touristic Urbanness" of Cities

Cities are now defined by what could be called a "touristic urbanness": these places are not only concerned with tourism but are built and function more and more around this dimension. Since the days of the Grand Tour, cities have been the first places to be concerned with tourism. Historically, we can observe that the tourism dynamic in cities is much more than a simple penetration of a new economy. As highlighted for American cities, a system of specific actors, techniques and places intended to welcome foreign people participates as a kind of civilization of American cities, a major improvement of their urbanity: "as a result, walking in an American city in the mid-nineteenth century was an act fraught with moral and political peril,

---

[2] To insist on the distinction, most of these prior studies about 'spatial knowledge' have modelling expectations through a 'behavioural' approach; we address this knowledge issue in a 'phenomenological' way within a 'theory of action'.

[3] Here, 'knowledge' is used in a broader sense as an equivalent of 'information'. Most papers do not define what they call 'knowledge'. Another fundamental point would be to discuss the distinction between 'spatial knowledge' and 'spatial cognition'.

[4] As the basic elements of the stock of knowledge are "universal and in principle invariant (…) they are on hand for everyone; they are the same in whatever relative-natural world view he was socialized"(Schutz and Luckmann 1973: 109), they are not a criterion that differentiates individuals. For that reason, in this paper, we will not take into consideration that kind of knowledge. Instead, we will focus on the two other groups of knowledge, which are "biographically articulated" (ibid.)

a danger the urban sketches of the period painted in the most lurid colors. Such cities were not amenable to nineteenth-century tourism (…) By 1915 urban tourism was not only thinkable, it was profitable. (…) Urban tourism presupposed and encouraged the domestication of public, urban spaces for the well-to-do" (Cocks 2001: 5). Until the early twentieth century, the American metropolis was perceived as a hostile space, or at least as a place not conducive to strolling and entertainment. It is the set of devices, equipment and other marketing strategies gradually put in place for tourists at that time that has contributed to a radical change in the perception society has of the American city – similar to what could have happened to the mountain and the coastline – by participating in the increase and reinforcement of sociability and norms in force in the heart of the modern American metropolis. This change constitutes a direct and genuine contribution to the domestication of the public space. To put it another way, this observation defends the following position: tourism has played an important role in increasing the urbanity of a number of American cities since the beginning of the twentieth century, both in terms of infrastructure and way of life: "the presence of tourists, afoot or clustered on trolleys and special 'seeing the city' cars, altered the composition and behaviour of city crowds. The cultivation of sights attractive to tourists altered the physical landscape to a small extent, and to a greater extent transformed the meaning of walking in the city in a way that affected many city residents" (Cocks 2001: 7). If we agree with this analysis, it is truly the presence and the practices of tourists that, by investing in the public space – most notably by strolling – contribute to changing the value of cities in the eyes of their own residents.

Tourism is not a simple activity set within an urban organization but rather a constituent element of the contemporary urbanity of cities (Lussault and Stock 2007). As asserted previously, "large cities are arguably the most important type of tourist destination across the world. They have always attracted visitors but until recently, with the exception of capital like London and Paris, the tourist industry has not been perceived as a significant one, nor have these cities been classified as tourist centres" (Law 2002: 1). Indeed, we may observe a radical change over a few decades, a *recreational turn* (Stock 2007b). This notion synthesizes the fact that today, an ever-increasing number of metropolises are shaped by the sphere of recreation: this is a radical change in the way cities are designed. The formerly annexed and residual tourist system has an increasingly important role in the functioning of these urban spaces and becomes a fundamental element of their dynamic: "Recreational turn" is therefore an expression that tries to back up the hypothesis that greater importance is given to different forms of recreation in contemporary society, particularly in European cities. The fundamental idea is that of a change in the quality of the urban space that is affected by recreation. European cities develop a new quality due to the relatively increased importance of recreation and, more specifically, of tourism. The quality of urbanness largely depends on the presence of tourists, tourist-related businesses and images informed by tourism. A 'real' city – a place defined by a certain quality of urbanness – is essentially defined by its touristic quality" (Stock 2007b). This 'recreational turn' underlines the fact that metropolises are all concerned (potentially or effectively) by the tourist practices that all aim to develop tourism. If this trend was initially restricted to Europe, we can now observe it in all cities of the world. Many metropolises in the United States, China, South America, etc. are driven by this process: tourism is inseparable from the way cities consider their status and income (Maitland & Newman 2009). However, how does tourism change the urbanness of cities? What is the tourist dynamic of the city?

Heritage and modernity are the two main components of the production and functioning of tourism cities (Duhamel 2007). As pinpointed by many works (cf. for instance, Ashworth and Tunbridge 2004; Leiper and Park 2010), the articulation between the taste for the old and for the new – from historic buildings (most European cities) to skyscrapers (US or Asian cities) –is definitely what tourists are looking for in cities. Recreational mega-events such as the Olympic Games or Universal Expositions are also true conveyors of this modern aspiration (this was as historically true for Paris as it is currently for London or Shanghai). Moreover, we can argue that tourists give value to what would probably be much less relevant for the local society because they become parts of everyday life. As a result, from its industrial roots, the city has been transformed into an entertainment machine (Clark 2004). While during the 1990s, some authors predicted the disappearance of the public space, the desire and the need to always welcome more tourists to cities required and provoked a full reassignment of this public space to recreational purposes. This process was conducted through generic amenities: fashion museums, "starchitecture", sports facilities, leisure events, regeneration of historic buildings, streetcars, sidewalk staging, pedestrian areas, green space, etc. This development generates a considerable transformation of the inner city: for example, all American cities are concerned with this type of improvement, with New York and Los Angeles being prime examples; consider how the urban dynamic of Downtown Los Angeles has changed in the last 20 years. While some researchers focus on the building of tourist precincts (Hayllar et al. 2008; González et al. 2013), we consider this dynamic as a rejuvenation of public space: most tourists do not want to be locked up in bubbles but prefer have the experience of one relatively neat and secure public space (which does not mean there is no tourist enclave). In that sense, we should think of tourist practices as revealing of the quality of a public space.

Tourism does not produce any type of urban space but rather produces urbanity at the highest level. In many cases, tourism is used by politicians as a lever of urban development: "the most visible effect of the increase in tourism concerns the modification of the urban landscape. Indeed, efforts to attract visitors have resulted in aestheticization and regeneration of parts of cities. (...) Decommissioned neighbourhoods and old industrial buildings have seen their heritage revalorized and rehabilitated into museums, art galleries, shops, cafes and lofts, while the redeveloped historic centres have seen new activities take hold behind their facades" (Maitland & Newman 2009). The change in the value of a space induced by tourism allows the legitimization of urban rehabilitation programmes established by local authorities. Tourism is therefore at the heart of the discourse of the various institutional players. This trend, which is very current, testifies to the increasingly pregnant participation of the sphere of recreation in the evolution of the urbanity of the metropolises. With the aim of attracting more diverse populations, recreation is a significant factor in the new valorisation of urban places through three main strate-gies: the enhancement of cultural heritage, the construction of iconic equipment and the launching of major events (Gravari-Barbas 2011, op. cit., tba). Tourism is more than ever a "great producer of urban spaces" (ibid.). Moreover, this dynamic can also be achieved spontaneously, without true planification, through a 'tourist diver-sion' of new buildings, or tourists investing in monuments or events that were not initially intended for them, as has happened for La Défense, the French National Library, or Paris-Plage, to take a few examples from Paris.

However, if 'off the beaten track' practices are growing (Maitland 2013; Matoga and Pawłowska 2018), tourists are still mainly concentrated in what has been called the *Central Tourist District*, or CTD (Duhamel and Knafou 2007a, b). This concept is a balanced proposition to describe places that are massively and visibly inhabited by tourists in one metropolis: the CTD may not consist of a single place and may not be in a compact form but is usually much more spread out or even stretched in a dominant direction. In addition, it is made identifiable not by a specific landscape (the forest of towers for the CBD) but by the significant and therefore easily identifi-able presence of tourists. In other words, the CTD is first and foremost the area of confirmed tourist practices; it combines places for sightseeing, strolling, shopping and, in part, residing (Duhamel and Knafou 2007a, b, op. cit., tba). Indeed, the majority of urban dwellers, and also tourists, no longer live downtown, and thus we could summarize tourism in the city as the visitation of peri-urban city centres (Knafou 2007, tba). In that sense, visiting a city means finding a new way to access centrality (ibid). Tourism development must be understood as a major element of the reconfiguration of the centrality of metropolises: it implies a centripetal dynamic within cities.

A strong hypothesis stems from this observation: tourism involves both a return *to* the centre and a return *of* the centre (Stock and Lucas 2012). The latter process, 'return *of* the centre', focuses on the material aspect: this place returns to the heart of the concerns of local society; it is the object of new development, particularly by urban policies and private investment. The political and economic ambitions to develop tourism lean on the regeneration of downtowns through a recreation-based urbanism, a trend that has been particularly impressive for US metropolises but more broadly for all metropolises in the world. This material return goes along with – as a consequence as much as an indispensable condition – a 'return *to* the centre' expressed by the return of populations who have long neglected it in favour of the suburbs: this corresponds to a change in the way societies look at this type of space. More than just a gaze, tourist practices in cities must be considered a new temporary way in which all social classes inhabit cities. After decades of sub- and peri-urbanization, it would correspond to a temporary recreational appropriation of a space. Downtowns are no longer accessible only to a small number of people but are potentially valued by all populations, with a strong social mix, where exposure to otherness is temporary but strong and powerful (Knafou 2007, op. cit., tba).

We can then conclude that both residents and tourists inhabit temporary cities, but each one in a specific way, with different intentions and motivations and with different resources (Stock 2007a, 2019). Inhabiting a city touristically means that

the city is charged with a certain degree of alterity: the city is encoded as an otherness, not as a familiar space (ibid). This is a crucial point: over all the post-tourism
and post-tourist discussions – arguing that nothing differentiates the tourist from the
local who strolls around taking a picture of a building in his own city – there is still
a huge difference. The local is used to this urban space while the tourist is just discovering it; she does not truly know where to go, what to do, etc. Alfred Schutz
explicitly considers this point:

> The man brought up in a town will find his way in its streets by following the habits he has
> acquired in his daily occupations. He may not have a consistent conception of the organiza-
> tion of the city, and, if he uses the underground railway to go to his office, a large part of the
> city may remain unknown to him. Nevertheless, he will have a proper sense of the distances
> between different places and of the directions in which the different points are situated rela-
> tively to whatever he regards as the center. (…) When a stranger comes to the town, he has
> to learn to orientate himself in it and to know it. Nothing is self-explanatory for him and he
> has to ask an expert, in this case a native, to learn how to get from one point to another. He
> may, of course, refer to a map of the town, but even to use the map successfully he must
> know the meaning of the signs on the map, the exact point within the town where he stands
> and its correlative on the map, and at least one more point in order correctly to relate the
> signs on the map to the real objects in the city (Schutz 1971: 66).

A question looms: how are tourists able to inhabit a city?

3.3 Inhabiting the City as a Tourist

For every individual, inhabiting any place as a tourist must be considered a "problematic situation". We use this expression following the opposition that Alfred
Schutz establishes with the "routine situation". The latter is when the situation "can
be sufficiently determined, with the aid of habitual knowledge, so that the plan-
determined interest is satisfied. All 'open' elements of the situation can be routinely
determined" (Schutz and Luckmann 1973: 115). The former is when "my knowledge is not 'clear' enough, 'sure' enough, not sufficiently free of contradiction, for
me to handle the current situation (…) In contrast to routine situations, I must here
either acquire new elements of knowledge or take old ones which are not sufficiently clarified for the present situation, and bring them to higher levels of clarity"
(ibid.). For each tourist, the alterity included in a tourist situation holds a certain
level of uncertainty: a city is a *problematic* place for tourists, and knowledge is at
the heart of the challenge of inhabiting the city.

The situation described above is particularly evident in Los Angeles, our case
study. Unlike the classic model of the tourist city as previously described, the geography of tourism in Los Angeles is highly dispersed: "Hollywood is the most visited
area within the county, but it still accounts for only 23% of all such visits. Beverly
Hills is second, accounting for 17% of non-resident tourist visits. Fewer than 10%
make a special trip to visit downtown Los Angeles, underscoring once again the
contrast with New York" (Fainstein and Gladstone 2001). More fundamentally,
three main features build the specificity of Los Angeles: first, this city was not

historically organized around a downtown; as a result, Downtown Los Angeles was traditionally not a major tourist destination – even if there has been a change in recent years with the renewal of this area. In relation to this point, the second distinctive element is that the tourist space of Los Angeles is not concentrated in one place but consists of a network of nodes that are separated by long distances – there are approximately 30 km between Downtown Los Angeles and Santa Monica. However, public transportation was insufficiently developed to address this problem (here again, we observe a very recent increase in the subway network): Los Angeles is the classic car-made city, and renting a car is the first thing most tourists do once they exit the airplane. Finally, in Los Angeles, not only do tourists not know the place, but they face an unusual spatial configuration (Lucas 2011).

The argumentation of this paper relies on approximately 70 semi-directive interviews that were performed during four field trips to Los Angeles between 2010 and 2013 (Lucas 2014). Most of these interviews were conducted at the Motel 6 hotel (Whitley Av., near the *Walk of Fame*) and in the public space around Hollywood Boulevard and Santa Monica – the two places that all tourists visit – to reduce a priori selection and bias. As this study used a qualitative approach, the priority was to obtain the broadest diversity of sociological profiles and a variety of ways of coping with space. Finally, the tourists interviewed were mostly from European countries and the United States, with very different profiles with respect to gender, incomes, ages and ways of travelling. These interviews were built to reveal the individuals' skills and knowledge through the lexical field of ability – for instance, the use of words such as "I couldn't" and "I didn't know". The fundamental idea was to put in perspective their discourses regarding their own practices, to guide the tourists to explain and justify their choices and trade-offs during their stays in Los Angeles, and to try to understand the motives, reasons and causes of their personal ways of inhabiting this urban space.

(i) *The guidebook as specific knowledge*

To focus on the knowledge challenge and develop a better understanding of the ways tourists make assemblages of different places inside the metropolis, the first step is to elucidate how tourists organize their navigation. The following extract, from the case of Marc and Amélie (Switzerland, 33 and 25 y.o.), offers a precise description of how tourists develop an itinerary in Los Angeles:

> We first searched individually, then we bought some guidebooks to see the selection of what we absolutely needed to do. This morning, we looked at the guidebooks to choose according to what we are interested in. We take inspiration in the guidebooks and then we make our choice with what we want. After that, we can make some pathways variations, but it is important to have a guiding principle. We focus on the areas we want to visit and we locate the places on the map. We define the places more or less in the same location. It is a transportation optimization perspective. We stay three days here, so if we want to see some things, we need to plan what we are going to do. You can't arrive in such a city as Los Angeles by saying you are going to stroll.

The atypical character of the spatial configuration of this metropolis, as it is perceived and lived by individuals, clearly comes through in this extract (*you can't arrive in such a city as Los Angeles by saying you are going to stroll*): in Los Angeles, tourists have to prepare and plan how and where to travel; navigation within the urban space seems to be, at least some tourists, an imperative, a necessity (with the role of improvisation – of random strolling – being inversely reduced). This spatial configuration has another direct consequence, also explicitly mentioned in these tourists' comments: the *transportation optimization perspective.* We explicitly understand how the logic of spatial optimization influences the ways (some) tourists deal with space in Los Angeles. Moreover, we also notice that they use guidebooks to organize their strategy. This observation is a good confirmation of the prescriptive role (*what we absolutely need to do*) of guidebooks for many tourists as they plan their stays and especially their routes. However, we also see that individuals use these tools critically: they do not strictly follow the guidebooks' advice but rather use the books to get ideas in order to plan a trip that is best adapted to the practices they want to apply. However, while owning a knowledge resource – knowing where to find the information one needs – is an important thing, being able to use and interpret that information is the next one. This is not evident, as we can observe in the next interview extract, from Joseph (24 y.o., French, living in Chicago, visiting L.A. for vacation with a group of friends):

> Well, in Los Angeles, I checked the guidebook… Well, you know, it seems we are far from the international famous stuff like in New York, or even in Chicago, where there is the Modern Art Institute, which is really famous… Here, I checked the *Routard* and it says 'we advice you to go to the animal cemetery, it's unique'… Ok, I can imagine, but… Well, that's it, Hollywood Boulevard, we quickly went around…

The reference to the Art Institute of Chicago shows that art centres are part of these visitors' cultural background. They were probably interested in visiting museums in Los Angeles, which is why they consulted the guidebook. It is surprising that they just pick an animal cemetery as a cultural destination, as there are internationally renowned museums in Los Angeles, and the guidebook definitely mentions them. Perhaps these tourists were not truly focused in their search, or perhaps they were caught up in the reputation of Los Angeles for 'sun, beaches, and palm trees.' This example shows that it should not be assumed that tourists can or will read a guidebook efficiently according to their purpose and tastes.

The first function of a guidebook is to identify places that the tourist must see in a particular metropolis, establishing a kind of homogenization of tourist practices at the global scale – all around the world, everybody is more or less focused on the same places. The guidebooks produce a discursive regime around such locations, creating, building and developing the social value of some places as well as the depreciation of others, instituting a true (touristic) hierarchy within the metropolis. Guidebooks go further in their recommendations by suggesting itineraries: they not only give advice about places to visit, such as autonomous locations, but also suggest different kinds of articulation between these places. Indeed, a guidebook could be very prescriptive, saying what a tourist *must* do: this is a powerful social prescription, as has been observed in the way a city is presented in mass media travel writing' (Stone 2018). Moreover, a guidebook's prescriptive character is not limited to places one must see, it can also dictate the order in which to visit them (some guidebooks, such as the *Frommers'* series, even point out in their route suggestions the streets tourists must take and the restaurants where they should stop). Such guidebooks truly answer the question of how to organize one's navigation within an urban space.

Research about the mobility paths of same-day visitors in Freiburg showed that visitors who are 'not well-prepared' stroll through the inner city, while 'well-prepared' visitors tend to engage in a wider range of activities (Bauder and Freytag 2015). The large difference in tourist navigation in Los Angeles due to individual skills has been previously highlighted in other studies (Lucas 2019a, b). However, let us analyse how the issue of knowledge influences the way tourists inhabit Los Angeles. To do this, we use two new cases. The first one is Keredin (26 y.o., Saint-Raphael, south of France), travelling with his wife, brother, sister-in-law and children:

- So it will have been just three days...
- Four days! Well, yeah, I tell you four days, but we arrived late afternoon, we were very tired, so we made a quick walk before to go to bed. After... uh... the second day, what did we do...? Uh... the same, the second day we visited a little bit like that! Yesterday we did...
- You visited a 'little bit like that' what?
- No, the same...
- Hollywood Boulevard?
- Yeah, Hollywood Boulevard, we did not do much... Our program was Universal Studio, but I did not want to go because it was very expensive and I expected it to be a museum. In fact, it was a theme park, I regret because they make me salivate at the prospect of. I thought it was more a visit of the movie sets when in fact it is an entertainment park with 3D and movies...
- So, you walked alone in Hollywood Boulevard?
- Yeah, but I do not feel comfortable. In Las Vegas and New York I was walking alone, it was different. I love the mix there, if you go to a bar they speak in all languages and it is a mythical place, it is also very beautiful at night visually. As soon as we arrived here, I did not feel very comfortable... I do not know, the people are weird, there are a lot of weird people. (...) Yes, in fact I feel better in the hotel, it's a kind of *refuge*. I was disappointed with Hollywood Boulevard, I was expecting something much more classy, there seems to be a lot of gangs... I've heard other people say the same thing too. There are plenty of places you cannot go, the night is dangerous.

This extract highlights a true area of confusion for this tourist: he does not know what a certain place (Universal Studios) is truly about. His stay in Los Angeles is not successful – he admits he missed out on something due to this misunderstanding. In that sense, the lack of knowledge is truly penalizing for this tourist's practice. The spatial configuration of Los Angeles seems to confront Keredin with too much alterity: he has an explicitly strong apprehension toward public space. According to his own words, the people are 'weird', he feels 'not comfortable', and the hotel is a 'refuge'. As a result, his experience in Los Angeles focused mainly on Hollywood, around Motel 6 (where the interview took place), with a tour in a tourist van and a day spent in Santa Monica, where he had to go right after the interview. This is a quite under-developed itinerary for a stay of 3 days (Fig. 3.1).

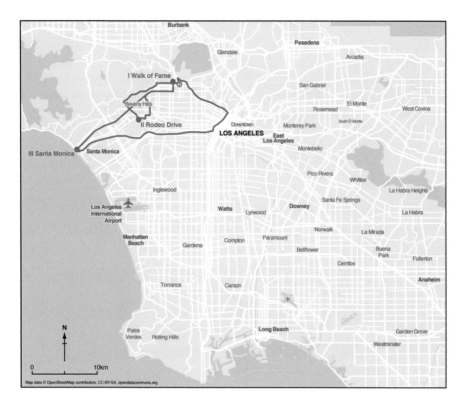

Fig. 3.1 Keredin's itinerary in Los Angeles

Tourist itineraries in Los Angeles can be much more ambitious and successful. This is the case for Elise (25 y.o., Paris, travelling alone). She spent the first 2 days of her stay at a friend's house in Santa Monica: "We went to the beach in Long Beach: it was far away, we took one hour… The next day I did the Pier, the canals… It's funny Venice Beach, people who play sports… near the canals it's very quiet, very nice". On the third day, she moved to new accommodations ("I prefer not to stay far from here") and settled at a hostel in a Hollywood ("because there is parking") neighbourhood where she spent the day walking on the Walk of Fame. If she get a rent car since San Francisco, she pays for a tour in a tourist van (the interview takes place on this occasion), "because I do not know the places without GPS, neither history, and with traffic I would not pay attention to what's around. At first I thought about walking, but it's hot and I'm tired". She visited the Griffith Observatory the next day before going to Downtown "to see the architecture". The day after, she planned to go to the Getty Center and most likely to LACMA, culture being a focal point of her practice in this metropolis: "yes, I like to walk in the streets, museums, exhibitions" (Fig. 3.2).

This broader itinerary results explicitly from her knowledge about the cultural resources available: she knows the places that interest her (museums, observatory,

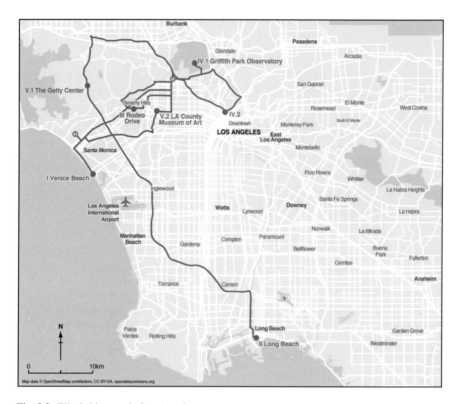

Fig. 3.2 Elise's itinerary in Los Angeles

etc.) and how to use her social network, a precious source of information. Moreover, she has a guidebook and is able to extract and interpret information according to her taste. She is not constrained in her way of inhabiting Los Angeles despite the vast expanse of its tourist space. However, distance is still a crucial issue, and placement and mobility are at the heart of her trade-off: she chooses an hostel to be close to the visited place and while she rented a car in San Francisco, she pays to take a bus tour: the knowledge issue is once again at the heart of her choice ('I do not know the places without GPS').

Elise and Keredin are two people of the same age and from the same country, but they have two different cultural backgrounds (she values museums, he avoids them). On the one hand, the young woman is travelling alone, but she acquires considerable knowledge about places she might be interested in and creates quite a broad itinerary to visit the places she wants to see. On the other hand, the young man, who is travelling in a group, does not truly know much about different places in Los Angeles. He says he is afraid of public space, which confines him to a limited itinerary in Los Angeles (relative to the length of his stay). These two cases show that the criteria of gender and travel mode (group/alone) cannot systematically explain the different ways in which individuals cope with space.

Obviously, guidebooks are particular to specific destinations. In that sense, we must think of them as containing specific knowledge, as "a cookbook for example is already a thematization and social objectivation of a specific knowledge" (Schutz and Luckmann 1973: 110). Indeed, Alfred Schutz calls this type of knowledge and its organization 'cook-book knowledge': "the cook-book has recipes, lists of ingredients, formulae for mixing them, and directions for finishing off. This is all we need to make an apple pie, and also all we need to deal with the routine matter of daily life" (Schutz 1971: 73). Moreover, we must recognize that while the guidebook is delivering some information, such as where to go and what to do, it does not explain how to use that information, i.e., how to *put knowledge into practice*. Knowledge[5] is essential to practice, but it is not enough.

(ii) *Habitual knowledge: a mastery of techniques*

Knowledge is just the first step in the achievement of a practice. Concurrently with 'specific knowledge', another element of the individual's 'stock of knowledge' is highlighted by Alfred Schutz when he distinguishes three types of what he calls 'habitual knowledge' (Schutz and Luckmann 1973: 107, op. cit.):

- *Skills* are the functional unities of bodily movement. Although kinetic experience is built on 'nonlearned' basic elements, these elements can be learned. Walking must be learned. Swimming must be learned, eating with cutlery must be learned.
- *Useful knowledge* no longer truly belongs to the usual functioning of the body. These types of knowledge were originally 'problematic' but have been 'definitively' solved. We do these activities 'automatically', and they are 'standardized': smoking, chopping wood, shaving, writing, playing the piano, riding, etc.
- *Knowledge of recipes* can be on hand for its 'self-evident' implications, especially regarding the end-horizons of situations, without becoming thematized: a hunter reading tracks, or a sailor or mountain climber orienting himself or herself to changes in the weather.

Two objections can be raised against this division. First, whether an individual is swimming (*skills*), playing the piano (*useful knowledge*) or reading tracks (*knowledge of recipes*), that is to say whether the practice requires tools or not, the action is always ultimately executed through the body. To draw a distinction between these actions is perhaps not relevant. Second, all these activities are indeed forms of knowledge, but they are knowledge of a radically different form in comparison with specific forms of knowledge: they consist much more in *know-how*. Tim Ingold develops a similar point of view when he regards skill "simply as a 'particular application of dexterity', in contrast to what he calls 'know-how', which refers to the capacity of the craftsman to envision forms in advance of their implementation" (Ingold 2011: 299). However, we could argue that each individual project is the

---

[5]These types of 'guidebook-knowledge' are not the only ones that individuals use within their tourist practices. Tourists also use what we could call 'personal knowledge' from their past experience – for example, tourists who chose their hotel in Los Angeles because of a successful and pleasant previous stay at the same chain in New York.

result of the craftsman's action when he plans and achieves it. Ingold uses 'dexterity' in opposition to 'technique' to critique a mechanical perception of the body and the idea of repetition suggested by the latter term.

However, swimming, playing the piano, or reading tracks are mostly questions of technique. Starting from the observation that he made "the fundamental mistake to think that there is technique only when there is an instrument", Marcel Mauss postulated that "the body is man's first and most natural instrument. Or more accurately, not to speak of instruments, man's first and most natural technical object, and at the same time technical means, is his body. (…) In this case, all that needs to be said is quite simply that we are dealing with techniques of the body" (Mauss 1973: 75). Indeed, we should not be duped by the fact that technique "has a bad name, it can seem soulless, and people whose hands become highly trained view technique [as] intimately linked to expression" (Sennett 2008: 149). Rather, we may call technique "an action that is effective and traditional" (Mauss 1973: 75). This is a crucial point pinpointed by Mauss: techniques of the body are not postures that are progressively and collectively constituted 'for the beauty of the gesture' but above all because they have been socially defined as the most effective ways of doing.

In that way, we consider all these skills as *mastery of (body) techniques* (Lucas 2019c). Ludwig Wittgenstein makes a fundamental observation about the importance of the latter expression when he describes the ability of one individual: "the grammar of the word 'knows' is evidently closely related to that of 'can', 'is able to'. But also closely related to that of 'understands' ('Mastery' of a technique). (…) To understand a sentence means to understand a language. To understand a language means to be master of a technique" (Wittgenstein 1953: §150 and §199). There is a strong link between 'to know' and 'to be able' according to Wittgenstein. However, it is not because a person knows something (a word, a gesture) that she is able to use it. We need to dissociate knowledge from ability. To know, either in the sense of getting information or understanding something 'in theory,' is a first step toward achieving a practice. In a second step, skills or know-how allow someone to use that information, to put theory into practice. Then, we join with the meaning of Schutz' 'habitual': to use knowledge to make a movement, to repeat it, is the only way to "master" something.

This mastery of techniques is another important element in understanding the different ways tourists inhabit Los Angeles. The big challenge when visiting a metropolis is to address distance: vehicles are one of the most obvious and important tools individuals need to cope with space. This is particularly true in Los Angeles: while in other cities, the tourist space is reachable within walkable distances and tourists can use a developed subway network, this is not possible in this metropolis. The main tourist places are spread throughout a very large area and are not accessible through the subway system: using public transportation means one must take the bus, which is more complicated. Table 3.1 highlights the differences in the mastery of techniques required by tourists when addressing this metric issue.

Here, again, in both cases, the social profile of the individual is similar: two young people using public transportation, and two middle-aged Americans renting a car. However, in both cases, we observe that individuals can easily and efficiently

Table 3.1 Tourists' different levels of ease of dealing with distance in Los Angeles

Mastery of techniques Metrics	Low	Strong
Public transportation	*"No, it's not easy to take public transportation!* Before I take a bus, I searched a lot on the internet, I saw all the maps and rides (…) *I wanted to visit Getty Center but it was too far to get there from my hostel.* I just used public transportation *so it was hard to get there, I couldn't go* (…) I didn't want to go far from my hostel, because I'm travelling by myself so the priority is on my safety so I stay around here." **(Sujin, 21 y.o., Séoul)**	"We don't have a car anymore. We left it yesterday. *Here you can travel with the subway,* it's cheap. If you have a car you have to pay the parking, it costs money. It's a big city, so you cannot walk to Venice Beach, it's impossible. Unless we miss the plane tomorrow." **(Jan, 26 y.o, Amsterdam)**
Car	"We're from Washington. I don't want to drive into the traffic so we decided to take the bus from Venice to Hollywood (…) in Washington if you get on the freeway if you take the wrong exit it's not a problem, but here you have to drive a lot to get back where you have to go. It's very confusing. (…) *Yes. It's not easier to move around if you're not used of the area.* (…) in the area where I live it's more residential and industrial. (…) It's very diversified here, a big cultural background." **(George, 40 ans, Washington State)**	"We do a lot of driving in Dallas, but it's not like in LA. In Dallas, the distance between things is so great that you're forced to drive, it's very similar from that perspective, you don't have great public transportation, so if you want to get from one place to another it's problematical and sometimes the distance could be 20 or 30 miles; unlike here, it could be 8 or 20 miles maximum. From here to Beverly Hills, it's not very far but it takes 30 minutes. It's very similar to Dallas, but Dallas is more spread out. What I've noticed about the traffic in LA vs Dallas is I think the people in LA come to the fact that there is always going to be traffic and so they are nice, friendly, they let you in, they let you off. In Dallas people are frustrated when there is a lot of traffic." **(Randle, 35 y.o., Dallas)**

Lucas (2014)

use the means of transportation they choose (to achieve the practices they wanted), and on the other hand, there are individuals for whom it is complicated to move around in Los Angeles whether by bus or car. The Sujin case is particularly illustrative: she *knows* and *wants* to visit the Getty Museum, but she felt *unable* to get there via public transportation. Her way of inhabiting Los Angeles and the fact that she ultimately does not visit the Getty is not a question of knowledge but rather how to implement the information she has. George, older and American (reducing the age and culture bias), also found it difficult to move around in this city: the crucial issue when visiting Los Angeles is not having a car but rather being able to use it efficiently.

We might think this situation is due to a lack of mastery of the situation, as these tourists are not used to the area. This is the reason given by George ("It's not easier to move around if you're not used to the area") to justify why he prefers to leave his car at his hotel and take the bus from Venice to Hollywood Boulevard. However, two questions arise from this interpretation: first, if two individuals are in the same unusual situation, why is it that one is able to cope and one is not? If 'mastery' of the urban space was necessary, no tourist should be able to easily inhabit Los Angeles. As shown in the previous cases, this is not the case. The second question is the following: can we say an individual has mastered a technique if he cannot use it everywhere?

To go further, we should examine in depth what we mean by 'master.' Can individuals ever master an environment, a place, a city, even when they are used to inhabiting it? As explicitly suggested by Schutz (cf. intra), they may have more or less important knowledge about it, but that does not mean they have mastered it. Their mastery would be for just part of the space, not the whole. Moreover, new events can occur, and one's routine can be disturbed even in a familiar environment. In this case, mastery just means developing some habits in one place. We can ask the same question about the technique: at what point can an individual be said to have mastered a technique? Here, again, a relative perspective must also be adopted, as suggested by Schutz and Luckmann: "such knowledge of mine indeed remains taken for granted as obvious, but the *performances* can again become 'problematic', if only in their execution. After a longer convalescence I have 'unlearned' walking; I must learn it again from the beginning. (…) If someone wants to ski again after 15 years, he will notice the discrepancy between his 'knowledge' and the performance" (Schutz and Luckmann 1973: 106). Two important points about individual capability occur in this quote: first, we must make a distinction between being physically able and being technically able. The authors are actually talking more about the first: an individual's body can never truly unlearn a technique (because he knows how to walk, ski), but he may not be physically able to apply it. The second element underlined here is that mastery is always proof of the situation: an individual *thinks* he can reproduce an action he previously achieved. However, he may fail to apply his previous technique if the new situation appears to be too complex. Therefore, if the mastery of one environment cannot be the criterion used to define and evaluate the skilled person, the environment remains a major component of the practice because it reveals the level that individual's mastery of techniques.

3.4   Conclusion: *Knowledge as a Capital*

The purpose of this chapter was to emphasize the importance of knowledge in the way tourists inhabit one metropolis. This chapter argues that these ways of inhabiting are not merely the results of taste or economic means; they are also matters of knowledge and skills. We might think it would be easy to find useful information because individuals now carry with them an incredible source of knowledge through GPS, the Internet and smart devices during their practice. However, finding such information is not easy: knowledge is still a challenge. First, there is the challenge of obtaining information, of sorting out the good (according to their needs) information from all the available information. Then, they must be able to use that information. Individuals do not master a situation but rather cope with space more or less easily, according to their level of knowledge and mastery of techniques. One more final idea must be outlined, as both knowledge seen as *stock* and skills seen as *mastery* imply a dynamic of accumulation. Schutz and Luckmann explicitly pinpoint this angle when they say that "the stock of knowledge is built on sedimentations of formerly actually present experiences that were bound to situations and biographically articulated" (Schutz and Luckmann 1973: 99). Consequently, we may argue that all the experiences lived by one individual are not a juxtaposition of distinct practices but are cumulative: they produce a capitalization on knowledge and techniques and contribute to progressive personal enrichment. Specifically, concerning the use of space, this last point strengthens the hypothesis suggested by Jacques Lévy (2014), following the theoretical framework of Pierre Bourdieu, of the possession by each individual of one *spatial capital*.

References

Ashworth, G. J., & Tunbridge, J. E. (1990). *The tourist-historic city*. London: Belhaven Press.

Ashworth, G. J., & Tunbridge, J. E. (2004). 'Whose tourist-historic city? Localizing the global and globalizing the local', in Lew, A. A., Hall, C. M. & Williams, A. M. (eds) *A companion to tourism* (pp.210–222). Oxford: Blackwell.

Bauder, M., & Freytag, T. (2015). Visitor mobility in the city and the effects of travel preparation. *Tourism Geographies, 17*(5), 682–700.

Bellini, N., & Pasquinelli, C. (2016). *Tourism in the City: Towards an integrative agenda on urban tourism*. Cham: Springer.

Clark, T. N. (ed.) (2004). *The city as an entertainment machine* (Vol. 9: Research in urban policy).

Cocks, C. (2001). *Doing the town. The rise of urban tourism in the United States 1859–1915*. Berkeley: University of California Press.

Colomb, C., & Novy, J. (2016). *Protest and resistance in the tourist city*. London: Routledge.

Duhamel, P. H. (2007). Patrimoine et modernité: double logique de la production et du renouvellement des villes touristiques. In P. H. Duhamel & R. Knafou (Eds.), *Mondes urbains du tourisme* (pp. 297–307). Paris: Belin.

Duhamel, P. H., & Knafou, R. (Eds.). (2007a). *Mondes urbains du tourisme*. Paris: Belin.

Duhamel, P. H., & Knafou, R. (2007b). Le rôle du tourisme dans la construction et le fonctionnement de la centralité parisienne. In T. Saint-Julien & R. Le Goix (Eds.), *La métropole parisienne. Centralités, inégalités, proximités* (pp. 39–64). Paris: Belin.

Fainstein, S., & Gladstone, D. (2001). Tourism in US global cities: A comparison of New York and Los Angeles. *Journal of Urban Affairs, 23*(1), 23–40.

Fodness, D., & Murray, B. (1999). A model of tourist information search behavior. *Journal of Travel Research, 37*(3), 220–230.

Freytag, T. (2008). Making a difference: Tourist practices of repeat visitors in the city of Paris. *Social Geography Discussions, 4*, 1–25.

Freytag, T. (2010). Being a tourist in Heidelberg: Exploring visitor activities and spatial mobility in the city. *Revista Geografica Italiana, 117*(2), 379–389.

Frisch, T., Sommer, C., Stoltenberg, L., & Stors, N. (2019). *Tourism and everyday life in the contemporary city*. London: Routledge.

Füller, H., & Michel, B. (2014). Stop being a tourist!' New dynamics of urban tourism in Berlin-Kreuzberg. *International Journal of Urban and Regional Research, 38*(4), 1304–1318.

Gillner, S., & Mallot, H. A. (1998). Navigation and acquisition of spatial knowledge in a virtual maze. *Journal of Cognitive Neuroscience, 10*(4), 445–463.

Golledge, R. G., Dougherty, V., & Bell, S. (1995). Acquiring spatial knowledge: Survey versus route-based knowledge in unfamiliar environments. *Annals of the Association of American Geographers, 85*(1), 134–158.

González, J. M., Salinas, E., & Navarro, E. (2013). The City of Varadero (Cuba) and the urban construction of a tourist enclave. *Urban Affairs Review, 50*(2), 206–243.

Gravari-Barbas, M. (2011). Le tourisme, un formidable producteur d'espaces urbains. In L. Cailly & M. Vanier (Eds.), *La France, une géographie urbaine* (pp. 325–366). Paris: Armand Colin.

Gravari-Barbas, M., & Delaplace, M. (2015). Le tourisme urbain 'hors des sentiers battus'. Coulisses, interstices et nouveaux territoires touristiques urbains. *Téoros* [Online] *34*, 1–2, available at: http://journals.openedition.org/teoros/2790

Gravari-Barbas, M., & Guinand, S. (2017). *Tourism and gentrification in contemporary metropolises: International perspectives*. London: Routledge.

Gursoy, D. (2003). Prior product knowledge and its influence on the traveler's information search behavior. *Journal of Hospitality and Leisure Marketing, 10*(3/4), 113–130.

Hayllar, B., Griffin, T., & Edwards, D. (2008). *City spaces–tourist places: Urban tourism precincts*. Amsterdam: Elsevier.

Hirtle, S. C., & Hudson, J. (1991). Acquisition of spatial knowledge for routes. *Journal of Environmental Psychology, 11*(4), 335–345.

Hoffman, L. M. (Ed.). (2003). *Cities and visitors: Regulating people, markets, and city space*. Malden: Blackwell.

Ingold, T. (2011). *The perception of the environment*. London: Routledge.

Ishikawa, T., & Montello, D. R. (2006). Spatial knowledge acquisition from direct experience in the environment: Individual differences in the development of metric knowledge and the integration of separately learned places. *Cognitive Psychology, 52*, 93–129.

Jansen, P., Schmelter, A., & Heil, M. (2010). Spatial knowledge acquisition in younger and elderly adults. A study in a virtual environment. *Experimental Psychology, 57*(1), 54–60.

Joas, H. (1997). *The creativity of the action*. Chicago: University Of Chicago Press.

Judd, D. R. (2003). *The infrastructure of play: Building the tourist city*. Armonk: Sharpe.

Judd, D. R., & Fainstein, S. S. (Eds.). (1999). *The tourist city*. New Haven: Yale University Press.

Kerstetter, D., & Cho, M. H. (2004). Prior knowledge, credibility and information search. *Annals of Tourism Research, 31*(4), 961–985.

Knafou, R. (2007). L'urbain et le tourisme: une construction laborieuse. In P. Duhamel & R. Knafou (Eds.), *Les mondes urbains du tourisme* (pp. 9–21). Paris: Belin.

Kolb, B. (2017). *Tourism marketing for cities and towns: Using social media and branding to attract tourists*. London: Routledge.

Law, C. M. (2002). *Urban tourism: The visitor economy and the growth of large cities*. London: Continuum.

Leiper, N., & Park, S.-Y. (2010). Skyscrapers' influence on cities' roles as tourist destinations. *Current Issues in Tourism, 13*(4), 333–349.

Lévy, J. (2014). Inhabiting. In R. Lee et al. (Eds.), *The Sage handbook of human geography* (pp. 45–68). London: Sage.

Lorentzen, A., & Hansen, C. (Eds.). (2015). *The city in the experience economy: Role and transformation*. London: Routledge.

Lu, A., & Chen, B. (2014). Information search behavior of independent travelers: A cross-cultural comparison between Chinese, Japanese, and American travelers. *Journal of Hospitality Marketing & Management, 23*(8), 865–884.

Lucas, L. (2011). Los Angeles ou l'hypothèse de la métapole touristique. *Mondes du tourisme* (Special Issue), pp 244–253.

Lucas, L. (2014) *Habiter touristique et agencement de l'espace urbain: le cas de Los Angeles. Recherche sur le concours des compétences des individus quant à leurs manières de faire avec les épreuves spatiales d'une métapole touristique.* Unpublished PhD Thesis, University of Lausanne, defended the 01.14.2014.

Lucas, L. (2018). Les bus touristiques, une technologie spatiale pour habiter les métropoles. Le cas de Los Angeles. *Mondes du Tourisme* [Online]: http://journals.openedition.org/tourisme/1671

Lucas, L. (2019a). The ordinary–extraordinary dialectics in tourist metropolises. *International Journal of Tourism Cities, 5*(1), 17–34.

Lucas, L. (2019b). 'I was not able to go there': Introducing a skills perspective about how tourists navigate in Los Angeles. *Tourist Studies, 19*(3), 357–377.

Lucas, L. (2019c). La maitrise des techniques du corps. Les pratiques des touristes au regard de leurs compétences. *EspacesTemps.net.* [Online]. https://www.espacestemps.net/articles/les-techniques-du-corps-des-competences-pour-faire-avec-de-lespace/.

Lussault, M., & Stock, M. (2007). Tourisme et urbanité. In P. Duhamel & R. Knafou (Eds.), *Les mondes urbains du tourisme* (pp. 241–245). Paris: Belin.

Lussault, M., & Stock, M. (2010). "Doing with space": Towards a pragmatics of space. *Social Geography, 5*, 11–19. https://doi.org/10.5194/sg-5-11-2010.

Maciocco, G., & Serreli, S. (Eds.). (2012). *Enhancing the city: New perspectives for tourism and leisure.* London: Springer.

Maitland, R. (2013). Backstage behaviour in the Global City: Tourists and the search for the 'real London'. *Procedia – Social and Behavioral Sciences, 105*, 12–19.

Maitland, R., & Newman, P. (2009). *World tourism cities: Developing tourism off the beaten track.* London: Routledge.

Manley, E. (2016). Estimating the topological structure of driver spatial knowledge. *Applied Spatial Analysis and Policy, 9*(2), 165–189.

Matoga, L., & Pawłowska, A. (2018). Off-the-beaten-track tourism: A new trend in the tourism development in historical European cities. A case study of the city of Krakow, Poland. *Current Issues in Tourism, 21*(14), 1644–1669.

Mauss, M. (1973). Techniques of the body. *Economy and Society, 2*(1), 70–88.

Maxim, C. (2019). Challenges faced by world tourism cities – London's perspective. *Current Issues in Tourism, 22*(9), 1006–1024.

Metro-Roland, M. (2016). *Tourists, signs and the city: The semiotics of culture in an urban landscape.* London: Routledge.

Moores, S. (2015). We find our way about: Everyday media use and 'inhabitant knowledge'. *Mobilities, 10*(1), 17–35.

Novy, J., & Huning, S. (2008). 'New tourism (areas) in the 'new Berlin. In R. Maitland & P. Newman (Eds.), *World tourism cities. Developing tourism off the beaten track* (pp. 87–107). London: Routledge.

Okazaki, S., Andrieu, L., & Campo, S. (2017). Knowledge sharing among tourists via social media: A comparison between Facebook and TripAdvisor. *International Journal of Tourism Research, 19*, 107–119.

Page, S. J., & Hall, M. C. (2003). *Managing urban tourism.* Harlow: Prentice Hall.

Pons-Obrador, P. (2003). Being-on-holiday: Tourist dwelling, bodies and place. *Tourist Studies, 3*(1), 47–66.

Richardson, A. E., Montello, D. R., & Hegarty, M. (1999). Spatial knowledge acquisition from maps and from navigation in real and virtual environments. *Memory & Cognition, 27*(4), 741–750.

Rossetto, T. (2012). Embodying the map: Tourism practices in Berlin. *Tourist Studies, 12*(1), 1–24.

Salas-Olmedo, M., Moya-Gomez, B., García-Palomares, J. C., & Gutierrez, J. (2018). Tourists' digital footprint in cities: Comparing big data sources. *Tourism Management, 66*, 13–25.

Schutz, A. (1971). *Collected papers II.* The Hague: Kluwer Academic Publishing.

Schutz, A., & Luckmann, T. (1973). *The structures of the life-world.* Evanston: Northwestern University Press.

Selby, M. (2004a). *Understanding urban tourism: Image, culture and expérience.* London: I. B. Tauris.

Selby, M. (2004b). Consuming the city: Conceptualizing and researching urban tourist knowledge. *Tourism Geographies, 6*(2), 186–207.

Sennett, R. (2008). *The craftsman*. London: Penguin Books.

Simpson, T. (2016). Tourist utopias: Biopolitics and the genealogy of the post-world tourist city. *Current Issues in Tourism, 19*(1), 27–59.

Smith, A. (2017). *Events in the city: Using public spaces as event venues*. London: Routledge.

Sommer, C., & Helbrecht, I. (2017). Seeing like a tourist city: How administrative constructions of conflictive urban tourism shape its future. *Journal of Tourism Futures, 3*(2), 157–170.

Stern, E., & Leiser, D. (1988). Levels of spatial knowledge and urban travel modeling. *Geographical Analysis, 20*(2), 140–155.

Stock, M. (2007a). Habiter touristiquement la ville. In P. Duhamel & R. Knafou (Eds.), *Mondes urbains du tourisme* (pp. 25–29). Paris: Belin.

Stock, M. (2007b). European cities: Towards a recreational turn? *Hagar. Studies in Culture, Polity and Identities, 7*(1), 115–134.

Stock, M. (2019). Inhabiting the city as tourists. Issues for urban and tourism theory. In T. Frisch, C. Sommer, L. Stoltenberg, & N. Stors (Eds.), *Tourism and everyday life in the contemporary city* (pp. 42–66). London: Routledge.

Stock, M., & Lucas, L. (2012). La double révolution urbaine du tourisme. *Espaces et Sociétés, 151*, 15–30.

Stone, M. J. (2018). Eat there! Shop here! Visit that! Presenting the city in mass media travel writing. *Current Issues in Tourism, 21*(9), 998–1013.

Stors, N., & Baltes, S. (2018). Constructing urban tourism space digitally: A study of Airbnb listings in two Berlin neighborhoods. *Proceedings of the ACM on Human-Computer Interaction, 2*(166), 1–29.

Thorndyke, P. W., & Goldin, S. E. (1983). Spatial learning and reasoning skill. In H. L. Pick Jr. & L. P. Acredolo (Eds.), *Spatial orientation. Theory, research, and application* (pp. 195–217). Boston: Springer.

Tlaukaa, M., Brolese, A., Pomeroy, D., & Hobbs, W. (2005). Gender differences in spatial knowledge acquired through simulated exploration of a virtual shopping Centre. *Journal of Environmental Psychology, 25*(1), 111–118.

Tsaur, S. H., Yen, C.-H., & Chen, C. L. (2010). Independent tourist knowledge and skills. *Annals of Tourism Research, 37*(4), 1035–1054.

Tverksy, B. (2000). Levels and structure of spatial knowledge. In R. Kitchin & S. Freundschuh (Eds.), *Cognitive mapping: Past, present, and future* (pp. 24–43). London: Routledge.

Vanolo, A. (2017). *City branding: The ghostly politics of representation in globalising cities*. London: Routledge.

Wearing, S., & Foley, C. (2017). Understanding the tourist experience of cities. *Annals of Tourism Research, 65*, 97–107.

Wen, W., Ishikawa, T., & Sato, T. (2011). Working memory in spatial knowledge acquisition: Differences in encoding processes and sense of direction. *Applied Cognitive Psychology, 25*, 654–662.

Wittgenstein, L. (1953). *Philosophical investigations* (3rd ed.). Oxford: Basil Blackwell.

Léopold Lucas is an Assistant Professor in geography at the University of the Littoral Opal Coast (France). Holding a PhD from the University of Lausanne (Switzerland), he has been successively a visiting research fellow in University College of London, a fixed-term lecturer at University of Lausanne, and a researcher with University of Paris (UMS RIATE 2414, CNRS). His work focusses on two main questions. First, an investigation of the individuals' actorial logics within spatial practices, in order to grasp the need of skills to "cope with" space. Second, an analysis of the urbanity of spaces, i.e. the urban assemblages shaped by the individuals' ways of inhabiting, particularly through tourism.

Chapter 4
Help or Hindrance? Media Uses and Discourses on Media in Outdoor Sport Tourism

Valérian Geffroy

4.1 Introduction

Although digital technologies have become essential to organising social life and mediate a substantial part of our interactions, dichotomies opposing the "virtual world" and "real life" persist in common discourses. An example of a practice commonly viewed as virtual would be an online video game: It involves distant individuals, actions performed through control devices, screens that display virtual territories and virtual bodies made of information flows. One example of a practice commonly perceived to be firmly anchored in reality is going downriver in a kayak. At first sight, information or media representations have little involvement in this specific practice. In most cases, however, the kayaker will have carefully studied a detailed and codified description of the river section in a guidebook or, more and more often, an online *topoguide*. Moreover, there is a non-negligible chance that such a run nowadays would be recorded with a video camera, most likely an "action camera", either by the kayaker her/himself using a device fixed somewhere on her/his gear or by a fellow paddler standing on the river bank. In the latter case, the leisure practice involves not only a human body performing complex and energy-demanding moves in a rapidly changing material environment but also the representational mediation of the camera; screens to watch the images afterwards; and, quite likely, digital transmission channels to store the video or share it on the Internet, through more or less public means of diffusion such as e-mail, a Facebook page or an Instagram account, thereby involving distant places and people. Rather than trying to identify in this second example a physical, real dimension and distinguish it from a virtual, informational one, we should try to analyse this complex networking of bodies, places, images and devices as a significant part of the outdoor sports

V. Geffroy (✉)
Institute of Geography and Sustainability, University of Lausanne, Lausanne, Switzerland
e-mail: valerian.geffroy@unil.ch

M. Stock (ed.), *Progress in French Tourism Geographies*, Geographies of
Tourism and Global Change, https://doi.org/10.1007/978-3-030-52136-3_4

practice. One major concept that will be used in this chapter to support this perspective is *media practices*, which Couldry (2004, p. 117) defines as "practices relating to, or oriented around media".

How to understand the pervasive integration of media practices into outdoor sport tourism, as well as the perceived incompatibilities between the two sets of practices? The aim of this chapter is to (1) acknowledge and understand, in the specific context of outdoor sport tourism, the common rejection and criticism of media practices as passive and/or detached from reality; (2) show the weaknesses of such views, given that media practices can be an integral part of the outdoor sport experience and, in most cases, are seen as enhancing or facilitating the practice; and (3) detail the crucial roles that media practices play in coordinating and communicating these practices, thereby constituting a significant part of their social dimension. These analyses are empirically grounded in the study of three different outdoor sports – paragliding, rock climbing and whitewater kayaking – through interviews with participants and examples of media contents and media uses from the same participants.

4.2   Theoretical Framework: Media and Space as Practices

This chapter is an account of how media are used – and sometimes refused – in specific leisure practices. On a theoretical level, it is rooted in theories of practice and their applications to two fields of research: media, and the geography of outdoor sport tourism. Practice theories, and more specifically the notion of *media practices* – that is to say all practices where media play a significant role without necessarily being central – allow to study the integration of media and representation in the course of action, and thus to overcome the virtual/real dichotomy. A geographical analysis of outdoor sport tourism, when informed by theories of practice, is suitable to explore the values attached to the practice of space, as well as its mundane and material aspects. Here, this geographical approach will help to explain the contrasted views on using media when experiencing nature, travel and sport altogether, while also grasping the deep practical implications of such media for actions performed through and with space.

4.2.1   Media as Practices

Theories of practice hold embodied, contextualised and interpretive action as the basis of the constitution of social life (Schatzki 2001); they consider that people act in certain ways because they are in certain contexts and have certain interpretations of how the rest of the world will respond to their actions. They are interpretive or cultural theories because they are attentive to "the symbolic structures of knowledge which enable and constrain the agents to interpret the world according to certain forms, and to behave in corresponding ways" (Reckwitz 2002, pp. 245–246). But they are also materialist theories in that they analyse the constant "relation between human agency and material environment", that is, a "coordination" (Thévenot 2001, p. 74) between ideas and materialities, between representation and action. "Understandings"[1] can lead actions in that they "organise" practices (Schatzki 2002), and media can take part in building understandings. However, understandings have no power outside the material world; they have no effect without being enacted through and with bodies. Consequently, theories of practice can in no way concur with a view of media contents as being detached from actual life and reality, nor with a view of media as content imposed on passive consumers.

As Couldry (2004) explains, adopting the theories of practice has been a way to renew the field of media studies. Couldry's criticism is directed at the excessive focus on the representational dimension of media and the blindness to what people actually do with media texts and devices. His main proposition is to "decentre media research from the study of media texts or production structures"; the notion of "media practices", as "the open set of practices relating to, or oriented around media" (Couldry 2004, p. 117), is the way to operate such a decentering. This suggests a diversity of practices, rather than assuming uniform experiences of reception or consumption determined only by media content and broadcasting technologies. It is also an effort to deconstruct the assumed specificities of mass media and to situate them in the long history of communication techniques and practices. This echoes Debray's theory (who names it "mediology") of studying the medium:

> Our mass media are fundamentally the contemporary, overinflated, deafening, over-visible variation of a basic invariant that is more shadowy and less showy but nevertheless present in every mode of communication, every chronological stage of the circulation of signs: the vehicle device. The organ of transmission. Let's call it medium[2] (Debray 1998, p. 12).

In contrast to the common understanding of "media" as an activity by corporations and professionals and as a process of mass diffusion, the study of the medium covers the full spectrum of mediated communication, all the way to basic inter-individual interaction. This does not mean undermining the structuring or "anchoring" role (Swidler 2001; Couldry 2004) of representations, nor the unequal power of the diverse actors who produce them; but with practice theories, the influence or strategic role of objects is understood by looking at how they are actually handled in the course of action, in the daily context of social life. Here, for instance, the notion of media practices will encompass reading or watching content from professional outdoor sport media; producing images or text about one's own sport travel practices, showing it *in situ* to peers, sharing it on social media; taking a paper

---

[1] A term that includes representations, ideas, discourses... in sum, ways of mentally grasping the world.

[2] Personal translation. Original quote: "nos mass-media sont au fond la variation contemporaine, hypertrophiée, assourdissante, surapparente d'un invariant de base plus ombreux, moins tapageur, et néanmoins coprésent à tous les modes de communication, tous les stades chronologiques de la circulation des signes: le dispositif véhiculaire. L'organe de transmission. Appelons-le médium."

guidebook out of a bag to look at it, adding comments on an itinerary described on an online collaborative *topoguide*; and so on.

This means that media must be studied without assuming *a priori* that the media content and objects are at the centre of all the practices that involve them. With this in mind, Morley (2009) advocates for a "non-media-centric media studies", its main characteristic being a much clearer take on materiality than in previous media studies. This materiality is not only about the technological networks and infrastructures that Morley focuses on: If informed by a theory of practice, the study of media should address every material involvement of media in practices, from undersea cables and satellites to the gesture of taking a smartphone out of one's pocket – as we will see with the example of outdoor sport, the latter is not always the unproblematic or meaningless gesture it appears to be.

After the era of mass media came another major technological and social change that made the practice approach even more necessary: the digital revolution. In short, the digital revolution is a spectacular acceleration of the "mediatization process", as defined by Krotz:

> Mediatization describes the process whereby communication refers to media and uses media so that media in the long run increasingly become relevant for the social construction of everyday life, society, and culture as a whole. (Krotz 2009, p. 24)

This increased relevance was particularly due to the digital format of data transmission, the Internet, and, subsequently, mobile devices and the rise of "Web 2.0", which is mainly characterised by the major role of user-generated content. In combination, these innovations have made the ability to produce and to share media content widespread. To address this new state of affairs, some authors have proposed "to see audiences as active cultural producers" (Bird 2011, p. 502).

4.2.2 Outdoor Sport Tourism as Geographical Play

The geographical perspective is crucial to understand the complex meanings and implications of leisure practices such as tourism and sport, where relations to place and environment are central to the enjoyment. Among the themes relevant to outdoor sport tourism, geographical research has explored the meanings of nature as a cultural and mystical construction of space, as opposed to urban space in particular (Bourdeau 2003), making nature a central category for the touristic enjoyment of places (Bourdeau et al. 2011; Laslaz et al. 2012). The geographical perspective has also yielded insights, through non-representational theory (Thrift 2007) in particular, in outdoor sport practices as bodily practices of immersion, of enjoyment of movement and contact (Thorpe and Rinehart 2010; Thrift 2000; Wylie 2005). Such work is in part inspired by theories of practice. A geography of practice, indeed, does not view space as a purely material context; it is also a resource (or constraint) and a material for action, as well as a subject of interpretations and of symbolic constructions (Lussault 2007; Stock 2007, 2015). To summarise the many ways in which space is involved in human action, Lussault and Stock (2010) propose the expression "doing with space". I proposed the alternative expression of "playing with space" (Geffroy 2017) to address the hedonist and aesthetic spatialities of leisure practices such as outdoor sport tourism.

In this geography of practice, leisure and tourism are treated as a set of physical movements and material actions, but also as "ways of making knowledge", part of a "process [of] 'lay geography'" where "the individual works and reworks, figures and re-figures an account of a place" (Crouch 2000, p. 65) and where such knowledge, beyond practical uses, may also be a source of enjoyment. In this regard, media practices hold an important role: tourism research has shown how they were a central means of the symbolic construction of places, especially tourists' practices of photography (Crang 1997). And a geography of practice should truly consider lay practices of photography as a *construction* of places, and not as mere representation or mirroring or in terms of accuracy or truthfulness. Crang calls for the following view to be adopted:

> Such a focus refuses to look on the mediated world as some fall from grace, some tragic loss of authenticity. Images are not something that appear over and against reality, but parts of practices through which people work to establish realities. Rather than look to mirroring as a root metaphor, technologies of seeing form ways of grasping the world (Crang 1997, p. 362).

For the author, it is best to avoid considering photographs only in their visual dimension, as they are not only seen but also taken, exchanged and discussed. They are not only objects but also practices. Furthermore, it is important to credit these practices with relevance in their relation to place: They are meaningful ways of experiencing places, of building attachments to and memories of them.

Some research works have already addressed in depth the relationship between outdoor sport and media practices, in terms of constructing places or identities, or as an aid to moving and acting in outdoor environments (Evers 2016; Laurier 2015; Mao and Obin 2018; Thorpe 2017; Woermann 2012). But none of these works have yet addressed the conflictual dimension of this relationship, the clash between the embodied experience of sport in nature viewed as an authentic experience of "reality" and media practices viewed as distanced or virtual engagements. This chapter will give empirical evidence of this conflict, in the discourse and practices of outdoor sport tourism participants, but also show the limits of this conflict's relevance to these leisure practices.

4.3   Empirical Insights: Methods and Outline

The ideas and examples I develop in this chapter are based primarily on a series of semi-structured interviews that took place between 2016 and 2018 and on images collected from the interviewees. I chose three sports based on their potential to induce travel: kayaking, paragliding and rock climbing. I conducted investigations at some of these sports' major sites, namely, places[3] that are world-renowned and attractive enough to the sport communities to attract people on a global scale.[4] I conducted 76 interviews, with more than 110 participants. The questions related to their travel and sport histories, their ways of conceiving the relation between sport and travel, their enjoyment of the places of practice and finally, their media practices during their mobilities for outdoor sports and in their daily lives.

Collecting pictures from these individuals was a way of building up research material that is more specific to media practices and was a direct illustration of the way participants spoke about their media practices. I asked participants to send me a few of the pictures they liked the most from their sports travels, mainly via e-mail after the interviews had taken place. It is a form of entirely "respondent-led photo-elicitation" (Scarles 2012), based on "participant-generated images" (Balomenou and Garrod 2019), where participants themselves are involved in the analysis, since I asked them to comment on their pictures. The aim was to grasp the visual ways of enjoying practices and places of outdoor sport tourism with the images providing information not only about what is valued and admired (landscapes, people, activities…) but also about how the practice of taking pictures is integrated into practices of sport and tourism. This means paying attention to what the pictures show but also to the circumstances of their capture. The interviews and the comments on the pictures help in this contextual work. For instance, the interviews give detailed information on the ways in which these pictures are shared, with whom, on what platforms and for what purpose. The interviews also help to understand the social interactions and the spread of information online: Thus, I explored a wide variety of online material based on the websites interviewees told me they visited and the tools they reported using. These included social media (mainly Facebook, Instagram and YouTube), specialised news websites, blogs, collaborative platforms for information about sport sites, weather apps, etc.

What follows will consist of three parts. The first is an account of general criticisms addressed to media practices, in common as well as scientific discourse, opposing them to the real or authentic experience. The second is an empirical study of the views expressed by outdoor sport tourists and grounded in, or related to, such criticisms. The third part, based on empirical material and providing elements of theoretical discussion, is an attempt to show how, on the contrary, media practices may be viewed as an essential means of constructing the reality of the outdoor sport experience – in particular through the diffusion of specific understandings of space.

---

[3] All bar one are located in the south-eastern part of France: for rock climbing, the Greek island of Kalymnos, and the Verdon gorges; for kayaking, the area of Hautes-Alpes; for paragliding, Annecy Lake and Saint-André-les-Alpes.

[4] The encountered population, though, was mostly European, or from other rich Western countries. This is due to the sites' locations and to the geographies of power and privilege that those sport and travel practices largely reflect.

4.4 Fake, Virtual, Passive: The Roots of Anti-media Discourses

Media contents and media practices are often viewed as a poor, untrustworthy way of accessing 'reality'. This wariness applies in particular to images, since in post-modern cultures, while the visual remains central, the "relation between seeing and true knowing has been broken" (Rose 2016, p. 4). The view of images as potentially deceptive rose to prominence in both scientific and common discourse (Boorstin 1961) in the era of mass media, which are perceived as a new central institution of influence – that is to say, of the manipulation of *messages* (Baetens 2014, p. 41) – and a major site for the creation of simulacra (Baudrillard 1981; Boorstin 1961). These ideas also blossomed in the field of tourism: Boorstin saw it as a particularly fertile ground for "pseudo-events" and fake images. Critics of Boorstin, like MacCannell (1976), rejected the accusations levelled at tourists that they are indulging in shallowness but recognised "staging" or "performing" as a fundamental characteristic of the tourist experience (Edensor 2000; Larsen and Urry 2011). Some authors imply that most tourists are condemned to an inauthentic and distanced relationship with people and places: "The connection with the unfamiliar is likely to be purely visual, and filtered through sunglasses and a camera viewfinder" (Graburn 1977, p. 31). Tourist photography, in particular, has repeatedly been analysed as essentially a reproduction of pre-defined dominant images; the idea of the "hermeneutic circle", in which tourists are "trapped", is one of the recurrent *topoi* of tourism studies (Albers and James 1988; Urry 1990) that are still frequently used today, although most of the time it is challenged by highlighting the ways in which tourists negotiate these representations (Stylianou-Lambert 2012).

The development of digital technologies and the Internet has added another layer of argumentation regarding views of media practices as disconnected from reality. This is because of the new and more efficient ways of handling and transforming information, and in particular because of the common conceptions of virtuality. Graham shows how the metaphor of "cyberspace" has helped to sustain the idea of the Internet as both "an ethereal alternate dimension" and an alternate system (because it is non-physical) of places and spaces (Graham 2013, p. 179). Such metaphors lead to a belief in the existence of a world of possibilities detached from "physical" reality or "real life". Kinsley details the specific issues this "life online" presents, in particular regarding "authenticity and identity": "The ability to bend and alter representations and performances of identity through mediated communication is [...] often treated as problematic" when accurate knowledge is sought, particularly in research (Kinsley 2013, p. 546). But this criticism is also ubiquitous in the public discourse, especially with regard to online social media as new stages for the narratives of the self.

Moreover, media practices are frequently accused of being passive and unhealthy behaviour; there have been multiple calls to restrict "screen time"[5] and to engage in other, more "active" activities, in particular those involving physical exercise and contact with *nature* (see, among others, Larson et al. 2018). Indeed, if media may be rejected from a common understanding of reality, nature is considered to be – at least, in contemporary Western cultures – one of the primary sites for experiencing reality. It is mostly a matter of feelings and stimulations of the body, as Crouch (2003, p. 1953) illustrates with the case of a gardener describing her experience:

> Working outdoors feels much better for you somehow… more vigorous than day to day housework, much more variety and stimulus. The air is always different and alerts the skin… unexpected scents are brought by breezes. Only when on your hands and knees do you notice insects and other small wonders.

The perception of the world seems enhanced here, the body and the mind more attuned to the diversity and versatility of life. Of course, this heightening of the bodily experience through contact with nature combines particularly well with other practices of physical activity. That is why outdoor sports are experienced as an intense commitment of body and mind (Geffroy 2017; Niel and Sirost 2008). Multisensoriality is a key part of enjoying physical activity in nature, unlike a modern body described as mostly "ocular" (Lewis 2000), that is, trained for a visual relation to the world – the media currently being a significant part of this relation.

These ideas and oppositions structured around the categories of reality *versus* abstraction and activity *versus* passivity are appropriated in various ways, as will become clear below, but they are common enough to constitute a strong discursive background. They are variations on the common dichotomy of image *versus* reality and representation *versus* action. The next part will study the occurrences and influences of such dichotomies in outdoor sport tourists' views.

Distrust or Distaste: Negative Views on Media Practices in Outdoor Sport Tourism

This section presents the main arguments put forward to oppose or limit media practices, as they emerged from my empirical study. Broadly, the participants may express indifference to representations of or discourses on the sport, as opposed to their view of the sport's actual practice; they may point to media practices that they view as excessive, particularly when they tend towards narcissism or hindering the physical or lived practice; and they may indicate a preference for more direct means of communication. Many of these views may thus be interpreted as a desire for a close relationship with space and the material environment through focused bodily activity; and many of these views reject communication-centered practices, as a form of disembodying or of staging the outdoor sport experience.

---

[5]While media are, of course, not restricted to television, computers and smartphones, these have assumed an increasingly dominant position in media practices, and the screen has become the symbol of the passive consumption of media content.

Media Practices: Poor Connection?

Some interviewees express indifference to representations of the sport or tourism practice, which leads to little or no consumption of such media contents. In rock climbing, in particular, the participants associate the specialised media mainly with accounts of extreme performances, which they consider uninteresting because of the wide gap between such activities and their own practices. Martine, for example, explains why she and her husband ended their subscription to a popular rock climbing magazine:

> It was increasingly clear that it was a quite elitist magazine, for the stars, and climbing starts at 7c [grade], but our climbing, which is 6a, for them it's hiking, not climbing![6]

Maike expresses her distaste for watching "climbing material", because of the unpleasant feeling of inferiority it elicits from her:

> I feel bad when I watch something about climbers, because then I always feel like, I'm the shittiest climber! Because most of the stuff they record and you can watch is about the, THE crags you know, the people that climb, 10 [grade] or whatever, and you're like, you're not even able to climb 5 [grade] at the moment!

To these people, it seems the media content is exceedingly oriented towards spectacular rather than regular practices of the sport; it is far from being representative of the sport as they experience it. Other climbers similarly report being unable to relate to media accounts of the practice, not even because it does not correspond to their experience but because, at a more fundamental level, their enjoyment of the sport is personal, and they do not find any form of satisfaction in watching or hearing about other people doing similar activities, as Henrik explains:

> I have zero interest in knowing how other people perform. [...] If I read magazines and watch TV, I watch the competitive aspect of climbing, and this is not interesting to me. I'm only interested in how well I perform.

Like Henrik, several of the interviewees state that, to media "consumption", they prefer their own physical, lived experience of the sport.

On a related note, many interviewees claim a preference for the more "embodied" means of communication. They strongly value the sport community as a space of exchange and social relations but dislike the distance and the lack of physical co-presence that characterise online interaction and/or the specialised media. Even to learn about rock climbing sites, Maike states she relies on word-of-mouth rather than professional media; when asked whether she reads magazines or any other types of specialised media, she replies:

> I don't. I like the, talking about things better. We say Mundpropaganda.[7] [...] Oh cool, so there's a different spot here, and now we look at the map together… It's better for me, works more than a magazine where they probably had paid a lot of money to put this article down.

---

[6] Some interview quotations are translated from French. Others are direct transcripts from English – often by non-native speakers.

[7] "Mund" (German) = "mouth".

She prefers to speak to fellow climbers with similar experiences; media representation, by contrast, appears to her to be prone to bending reality for commercial purposes. And not only does she hope for more accurate information, but she also seems to find direct human contact more enjoyable and more lively, much like Jérôme, a kayaker who answers as follows when asked about his means of communicating with other kayakers:

> Telephone, mate! Telephone, and when you see boats, you run after them [...] wherever you go, you take phone numbers. In that way, you have a contact. [...] And I'm thinking, telling people, come on, bring me to your place, and I'll bring you to mine, see, we have things to exchange... I like that. Facebook and all that, first you need Internet, and then it's less fun, and you don't know who you're going to navigate with, on the phone you quickly see who you are...

Again here, direct conversation rather than mediated exchanges, or speaking (on the telephone) rather than writing (that is, more embodied ways of communication), are preferred because they are viewed as deeper, more honest and more open.

Hindrance to Lived or Physical Practice
But this reluctance also often applies to "productive" media practices, in particular when capturing images is seen as hindering other, more important dimensions of the practice. In such cases, people seem to value the material over the discursive; the mental memory over the documentary memories; and *living the moment* over recording it or showing it. Micaela puts it as follows: "when we travel, we live the moment intensely, we are here for what we came to do, and not for, afterwards showing 'Oh, I was there', or for remembering"; and her husband, Théo, adds "I don't have Facebook, she doesn't post anything on Facebook... we're not the type to show, today a multi-pitch route..." For them, the time and effort needed to capture pictures threatens the full enjoyment of the practice as they conceive it; it is almost incompatible with "what [they] came to do", and they have little interest in sharing and displaying what they did. Though it is rather rare among the interviewees to express incompatibility on such a general level, many of them explain how the production of images may sometimes conflict with the sport activity, in particular because of the complex or even perilous material and bodily circumstances. Paragliders, in particular, if handling photo or video gear, face the risk of dropping it, like Francis who "lost two smartphones, each time [he] tried!", and face the risks related to a lack of focus on the control of the wing, as Vivien explains:

> When it's crowded in the air or when the air conditions are turbulent, it is better to be focused on what happens around you because it might be dangerous, to take a selfie and not see someone coming just in front of you.

Besides, while the material conditions can make it difficult to take pictures in general, it is particularly hard to take good pictures. Several interviewees explain that the result is not worth the trouble if the proper gear and techniques are not used, and that it can be a major effort. In rock climbing, in particular, they often note that high-quality pictures need to be shot from above, requiring a third member outside of the belayer–climber party and some rope handling; otherwise, as Michel puts it, the images produced by the belayer are "always the same" and restricted to "butt pictures"!

Criticising Narcissism

Criticism directed at media practices may also take on an ethical, if not moralistic, dimension. Social media are the main target: as a platform of public or semi-public display of the self, they attract accusations of narcissism and concerns about privacy. Many of the interviewees consequently claim that they use these tools with caution or even dislike the general tone of the contents and exchanges on these platforms, while still using them, as is the case for Marius:

> I've registered on Facebook, but I find it's too much navel-gazing. [...] It annoys me. It's too much about showing off.

Indeed, although most of the interviewed people have a social media account (mostly on Facebook), there seems to be a general desire not to engage in excessive habits of posting – of course, what is "excessive" may depend on the point of view – and to restrict most of their communication to their closest social circles. Some people quite clearly reject any form of display of their "life" to broader circles. The idea is that social media are not a legitimate space for personal matters. That leads several people, like Javier, to stay off social media:

> I have no Facebook; I don't like to share my life with people I don't know [...]. I want to share my pictures with friends, or my family, and no more people.

Micaela and Théo develop their own view on the media-related behaviours they see as excessive, in a way that echoes what I call here the narcissistic tendency:

> T: It's also consumption society, kind of [...]. I did this, and this, and this, and this, people show that, they do lots of things...
> M: I want to taste this, I want to have access to that. Where it becomes annoying is that, they don't want to taste for the sake of tasting, they want to taste for the sake of showing.

They analyse media practices as part of a broader process of accumulation of symbolic capital, that works through displaying and reporting numerous visited places and lived experiences. Such analyses are well-documented in literature: Sport and tourism, in particular sports perceived as risky (Kane and Zink 2004) and tourist behaviours viewed as adventurous and autonomous (van Nuenen 2016), are an important source of symbolic capital and, as such, are heavily mobilised in media practices, especially when it comes to "self-branding" (van Nuenen 2016). But in Micaela and Théo's opinion, this is a shallow relationship to the world, and it is encouraged, or at least supported, by media practices.

Attitudes of distrust or distaste towards media practices are undeniably present – and even common on certain particular topics – in outdoor sport communities. However, most of the time, such a reluctance is presented as a matter of personal preference rather than a general, socially relevant criticism. And they co-exist with many neutral or positive opinions on the matter, and first of all, with multiple uses that make media an essential part of the outdoor sport practice – as the following section will show.

4.5 Media Practices: Sharing Spatialities, Sustaining Communities

It is insufficient to address media practices in terms of taste or to ask whether they are hindering or enabling aspects of outdoor sports tourism, given that they now are a major component of much of human action rather than a set of tools. I will show here how media contents and technologies are enmeshed in practices of outdoor sport tourism, and in particular how they contribute to the construction of places and spatialities in this leisure field. I have made a similar argument before (Geffroy 2017), which is developed here in greater detail. In particular, I will interpret media practices, in line with practice theory, as a means of *coordinating* and *communicating* practices on both the individual and the collective level.

4.5.1 Mythologies of Places, Mythologies of the Self

In outdoor sport tourism, a large share of media practices consists of circulating sport sites' images. These images' influence relates to the general landscape aesthetics and to the specific aesthetics of each sport practice, including criteria relating to the terrain's suitability for the sport. It is also related to the people circulating these images and to the events and stories situated in these places and narrated through pictures and text. It is in such a circulation that *myths* are formed, and it is of such material that the dreams of sport tourists are made. Media practices are a central node for the cultural construction and ordering of space, especially because they create places of reference. The Verdon canyon is a good example of such a famous place. It owes its symbolic power within the rock-climbing community to its spectacular cliffs, to its history, which rests on exceptional sport performances and key cultural developments, and to prominent images of the area. In the Verdon, when I asked rock climbers what had brought them there for the first time, the answers frequently contained adjectives such as "mythical", "famous" and "historical". In several cases, the reputation was given as an explanation in itself, as with Tim: "Because it's super famous! I don't know, yeah, it's like, it's one of those places, you have to be there once in a lifetime pretty much, at least." Two different pairs of climbers elaborated a little more and cited among the "big names" that of Patrick Edlinger, a key influence in popularising both rock climbing and the Verdon in the early 1980s, through films (Janssen 1982, 1983) depicting the climber's lifestyle along with spectacular climbing sequences. The importance of strong visual impressions is evident in the vocabulary used by the interviewees to describe the power of this place's appeal: Martin and Gabriel mention "the grey" (in reference to the dominant colour of the cliffs), the "beauty of the rock" and the "grandiose atmosphere".

Of course, the sport sites' cultural construction has a material reality: The Verdon's reputation has attracted many rock climbers from around the world and has strongly structured the (modest) development of the area around the activity of rock climbing (Mao et al. 2003). Media practices, by carrying positive values through images, discourses and stories, have played a significant role in the material appropriation by the climbing community. While the spread of media content accounts for part of the places' symbolic value, the physical practice also contributes to actualise these meanings. By travelling there, staying there and climbing in the cliffs, the climbers experience and rethink their own conceptions; in the eyes of others, their bodily presence and their specific sport actions confirm the identity of the place. This is particularly visible in the Verdon, where viewpoints along a scenic road offer non-climbing tourists the chance to watch climbers emerge from the deep ravine; and by producing the images themselves and circulating them, climbers reproduce, perpetuate or transform the representations. Lamont (2014), using the case of cycling tourists on the Tour de France's roads in the French Alps, shows how a place's mythical status is validated through physical experience and expressed through discursive categories of authenticity or even sacredness. He also shows that these global representations draw their power from the intense joy they provide when put into action and, eventually, from the images shot during these meaningful moments and shared afterwards. Martin and Gabriel shared with me pictures and comments that demonstrate the same kind of relations with the Verdon and also with Yosemite. During the interview, they explicitly stated their personal appropriation of the myth of Yosemite prior to visiting it. They went there and captured spectacular pictures of themselves climbing cliffs. They found intense pleasure in the environment's exceptionality (Gabriel: "Arriving on one of the most aesthetic and most exposed summits I've ever known") and in its mythical value (Martin's comment on Fig. 4.1: "The myth finally within reach of our hands"). They shared these pictures, that they count among their dearest memories, with a pride they do not try to conceal.

Ness (2011), in her study of meaning-making processes in Yosemite, offered to go beyond the "representationalist-constructivist bias", which is the belief that landscape meanings are the result of public, conventional symbolisms. While acknowledging that place symbolisms are internalised ("inward" meaning-making), she also shows that the bodily act of climbing itself produces spontaneous, "unmediated", "outward" meanings. The value of such an analysis lies in its emphasis on freedom, spontaneity and pre-conscious processes in the constitution of places' significations. In particular, it may challenge a view of professional media representations as hegemonic. However, as soon as the meanings processed at an individual level are expressed through a medium and shared, these meanings enter the global sphere of the collective constitution of understandings and symbolisms. For instance, Martin and Gabriel have no authority regarding the representations of Yosemite, a US national symbol and rock-climbing mecca, since they are French, non-elite climbers and do not engage in any media coverage. However, they did partake in the collective constitution of Yosemite's meanings through sharing their personal pictures. Social media and other technologies that facilitated the handling of pictures probably helped bridge the gap between the authoritative and lay practices of meaning-making.

Fig. 4.1 Martin and Gabriel at the foot of Half Dome in Yosemite National Park, US. Source: M. Berthelot

These media practices not only contribute to collective understandings of places or landscapes but also negotiate the collective understanding of the sport participant's identity and the sense of community (McCormack 2018). Social media, in particular, are one of the main spaces of self-presentation. Within outdoor sport communities, "profile pictures" often display the individual's body in action in a natural environment. Such representations forge close ties between socially valued personality features and terrains of practice. Indeed, they embody the skilful negotiation of risk, the aesthetics of the functional body and an intimate connection with the natural environment. Martin and Gabriel offer an explicit illustration of this with Martin's picture of Gabriel (Fig. 4.2) and comments made during the interview that seem directly related to such pictures: "We also stage ourselves a little bit, so that means we give in to the common temptation of heroism. So yeah, like, "Oh fuck, it's exposed, take a picture of me…!"".

Based on this material, media practices may be interpreted as ways of creating and sustaining shared aesthetics, symbols and stories among the participants in outdoor sports, especially regarding places and ways to act in these places – in other words, the spatialities of the practice. In line with Schatzki, such frames of thought and action may be called "teleoaffectivities", that is, an association of ends and emotions (Schatzki 2002, p. 80). Teleoaffectivities are the "desired horizons" of a practice; the concept is one way of explaining the normativity of practice: how shared

Fig. 4.2 On the "Snake Dike" route on Half Dome's south face, Yosemite. Source: G. Moncaubeig

understandings lead to similar actions. In tourism and in sport subcultures, teleoaffectivities are heavily loaded with place symbolisms and hedonic values, which media practices contribute to establishing and transmitting in the form of appealing images and promises of pleasure. But in a theory of practice, teleoaffectivities must be viewed as engaged in the course of action and always in specific contexts; relatedly, media representation must be understood as the focus of constant work by the actors rather than distant images and discourses determining motives and desires. Media practices build a sphere of immaterial, discursive relations concurrently with tourist mobilities and sport movements. And one of the elements of criticism of media practices is that they substitute an alternative world of such relations to the physical experience. My observations show that, rather than being a substitute, media practices support and complement the sport and travelling experience (Thorpe 2017), make it possible to share experience and conceptions of the activity and, in some cases, may be a *continuation* of outdoor sport tourism outside the timespaces of the physical sport practice, e.g. at home or off-season. Some interviewees underscore how important it is for them to "daydream" about their sport and travels when they cannot be away or outside. Apart from holidays, Vivien, who lives in Belgium, has almost no opportunity to fly, and he explains his habits of reading and watching paragliding media as follows: "since I don't fly much during the year, I need to feed myself with paragliding." Michel, who is also Belgian, jokes with his wife, Martine, about his imaginary climbing during winter months:

Martine: All winter long, he reads the guidebooks, he dreams about doing this and that, that's true…

Michel: I climb much more in winter than in summer, you know!

4.5.2 Encoding Terrains into Playgrounds

Outdoor sport tourism is a highly specialised geographical practice as it is grounded in a specific knowledge and reading of the terrain corresponding to the modalities of a sport practice. To be shared and accessed in efficient ways, such information needs to be "encoded" in an adequate vocabulary and/or adequate media representations. Thus, a part of media practices in outdoor sport tourism may be analysed as an encoding/decoding of the terrain.

On a global scale, such information may be shared through online platforms. Among the main media tools used by the people I interviewed are online "topoguides" and reports on weather and other conditions. Rivermap (see Fig. 4.3) is one example of such a tool. It is not a comprehensive guide for kayaking routes but focuses on displaying a precise set of data, namely *water levels*. It aggregates a large set of public data from different countries and regions – in particular, measures from hydro-electrical companies. The main aim is to display rapidly changing geographical information (river levels) on a base map by using an efficient visualisation: colour lines on the river sections and easy-to-read charts of water level variation. Part of the contextual information is provided on a collaborative basis: the geographical coordinates of the routes (start and end of river sections), the name of the river, the grade of difficulty etc. Other complementary information or sources of information may be added to each river section, such as links to a description of the route, temporary obstacles or hazards, video footage of a kayak run. Indeed, although it is useful to have a quick, multiple-scale glance at this essential indicator (water levels), it is only one part of the information needed to find kayaking routes and practice them. Such a website is generally supplemented by other sources, mainly guidebooks or "topoguides" in paper or digital format,[8] which provide a more thorough description of the river: additional information about put-in/take-out (embarkation/disembarkation) points, features of the river, infrastructure etc. These platforms may be described as "spatial media"; these technological developments, built on the digital processing and displaying of geographical information, are "increasingly intrinsic to how it is that places/spaces are accorded variable importance" (Leszczynski 2015, pp. 745–746). For outdoor sport practices among others, they greatly contribute to make our spatialities increasingly mediated. The concept of "spatial media" is a way to undermine the description of such technologies as "'virtual' – 'real' spatial hybrids", and to acknowledge "spatiality […] as always-already mediated" (Leszczynski 2015, p. 729).

---

[8] For instance, eauxvives.org and kajaktour.de.

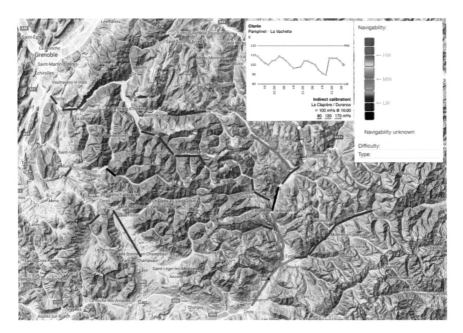

Fig. 4.3 The state of some rivers in the Hautes-Alpes on 22 June 2017, as seen on rivermap.ch. Example of reading: The River Clarée currently flows at 100 m³/s. This river's navigability is between medium and low, and has been the same for the few past days. Licence CC-BY-SA

The micro-geographies of the body in the biophysical environment are also a significant focus of media practices. There are means of expressing skilled, embodied relationship to the terrain – visual means, in particular. A whole field of media practices is built around certain technologies, principally the combination of light mobile devices and online sharing platforms – the iconic brands being GoPro and YouTube. Video footage may be used, for example, when preparing a climb, flight or river run. Fabrice, a climber and mountaineer, says he frequently searches the Internet for videos of ascents he plans to do: "it's reassuring, but sometimes I've told myself it's not good because you don't discover, sometimes I've watched the climb and I could almost bluff someone and tell him I've done this ascent." Once again, despite the usefulness of this pre-visualisation technique, it is criticised for potentially reducing the first-hand physical experience. Several interviewees explained how they use their own first-person video footage to reflect on their practice and learn from their own mistakes. For instance, Jérôme, Valentin and Gabriel discuss using GoPros while kayaking:

V: It's mainly to watch in the evening. Like later, we're going to watch what we did today, look at the passages…

J: […] The things today, the mistakes, I'm sure it's this damn left hand that threw me in the hole…

G: Yeah you clearly see all the mistakes you make.

Didier has a similar habit: He records all his paragliding flights on video, not only to improve his technique but also to "re-enjoy the flight". It seems, then, that such videos are viewed as particularly realistic and immersive representations of the outdoor sports experience. It allows access to precise details of the body's movements, some of which might even be unconscious or uncontrolled during the action. It may also provide a part of the pleasure of the lived experience through the visual impressions and some other sensorial or emotional evocations of the bodily relation to the environment. In that perspective, wearable or "action" cameras have been a crucial innovation (Evers 2016; Thorpe 2017).

4.5.3 Communicating and Coordinating Spatialities

As can be seen, media practices are involved in multiple instances of conceptual, as well as pragmatic, understanding of environments of outdoor sport tourism; in other words, they are a key element in defining the spatialities of this leisure practice. Media practices do not only have a representational role to play as a distant, informational reproduction of reality; this is a misconception at the root of many negative views of media practices. In the framework of a theory of practice, they should rather be conceived as central means of *communication* and *coordination* of practice, as defined by Thévenot (2006, p. 6):

> [Communication] designates the variety of ways of putting things in common: through the movement of a body communicated to the other it embraces, through the opening of a room communicating with another. The notion of communication then becomes more concrete, more material and plural, than its narrow informational meaning implies.[9]

In that sense, communication is the basis of social action and phenomena: Communication happens whenever we take something out of the strictly individual realm. *Coordination* designates all the ways of establishing schemes of interaction – orders, but orders always viewed as doubtful and problematic, relying on the whole set of communications and not only on rules, formal hierarchies and agreements (Thévenot 2006, p. 12). Coordination concerns interactions not only between actors but also between the actor and his or her environment (*idem*).

As illustrated above, outdoor sports are coordinated activities in that they rely on conventions on how to move in a specific environment. Since they take place in non-standardised and sometimes rapidly changing environments, they have always relied on geographical conventions of representation. Recent technological innovations have enhanced and developed the means of *communicating* spatialities of practice: As seen with the example of Rivermap, digital, online, interactive formats

---

[9]Personal translation. "Le terme [communication] désigne des façons diverses de rendre commun: par le mouvement d'un corps communiqué à l'autre qu'il étreint, par la liaison d'une pièce qui communique avec une autre dans laquelle elle donne. La notion de communication se fait alors plus concrète, matérielle, et plurielle dans ses canaux, que ne l'implique son acception informationnelle étriquée."

make it possible to efficiently aggregate large sets of data, to regularly update them, and to build them in a collaborative way. The same technological developments opened up a field for an efficient communication of grounded, bodily schemes of understanding the environments and movements of practice; in that sense, media practices are closer than ever to physical practice. The contemporary flourishing of self-shot pictures and videos may, therefore, be interpreted as the expression of a renewed interest in a bodily aware communication of practices. In it, participants often find precious material to develop their own practice or simply the pleasure of sharing or recognising enjoyable modes of body–environment coordination. Such media practices are collective (Laurier 2015) in that they refer to and actualise common ways of enjoying places, landscapes and movements.

4.6 Conclusion

As a practice of the body, of nature and of immersion, outdoor sports tourism is particularly likely to attract criticism about media practices being disembodied, artificial and isolating. My research showed that such critical views are undoubtedly common among participants in this leisure practice. These views are, however, far from being universal, and the participants' discourses show, in general, a more nuanced consideration of the multiple ways in which media practices are integrated to outdoor sport projects and actions: media practices help building aesthetics of the sport environment; they may become tools supporting and improving the skilled bodily practice; they are instrumental in connecting people around shared practical understandings of space. I do not want to suggest that there is a natural and frictionless integration of technological innovations in practices of leisure, nor that the evolution of outdoor sport tourism is now and forever linked to the evolution of media practices. Rather, I suggested here that leisure practices have their own specific ways of appropriating media and technologies; tools and uses are defined in relation to particular needs and aspects of the practice. This is precisely what the conceptualisation of media as practices allows to grasp: how media content and uses are embedded in contexts, in practices where media are not necessarily an end in itself. Here, the specific context of outdoor sport tourism, its specific values, needs and constraints account for a large part of the reluctance to or acceptance of media practices. On the individual level, viewing certain media practices as hindrance to or enhancement of outdoor sport practices equates to attributing different sets of values to those media practices within a more general project of action. And on the collective level, media practices are essential for defining the frames of such projects of action—expectations, values and understandings related to codified physical movement in the biophysical environment, in the case of outdoor sport tourism. The approach of the geography of practice also helps to discern the importance of media practices within this specific leisure practice: this approach moves the discussion away from the dichotomy or virtual against physical relationship to the environment and acknowledges the full diversity of spatialities that are at stake in outdoor sport tourism practices. These spatialities indeed involve aesthetics and representations, affects and perceptions and physical contacts and material resources.

Hence, this chapter contributes to the science of digitally and informationally mediated social life, a social science that fully tackles the contextualisation of technologies and representations in human action. To that end, geography has an important role in spatially grounding technologies that may seem detached from materiality; and studies of bodily-focused practices, such as sport practices, can be instrumental in recognising the interlocking of the conceptual-informational sphere and the bodily-material one.

References

Albers, P. C., & James, W. R. (1988). Travel photography. A methodological approach. *Annals of Tourism Research, 15*(1), 134–158. https://doi.org/10.1016/0160-7383(88)90076-X.

Baetens, J. (2014). Le médium n'est pas soluble dans les médias de masse, "the medium" is not soluble in "the mass media". *Hermès, La Revue, 70*(3), 40–45.

Balomenou, N., & Garrod, B. (2019). Photographs in tourism research: Prejudice, power, performance and participant-generated images. *Tourism Management, 70*, 201–217. https://doi.org/10.1016/j.tourman.2018.08.014.

Baudrillard, J. (1981). *Simulacres et simulation*. Paris: Galilée.

Bird, S. E. (2011). Are we all Produsers now? *Cultural Studies, 25*(4–5), 502–516. https://doi.org/10.1080/09502386.2011.600532.

Boorstin, D. J. (1961). *The image: A guide to pseudo-events in America*. New York: Harper & Row.

Bourdeau, P. (2003). Territoires du hors-quotidien: une géographie culturelle du rapport à l'ailleurs dans les sociétés urbaines contemporaines; le cas du tourisme sportif de montagne et de nature. Université Joseph-Fourier-Grenoble I. Retrieved from http://tel.archives-ouvertes.fr/docs/00/18/16/68/PDF/HDR_Philippe_Bourdeau_2003.pdf.

Bourdeau, P., Mao, P., & Corneloup, J. (2011). Les sports de nature comme médiateurs du « pas de deux » ville-montagne. Une habitabilité en devenir ? *Annales de géographie, n°, 680*(4), 449–460.

Couldry, N. (2004). Theorising media as practice. *Social Semiotics, 14*(2), 115–132. https://doi.org/10.1080/1035033042000238295.

Crang, M. (1997). Picturing practices: Research through the tourist gaze. *Progress in Human Geography, 21*(3), 359–373. https://doi.org/10.1191/030913297669603510.

Crouch, D. (2000). Places around us: Embodied lay geographies in leisure and tourism. *Leisure Studies, 19*(2), 63–76. https://doi.org/10.1080/026143600374752.

Crouch, D. (2003). Spacing, performing, and becoming: Tangles in the mundane. *Environment and Planning A, 35*(11), 1945–1960. https://doi.org/10.1068/a3585.

Debray, R. (1998). Histoire des quatre M. *Les cahiers de médiologie, 6*(2), 7. https://doi.org/10.3917/cdm.006.0007.

Edensor, T. (2000). Staging tourism: tourists as performers. *Annals of Tourism Research, 27*(2), 322–344. https://doi.org/10.1016/S0160-7383(99)00082-1.

Evers, C. (2016). Researching action sport with a GoPro™ camera: An embodied and emotional mobile video tale of the sea, masculinity, and men-who-surf. In I. Wellard (Ed.), *Researching embodied sport: Exploring movement cultures* (pp. 145–162). London: Routledge.

Geffroy, V. (2017). 'Playing with space': A conceptual basis for investigating active sport tourism practices. *Journal of Sport & Tourism, 21*(2), 95–113. https://doi.org/10.1080/14775085.2016.1271349.

Graburn, N. H. H. (1977). Tourism: The sacred journey. In V. L. Smith (Ed.), *Hosts and guests. The anthropology of tourism* (pp. 17–31). Philadelphia: University of Pennsylvania Press.

Graham, M. (2013). Geography/internet: Ethereal alternate dimensions of cyberspace or grounded augmented realities?: Commentary. *The Geographical Journal, 179*(2), 177–182. https://doi. org/10.1111/geoj.12009.

Janssen, J.-P. (1982). *La vie au bout des doigts*. Documentary film, France Télévisions.

Janssen, J.-P. (1983). *Opéra vertical*. Documentary film, France Télévisions.

Kane, M. J., & Zink, R. (2004). Package adventure tours: Markers in serious leisure careers. *Leisure Studies, 23*(4), 329–345. https://doi.org/10.1080/0261436042000231655.

Kinsley, S. (2013). Beyond the screen: Methods for investigating geographies of life 'online'. *Geography Compass, 7*(8), 540–555. https://doi.org/10.1111/gec3.12062.

Krotz, F. (2009). Mediatization: A concept with which to grasp media and societal change. In K. Lundby (Ed.), *Mediatization: Concept, changes, consequences*. New York: Peter Lang.

Larsen, J., & Urry, J. (2011). Gazing and performing. *Environment and Planning D: Society and Space, 29*(6), 1110–1125. https://doi.org/10.1068/d21410.

Lamont, M. (2014). Authentication in sports tourism. *Annals of Tourism Research, 45*, 1–17. https://doi.org/10.1016/j.annals.2013.11.003.

Larson, L. R., Szczytko, R., Bowers, E. P., Stephens, L. E., Stevenson, K. T., & Floyd, M. F. (2018). Outdoor time, screen time, and connection to nature: Troubling trends among rural youth? *Environment and Behavior*. https://doi.org/10.1177/0013916518806686.

Laslaz, L., Depraz, S., Guyot, S., & Héritier, S. (2012). *Atlas mondial des espaces protégés: les sociétés face à la nature*. Paris: Autrement.

Laurier, E. (2015). Owning and sharing experiences of adventure: Tourism, video and editing practices. In S. P. Mains, J. Cupples, & C. Lukinbeal (Eds.), *Mediated geographies and geographies of media* (pp. 433–445). Dordrecht: Springer. https://doi.org/10.1007/978-94-017-9969-0_26.

Leszczynski, A. (2015). Spatial media/tion. *Progress in Human Geography, 39*(6), 729–751. https://doi.org/10.1177/0309132514558443.

Lewis, N. (2000). The climbing body, nature and the experience of modernity. *Body & Society, 6*(3–4), 58–80. https://doi.org/10.1177/1357034X00006003004.

Lussault, M. (2007). *L'homme spatial: la construction sociale de l'espace humain*. Paris: Seuil.

Lussault, M., & Stock, M. (2010). 'Doing with space': Towards a pragmatics of space. *Social Geography, 5*(1), 11–19. https://doi.org/10.5194/sg-5-11-2010.

MacCannell, D. (1976). *The tourist: A new theory of the leisure class*. New York: Schocken Books.

Mao, P., & Obin, O. (2018). La transition numérique des sports de nature, vers des sportsnature 3.1. *Nature & Récréation, 6*, 13–25.

Mao, P., Corneloup, J., & Bourdeau, P. (2003). Analyse des processus de territorialisation des hauts lieux de pratiques touristiques et sportives de nature: l'exemple des gorges du Verdon. *Téoros, 22*(22–2), 52–62.

McCormack, K. (2018). Building community online and on the trail: Communication, coordination, and trust among mountain bikers. *Information, Communication & Society, 21*(4), 564–577. https://doi.org/10.1080/1369118X.2017.1290128.

Morley, D. (2009). For a materialist, non – Media-centric media studies. *Television & New Media, 10*(1), 114–116. https://doi.org/10.1177/1527476408327173.

Ness, S. A. (2011). Bouldering in Yosemite: Emergent signs of place and landscape. *American Anthropologist, 113*(1), 71–87. https://doi.org/10.1111/j.1548-1433.2010.01307.x.

Niel, A., & Sirost, O. (2008). Pratiques sportives et mises en paysage (Alpes, Calanques marseillaises). *Etudes Rurales, 181*(1), 181–202.

Reckwitz, A. (2002). Toward a theory of social practices. A development in culturalist theorizing. *European Journal of Social Theory, 5*(2), 243–263.

Rose, G. (2016). *Visual methodologies: An introduction to researching with visual materials*. London: Sage.

Scarles, C. (2012). Eliciting embodied knowledge and response: Respondent-led photography and visual autoethnography. In T. Rakic & D. Chambers (Eds.), *An introduction to visual research methods in tourism* (pp. 70–91). London: Routledge.

Schatzki, T. R. (2001). Introduction: Practice theory. In T. R. Schatzki, K. Knorr-Cetina, & E. Von Savigny (Eds.), *The practice turn in contemporary theory* (pp. 10–23). London/New York: Routledge.

Schatzki, T. R. (2002). *The site of the social: A philosophical account of the constitution of social life and change.* University Park: Pennsylvania State University Press.

Stock, M. (2007). Théorie de l'habiter. Questionnements. In T. Paquot, M. Lussault, & C. Younès (Eds.), *Habiter, le propre de l'humain* (pp. 103–125). Paris: La Découverte. http://www.cairn.info/article.php?ID_ARTICLE=DEC_PAQUO_2007_01_0103.

Stock, M. (2015). Habiter comme "faire avec l'espace". Réflexions à partir des théories de la pratique. *Annales de Géographie, 704*(4), 424–441.

Stylianou-Lambert, T. (2012). Tourists with cameras: Reproducing or producing? *Annals of Tourism Research, 39*(4), 1817–1838. https://doi.org/10.1016/j.annals.2012.05.004.

Swidler, A. (2001). What anchors cultural practices. In T. R. Schatzki, K. Knorr-Cetina, & E. Von Savigny (Eds.), *The practice turn in contemporary theory* (pp. 83–101). London: Routledge.

Thévenot, L. (2001). Pragmatic regimes governing the engagement with the world. In T. R. Schatzki, K. Knorr-Cetina, & E. Von Savigny (Eds.), *The practice turn in contemporary theory* (pp. 56–73). London: Routledge.

Thévenot, L. (2006). *L'action au pluriel: sociologie des régimes d'engagement.* Paris: La Découverte.

Thorpe, H. (2017). Action sports, social media, and new technologies: Towards a research agenda. *Communication & Sport, 5*(5), 554–578. https://doi.org/10.1177/2167479516638125.

Thorpe, H., & Rinehart, R. (2010). Alternative sport and affect: Non-representational theory examined. *Sport in Society, 13*(7–8), 1268–1291. https://doi.org/10.1080/17430431003780278.

Thrift, N. (2000). Still life in nearly present time: The object of nature. *Body & Society, 6*(3–4), 34–57. https://doi.org/10.1177/1357034X00006003003.

Thrift, N. (2007). *Non-representational theory: Space, politics, affect.* London/New York: Routledge.

Urry, J. (1990). *The tourist gaze.* London: Sage.

van Nuenen, T. (2016). Here I am: Authenticity and self-branding on travel blogs. *Tourist Studies, 16*(2), 192–212. https://doi.org/10.1177/1468797615594748.

Woermann, N. (2012). On the slope is on the screen: Prosumption, social media practices, and scopic systems in the Freeskiing subculture. *American Behavioral Scientist, 56*(4), 618–640. https://doi.org/10.1177/0002764211429363.

Wylie, J. (2005). A single day's walking: Narrating self and landscape on the south west coast path. *Transactions of the Institute of British Geographers, 30*(2), 234–247. https://doi.org/10.1111/j.1475-5661.2005.00163.x.

Valérian Geffroy has completed a PhD thesis in Geography at the University of Lausanne (Switzerland). His thesis explored the spatialities and communities of practice in outdoor sport tourism. His research interests cover leisure, mobilities, geographical and sociological theories of action, and the digital mediation of space.

Chapter 5
Challenging Connectivity During Nature-Based Tourism: (Dis)connection at Banff National Park

Morgane Müller-Roux

5.1 Introduction

Mobile technology has changed the way people travel, move to unfamiliar places and immerse into environments, look for information and resolve practical problems. In particular, it has modified practices when people are away from home. Connectivity has become central to tourist practices and the different ways of make do with unfamiliar spaces (Lussault and Stock 2010). As a result, this phenomenon has required new strategies from the tourism industry. Following this new enthusiasm for the digital age, actors from the industry saw an opportunity to satisfy new demands and began proposing new activities and discourses on certain places (e.g. Gretzel 2010). In response, a growing amount of scientific research has focused on the actual use of various mobile applications for travellers (e.g. digital tourist guides) and offered a critique of these applications' effectiveness (Germann Molz and Paris 2015; Dickinson et al. 2016). Especially, the interpretation of this ubiquitous connectivity as overwhelming and the question of its desirability has been studied (Jauréguiberry 2003, 2014; Jauréguiberry and Lachance 2016). Some studies have found, for example, that staying connected could cause tourists anxiety during moments of relaxation (Pearce and Gretzel 2012; Jauréguiberry 2014). In addition, Gretzel (2010) argues that permanent connectivity can disengage people and lead to disembodied experiences and a lack of interaction with others who are physically present. In this way, terms like "digital detox" and "disconnection" have appeared in common discourse and on various social media platforms (Turkle 2011; Jauréguiberry 2014). This hyperconnectivity coupled with global mobility creates new issues regarding human relations, which can now be continuously maintained even when people are separated by great distances and without physical

M. Müller-Roux (✉)
Institute of Geography and Sustainability, University of Lausanne, Lausanne, Switzerland
e-mail: morgane.muller.1@unil.ch

© The Editor(s) (if applicable) and The Author(s), under exclusive license to
Springer Nature Switzerland AG 2021
M. Stock (ed.), *Progress in French Tourism Geographies*, Geographies of
Tourism and Global Change, https://doi.org/10.1007/978-3-030-52136-3_5

87

co-presence. It leads to "sociality at a distance", as underscore Larsen and Sandbye (2014) in their study on digital photography.

By making use of digital photography and smartphones, tourists now have the opportunity to capture and instantly share intangible memories with their loved ones or the rest of the world at every step of their journey (not only during but also before and after their holiday). In this context, a new form of tourist practice has been emerging, which consists of disconnecting from any form of information and communication technologies (ICT) in order to escape daily life (Jauréguiberry 2014). This decision to disconnect tends to come from a desire not to be over-whelmed by an uncontrolled, continuous flow of information and communication when on holiday; as a result, partial disconnection is perceived as a way to grasp some kind of control over this situation. National parks, such as Banff National Park (Canada), appear to be the ideal place for this type of tourism practice because of eventual "technological dead zones" in the wilderness on the one hand, and, on the other hand, because "nature" is nowadays perceived, in the collective human psyche, as beneficial for the body and the mind and symbolizes a break with the daily life. Moreover, as Saarinen puts it:

> elements such as experiencing peace and quiet and natural beauty, wildlife viewing, [...] and spiritual encounters are among the main motivations for nature-based tourism (Saarinen 2014, p. 505).

Voluntary disconnection can therefore be viewed as a good way to escape the rou-tines of daily life and fully experience nature-based tourism and the feeling of being away. Additionally, up until recently, tourism research has focused on the fact that mobile technology is, in many ways, essential/useful to tourism (among others, Jacobsen and Munar 2012; Munar and Jacobsen 2014; Vincent 2014).

There has been little research into these new practices – more specifically, this desire to "disconnect from it all" and tourists' will to reduce or at least mediate their connectivity while being away from their everyday lives (Pearce and Gretzel 2012; Jauréguiberry 2014; Paris et al. 2015; Dickinson et al. 2016). Moreover, since the rise in popularity of (new) social media (e.g. Instagram, TripAdvisor and Facebook), studies have more concentrated on the many possibilities of promoting a destina-tion, as social media have made it possible for one person to instantly communicate with people around the world and share information about a tourism product (Fatanti and Suyadnya 2015). However, few studies have tried to show how social media influence tourist practices in specific places around the world, more especially in natural spaces. The question that is then risen here is: what is at stake when choos-ing to disconnect with home, daily life and the world during nature tourism prac-tice? Or in the opposite, how do tourists 'maintain their connectivity while being away?

This chapter will fill in two gaps in tourism research by focusing on these issues around the ubiquity of mobile technology. *First*, I will describe tourists who choose to share Banff National Park (and their experience in the wild) with their loved ones or the rest of the world. I then explore how tourists' use of social media requires new strategies to capture the materiality of the wilderness and, in so doing, creates new ways of engaging with it. Furthermore, I show how actual representations of the tourists' engagement with nature are produced in a very particular way so as to be shared with the rest of the world in a way that is in keeping with the imaginary produced by social media while simultaneously reproducing it. *Second,* I will try to understand tourists' interactions with nature and the way in which their stay in the wild allows them to disconnect from daily life. I will also show that tourists implement these types of practices through various tactics aimed at disconnecting and reclaiming a certain level of control over their use of ICT. I will also show that these practices take place in spaces that are considered part of the "wilderness" and are often remote. These last points will be supported by several examples collected throughout my multiple fieldworks in Banff National Park in Canada, where connectivity is managed in various ways by visitors.

5.2 Nature's Healing Power in a Connected World

Related to this reflection on the implications of the continuous use of digital technologies, I will also shed light on the strong link between nature's discourses and tourist imaginaries of nature practice. The past few decades, the Western world started seeing nature as something to preserve and cherish rather than exploit (Arnould and Glon 2006; Depraz and Héritier 2012). Indeed, there is a dominant discourse that states that being in and practising nature is an authentic and intense 'being-in-the-world', while the city is seen as a place of extreme "anthropisation". Especially, the national parks have been created with this idea in mind (MacLaren 2007): in response to the artificiality of modern life, there is an increasing interest in the role of nature for health.[1] The idea that the pure air, the absence of stress, physical activity and so forth associated with nature could help to improve our health and general happiness continues today (Chen and Prebensen 2017). The discourse around nature as something beneficial for our society has led to a rise in the number of studies with a focus on the relationship between nature and quality of life. It has even been elevated to a medical level as there is scientific evidence of the benefits of nature (Smith in Chen and Prebensen 2017). More importantly, it is also a moral discourse with a strongly anchored value: the idea that engaging with nature is essential. Popular press publications like National Geographic and the GEO magazine have addressed this subject numerous times (Williams 2016; Romberg 2018). Every time, they explain how essential nature is to our well-being in an almost "mystical" way. National Geographic also describes how some countries, like Finland and South Korea, and their governments take this subject very seriously and are promoting nature experiences as public health policy (Williams 2016).

---

[1] As the environmentalist John Muir states in 1898: « *Thousands of tired, nerve-shaken, over-civilized people are beginning to find out that going to the mountains is going home, that wildness is a necessity, and that mountain parks and reservations are useful not only as fountains of timber and irrigating rivers, but as fountains of life* » (John Muir, 1898, cited after Runte, 1920).

According to scientific literature (Bulbeck 2012; Fletcher 2014; Nepal and Saarinen 2016; Dickinson et al. 2016), this discourse on nature is pushing more and more tourists to visit places considered part of the wilderness; in this way, it also feeds into the tourist imaginary around nature practices. Indeed, with sustainable development as the current ideology, we no longer perceive nature as something we have to exploit but as something beautiful, calming and liminal; our society then finds itself again in a logic of contemplating nature, as the romantics used to do. Natural spaces, such as national parks, are currently appreciated for their aesthetic value, and, gazing remains one of the most important aspects of tourist practices (Urry and Larsen 2011).

This appreciation of the sublime and the picturesque follows a long tradition of promotional materials for Banff that includes framed landscapes, and this dimension of "the beautiful to look at" now also turns up in social media culture, where aesthetics plays a big part in how popular an account can be. Indeed, as posters and brochures used to do, photographers and influencers on Instagram can now provide a genuine expression of a destination (and, in this way, reach a large audience). Therefore, I argue the digital technologies allow for the creation and/or regeneration of tourist imaginaries in places considered part of the wilderness (Fatanti and Suyadnya 2015; Miller 2017).

5.3 Assisted Practices and Performance

My study adopts the perspective from "practice theory" as a conceptual foundation to study the practices of individuals identified as tourists. This framework will help us to solve two issues with respect to the field of geography: (1) the use and management of the physical and symbolic space and (2) the construction of a relational space through practice (Stock 2003, 2015). With these two objectives in mind, Lussault and Stock (2010) propose an approach to practices that illustrates individuals' relationship with space. By mobilising the expression of "doing with space", the two authors connect with the notions of practices traditionally used in geography that had previously mobilised "spatiality" as "spatial practices" by insisting on the the reflexive, intentional and tactical nature of practices. Individuals actually do something *with* space in they mobilise it as a resource or a problem. It also permits us to understand the ways in which the spatial dimensions of human societies are "active" and describes the ways in which the spatial dimensions of human societies are "active" within, "integrated" in and "co-constitutes" practice, for instance regarding landscape, place, location, distance, limits etc.. It means that people "have to make do with it" (« *il faut faire avec* », in French), meaning one has to do something even though it might not be very pleasant or desirable. Therefore, people must face up to "space" and find ways to deal with it (Certeau 1990; Lussault and Stock 2010, pp. 14–15).

This notion of "doing with space" mainly relies on Michel de Certeau's (1990) approach to practices as being of a "tactical" nature beyond the disciplinary productions of society. De Certeau (1990) calls it *"manières de faire"* – arts of doing – and deploys his analysis on the arts of doing with space and place. Individuals are not considered as passive, but on the contrary as active as they utilise a series of tactics and strategies in their daily lives in order to face "power". Throughout this chapter, this notion of tactics will be illustrated through examples of tourist practices that are strengthened by various forms of technology to deal with space in innovative ways. Moreover, we insist on the fact that tourist practices can be analysed through this conceptual framework as, according to Stock et al. (2017), "an individual can be considered a 'tourist' when he or she performs tourist practices, which can be analysed in their spatialities" (Stock et al. 2017).[2] This term, "spatiality", is essential to our analysis because it permits us to grasp all the different symbolic dimensions, meanings, interpretations, representations and imaginaries linked to geographical places, landscapes, distances, locations, limits, milieus, natures etc. In this research, working on the spatial practices of tourists means we would be able to understand their way of dealing with space and also emphasises that there are specific imaginaries embedded in their practices (Lussault and Stock 2010).

A second element will dwell on the notion of performance. I understand tourism here as a process involving the construction and/or the integration of new practices. In order to illustrate these practices as well as possible, the metaphor of performance will also be used to identify these various tourist practices. In tourism studies, the notion of performance has grown rapidly in popularity. Dean MacCannell (1976) develops the idea of tourist practices as theatrical representations and questions the notion of "authenticity" because tourists are faced with a "staged authenticity", meaning here that he establishes a distinction between front regions (where the performance takes place) and back regions (where one can be "oneself") (Coleman and Crang 2002; Chapuis 2010). Edensor (2000, 2001), for his part, describes tourist practices as fixed and codified performances that produce norms by virtue of repetition. However, in his example of the Taj Mahal (Edensor 1998), the tourist is not reduced to the role of a spectator who only "looks" and does what is excepted of him (in contrast to MacCannell's account of tourism): He is, in fact, aware of this etiquette and the standards to be respected but allows himself to improvise and to leave the frame when he has the opportunity or the desire to do so. This last point echoes the practices and photographic performances of some tourists in Banff National Park who develop specific tactics in order to move beyond codified performances. In line with Bærenholdt et al. (2004, p. 70), I will consider tourism photography as a complex amalgam of materiality, technology, discourse and practice (by both humans and non-humans). I will also show, as stated before, that a performance of such photography can be either improvised or staged in response to dominant "tourist" gazes, imaginaries or representations circulating on social media, in magazines etc. (Urry 1990; Bærenholdt et al. 2004). Lastly, I will argue

---

[2] My translation from French: *"l'individu est appréhendé en tant que touriste lorsqu'il effectue des pratiques touristiques; celles-ci peuvent être analysées dans leurs spatialités"*.

that these specific imaginaries condition not only tourist practices but also visitors' photographic performances inside the park.

5.4   Methods and Fieldwork

Using a framework combining the imaginary, the material and the immaterial, the instantaneity and the disconnection, this chapter examines tourists' photography practices. The research was conducted inside Banff National Park, which is situated in the province of Alberta in western Canada. The results presented here rely on mixed qualitative methods that were applied over the course of four fieldworks between the summer of 2016 and the winter of 2018.[3] The first stage involved participant observation. This method is interesting because it can be applied to an everyday life context that is punctuated by routine activities; however, in order to study tourists and tourism in general, it means analysing non-daily practices. In this case study, my role as a researcher was to observe tourists in a context where new tactics are implemented in order to tackle new realities and to engage in a certain practice in a place considered as "away" or "the wilderness". More concretely, these observations were made during a variety of group activities for tourists (sightseeing, kayaking and horseback riding). Two of these group activities proved to be really useful for the research. The first was a trip into the backcountry during which I experienced a complete disconnection in the company of a small group of tourists (about 15 in total). The second was a photography workshop by Paul Zizka, a well-known local photographer, during which I was able to interact with 20 other people interested in photographing the Canadian Rockies. During each of these group activities, I "acted" like a tourist while keeping in mind my main role as a researcher. The second stage of this study involved exploratory in-depth interviews (semi-structured interviews of varying lengths) that raised questions about wilderness, the park as well as digital connection/disconnection in a tourism context. Some of these interviews were conducted in French, I then translated them for the purpose of this chapter. Finally, I also collected various visual materials related to the park, such as tourist brochures, paperback guidebooks, local archives, websites etc., on each of my stays. Banff National Park was the ideal place to conduct this study because it makes it possible to combine different aspects of this research. First, this park offers an immense space where you can find never-ending nature and easily confront yourself with it. Second, the park is a popular "hub" on Instagram and is frequently cited as a "place to visit" on social media. In particular, Lake Louise and Moraine Lake, two well-known hotspots inside the park, are highly appreciated, and pictures of them are widely shared on Instagram because they are so visually striking. To date,[4] the hashtag "Banff" has been associated with more than two million posts on

[3] In total, the fieldwork lasted 3 months.
[4] Numbers were collected in February 2019.

Instagram, which demonstrates the importance of mobilising this social network to gain a better understanding of how visual content can influence the imaginary of the wilderness. Moreover, Banff National Park and the Canadian Rockies are considered emblematic spaces throughout North America for discovering "pure wilderness" and engage in tourism activities. Banff National Park was created in 1885, making it the second-oldest national park in the world, right behind Yellowstone in the United States, which was established in 1872. Since the beginning of the twentieth century, its popularity has never stopped growing and experienced considerable growth in the 1960s.[5] Banff National Park attracts more than four million visitors per year, a figure that rises to nine million if attendance at all seven of the mountain parks that make up the Canadian Rocky Mountains Park is taken into account (Héritier 2006; Agence Parcs Canada 2015). These impressive numbers certainly bear witness visitors' interest in parks and nature. However, despite this popularity, the number of visitors has dropped at the national level over the past decade. Consequently, new marketing and communication strategies[6] have been implemented by the governmental agency, Park Canada, and the most recent ones have proved to be efficient at (some) local level sites as the numbers have seen an increase since 2009 (Agence Parcs Canada 2012). Moreover, 2017 was announced as "record year" because all the parks were open for free to the public due to the 150th anniversary of Canada. In relation to what I argue in this paper, I believe that that the number of visitors has risen not only thanks to the actions mentioned before but also thanks to the actual representation of nature and the wilderness in common discourses.

5.5 Being Connected to the Wilderness

Destinations described as "natural" or "wild" on social media sites are typically pictured as something pure and untouched. These representations attract more tourists and, in turn, generate new tourist practices. Indeed, a user scrolling down his Instagram feed with the hashtag #wilderness, #nature or #wildernessculture[7] will almost certainly realise that most of the photos have a lot in common as Instagram produces very similar, normative representations of outdoor tourism aesthetics. One of the most important elements is the absence of people. As you can see in the images below (Fig. 5.1), the mountains are represented as something magnificent and quasi-mystical that should be gazed at. Most of them show only nature without any or with just a single protagonist. Some Instagram' accounts contributes to

---

[5]This growth can be explained by the fact that car ownership became more and more common.

[6]Attractive visitor policies, new programmes, new infrastructure, packages for family, free access for young people, free pass for 2017 etc.

[7]If he mostly looks at the most "popular" ones selected by Instagram's algorithm.

Fig. 5.1 Normative representations of nature on Instagram. (Source: @paulzizkaphotography and @kahliaprilphoto, 2019) With permission from the authors

creating particular outdoor tourist aesthetics with a series of very similar and normative representation of nature.

Of course, seeking to depict "nature" or "the wilderness" while engaging in tourism is becoming more and more common: In Banff National Park, searching for iconic places and photographing them in a way that shows them to be as "natural" and "beautiful" as possible has fast become an obsession among visitors. Tourists are immortalising hotspots like Moraine Lake, Johnston Canyon and Lake Louise in a very deliberate and carefully planned way: The main focus is the art of posing alone in order to mimic peacefulness and underline this division between man and nature. For example, John, who was travelling on his own and is passionate about outdoor tourism, wanted to capture Johnston Canyon when it was as quiet as possible, meaning without the presence of other tourists:

> I try to get nobody else in the shot. Sometimes it's a bit tricky, as you can see (John, July 2017).

The tactic here seems to be to take a picture of this exact spot without anybody else in the shot, thereby fitting with the imaginary of the wilderness (an absence of people). Adventure photographer Paul Zizka[8] confirmed to me that he could see in narratives and various representations that the art of posing alone while facing the "wilderness" has grown popular on social media. The effect is achieved by using different tactics, which sometimes means illegally trespassing by leaving the trail, to fit the different imaginaries of it on social media (see below Fig. 5.2). In this particular example, we must also keep in mind that this imaginary of wilderness did not originate on social media. This way of depicting and picturing Banff's

---

[8] Paul Zizka's work can be accessed via Instagram or Facebook under the handle @ paulzizkaphotography.

Fig. 5.2 Tourists' strategies to get the "alone and facing the wilderness shot". (Source: author, 2017)

landscapes flows from a long legacy of promotional materials (e.g. National Railway Canada), most of which include a single protagonist facing the natural setting. The inclusion of the human component allows potential tourists to project themselves into this situation and produce an imaginary of the natural world that they can understand but also manipulate (MacLaren 2007, p. 246). Tourist brochures, pamphlets and guidebooks also play their part in encouraging a drive for "this never-ending nature" (author's material). For example, Park Canada promises that "Moraine Lake offers dramatic photographic opportunities", Banff and Lake Louise Tourism agency also present Moraine Lake as a quiet place and provoking a special effect on its visitors: "you felt at peace as the stillness of the surroundings overcame you » (Banff and Lake Louise Tourism 2016; Parks Canada Agency 2019). These examples reveal the paradox between the wilderness – a place that is desirable because of the absence of humans – and wanting to explore it along with other tourists.

This representation of Banff may also have resulted in certain places being overexposed on Instagram. Indeed, when I spoke to several tourists about a particular place located in Johnston Canyon, many of them referred to a "secret cave" that has become particularly trendy on Instagram over the past few years. This "Instagram effect" was just starting to become problematic: The cave is located off the main trail in Johnston Canyon, and the frequent visits were disturbing the wildlife. A volunteer who was working for the park at the time told me that local authorities were aware of the problem but only recently realised the influence of social media on tourist practices and the environment (field notes, June 2017). However, the number of photos of this place that continue to be posted, as well as advertisements by the park itself, draws attention to it and further encourages tourists to visit and take their own photos to share online.[9] A direct result of these "ways of doing", as one of my interviewees puts it:

> It is very clear that if you go to Johnston Canyon, it will be crowded. If your travel ideas for Banff come from Instagram, then it is absolutely certain that you won't be alone there. Then again, if you do more research on the side, it's really not difficult to find a place where you can experience solitude (workshop, December 2018).

We understand that this kind of practice, helped along by social media and a long-time imaginary of the wilderness, is (being) reproduced all over the main hotspots in the park[10] and causes "the Instagram effect", which consists of visitors over-crowding certain places in the park.

5.6 Playing with the Wilderness

The examples above show that pictures can often be staged in a particular way that is similar to how they are symbolised (in brochures and magazines, for example), and this practice has institutionalised how tourist attractions should be "gazed at" and photographed (Edensor 2000). Besides the classic "person standing alone and facing the wilderness", other types of digitally equipped performances have recently taken place in Banff National Park. They are produced as the tourist deploys differ-ent tactics in the wild on a visit to the park. All of these performances have some-thing in common: The main protagonist "plays" with the wilderness and goes beyond the ritual and symbolic performance. Indeed, what I found most interesting in the narratives is that people want to immortalise "a certain feeling" – something that would mark their stay in the park and make them stand out from the crowd on social media: "You have to get creative; otherwise, we always take the same picture over and over again."[11] One of the ways of getting "outside the boundaries" of the classic shots would be to represent yourself in an original or unusual situation, like going for a swim in freezing water (see Fig. 5.3). Three Canadians actually jumped into a glacier-fed river together, screamed at the top of their lungs and explained to me afterwards that "it was the best feeling in the world and worth every second of it". Their performance was so unexpected at the time that a small crowd started to

---

[9] This cave is one example among many others. Moraine Lake, Lake Louise and Peyto Lake are also affected by similar issues.

[10] It might be important to note here that these places offer reception.

[11] "People are, like, well, I think they're doing this to gain followers on Instagram. Banff National Park is most likely at the centre of this trend (nature and tourism on Instagram). They have this desire to go to a place so that they can take a 'special' picture and increase their own popularity." (Paul Zizka, photographer)

Fig. 5.3 Friends immortalising their cold river shower as well as paddling on a thawing lake. (Source: author, 2018)

form around them, and their performance was immediately shared on Instagram (field notes and interview, July 2017).

Paddling across a thawing lake (see Fig. 5.3), lighting a fire next to a lake or kayaking while wearing a special shirt (here red flannel shirts) are all good examples of this desire to "go beyond" the traditional vision and representation of certain hotspots. These innovative performances actually take place in well-known spots, where some tourists may refuse to conform to routinised performances. These examples can remind us to consider Michel de Certeau's work on ways of doing with space; his way of apprehending practices can underline this rejection of "conventional" tourist practices. We also understand here that tactics – assisted by digital equipment – are used by tourists in the park to (re)create "technocratically constructed, written and functionalized spaces" (Certeau 1990).

5.7 Disconnecting from It All

Remaining connected while on holiday can be described as a common practice; the majority of my interviewees confirmed that they were keeping in touch with their friends and family. For a young Canadian girl, the possibility of staying connected while discovering Banff was important:

> sharing my experiences with my loved ones is important to me; I love that they can also discover a piece of the country that they've never seen before. It is precious for m" (Judy, July 2017).

Some other tourists pushed these connected practices even further by sharing it simultaneously with others; FaceTiming is not an uncommon thing to witness, and I documented this behaviour numerous times during my fieldwork. My interlocutors also demonstrated this desire to manage their connectivity, especially in this temporality paced by relaxation. These connections were mostly managed by the tourists themselves; just as some of them chose how they would practice the park, others tried to limit having a permanent connection to their daily life:

> I try to disconnect when I'm on holiday. It takes time at first to get used to it, but I love it (…), that being said, I try to send news to my family once a day, so they don't worry (Anne, July 2017).

Most of the tourists realised there is a contradiction in staying connected while being in the wild and on holiday; nonetheless, they still felt compelled to do it:

> even if it bothers me, I have to do it (speaking about sending news), even on holiday. I can't do in some other way, 'cause I'm stuck (…) it's a social constraint. It's rude not to answer a WhatsApp (Theo, July 2017).

This notion of trying to be (or at least to feel) disconnected in order to be more engaged in nature tourism practices is embedded in visitors' narratives, official discourses and social media posts (material collected in the field). However, the visitors realise that this philosophy relies on a particular vision of nature tourism – one that appears to be profoundly different from our hyperconnected ways of doing things in daily life:

> Yeah, I think this contrast is interesting, the contradiction between 'being in nature to the maximum', but I clearly see that people who are posting images frequently are really not far into nature. Because let's face it, you have to have service in order to post, write a caption and answer comments. Then, eventually, you understand that … you see that it's contradictory for people to speak about (really being in) nature all the time! (Sam May 2018).

What is interesting is that this fundamental contradiction pushes certain visitors to deploy particular tactics in order to experience a break with the connectivity they otherwise experience everywhere around them. The tourists who had deliberately chosen to undergo a complete disconnection in Banff National Park were quite rare, as the main condition of this type of practice suggests (an experience of) remoteness. However, I was able to witness it on a trip to a lodge located in Banff's backcountry, where the absence of reception greatly contributed to the experience. There, the aim was for the tourist to feel disconnected on different levels. In fact, the majority of the interviewees underlined the importance of being "away from everything", and the *remoteness* from constant crowds of tourists was often mentioned:

– Is that why you came here?
– (Husband) Sure, I guess. It was part of our programme. We wanted to have an experience in the backcountry, to be able to be away from all these tourists and enjoy the quiet. Here we are away from everything, there are only a few people, and you can hike almost every day.
– I see. You chose the right place then.
– (Wife) I agree with you, I completely lost track of time. I don't know what day it is, what date we are, but that's a good sign, right? Yes, it's perfect for that. You have the quiet, the view and nature. Here, we are disconnected from everything. Magnificent. (pause) I don't get how the tourists can stand meeting so many other people. It's so crowded. I mean, last year I was in Yellowstone, sure there were some tourists, but it was never like that. It was in May, I guess, but even so.

As the lodge is located more than 30 km away from Banff and has no reception, the location is ideal for these types of tourists who are looking to unwind and disconnect. In this last extract, the two retreaters underlined how this experience enabled them to get away from day-to-day life, and in doing so they completely lost track of time. Plus, this backcountry lodge experience is presented as a chance to disconnect, venture out onto a trail without (almost) anybody else – in this case, any other "tourists" (fieldnotes, 2017). Many others evoked the pleasure of being able to relax without distractions from any kind of connection device; for example, two New Yorkers discussed with me how pleasant it was to properly disconnect from work:

– (Mary) I'm not looking forward at all to going back to "civilisation".
– Why is that?
– (Mary) Well, because I'll have to go through my e-mails.
– Your personal e-mails?

- (Mary) No, my work e-mails. If I don't check them for 2 days, I get about 200 of them, so I check them regularly, even when I'm on holiday. That's kind of bad, right? But I don't really have a choice.
- (Jess) Yes, me too. I enjoyed the break. I mean, I took my iPad with me, but that was only for reading.

For some workers, ICT have rapidly become a source of constant pressure, as e-mail and phone calls can quickly result in an information overload even holidays cannot interrupt (Jauréguiberry 2014). The conversation above clearly illustrates this issue. In Mary's case, she feels obligated to read her e-mails, even when she is on holiday, for fear of having to deal with too many of them upon her return. Remoteness and being able to completely connect with nature during this type of tourist practice also seemed essential to this experience:

> This place is by far my favourite from this trip. Because there's nothing else to bother you, you know. In the evening, I just stood there, on my own, listening to the little noises coming from the forest and just looking at this picture-perfect landscape. And that was enough for me, you know (Albert August 2017).

Overall, this sudden change in tourists' usual daily practices permitted them to confront nature, loneliness and remoteness. In doing so, they left more room to share with others over dinner the anecdotes they had collected during the day spent in the wild, and, inevitably, technologies were left aside. During these "intimate" moments, a certain nostalgic vibe was shared. Nelson, for example, reminisced as follows about his prior travel experience:

> When we travelled, there were no cell phones, no Internet. We were lucky if we could even find a phone. My wife and I got married in New Zealand, just with some friends. We told everyone else the news later. (laughs) Yeah, good memories! (Nelson August 2017).

These moments seemed to be ideal for unwinding and reflecting on each other's life without any form of distraction other than "walk, eat and sleep" (fieldnotes, August 2017). The narratives here relate the importance of experiencing a break with day-to-day practices while travelling. As a result, this particular experience of the wilderness and of "living" in the backcountry (for a short period of time) allowed the individuals to disconnect from all forms of technological communication while simultaneously allowing them to re-appropriate the main purpose of tourism: experiencing a break from daily life.

5.8 Conclusion

This chapter has shown how the wilderness has become an important symbol within the tourism industry because signifying a disconnection from the stress of daily life. Common discourse around nature incites more and more tourists to visit places considered to be a part of the wild outdoors. Moreover, big social media platforms such as Instagram allow for the creation and regeneration of tourist imaginaries considered as natural spaces, consequently, contribute to creating particular outdoor tourist aesthetics through a series of normative and very similar representations of nature. In all the examples provided, we understand that photography and "connected practices" are not simply ways to document pre-existing experiences at a tourist attraction but are part of producing them as concrete bodily performances and tangible memories, often with the assistance of various kinds of technological equipment.

Furthermore, the examples of photography performances provided in this chapter emphasise that these tactics and strategies are not really new but more likely "renewed", as the practice of sharing pictures of the Rocky Mountains with the rest of the world has been around for a long time. What is changing, however, is the speed at which it is done: the form of communication and the channel of communication have been profoundly affected by the digital revolution. Tourists nowadays have the opportunity to capture and share intangible, immaterial memories instantly with the rest of the world and their loved ones. This new publicness of images also affects the very tourist practices. Visitors are actually aware of these staged and scripted performances. So, in order to "go beyond" the traditional vision and representation of certain hotspots, improvised performances take place at Lake Louise, Moraine Lake, Johnson Canyon and Peyto Lake, mainly because certain tourists may refuse to conform to routinised performances. Therefore, it goes beyond mere sightseeing or "gazing" at a site and becomes a bodily performance, technologically equipped and globally shared.

In addition, in response to this ubiquitous connectivity during moments considered to be suitable for unwinding and marking a break with daily life, people implement different strategies in order not to feel too overwhelmed by technology. Immersing oneself in a natural and remote setting helps some visitors to "unplug" from technology and to "connect" to nature, which mimics tourism's first essential purpose. This last part suggests that even with this hyperconnectivity, the search for "escape" continues to be a powerful motive in tourism.

References

Agence Parcs Canada. (2012). *Parcs Canada – Évaluation de l'offre de services aux visiteurs de Parcs Canada*. https://www.pc.gc.ca/leg/docs/pc/rpts/rve-par/78/index_f.asp#section2. Accessed 19 Feb 2019.

Agence Parcs Canada G du C. (2015) *Loi et règlements – Agence Parcs Canada*. https://www.pc.gc.ca/fr/agence-agency/lr-ar. Accessed 28 Jun 2018.

Arnould, P., & Glon, É. (2006). Wilderness, usages et perceptions de la nature en Amérique du Nord. *Annales de géographie, 649*, 227–238.

Bærenholdt, J. O., Haldrup, M., Larsen, J., & Urry, J. (2004). *Performing tourist places*. London: Ashgate.

Banff and Lake Louise Tourism. (2016). Moraine Lake | Banff Alberta. In *Banff & Lake Louise Tourism*. https://www.banfflakelouise.com/moraine-lake. Accessed 9 Sept 2019.

Bulbeck, C. (2012). *Facing the wild: Ecotourism, conservation and animal encounters*. London: Earthscan.

Chapuis, A. (2010). Performances touristiques. D'une métaphore à un cadre de pensée géographique renouvelé. *Mondes du Tourisme*, 44–56. https://doi.org/10.4000/tourisme.274.

Chen, J. S., & Prebensen, N. K. (2017). *Nature tourism*. New York: Taylor & Francis.

Coleman, S., & Crang, M. (2002). *Tourism: Between place and performance*. New York/Oxford: Berghahn Books.

de Certeau, M. (1990). *L'invention du quotidien, I : Arts de faire, Nouvelle éd*. Paris: Gallimard.

Depraz, S., & Héritier, S. (2012). La nature et les parcs naturels en Amérique du Nord. *L'Information géographique, 76*, 6–28.

Dickinson, J. E., Hibbert, J. F., & Filimonau, V. (2016). Mobile technology and the tourist experience: (dis)connection at the campsite. *Tourism Management, 57*, 193–201. https://doi.org/10.1016/j.tourman.2016.06.005.

Edensor, T. (1998). *Tourists at the Taj: Performance and meaning at a symbolic site*. London/New York: Routledge.

Edensor, T. (2000). Staging tourism: Tourists as performers. *Annals of Tourism Research, 27*, 322–344. https://doi.org/10.1016/S0160-7383(99)00082-1.

Edensor, T. (2001). Performing tourism, staging tourism (re) producing tourist space and practice. *Tourist Studies, 1*, 59–81.

Fatanti, M. N., & Suyadnya, I. W. (2015). Beyond user gaze: How Instagram creates tourism destination brand? *Procedia – Social and Behavioral Sciences, 211*, 1089–1095. https://doi.org/10.1016/j.sbspro.2015.11.145.

Fletcher, R. (2014). *Romancing the wild: Cultural dimensions of ecotourism*. Durham: Duke University Press.

Germann Molz, J., & Paris, C. M. (2015). The social affordances of flashpacking: Exploring the mobility Nexus of travel and communication. *Mobilities, 10*, 173–192. https://doi.org/10.1080/17450101.2013.848605.

Gretzel, U. (2010). Travel in the network: Redirected gazes, ubiquitous connections and new Frontiers. In M. Levina & K. Grant (Eds.), *Post-global network and everyday life* (pp. 41–58). New York: Peter Lang.

Héritier, S. (2006). La nature et les pratiques de la nature dans les montagnes canadiennes : le cas des parcs nationaux des montagnes de l'Ouest (Alberta et Colombie Britannique). *Annales de géographie, 649*, 270–291.

Jacobsen, J. K. S., & Munar, A. M. (2012). Tourist information search and destination choice in a digital age. *Tourism Management Perspectives, 1*, 39–47. https://doi.org/10.1016/j.tmp.2011.12.005.

Jauréguiberry, F. (2003). *Internet, nouvel espace citoyen?* Paris: L'Harmattan.

Jauréguiberry, F. (2014). La déconnexion aux technologies de communication. *Réseaux, 186*, 15. https://doi.org/10.3917/res.186.0015.

Jauréguiberry, F., & Lachance, J. (2016). *Le voyageur hypermoderne. Partir dans un monde connecté*. Toulouse: Erès.

Larsen, J., & Sandbye, M. (2014). *Digital snaps: The new face of photography*. London: Tauris.

Lussault, M., & Stock, M. (2010). "Doing with space": Towards a pragmatics of space. *Social Geography, 5*, 11–19. https://doi.org/10.5194/sg-5-11-2010.

MacCannell, D. (1976). *The tourist: A new theory of the leisure class*. New York: Schocken Books.

MacLaren, I. S. (2007). *Culturing wilderness in Jasper National Park: Studies in two centuries of human history in the upper Athabasca River watershed*. Edmonton: University of Alberta.

Miller, C. (2017). *How Instagram is changing travel*. National Geographic. http://www.nationalgeographic.com/travel/travel-interests/arts-and-culture/how-instagram-is-changing-travel/. Accessed 15 May 2017.

Munar, A. M., & Jacobsen, J. K. S. (2014). Motivations for sharing tourism experiences through social media. *Tourism Management, 43*, 46–54. https://doi.org/10.1016/j.tourman.2014.01.012.

Nepal, S., & Saarinen, J. (2016). *Political ecology and tourism*. London/New York: Routledge.

Paris, C. M., Berger, E. A., Rubin, S., & Casson, M. (2015). Disconnected and unplugged: Experiences of technology induced anxieties and tensions while traveling. In I. Tussyadiah & A. Inversini (Eds.), *Information and communication technologies in tourism 2015* (pp. 803–816). Cham: Springer.

Parks Canada Agency. (2019). 10 things you have to see in Banff National Park (...and a few more) – Banff National Park. https://www.pc.gc.ca/en/pn-np/ab/banff/visit/les10-top10. Accessed 12 Mar 2019.

Pearce, P. L., & Gretzel, U. (2012). Tourism in technology dead zones: Documenting experiential dimensions. *International Journal of Tourism Sciences, 12*, 1–20. https://doi.org/10.108 0/15980634.2012.11434656.

Romberg, J. (2018). Warum wir Natur brauchen. *GEO Magazin.* https://www.geo.de/magazine/ geo-magazin/31860-geo-nr-09-2018-warum-wir-natur-brauchen. Accessed 6 Nov 2019.

Saarinen, J. (2014). *Tourism and tourists in nature, national parks, and wilderness.* The Wiley Blackwell companion to tourism, pp. 500–512.

Stock, M. (2003). Pratiques des lieux, modes d'habiter, régimes d'habiter: pour une analyse trialogique des dimensions spatiales des sociétés humaines. *Travaux de l'Institut de Géographie de Reims,* (115), 213–230. https://doi.org/10.3406/tigr.2003.1473.

Stock, M. (2015). Habiter comme « faire avec l'espace ». Réflexions à partir des théories de la pratique. *Annales de géographie, 704*, 424–441. https://doi.org/10.3917/ag.704.0424.

Stock, M., Coëffé, V., & Violier, P. (2017). *Les enjeux contemporains du tourisme: Une approche géographique.* Rennes: Presses Universitaires de Rennes.

Turkle, S. (2011). *Alone together: Why we expect more from technology and less from each other.* New York: Basic Books.

Urry, J. (1990). *The tourist gaze: Leisure and travel in contemporary societies.* London: Sage.

Urry, J., & Larsen, J. (2011). *The tourist gaze 3.0.* London: Sage.

Vincent, J. (2014). L'appropriation des nouvelles technologies de la mobilité par le tourisme: Nouveaux enjeux créatifs. *Mondes du Tourisme,* (10), 62–74. https://doi.org/10.4000/ tourisme.380.

Williams, F. (2016). *This is your brain on nature.* National Geographic. https://www.nationalgeographic.com/magazine/2016/01/call-to-wild/. Accessed 28 Feb 2017.

Morgane Müller-Roux a PhD student and research assistant with the Institute of Geography and Sustainability at Lausanne University (Switzerland), where she participates in the research group "Cultures and Natures of Tourism". Her research deals with the entanglement of digital technologies with tourist practices.

Chapter 6
Tourism Territory/*Territoire(s) Touristique(s)*: When Mobility Challenges the Concept

Dominic Lapointe

6.1 Introduction

Tourism is about mobility, moving for leisure and consuming places (Urry 2002). The place-based dimension of tourism has focused research on localization where tourism happens and is performed, looking at tourism in terms of place (fixity) instead of mobility (Franklin 2014). It can be seen in the importance of the destination concept for tourism studies as the place within which the tourists' desire is destined to happen (Kadri et al. 2011). It is also epitomized in the generalization of the terms of destination management, the famous DMO's (destination management organisation). This destination centred view of tourism constructs tourism's space as a place in itself. Destinations are objects that need to be developed and managed, almost as if they were apart from the space and society where it happened. This have brought some authors to talk about enclave tourism (Saarinen 2017; Minca 2009) when they are actually set apart by different forms of boundaries (Manuel-Navarette 2016), be it physical, political, economic and psychological, but also of tourism bubbles (Judd 1999) when the tourism zone becomes circumscribed and tourism becomes the main function of the area. This form of tourism planning and management has raised criticism and called for more relationship with host communities. This criticism and the rise of territorial marketing (Vuigner 2016) have seen a sliding from the concept of destination towards tourism territories (Knafou et al. 1997). This chapter aims to unpack what tourism territory implied conceptually.

The concept of territory is mobilized by different disciplines, especially geography and political science, but also has different meanings and use in different linguistic scientific traditions. To unpack tourism territories, we will first look at the territory as conceptualized by anglosaxon geography, with a particular attention of

D. Lapointe (✉)
Université du Québec à Montréal, Montreal, Canada
e-mail: lapointe.dominic@uqam.ca

M. Stock (ed.), *Progress in French Tourism Geographies*, Geographies of
Tourism and Global Change, https://doi.org/10.1007/978-3-030-52136-3_6

the work of Stuart Elden and David Harvey. Afterwards we will turn to the French tradition and their use of the concept of *territoire* with a particular accent to the work of the members of the *Centre de recherche sur le développement territorial* based in Québec in Canada. Then, we will address the interaction of tourism with territory, more precisely how alterity and mobility of tourism conjugate with the fixity of territory.

6.2   Territory

Territory and *territoire* come from the same latin roots, *terra* which means land, and *territorium*, which is land under the control of a city, judge, etc. Its generalization in both French and English language is around the end of the seventeenth century (Robert et al. 1990). The concept of territory is a central contemporary concept used as the main way to divide the world and to politically control it (Elden 2013), but also to address power relationship in space and through space (Raffestin 1980). Its evolution and instalment is closely related with the expansion of the Nation-State from the eighteenth and nineteenth century onward. The notion of territory is based on the assumption of a stable and non-ambiguous spatial form to situate the political action of the State (Harvey 2009). Therefore, it is a spatial extension of sovereignty. A territory is then a space of power, bound to contain the power (Giddens 1981 in Elden 2013) and to regulate human activities within, and the relationship with the outside. It's a way to separate and distinguish societies (Gottmann 1973). In this respect, Elden (2013) defines territories as a political technology, in the sense of Foucault (2004), to control and manage space politically.

David Harvey (2009) also situates territories as the functional apparatus of Nation-State power. Indeed, it is through the State that territorializing behaviour are transformed in fixed and stable form of territory:

> The rise of modern state forms, and political claims to state jurisdiction and sovereignty (as exemplified in the Treaty of Westphalia of 1648), coupled with the instantiation of a legal and administrative system of private property rights, amounted to an administrative and institutional revolution in and codification of territorializing behaviors, the primary requirement of which was the construction of territorial forms that were unambiguous, fixed, and secure. (Harvey 2009: 172)

It is through this instantiation that territories, in Harvey's sense, are produced as nodes in the system of capitalist accumulation through the production of regionality (Harvey 2006). In these regional systems:

> Regional consciousness and identities, even affective loyalties, may build within this region and, when it is overlain by some apparatus of governance and state power, the regional space can evolve into a territorial unit that operates as some kind of defined space of collective consumption and production as well as political action. (Harvey 2006: 75)

In this view of territory, it is about a structuring of productive and consumption forms in a specific space within the capitalist accumulation structure.

In his review of space, place and territory, Duarte (2017) situates territory at the intersection of space and place. While keeping Harvey's (2009) and Elden (2013) conception of territory as an apparatus of Nation-State to assume power and control over space, he does add a significant relational dimension to it. Duarte (2017) states that within the technology of power called territory, there is a whole symbolic layer imposed through symbols, rituals, language and morals. These elements of the symbolic layer are shared and accepted by those who called the territory their homeland. According to this author, this layer is institutionalized through central power and a clear boundary as well as the recognition from other territories of these boundaries and sets of rules as specific to the territory. It works at two levels: outwardly with other territories and inwardly for the population. Therefore, territories are the translation of experience (place) through symbolic action within a bounded space.

As we can see, territories are mostly defined as a geopolitical concept by the anglo-saxon tradition, the concept referring to a defined, close and bounded space of power, even a space that the boundaries separate some sort of Us and Them, some sort of subject and object of the sovereign power in space. One noticeable divergence from this conceptualization of territory within the anglo-saxon understanding of territory is the book of Friedmann and Weaver (1979) *Territory and Functions*. As a strong influence of the Sciences du *territoire*, which are enacted through the *Centre de recherche sur le développement des territoires* (CRDT) in Québec, those authors offer a different perspective of the concept of territory. First, they make a distinction between Territories and Functions, where the latter refers to what Harvey's call the spatial division of labour and the creation of regionality. Where Harvey oppose territories to space, Friedmann and Weaver oppose it to functions, where space and place are integrated as specializing functions within larger continental and global systems of value production, where place and space echo the language of management as raw material pools, site of production, etc. Planning and development through functions is not about living somewhere but about serving a disembodied economical structure. On the opposite, territory is about the particular way of living somewhere with its physical particularities, and limits, its relationalities and possibilities. Friedmann and Weaver (1979) situate territory as the organization of life within a set space, with possibilities and constraints. It becomes a unit of life reproduction, social and biological, within a particular place. Although calling for a higher level of autonomy, material and social, they did not involve a notion of inward-looking parochial conceptualization of territories, they are not the space of us and them, but mostly a forecasting of some sort of contemporary environmental values of short circuit economy based on wellness and local capacities.

6.3 Territoire(s)

The French writing geographers engage with the notion of territory differently, their conceptualization is somewhere between place and territory, a more relational and less structural conceptualization of territory (Raffestin 1980), closer to Friedmann and Weaver (1979), but also bounded to the nation-state, mostly by its transformation post-1989 and onward in its hollowing out and reconfiguration (Hardt and Negri 2000).

Le territoire refers to a complex system of stakeholders, a space and how those stakeholders use this space in their daily life (Moine 2006). Territories is a lived space, close to the idea of place, that includes the subjective experience of its inhabitants. It is embedded in cultural values associated with a localised group. This interrelation includes also economical, political and social appropriation of space by a group and how they represent themselves, their histories and their subjectivities (Di Méo 1998). It revolves around actions and representations structured in a *projet de territoire,* a system of shared understanding of spatial units (Raffestin 1980).

Territorial development expresses the recognition of the strong link between the dynamics of development and the multiple characteristics of the territories on which they unfold. This concept recognizes the localized nature of the stakeholders and the use of this reference in their interactions. It also acknowledges the emergence of this reality that facilitates, between local aspirations and more global political incentives, a coherence of the actions and stakeholders that constitute territories. The process of making territories by stakeholders who identify with them, on a scale defined not by an administrative body, but by a project carried by stakeholders (Jean 2008). In this view, territories are not only bounded to the nation state and its administrative division, its form are not as stable because stakeholders will intersect their lived space with politically supported projects carried within a situated shared cultural environment.

> The notion of territory in its most complete sense includes resources, living environment, activities, stakeholders, their interrelations, their awareness that they belong to the same development entity, finally the projects that they collectively design and implement to ensure this territorial dynamic. (Boiffin 2006, 224)[1]

The territory is at the intersection of physical space and social web of relations (Poche 2000; Jean 2008), it involves addressing the interactions between structures and stakeholders (Fournis 2012). For the proponents of this approach, the territory is not limited to an administrative or physical division of space: "[…] the territories are socio spatial entities that are related to human activities in space and therefore reflect an approach of political construction" (Jean 2008: 283). It is not only a result of a political construction, but also "[…] a structured, occupied, regulated and developed by a community. Territories plays both a role as a physical frame and a stakeholder in reproduction of it" (Klein 2008: 317). The territory would come under the mechanisms of space production as a framework for social processes, because it "mediates the relationship of society to space" (Klein 2008: 317). A territorial approach therefore requires "[…] making intelligible the processes of social

---

[1] Author translation of: « La notion de territoire dans son acception la plus complète englobe à la fois les ressources, le cadre de vie, les activités, les acteurs, leurs interrelations, la conscience qu'ils ont d'appartenir à une même entité de développement, enfin les projets qu'ils conçoivent et mettent en œuvre collectivement pour assurer cette dynamique. »

construction of the territory as a significant reality for a given social group or society" (Jean 2008: 286). This effort to understand the meaningful realities for a social group requires us to look at the constructions and representations of space, thus to examine the material, discursive and symbolic practices associated with it and the institutional construct that sustain it.

Sweetland (Crummey 2015) is an expression of this sense of territory. Surprisingly, very few authors express in a clearer way this way of understanding territory than this 2015 novel. In this novel, M. Sweetland is the last denizen of an island, also called Sweetland, that refuse to take the government compensation to leave the island and allow the provincial government to close it and cease offering services. One of the conditions is that all denizens accept, it is an all or nothing situation. The novel is an illustration of a State using its power and sovereignty on a part of its territory, in the sense of Elden and Harvey, to cease all activities, the functions of this island being no longer considered worthy in a world where commercial fisheries are close by moratorium. Facing this State, the novelist describes with sensitivities how this territory has shaped its denizen creating meaning and identity, beyond the functions, but also how, the same space, without its denizens, is failing reproducing and maintaining sense to the lonely Sweetland after is illegal return on the emptied island. Territory not being tied to content of power, to functions in the capitalist production system but to the very human experience situated in space and with the end of a whole institutional construct interacting at different scales to maintain in time this human experience in place. Territory being in this sense an institutional construct from the place based consciousness that negotiates with State power and spatial structure of late capitalism.

From this short and non exhaustive review of two scientific tradition tackling the idea of territories/*territoires*, we can state that territory is standing conceptually in a spectrum that goes from a simple container of power over land to a complex assembly at the intersection of lived space and structural forces (politics, capitalism, resource regime). Indeed, the idea of territory in the anglo-saxon tradition is based on an entity of power which can define borders and rules within those borders. It also regulates production and exchange while looking for recognition from its neighbours. On the other side, the French tradition refers to territories as the way the state draws its different space of action but mostly as a particular way of living in place that is translated politically and socially. This particular way is expressed through political projects called *projet de territoire*, that define how a specific place translated its value in a productive system and how it negotiated its interactions with the different flux coming from other scales, from the enactment of global issues like climate change, migration, tourism to the very local issues like identity formation and life reproduction like we saw in Sweetland. It is not confined to the State and its administrative division. This spectrum always involves some kind of persistence in time, of a fixity expressed through more or less stable boundaries. Then, what does territory involve when it is paired with tourism in the more recurrent pairing of Tourism territories/*Territoires touristiques*? Tourism being about leisure mobility, alterity and encounter within a consumption practice.

6.4   Tourism Territories/*Territoire(s) Touristique(s)*

Although it seems a simple expression at first glance, the pairing of tourism and territories open up some serious contradictions. First of all, tourism is about alterity (MIT 2008). Indeed, tourists are in search of alterity, of experiencing otherness out of their ordinary, daily life. This alterity is expressed geographically, in going somewhere that is not within the live space of daily life, but also culturally, in the encounter with different ways of living, speaking, dwelling, eating and different forms of leisure. Tourism is also about leisure mobilities and a fluid non political inscription in place (Ek and Tesfahuney 2016). Therefore, how can we see territories being tourism territories if territories are about fix and stable bounded space, daily life in place and socio-political appropriation, while tourism is about mobility and alterity?

First, territories can be markers of alterity. Through their boundaries they are setting geographically the difference. In their political technology dimension, they define where is the other, the limit of nations, of the administrations. That creates a readable space to cross; to enter in some forms of alterity. In the French tradition of *territoire*, the alterity is more flexible in its relationship to the different scales of political and state actions. *Territoire* get define in their alterity associated with the way of living but also with the political appropriation of a space by a group. Tourism is also looking for these alterities as express in the different *territoires* that tourists are crossing, experiencing differences, sometime subtle, from one *territoire* to another. Alterity is not always associated with distances (MIT 2008). Sometimes, the experience of alterity is at the turn of the corner, where one can find differences and alterity. This situation was clearly expressed in our work with the communities of Ile Verte and Isle-Verte in Québec (Lapointe et al. 2017). Where two neighbouring communities, with almost the same name, one being an island the other one being on the continent facing the island, were having non overlapping representations of each other tourism activities and potentials. Moreover, the tourists were having their own conceptions of those two communities, creating complex juxtapositions of understanding and practices with at the core one common point, a lighthouse. Like in our example, alterity can become some form of recoding of the *territoire* (Hollinshead and Suleman 2018). This recoding can accentuate alterity to satisfy tourists and their demands in evacuating the daily life dimension in a spectacularisation of space (Judd 1999) or reduce alterity in touristifying daily-life (Bélanger et al. 2020; Russo and Scarnato 2018).

Mobilities on its side, is in contradiction with the *terra*, land-based, of territories. As a central part of the tourism phenomenon, Korstanje (2018) expose how mobilities transform societies:

> The concept of mobilities alludes to much deeper mechanisms of political dominance, which are encapsulated on an aesthetic modernity but also because tourism seems to be associated with a saturation of landscapes that meets a new type of psychological need: the curiosity for novelty. To put this in slightly different terms, in a postmodern society which is characterized by the codominance of spectacle and multiculturalism, nation-states delineate new borders toward a global form of identity. (Korstanje 2018: 14).

This description is how tourism mobilities is on one side feeding on alterity but also eroding alterity in emerging a new form of mobile identity. This mobile identity is recoding people and space alongside tourism standard, discourses and constructs:

> Mobilities II not only democratised international tourism within the West and elsewhere, but began to identify almost everyone in the world as a tourist and every place as configured for tourism consumption. This means that the binaries that once defined tourism in Mobilities I, particularly home/destination; everyday/tourism spaces; familiarity/difference; stationary/mobile, began to break down as tourism became a more socially, economically, culturally and spatially distributed form of experience. (Franklin 2014: 77)

In this breakdown, the spatial expansion of tourism is not just changing the tourist within their mobile subjectivities but also the daily-life:

> The subjective experiences of tourists are not only part of a broader macro-social mobile background, but also they transform the day-to-day life for consumers. This is the reason why tourism recycles citizens' frustrations into commoditized forms of cultural entertainment. In this process, the sense of attraction and attractiveness are vital forces that determine what destination is desirable and what is avoided. (Korstanje 2018: 14)

Henceforth, tourism territories are about weaving this space of entertainment within the productive localized system through investment in symbolic values and infrastructures (Lapointe et al. 2015). One example of this transformation around tourism can be seen in tourism in and around protected areas. As Tardif and Sarrasin (2014) state, tourism, in the form of ecotourism in their case, is transforming territories and territoriality. The setting up of protected areas is layering a whole discourse on nature, environment and place (Lapointe 2011) where what once was daily-life activities for local communities is transformed on spectacular nature for tourists, where vernacular knowledge and uses of the environment are reframed as possible threat, and tourism contemplation about protection and development (Lapointe and Gagnon 2009; Sarrasin 2013). It is a rearrangement of language and symbols in order to get environment and space readable and consumable for mobile subjects, aka tourists, while transforming daily life around the protected areas. This form of territories is about serving tourism as an industry, it echoes the functional dimension (Friedmann and Weaver 1979) of space, or what Harvey (2006) called regionality. In this case we see territories as being a result of tourism, in its functions within the capitalism accumulation system (Mowforth and Munt 2008; Jeannite and Lapointe 2016) but lack the political dimension of the "*projet de territoire*".

As seen previously, the concept of *territoire* have a political dimension beyond the container of power of the geopolitical sense of territory. The *territoire* has a political dimension as a forum to debate, exchange, and participate in defining the *projet de territoire*, the socio-political appropriation of space by a community. This dimension is in contradiction with the fact that tourists:

> (...) stands beside the political subject, the citizen of the polis, as the post-political figure par excellence. The tourist is in this sense an agent of de-politicization or side-lining of politics: the reductions of politics to management and the administration of difference (Ek and Tesfahuney 2016: 115).

The tourists are not anchored to land in their transient nature, mobile subjects moving from jurisdiction to jurisdiction. A tourism territory is about the territoriality of the tourists practices.

In their leisurely transhumance they are mobile subjects, normalizing force but also transforming force, searching for alterity but also for daily life. The *"projet de territoire"* for a tourism territories is about the community stakeholders defining their projects to fulfil tourism demands, building a regionality around the economic incentive of tourism, especially to restructure declining resources economies at the periphery. Indeed:

> In a world that has become more or less thoroughly touristified, the tourist becomes its ideal subject. Increasingly, territories, societies, and economies are ordered by and coded under the sign of tourism, with the tourist subject as axiomatic for ways of being and living (Ek and Tesfahuney 2016: 127).

Tourism has become the projects, but also the depoliticizing force. Imposing forms of management around resources that are sometimes contested within large frame and scales of power (Sarrasin 2009). As we state in a previous article (Lapointe et al. 2018), tourism is about bringing subjectivities in the market. Where subjectivities in place was political, and is the main reason for the political dimension of the *"projet de territoire"* expressing in a future-oriented project shared subjectivities and institutionnalizing it in some forms, in the market subjectivities become economic. The tourism territories are about this transformation of subjectivities, within a market hierarchy. The *projet de territoire touristique* will be competing with other subjectivities in the market, but will be strip politically becoming one of the many ways to live in space, recoding people, place and history (Hollishead and Suleman 2018), while letting aside some others subjectivities and productive activities within this space. The tourism territory is an appropriation of space by the tourist's practices and mobilities while the political embedness of territories are mostly about living (and ownership) in place, creating space that are politically close while economically living from openness (Knafou et al. 1997)

We observe this situation acutely when faced with mono industrial communities where tourism is the main, if not the only, industry. The situation of Tadoussac in Québec, Canada, is quite exemplar of this. While being a tourism success with around 300,000 visitors for a resident population of 799 inhabitants in 2016, there are major issues for the resident populations (Lebon and Lapointe 2018). High seasonality, exogenous stakeholders and a small agency over tourism of local political institutions. While tourism grows in Tadoussac, year-long services and resident populations decline. Basic commercial services, like food, become an important issue during low season. The whole development is based on tourism, pushing the development, planning and public actions along satisfying the demand for alterity of a mobile non voting subjects who are the main beneficiaries of the community amenities. This creates a deficit of legitimacy for all other initiatives, but also transformed local authority on manager of basic services (road, water, garbage collections) for those mobile subjects whom their needs guide the development. Local authorities have their political prerogative as constructing a collective project to live in place – *le projet de territoire* – and become mere managers of services. Tourism, in this context, is post-political in contributing to the transformation of politics as managing functions with limited telos functions (Ek and Tesfahuney 2016).

6.5   Concluding Remarks

From this short overview of the concept of territory, we witness a difference between the English written tradition, where territory is more about geopolitical and structure, and the French written tradition, where territory is more about a relational live space interacting with political structure. A space intertwined with identity and alterity, in a politically driven project of lived space. In this context, the construction of tourism territories is more complex than it appears, tourists being mobile and not directly rooted in political subjectivity of the territories they cross.

As we have seen, the expression of tourism territory is slowly replacing the one of destination. The discourse on destination management implicitly stipulates a standalone spatial configuration, the destination, the place destined for tourists (Kadri et al. 2011). While the destination being still largely used, we come across more and more the concept of tourism territories, which implicitly suggest a weaving of tourism within resident communities, rural or urban, where tourism is an integral part of the "*projet de territoire*". This being misleading in some sort because of the interactions of alterity and mobility as core constituent of tourist practices which is dislocating tourism from political embedding at the scale of territories (Renaud and Sarrasin 2019). Which calls for a different look at tourism and how we spatially construct it understanding and knowledge.

Indeed, as we have seen before, the study of tourism has been strongly locality based (Franklin 2014), but would gain to develop towards a more relational and mobile perspective, centred on flux of social relation and practices, instead of dots where tourism happens.

> Here, particularly, tourism could be related positively to other distributed social relations that had become detached from particular sites and the 'mycelium-like' orderings of large companies and nation states to become enrolled in the wider orderings of cosmopolitanisation, global consumerism, aestheticisation, and the liquefaction of many modern orderings and to become implicated in all manner of subjectivities of mobility. (Franklin 2014: 75)

In this reordering, tourism, and tourists move from peripheral subjects, as a benign substrate of daily-reproductive life under a capitalist (re)production of society, to core subjects of this late mobile dematerialized capitalism in a post-political era (Ek and Tesfahuney 2016). Tourism is a clear marker of the transformation and reordering of the late capitalism economy from a material production of value economy to a mobile sign consuming economy (Meethan 2001), which happen at points of contact, through presence, while the structuring and production of those signs can be disconnected from the place of consumption (Pecqueur and Talandier 2011).

The understanding of this reordering of society and politics as a whole, and the role of tourism ask researchers to look at their conceptual frameworks and reorder them, especially the different binaries exposed by Franklin (2014). If tourism practices definitely have a territoriality, the post-political nature of tourists might be better served by Deleuze and Guattari (1980) and the binary of territorialization and deterritorialization. Tourism might be acting as a deterritorialization of daily-life and political subjectivities. Yet, we still need to find how it is reterritorialized through mobilities and how to reconceptualize the notion of territory in highly mobile, but unequally mobile, societies.

References

Bélanger, H., Lapointe, D., & Guillemard, A. (2020). Central neighbourhoods revitalization and tourists bubble: From gentrification to touristification of daily life in Montréal. In J. Bean (Ed.), *Critical practices in architecture: The unexamined* (pp. 71–94). Newcastle upon Tyne: Cambridge Scholars Publishing.

Boiffin, J. (2006). Conclusions et perspectives. In A. Mollard, E. Sauboua, & M. Hirczak (Eds.), *Territoires et enjeux du développement régional* (pp. 221–224). Versailles: Editions Quæ.

Crummey, M. (2015). *Sweetland*. New York: WW Norton & Company.

Deleuze, G., & Guattari, F. (1980). *Mille plateaux*. Paris: Les éditions de minuit.

Di Méo, G. (1998). De l'espace aux territoires : éléments pour une archéologie des concepts fondamentaux de la géographie. *L'information géographique, 62*(3), 99–110. https://doi.org/10.3406/ingeo.1998.2586.

Duarte, F. (2017). *Space, place and territory: A critical review on spatialities*. London: Routledge.

Ek, R., & Tesfahuney, M. (2016). The paradigmatic tourist. In A. M. Munar & T. Jamal (Eds.), *Tourism research paradigms: Critical and emergent knowledges* (pp. 113–129). Bingley: Emerald Group.

Elden, S. (2013). *The birth of territory*. Chicago: University of Chicago Press.

Équipe, M. I. T. (2008). *Tourismes 1. Lieux communs*. Paris: Belin.

Foucault, M. (2004). *Naissance de la Biopolitique: Cours Au Collège De France (1978–1979)*. Paris: Seuil.

Fournis, Y. (2012). Le développement territorial entre sociologie des territoires et science régionale: la voix du GRIDEQ. *Revue d'Economie Regionale Urbaine, 4*, 533–554.

Franklin, A. (2014). Tourist studies. In P. Adey (Ed.), *The routledge handbook of mobilities* (pp. 74–84). London: Routledge.

Friedmann, J., & Weaver, C. (1979). *Territory and function*. Berkeley: University of California Press.

Gottmann, J. (1973). *The significance of territory*. Charlottesville: University of Virginia Press.

Hardt, M., & Negri, A. (2000). *Empire*. Cambridge: Harvard University Press.

Harvey, D. (2006). *Spaces of global capitalism*. London: Verso.

Harvey, D. (2009). *Cosmopolitanism and the geographies of freedom*. New York: Columbia University Press.

Hollinshead, K., & Suleman, R. (2018). The everyday instillations of worldmaking: New vistas of understanding on the declarative reach of tourism. *Tourism Analysis, 23*(2), 201–213.

Jean, B. (2008). Le développement territorial : une discipline scientifique émergente. In *Sciences du territoire: perspectives québécoises* (pp. 283–314). Québec: Presses de l'Université du Québec.

Jeannite, S., & Lapointe, D. (2016). La production de l'espace touristique de l'Île-à-Vache (Haïti): illustration du processus de développement géographique inégal. *Études caribéennes*, 33–34.

Judd, D. R. (1999). Constructing the tourist bubble. In D. R. Judd & S. S. Fainstein (Eds.), *The tourist city* (pp. 35–53). New-Haven: Yale University Press.

Kadri, B., Khomsi, M. R., & Bondarenko, M. (2011). Le concept de destination: diversité sémantique et réalité organisationnelle. *Téoros, 30*(1), 12–24. https://doi.org/10.7202/1012104ar.

Klein, J. L. (2008). Territoire et développement : du local à la solidarité territoriale. In *Sciences du territoire: perspectives québécoises* (pp. 315–334). Québec: Presses de l'Université du Québec.

Knafou, R., Bruston, M., Deprest, F., Duhamel, P., Gay, J.-C., & Sacareau, I. (1997). Une approche géographique du tourisme. *L'Espace géographique, 26*(3), 193–204. https://doi.org/10.3406/spgeo.1997.1071.

Korstanje, M. E. (2018). *The Mobilities paradox: A critical analysis.* Northampton: Edward Elgar.

Lapointe, D. (2011). *Conservation, aires protégées et écotourisme des enjeux de justice environnementale pour les communautés voisines des parcs?* (Doctoral dissertation). Université du Québec à Rimouski.

Lapointe, D., & Gagnon, C. (2009). Conservation et écotourisme: une lecture par la justice environnementale du cas des communautés voisines du Parc national de la Guadeloupe. *Études caribéennes, 12.*

Lapointe, D., Sarrasin, B., & Guillemard, A. (2015). Changements climatiques et mise en tourisme du fleuve St-Laurent au Québec. Analyse critique des représentations. *VertigO - la revue électronique en sciences de l'environnement, Hors-série 23.*

Lapointe, D., Gueugneaud, F., & Guimont, D. (2017). Les convergences et les divergences des représentations touristiques: le cas des Iles Vertes du Bas-Saint-Laurent au Québec. In M. Delaplace & M. Gravari-Barbas (Eds.), *Nouveaux territoires touristiques: Invention, reconfigurations, repositionnements.* Québec: Presses de l'Université du Québec.

Lapointe, D., Sarrasin, B., & Benjamin, C. (2018). Tourism in the sustained hegemonic neoliberal order. *Revista Latino-Americana de Turismologia, 4*(1), 16–33.

Lebon, C., & Lapointe, D. (2018). Community well-being between climate risk and tourism development. In B. S. R. Grimwood (Ed.), *Tourism and wellness: Travel for the good of all?* Lanham: Lexington Book.

Manuel-Navarrete, D. (2016). Boundary-work and sustainability in tourism enclaves. *Journal of Sustainable Tourism, 24*(4), 507–526.

Meethan, K. (2001). *Tourism in global society: Place, culture, consumption.* London: Red Globe Press.

Minca, C. (2009). The island: Work, tourism and the biopolitical. *Tourist Studies, 9*(2), 88–108.

Moine, A. (2006). Le territoire comme un système complexe : un concept opératoire pour l'aménagement et la géographie. *L'Espace geographique, 35*(2), 115–132.

Mowforth, M., & Munt, I. (2008). *Tourism and sustainability: Development, globalisation and new tourism in the third world.* London: Routledge.

Pecqueur, B., & Talandier, M. (2011). Les espaces de développement résidentiel et touristique, état des lieux et problématiques. In *Territoires 2040: revue d'études et de prospective* (Documentation française, DATAR., pp. 121–138). Paris.

Poche, B. (2000). La sociologie et la question de l'espace. In N. Pélissier & D. Pagès (Eds.), *Territoires sous influences* (pp. 25–43). Paris: L'Harmattan.

Raffestin, C. (2019). *Pour une géographie du pouvoir* (1st edition 1980). Lyon: ENS Éditions https://books.openedition.org/enseditions/7627; https://doi.org/10.4000/books.enseditions.7627.

Renaud, L., & Sarrasin, B. (2019). La géographie politique du tourisme de croisière en Gaspésie : une lecture critique des enjeux. In D. Lapointe & H. Bélanger (Eds.), *Perspectives critiques et analyse territoriale: Applications urbaines et régionales* (pp. 97–121). Québec: Presses de l'Université du Québec.

Robert, P., Rey, A., & Debove, J. R. (1990). Le Petit Robert. Société du nouveau Littré.

Russo, A. P., & Scarnato, A. (2018). "Barcelona in common": A new urban regime for the 21st-century tourist city? *Journal of Urban Affairs, 40*(4), 455–474.

Saarinen, J. (2017). Enclavic tourism spaces: Territorialization and bordering in tourism destination development and planning. *Tourism Geographies, 19*(3), 425–437.

Sarrasin, B. (2009). La Gestion LOcale SÉcurisée (GELOSE): L'expérience malgache de gestion décentralisée des ressources naturelles. *Études caribéennes, 12*.

Sarrasin, B. (2013). Ecotourism, poverty and resources management in Ranomafana, Madagascar. *Tourism Geographies, 15*(1), 3–24.

Tardif, Jonathan, & Sarrasin, B. (2014). La territorialisation par et pour l'écotourisme dans les aires protégées (pp. 354–359). Presented at the CIST 2014 – Fronts et frontières des sciences du territoire, Collège international des sciences du territoire (CIST).

Urry, J. (2002). *Consuming places*. New York: Routledge.

Vuignier, R. (2016). *Place marketing and place branding: A systematic (and tentatively exhaustive) literature review*. Lausanne: Working paper de l'IDHEAP.

Dominic Lapointe is a professor in the Department of Urban and Tourism Studies at Université du Québec in Montréal (Canada). He holds the Research Chair on *Dynamiques touristiques et les relations socioterritoriales* and leads the *Groupe de recherche et d'intervention tourisme territoire et société* (GRITTS) at UQAM. He is also the editor-in-chief of the scientific journal *Téoros*. His work explores the production of tourism space and its role in the capitalist system expansion and its biopolitical dimensions. His latest research looks at climate change, social innovations, indigeneity and critical perspective in tourism studies.

Chapter 7
Living Treasures, Common Goods and Tourism Development of the Agdal of Yagour, Zat Valley, High Western Atlas, Morocco

Saïd Boujrouf, Ayoub El Ouarti, Fatima El Khadali, Saïd Abbanay, Nada Baki, Mari-Carmen Romera, and Veronica Blanco-Magariños

7.1   Introduction

The plateau of Yagour is one of the main cultural and natural heritage sites of the northern watershed of the High-Atlas of Marrakech. Through its heritage, Yagour demonstrates the extensive adaptation of humans to their environment. Indeed, since prehistory, residents of Yagour have adopted agropastoralism as a lifestyle. With their ancestral know-how, they maintain a symbiosis between two productive systems, agriculture (market-gardening, cereal and fruit growing, ...) and extensive livestock farming. As a common good shared and managed by its right-holders from the neighbouring valleys, Yagour constitutes a resource of reserve and survival during the dry season. Villagers move then to the mountain pastures of Yagour, the access to which is generally restricted from early spring until early summer. In addition to this natural resource management system, locally called "Agdal", Yagour abounds with heritage treasures among which the oldest rock engravings date back more than 2000 years B.C.E. These display the history and evolution of mountain populations' predecessors around Yagour.

This paper is translated and adapted for an Anglophone public from our publication in the journal *Maghreb-Machrek* (n° 240, 2019).

S. Boujrouf (✉) · A. El Ouarti · F. El Khadali · S. Abbanay
LERMA FLSH – Université Cadi Ayyad de Marrakech, Marrakech, Morocco

N. Baki
LERMA and University Hassan I Settat, Settat, Morocco

M.-C. Romera
LERMA FLSH – Université Cadi Ayyad de Marrakech, Marrakech, Morocco

ICTA – Universitat Autònoma de Barcelona, Barcelona, Spain

V. Blanco-Magariños
Universidad Santiago de Compostela-La Coruña, La Coruña, Spain

Nowadays, this place of sacredness and ancestral culture undergoes various socio-spatial changes which force the perpetuity of its heritage and its landscapes. In addition, Yagour is experiencing the transition from an agrarian and pastoral seasonal activity to a sedentary one. This transition generates a change in the structure of land ownership because as this common territory of pastoralism is transformed into patches of cultivable land, families appropriate it. These changes are further emphasized by the Yagour's process of openness to the outside world. The development of the accessibility of Yagour promotes the mobility of bordering populations (reinforcing flows of emigration, especially young people) and tourists. Straddling between a valley of mass tourism like "Ourika valley" and a hardly touristic one like "Zat valley", the plateau of Yagour might face the challenges of its tourism development in the near future.

Faced with these upheavals and committed to long-term sustainability and valorisation of different heritage resources; this paper will initially question the changes and evolution of the different production systems, their trends of convergence or divergence as well as synergies and competitions which result from it. Secondly, we will look at the contributions that tourism valorisation could bring to this territory, its heritage and local populations. Lastly, we will consider the role of mediation among actors, within their embedded hierarchical system, to cope with the new challenges of this territory, as well as the role of tourism as a "facilitator" of this mediation.

7.2 Agdal of Yagour: A Changing Territory with Specific Heritage Resources

The landscape heritage of the High Western Atlas owes its cultural character to the agro-silvo-pastoral lifestyle (Mahdi 2010). The plateau of Yagour appears like one of the remarkable landscapes and cultural products of this lifestyle. In fact, the ancestral practice of pastoralism on this site, as certain rock engravings illustrate, is what has shaped the various landscape facets of today's Yagour. The engraved landscapes, dating back nearly 4000 years for the oldest ones, refer to pastoralism via the representation of bovids and to transhumance via the representation of "engraved borders" (Malhomme, 1950 in Auclair et al. 2013). Since these old times, bordering agro-pastors of Yagour have continued to maintain these landscapes inhabited thanks primarily to the practice of summer transhumance.

The ascension of transhumant to the summer pastures of the plateau of Yagour is governed by a specific community management system called "Agdal". It is an agro-pastoral prohibition which consists of protecting the pastoral space from the beginning of spring until early summer, aiming the regeneration of pastoral resources essential for the survival of herds during the dry seasons. The closing and opening dates of Agdal depend on the pluviometric conditions of each year, according to the

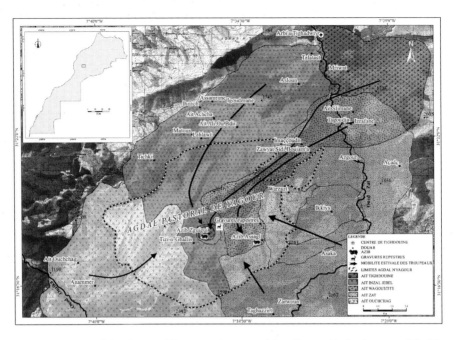

Fig. 7.1 Location of the plateau of Yagour study area and the tribes entitled to its pastoral Agdal. Source: Map based on research by Dominguez, P. (2007)

agreements of the local communities. In addition to fixing the calendar of protection, Agdal also governs the territorial delimitations as well as the access rights of the different rights-holders. The summer pasture of Yagour is a common pastoral territory shared between 5 fractions of tribes (Ait Wagustit, Ait Inzal Aljabal, Ait Oucheg, Ait Tighedouine, Ait Zat) (Fig. 7.1).

According to Ostrom (1999), the concept of common good refers to a system of relatively abundant resource so that it is difficult to exclude a potential recipient (principle of non-exclusion) and whose overexploitation makes decrease the stock of the resource to thus limit the pleasure of the benefit to the whole of the potential recipients (principle of competition). The same author specifies the management of common goods and the establishment of rules of access concerns the users' communities. Therefore, via the Agdal system, agro-pastoral communities of the High Atlas, including those whose common good is the Yagour, usually manage their common pastoral resources inherited from their predecessors. As shown by Aubert and Romagny (2012) in Auclair and Alifriqui (2012, pp. 254–253), this community management of the common resources is effective and durable because it addresses each of the seven criteria for effective management of common goods stated by Ostrom in 1990. Ostrom's criteria, brought closer and adapted to local practices in the valleys of the High Western Atlas around the pastoral plateaux of Zat and Ourika, are:

1. Existence of limits recognized by the communities but which are mobilized only for periods of conflicts or intense competition for the resource. The five tribal fractions sharing the space of Yagour acknowledge the rights of access and occupation of each fraction;
2. Use and access rules to resources adapted to the local socio-ecological context by the development of a calendar to manage the space and the resource;
3. The community assemblies or Jmâas constitute, since centuries, local institutions of participative decision making concerning the rules of use of the resources;
4. Development of a Community control and compliance justice system;
5. The precision of sanctions as for the case of fines locally called Azzayen;
6. The Jmâa represents the institution of conflict management and mediation. The recourse today to local authorities, the Caïd, is increasingly made like an intermediate stage before addressing itself to justice;
7. Conflict resolution related to Agdal by local social management is generally recognized by the positive law.

The traditional system of Agdal, still in practice in the Yagour, also represents "a community heritage answering the insecurity related to the use of the natural resources, contributing to the construction of resilience and adaptability of the socio-ecological system" (Auclair and Alifriqui 2012). The perpetuity of this heritage lies with the intergenerational transmission of the traditions and customs for several centuries and continues until today. This transmission results at the same time from the need for regeneration of the herbaceous resource (to guarantee the durability of the economic resource which the pastoralism represents) and also from the need to establish the right of access and use of this pastoral resource. Beyond pastoral resources, Agdal also applies to other specific resources, as for the case of fruit-bearing, agricultural and forest Agdals, among others. This ancestral system of community management holds know-how which converges with several modern concepts such as (1) sustainability, which appears in the sustainable management of natural resources, (2) good governance which is palpable in the common management of collective goods; as well as (3) customary law, which specifies the access rights of the rights-holders.

Cultural heritage in its modern approach is interested not only intangible goods and immaterial aspects but also includes original approaches integrating at the same time natural and cultural landscapes as well as know-how and local specificities (Skounti and Tebbaa 2011). The agro-pastoral landscapes recently profited from this interest via the UNESCO label of "cultural landscape of Mediterranean agro-pastoralism" awarded to Causses and Cevennes in France 2011 (Mahdi 2015). This site was registered in the world heritage list based on criterion (v)[1] appearing in the world list of heritage selection criteria which was established by UNESCO at the

---

[1] **Criterion (v):** be an outstanding example of a traditional human settlement, land-use, or sea-use which is representative of a culture (or cultures), or human interaction with the environment especially when it has become vulnerable under the impact of irreversible change; http://whc.unesco.org/en/criteria/

convention of 1972. Beyond this criterion, Agdal of Yagour is also in line with the criterion (iii)[2] making this practice and this territory an exceptional testimony of a traditional civilisation in perfect balance with its natural environment.

In parallel, the definition of the "living human treasures" of UNESCO applies to the holders of this heritage. It specifies that "living human treasures are people who have a prominent level of knowledge and know-how necessary to interpret or to recreate specific elements of the immaterial cultural heritage". This definition was produced by the executive council of UNESCO in 1993 within the framework of the program "Living Human Treasures System" which invites the Member States to its implementation within the national scale.

The Kingdom of Morocco, having ratified the Convention for the Safeguarding of Intangible Cultural Heritage in 2006,[3] is therefore involved in the implementation of this program. Within this framework, it proposed a draft law on living treasures which was elaborated by the Ministry of Culture. In addition to the exogenous territorial changes and challenges cited previously, it is noteworthy that Yagour, a common good of the Mesfioua tribe fractions, currently knows upheavals of endogenous nature. Among the more striking issues, emerge the change and evolution of production systems and those with the status of collective lands. Historically exclusively reserved for pastoralism, Yagour knows the beginning of parcelling its pastoral surfaces as crops (mainly cereal). This progressive fragmentation of pastoral lands, which should be checked and quantified further,[4] reflects "the appropriation" by the right-holders of the common lands and, thus, the beginning of a transition of Yagour from a common good to an individualized good around villages and Azibs.[5]

Other social phenomena concerning changes in the right-holders' system of values, their relationship with traditions and local customs (guarantors of the maintenance of the practice of Agdal and its transmission), are mainly globalization, the search for modernity and temporary or permanent migration. The latter involves, indeed, a local de-heritagization of Agdal practice and agro-pastoral know-how (Auclair 2012). Consequently, the result of exogenous heritage dynamics undertaken on and for this territory are not felt in terms of conservation of this community heritage. Tourism, which evolves slowly but surely in the area, is not yet properly committed to the heritagization of these specificities.

---

[2] **Criterion (iii):** bear a unique or at least exceptional testimony to a cultural tradition or to a civilization which is living or which has disappeared;

[3] **Law n°39-04** promulgated by the dahir n°1-05-193 of 15 Moharrem 1427 (February 14th, 2006) Official Bulletin N°5404–15 afar 1427 (March 16th, 2006) bearing approval, as for the principle, of the ratification by the Kingdom of Morocco of the Convention for the Safeguarding of Intangible Cultural Heritage.

[4] Clarification should also accompany these reviews by considering current development of the emigration phenomenon towards other areas of Morocco, change of the extent of these agricultural surfaces according to wet or dry years and for how many decades has started the cereal culture to nibble Agdal grounds.

[5] Azib: Berber term for refuges or shelters with sheepfold.

7.3 Heritagization and Tourism Development Among Socio-economic Changes

The *agdal* Yagour is a socio-ecological heritage which covers a resource area necessary for animal feeding and the satisfaction of the population's basic needs of cereal, as it provides also many other ecosystem services. For that reason, it is at the heart of social, ecological, economic and political balance-related issues. Yagour has lately witnessed changes leading to new dynamics.

7.3.1 Changes Within a Space of High Cultural Value

The territory of Yagour has a climatic pattern characterized by a stable summer period and an irregular winter. Consequently, this steppe area is vulnerable to extreme periods of great droughts or strong rains. In this difficult climatic context, forage and water resources are relatively limited and subject to increased exploitation. This specific quality of the physical environment has strongly conditioned the lifestyles developed by local populations. Another key phenomenon that influences the procedure for occupying the area and using the resources is climate change. It appears among the big challenges of the twenty-first century. The plateau of Yagour, having for a long time constituted a place of pasture and agriculture, reveals the experience of techniques and know-how related to surface waters used for irrigation. The agro-silvo-pastoral system constitutes the keystone of local population lifestyle, which is based on the extensive breeding (ovine, caprine and bovine), the practice of an irrigated food agriculture and a rain-fed grain. This lifestyle is founded on:

– Intensive exploitation of local resources still dependent on pluviometric variations and spatio-temporal patterns of rainfall;
– Collective mobility of men-women-children and herds between the neighbouring villages and Yagour;
– Traditional modes of community management at the level of tribes' right-holders (Mesfioua and Ourika tribes) within the framework of rules and standards of solidarity and inter-tribal alliance.

This traditional lifestyle in harmony with the natural environment has experienced new socio-spatial dynamics during the twenty-first century, expressed in the traditional modes of management and the functioning of customary institutions. Consequently, the following difficulties were accentuated in recent years: a reduction of foraging, a modification of the transhumance calendar, a trend to the settlement of several families from the douars located between Ikkis and Warzazt, a reduction of surface water resources and grazing area, etc.

Today the situation in the Agdal of Yagour is worrying due to the conflicts' frequency around land and water resources necessary for the culture's irrigation. For instance, people from douar Asaka, users of "Azib Tamsna" refused during 2016 to install an irrigation channel (locally called "séguia") to feed the douar Warzazt, since this channel would be built out of reinforced concrete. This structure would not allow water infiltration, which is a historical right of the first douar, thus allowing the irrigation of grass of its courses. Despite being in crisis today, the "Jmâa" in the rural world in Morocco, has always been the cornerstone of common goods management and decision making related to the developments. The crisis has facilitated to appeal to the local authorities' recourse, the territorial collectivities or to the new structures like those of the civil society and the social economy (associations and cooperatives).

If these changes have effects over the community management choices and the local economic life, globalization has also contributed to deep socio-economic changes like the arrival in the region of tourism (Bellaoui 1996; Boujrouf 2004, 2014). Tourism has promoted the emergence of new networks of actors organized so as to connect the local to the global, without the local population being prepared. This situation questions the sustainability of resources and local ecosystem services. Moreover, new identities question the local culture in order to produce a new system of readjustment and re-appropriation of locally-produced innovations. The content of the relationship to the other (individuals, families, groups, foreigners or tourists) through the relationship to territories poses a problem as to the nature of the governance system to be set up and accepted by everybody (Boujrouf 2015).

All these transformations on a very sensitive plateau, full of history and rich in patrimonial resources, poses the big challenge of succeeding – in spite of the difference of stakes and representations of actors – the production process for a territorial project with the least risk of conflicts possible, in order to avoid any blocking of the territorial system.

7.3.2   Heritagization and Touristification as Two Slow Processes of Territorial Revitalisation and Innovation

The Agdal of Yagour shelters a natural and cultural heritage that is integrated today in processes of economic and sociocultural valorisation. Its heritage seems to be a privileged vector of projects and mobilization, particularly in the touristic sector. For this reason, the High Atlas of Marrakech and, particularly, the plateau of Yagour constitutes a favourable study area to observe the relation between heritage and tourism.

Heritagization of natural and cultural spaces of Agdal of Yagour and its tourism development refer to a certain antagonistic relationship (Duval 2008). We witness today a beginning of heritage valorisation by a diversity of actors who reinvent, enhance, safeguard and mobilizes elements of culture and nature. A process of "heritagization" reflects a shift of natural and cultural goods into services, which acquire the quality of a specific heritage. In this context, the heritagization phenomenon constitutes one of the contemporary methods for the reinvention of new collective territorialities (Gravari-Barbas 2002), making it possible for a group to collectively reinvest or re-appropriate resources considered to be essential for the (re)production of its identity (Berriane et al. 2015).

In this sense, heritagization of territorial resources by actors constitutes a key instrument for the activation of resources and redefinition of the territory. It could be at the base of the production of a public policy of sustainable development and conservation which allows for better governance of resources and territories (Auclair 2012) in order to develop tourism in the marginalized areas of this region. Today, public authorities have not yet shown interest regarding registration of heritage resources of Yagour on the lists of national heritage or world heritage.

The plateau of Yagour conceals diversified touristic potentialities characterized by a rupestral heritage of high cultural and historical value and by an atypical agro-silvo-pastoral landscape, able to make of this territory an attractive tourist destination. These heritage features are regarded as economic and symbolic wealth which external actors seek to mobilize. On the other hand, these symbols of wealth are not considered with their right value by the local population, which puts them at risk of strong degradation. Thus, the combined effects of natural and anthropic factors accentuate their degradation and their progressive disappearance. As an example, and after several interviews carried out with some users of this space, in the imaginary or even in the everyday life of populations, rock engravings do not really constitute a treasure for the local population and do not have any value, neither heritage nor even commercial.

In this context, endogenous factors do not appear in the process of heritagization of this territory. On the other hand, the exogenous factors appear through the external initiatives of actors, particular scientists and Tour Operators, which contribute to the development of the territorial resources. The creation of touristic routes as well as the presence of tourists in this territory attests of a heritage conscience. Heritage recognition of this territory constitutes a vector of both, sustainable and touristic development. Indeed, the re-appropriation of these resources can generate a territorial dynamic which could have socio-economic benefits for the whole of local actors.

For heritagization to succeed, criteria of legal recognition should be controlled as well as the tools which ensure a better safeguard and transmission of heritage. The actors' scale of intervention in this process is, however, relevant to understand their concerns, strategies and motivations (Di Méo 2007; Berriane 2010). The emergence of tourism activity in the Yagour and its surroundings, even though it is in its embryonic stage, confers to this space a new dynamic. Indeed, tourism could have a great influence on the local population's practices, especially as a means of the revival of local memory. Tourism development of this territory depends on the involvement of a multitude of actors who play a significant role in this process of territorial reformulation by setting up territorial projects. Thus, the creation of dynamics around these natural and cultural resources presents today a need to resurrect this long-neglected territory and to integrate it into new management and development plans (Fig. 7.2).

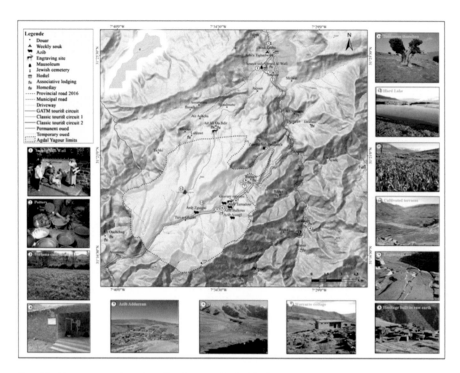

Fig. 7.2 Resources and tourism development in the Zat Valley. Source: Own elaboration

At the local level, various actors take a fresh look at this cultural patrimonial resource represented by Agdal of Yagour. They mobilize or try to mobilize this resource, according to their own interests and concerns through initiatives in the framework of national strategies. The creation of at least 14 rural B&B's on and around the plateau as well as the development of responsible tourism, walking tourism and diffused tourism attest perfectly the mobilization of cultural and landscape heritage resources in the tourism development of Yagour and neighbouring valleys (Table 7.1). The establishment of a certain number of local and trans-valley tourist routes (tourist map of the Zat valley) reinforces this trend.

Regarding this longing for heritage Agdal of Yagour, it becomes strategic for the operators to highlight the role of these human living treasures and for the holders of heritage in the upkeep and maintenance of their own common goods. According to Eychenne and Lazaro (2014), because of the development of recreational uses of pastoral areas and the interest for heritage safeguard (biodiversity, culture...), it tends from a transition of these common goods (pastoral areas) of which the only managers are the agro-pastors towards global collective goods asserted and managed by various actors belonging to various scales (international, national, regional or local). In parallel, heritage dynamics, particularly those integrated into their tourism development, endorsed by the various actors involved, could contribute, positively or negatively to the maintenance of these human living treasures, to the

Table 7.1 First small tourist accommodation facilities in the High Zat Valley

Douar	Associative B&B	B&B with the locals
Warzazt	X	X
Tizirt	X	X
Ansa	–	X
Taghzirt	–	X
Ait Ali	X	X
Tighdouine	X	–
Iwossouden	–	X
Izerfan	–	X
Ait Oucheg	–	X
Anamer	–	X
Lalaout	X	–

Source: Own elaboration

promotion of their know-how, and to the transmission and safeguard of their common goods. Therefore, tourism would be an opportunity to make the territory of Yagour a genuine heritage and thus build its brand image.

The question which arises here is how to integrate the heritage dimension and the rock engravings safeguard in the tourist development projects? Could the tourism offer be integrated in order to constitute together with the initial offer a basket of goods and services helping to consolidate the actors' project? How could tourism, which is still embryonic on the plateau of Yagour, cohabit with local practices?

7.4 A Territorial Project that Demands Territorial Mediation

The plateau of Yagour features a natural and landscape heritage and shelters material (rock engravings) and immaterial (atypical lifestyle and natural resources management) cultural treasures able to confer a territorial development and spatial significance at several scales. This enclosed "living space", managed and maintained by local population since millennia, has become on the last decades increasingly accessible thanks, *inter alia*, to the development of road and electrification infrastructures and telecommunication networks. These changes have generated others, mainly of socio-economic nature. Among them, in this case, is the emergence of a tourism activity orchestrated by external actors and coveted by local actors. The latter plays a fundamental role in the heritage presentation of local resources, however, the mobilization of tourism by various actors is driven by both divergent and convergent visions and concerns. This third part aims at the analysis of the configuration of territorial actors' map in relation to tourism development, of the heritage presentation of territorial resources and, finally, of the ability of this system of actors to converge towards a territorial project so far dormant.

7.4.1   The System of Actors: Convergences or Divergences?

The introduction of tourism activity into the plateau of Yagour dates back to the late 1970s during which the locations of the Great Crossing of the Moroccan Atlas (GTAM) were conducted. It is thus through the tourist actors and on the basis of scientific research undertaken since the time of French rule in Morocco that we recognize today the heritage and historical values of Yagour and that it has become so attractive for tourists. More recently, although these professionals of tourism are profit motivated, they have indirectly contributed to awake a certain heritage conscience in the local population. The numerous visits and long stops of tourists close to rock engravings have arisen the curiosity of inhabitants regarding the special interest given. Furthermore, the magnitude of the mobilization of state powers in situ, due to the rumour concerning the theft of one of the most important rock engravings of the site, has generalized this awareness and supported the appropriation of rock engravings by the local population. Previously, the engraved flagstones did not have a value to the eyes of bordering populations of Yagour. They made use of them to build the sheepfolds or to spread out the salt intended for cattle. Moreover, the surveys conducted to right-holders of Yagour revealed that they were unaware, on the one hand, that these rock engravings were made by their ancestors; and on the other hand, they did not understand why researchers and tourists pay so much attention to them. Today, conscious of their heritage value, local populations, in collaboration with local authorities, have become guardians and guarantors of this treasure's perpetuity.

The emergence and development of hiking tourism on Yagour, mainly by external tourism actors, has also taken part in the increase will of the local population to integrate tourism networks. Following a study carried out by the Association of Zat's Friends in 1996, in which local population expressed its will to engage with tourism activity, three rural B&Bs, including two bordering with the plateau of Yagour, were created from a point of view of interdependent tourism (funding community projects via the tourism incomes from the rural B&Bs). The need for tourism services in situ has generated local tourist businesses, as it is the case for guides, accompanying-guides and B&B owners. More recently, and following the evidence of tourism in terms of living conditions' development of certain families who really got involved in it, many other people try to collect tourism flows by offering services of transport on mules as well as community-based home-stay accommodation and catering. Indeed, they consider it a means of diversifying their income sources and improving their living conditions. However, language and capacity of financial investment remain the main factors limiting access of local populations to this system of services.

Convinced of the positive effects of tourism regarding economic and human development, public authorities, including those concerning tourism, have implemented tourism development strategies. Thus, the regional programme contract came out in 2016. It brings together the region of Marrakech, ministerial delegations and territorial collectivities, including the commune of Tighdouine. Yagour will be one of the territories objects of public action within the framework of this program. It is envisaged to build a road crossing the Yagour to connect the Zat valley to the touristic Ourika valley, and then to create a museum of rock engravings and a high mountain tourist resort at the centre of Yagour.

These new prospects which are offered to this agro-pastoral territory raise convergences and divergences of actors regarding their future. The road project constitutes a true hope for the local population who acknowledge their easier access to their mountain pasture and a potential opening of tourist activity via the sale of local products and the construction of shops and coffees/restaurants by this road. For walking tourism actors, this road project would limit the number of routes crossing Yagour. The mule-drivers see there fewer hikers but more request for services of one-day excursions, half-day or even walks of a few minutes with the excursionists from Marrakech. Regarding the construction of the tourist resort, public authorities consider it as a means of diversification of Marrakech's tourist offer and driving force of local employment. While for the right-holders in Yagour, traditionally very involved in the pastoral activity, the aforementioned resort would occupy part of their pastoral territory and would thus limit their right of use and access to this portion of the pastoral resource. Lastly, for a share of public opinion, *inter alia* militant associations and scientists, this new tourist development of Agdal of Yagour is regarded both, as a distortion of the agro-pastoral landscapes and as a constraint for the continuity of this living heritage.

Fundamentally, tourism is a desired activity by the various spheres of actors. However, the latter stick still and independently to their own interests. Territorial development via tourism development and heritage valorisation remains a wish, a "latent and implicit" consensus. Because a project of territory must be part of active territoriality, "which refers to the capacity to capitalise the widest range possible of resources and actors through inclusive strategies aiming to local autonomy" (Courlet et al. 2013) and to the development of capabilities. However, the current project of tourism development of Yagour does not integrate the whole of actors' visions on this common territory and does not encourage yet a synergy in this actors' map.

7.4.2   Could Committed Tourism and Common Heritage Engage the Mediation Among Actors?

Yagour is subject today to a latent territorial project of tourism development and heritagization of territorial resources. It is thus an implicit consensus and a shared vision of local actors, seeking to meet their economic, social and cultural needs by mobilizing their local specificities. However, the lack of communication and articulation among actors does not foster a synergetic effect, which is the key to the success of the territorial project.

Mediation refers from this point of view to deal with conflicts of interest and difficulties to ensure implementation of projects and guarantee their success. According to Muttenzer (2002), mediation is a method of negotiation which utilizes a neutral third person to achieve agreement among stakeholders; it relies on translation among actors of their respective representations of the question or problem. Indeed, mediation promotes dialogue and information transfer, by creating a climate of trust and by maintaining transparency as regards the roles and issues of each group of actors. This process of conflict regulation recognized and institutionalized, for a few decades already, in many Western countries, has been intuitively practised in the plateau of Yagour.

In terms of population and at various levels (tribe, fraction and village), it has always existed a customary assembly called "Jmâa", whose members are designated among social structures themselves to assume the role of dialogue and mediation. The Jmâa guarantees, in the case of the plateau of Yagour, everything related to the community affairs and more mainly those related to the management of Agdal and the conflicts of use. Today, with the increasing emergence of local associations following a recurring need for the formal institutions, Jmâa starts to lose a share of the roles which were assigned to him formerly.

Currently, there are associations who assure mediation in the small-scale planning and development projects but their scope (of action) remains limited to the village level. To date, it lacks great projects which can extend to the entire territory. Various existing associations on the Yagour operate separately and would need themselves a mediator helping to transfer experience and information and promoting synergies. Moreover, certain associations have a political affiliation and are not neutral. Others were created just aiming for funding or a specific call for proposals. They are "ephemeral" associations which conduct a single action without long term or short-term associative projects including sets of actions.

Moreover, the Caïd (who is the head of local authorities) intervenes in case of use conflicts and rules violation (pre-determined rules unanimously approved by the local population). He may impose sanctions in certain cases. The Caïd does not act as a mediator but rather as arbitrator. He generally acts when the concerned parties cannot find a conflict resolution (conflict intra-Jmâa or conflict inter-Jmâas). The mediation is thus practised here in terms of conflict regulation and not as a means of dialogue and negotiation around a common project.

Nevertheless, it can be considered that both locals and foreigners tourist actors have been playing a role as mediators by increasing awareness among the local population regarding the value of their rock art heritage and the agro-pastoral landscapes over which they have sovereign rights. On the other hand, except for some actors of solidarity tourism, tourist actors carry a capitalist vision of tourism development of Yagour. Their thirst for profit maximization is sometimes done to the detriment of guarantor populations, producers of landscapes which attract tourists.

Mediation practices on the Yagour take place on limited scales. Considering the variety of actors concerned with the project tourism development, there is a total absence of information transfer, dialogue or negotiations implying all territorial actors. Local actors aspire to an improvement of their living conditions without asking for the institution of a mediation committee at a broader scale. The challenge that mediation can address in the case of Yagour is to create synergies among actors and bringing them together around an inclusive development project (that benefits all). Only when each group of actors finds there a self-interest, tourism development and heritage resource valorisation will be unanimously desired. Therefore, the existence of a real "latent" territorial project supports mediation among territorial actors of Yagour.

7.5 Conclusion

Pastoral Agdal of Yagour is a territory with living heritage resources, attested by its thousand-year-old rock engravings, ancestral transhumance landscapes and management of the common goods perpetuated by the "Jmâas" through customary regulation. Empirically in line with certain notions of heritage promoted by UNESCO (immaterial cultural heritage, cultural landscapes of Mediterranean agropastoralism, living treasures) and with various theories and concepts displayed in this article (effective management of common goods, specific heritage resources, socioecosystem), the territory of Yagour experiences new changes that place it towards new emerging issues.

Valleys' accessibility and their openness to the outside world accentuate changes by encouraging villagers' mobility and migrations. Globalization also modifies the relationship of rural communities to their living spaces and resources, resulting in a metamorphosis of productive systems and the emergence of new income-generating activities for local populations. Thereby, traditional methods of resources use and management give gradually way to so-called "modern" systems. In addition, the "Jmâa", a customary assembly considered as the cornerstone of the social structure management, seems unable to manage the various conflicts around land and resources and the intervention of local authorities in the conflict management becomes increasingly determining. Meanwhile, Moroccan law associations are in progress to replace customary assemblies regarding the implementation of community projects.

Indeed, the territory of Yagour is subject today of heritage covetousness and tourism development. Even though recreational uses and heritage mobilization of resources is orchestrated by external actors, certain local actors assert their identity and are involved in tourist networks. This covetousness may create development opportunities for territories, resources and bordering communities of Yagour. However, in the absence of mediation among actors, tourism development and heritage valorisation of resources remain a latent project of territory buried under challenges and divergent views.

In this context, further fundamental research and action-research are needed to support local actors still not used to work together around a common project, as well as a comprehensive analysis regarding a future process of mediation among actors, how this could be successfully conducted and by whom. Finally, more thought is needed to determine the real relevance of local heritage and processes of heritagization and how to enhance them, by which means the local population can be fully aware of its heritage resources and their importance and who should oversee this process. Once this is properly analysed and understood, it will be feasible to foster a synergetic effect driven by a mediation process which seems to be the key for the success of the latent territorial project of tourism development and heritagization of territorial resources in the Agdal of Yagour.

References

Auclair, L. (2012). Un patrimoine socio-écologique à l'épreuve des transformations du monde rural. In Auclair, L., Alifriqui, M. (Eds.), *Agdal. Patrimoine Socio-Écologique de l'Atlas Marocain. Rabat, Morocco* (pp. 23–72). https://doi.org/10.1017/CBO9781107415324.004.

Auclair, L., & Alifriqui, M. (Eds.). (2012). *Agdal: patrimoine socio-écologique de l'Atlas marocain*. Rabat: IRD-IRCAM.

Auclair, L., Lemjidi, A., & Ewague, A. (2013). *Paysages gravés: 4000 ans de transhumance dans les alpages du Haut Atlas (Maroc)*. In PAPERS XXV Valcamonica Symposium (pp. 293–299).

Bellaoui, A. (1996). Tourisme et développement local dans le Haut-Atlas marocain : questionnement et réponses / Tourism and local development in the Moroccan High Atlas Mountains : some questions and answers. *Revue de Géographie Alpine, 84*(4), 15–23. https://doi.org/10.3406/rga.1996.3882.

Berriane, M. (2010). Patrimoine et patrimonialisation au Maroc. *Hesperis-Tamuda, XLV*, 11–17.

Berriane, M., Michon, G., Skounti, A., Moizo, B., Romagny, B., & Tebbaa, O. (2015). Les "patrimoines ruraux" au Maroc : un nouveau produit des mobilités contemporaines ? *Géo-Dév.ma, 3*. http://revues.imist.ma/?journal=GeoDev&page=article&op=view&path[]=4086

Boujrouf, S. (2004). Tourisme de montagne au Maroc: enjeux de la durabilté. In R. S. Bousta (Ed.), *Le tourisme durable: réalités et perspectives marocaines et internationales* (pp. 273–284). Marrakech: Centre de Recherche sur les Cultures Maghrébines.

Boujrouf, S. (2014). Ressources patrimoniales et développement des territoires touristiques dans le Haut Atlas et les régions sud du Maroc. *Journal of Alpine Research, 102*(1). https://doi.org/10.4000/rga.2259.

Boujrouf, S. (2015). Introduction. In S. Boujrouf & O. Tebbaa (Eds.), *Le rapport aux autres à travers le rapport au territoire. Des entrées à des cas marocains par les ressources territoriales, le développement et la gouvernance*. Marrakech: LCPT, LERMA-TDD, FLSH.

Courlet, C., El Kadiri, N., Fejjal, A., & Jennan, L. (2013). Le projet de territoire comme construit d'acteurs et processus de révélation des ressources: l'exemple marocain. *GéoDév. ma, 1*. revues.imist.ma/index.php?journal=GeoDev&page=article&op=view&path%5B%5D=612

Di Méo, G. (2007). Processus de patrimonialisation et construction des territoires. Presented at the Colloque 'Patrimoine et industrie en Poitou-Charentes : connaître pour valoriser'. https://halshs.archives-ouvertes.fr/halshs-00281934.

Dominguez, P. (2007). Transformación de instituciones religiosas tradicionales en el Alto Atlas de Marrakech (Marruecos) y su impacto en los ecosistemas sub-alpinos. Caso del sistema pastoral del agdal. *Perifèria. Revista d'investigació i formació en Antropologia, 7*(2), 1–26. https://doi.org/10.5565/rev/periferia.666.

Duval, M. (2008). Patrimonialisation et mise en tourisme des espaces naturels. L'exemple des gorges de l'Ardèche. *Géographie et cultures, 66*, 61–78.

Eychenne, C., & Lazaro, L. (2014). L'estive entre « biens communs » et « biens collectifs ». Représentations des espaces pastoraux et modalités d'action publique. *Journal of Alpine Research | Revue de géographie alpine, 102*, 2. https://doi.org/10.4000/rga.2297.

Gravari-Barbas, M. (2002). *Le patrimoine territorial. Construction patrimoniale, construction territoriale: vers une gouvernance patrimoniale* (Vol. 18). *Lettre d'ESO*.

Mahdi, M. (2010). Patrimonialisation de la transhumance à l'Oukaïmeden! In *Pastoralisme méditerranéen: patrimoine culturel et paysager et développement durable* (pp. 73–83). Montpellier: CIHEAM / AVECC / UNESCO. http://om.ciheam.org/om/pdf/a93/00801268.pdf

Mahdi, M. (2015). *Paysages culturels de l'agropastoralisme du Haut-Atlas, un patrimoine à valoriser!* https://www.academia.edu/12358393/Paysages_culturels_de_lAgropastoralisme_du_Haut-Atlas_un_patrimoine_%C3%A0_valoriser

Muttenzer, F. (2002). La mise en œuvre de l'aménagement forestier négocié. In E. Le Roy (Ed.), *Retour au foncier* (pp. 135–186). Paris: Karthala.

Ostrom, E. (1999). Coping with Tragedies of the Commons. *Annual Review of Political Science, 2*(1), 493–535. https://doi.org/10.1146/annurev.polisci.2.1.493.

Skounti, A., & Tebbaa, O. (2011). *De l'immatérialité du patrimoine culturel.* Marrakech: Equipe de Recherche Culture, Patrimoine et Tourisme de la Faculté des Lettres et des Sciences Humaines, Université Cadi Ayyad\Bureau Régional de l'UNESCO.

Saïd Boujrouf is a professor of Geography and director of "Resources, mobility and attractivity studies laboratory" (LERMA) at University Cadi Ayyad de Marrakech (Morocco). He studied management and territorial development in Morocco. He was director of the Geography Department and is currently working on issues of specification, qualification, patrimonial and tourist exploitation in areas of the margin south of Morocco. His research interests include tourism development and its socio-cultural and economic impact, sustainability and the construction of local identities, culture and nature in tourism.

Ayoub El Ouarti is a PhD student at University Cadi Ayyad de Marrakech (Morocco) with "Resources, mobility and attractivity studies laboratory" (LERMA). His research deals with the issues of tourism and heritage in the agro-pastoral and mountainous areas, especially in the High Atlas mountains and Corsica island.

Fatima El Khadali is a PhD student at University Cadi Ayyad de Marrakech (Morocco) with "Resources, mobility and attractivity studies laboratory" (LERMA). Her research deals with vulnerability and resilience of touristic mountain territories through territorial trajectories of three models of tourism development in the Moroccan High Atlas.

Saïd Abbanay is a PhD student in geography with the "Resources, mobility and attractivity studies laboratory" (LERMA), Faculty of Letters and Human Sciences, Cadi Ayyad University Marrakesh (Morocco). He holds a master's degree in geography. His doctoral thesis currently is on: "The common between innovation and heritage and the contribution to sustainable territorial development: the case of the Zat and the Ourika Valleys".

Nada Baki is a higher education teacher at the National School of Business and Management (ENCG) University Hassan I Settat. Her research deals with communication, tourism and regionalization in the region Marrakesh-Safi (Morocco).

Mari-Carmen Romera is a socio-environmental scientist interested in rural commons, community conserved areas (ICCAs), heritization procedures and political ecology issues in the Mediterranean. She's a PhD candidate, holder of a FI grant associated with the LASEG research group, under the supervision of Dr Roser Maneja, Dr Pablo Domínguez and Dr Said Boujrouf, working on ICCAs, governance and biosphere reserves in Morocco. She holds a Degree on

Environmental Sciences from the University of Almería, a Postgraduate on Climate Change from the University of Salamanca and FLACSO España and a Masters in Ecological Economics from the Autonomous University of Barcelona (ICTA-UAB).

Veronica Blanco-Magariños is a PhD student with University Santiago de Compostela (Spain). Her research interests include cultural-natural heritage management and mediation on the Urban Region of La Coruña. She holds a Master's Degree in management and mediation of cultural heritage in Europe and also completed a Master of Advanced Studies in History of Art at UNED.

Chapter 8
From Tourist Gaze to Tourist Engagement, A Relational Approach to Heritage

Maria Gravari-Barbas and Sébastien Jacquot

8.1 Introduction

The fire at Notre-Dame cathedral in Paris on 15 and 16 April 2019 aroused strong feelings worldwide. Some of those who voiced their deep sorrow on social media had forged a relationship with this monument as tourists on trips to Paris. Some posted photographs of themselves taken in front of Notre-Dame as proof of their emotional relationship with the monument. Photographs taken with their families, lovers or friends show what Notre-Dame meant to them and the personal effect the destruction caused by the fire had on them.

Heritage emotion in a tourism context offers a lens for re-examining the assumption that heritage, territory, and identity are connected. Heritage has generally been studied in terms of its connection to local and national identity-building (Thiesse 1999), and as a driver for the creation of imagined communities (Anderson 1991), usually rooted in a national or local space. According to the philosopher Régis Debray, the monument which is the archetypal seat of heritage emotions is the funerary monument, which recalls and forges ancestral links with the land (1999). Territorial conflicts characterised by the destruction of heritage belonging to others demonstrate this logic of feeling rooted via a monument and heritage, and the loss of heritage is experienced as a form of delegitimisation of presence (Jacquot 2010). But can we rethink this connection between heritage, identity and territory from a tourism perspective?

The contribution of tourism to heritage production, and the construction upstream of an ideal prescriptive gaze as the driver for types of heritagization has been highlighted (Gravari-Barbas 2018). The aim of this article is to look beyond the dynamics of heritage recognition and to identify the relationships forged between tourists and heritage elements, focusing on two lines of enquiry. The first of these is the tourist experience and the feelings aroused by a site or its future. What type of

M. Gravari-Barbas (✉) · S. Jacquot
Université Paris-Panthéon Sorbonne, Paris, France

M. Stock (ed.), *Progress in French Tourism Geographies*, Geographies of
Tourism and Global Change, https://doi.org/10.1007/978-3-030-52136-3_8

135

Fig. 8.1 Tourists in front of Notre-Dame after the fire. April 2019 © MGB

attachment do tourists form with a heritage site or element which has no connection with their everyday lives? The aim here is to reconsider the distinction between proximity and distance as a means of explaining or legitimising heritage attachment. Secondly, does this attachment based on a tourist experience create a desire for action, and if so in what ways does this manifest itself? Does heritage emotion result in a form of empowerment or mobilisation? This raises the issue of the political aspect not only of tourism but also of tourists.

This article adopts both a phenomenological and a pragmatic reading of tourism by applying to aspects of the tourism field methods and ideas emerging from research into engagement, and also by exploring the tourist experience and relationships forged with heritage (Fig. 8.1).

8.2 A Relational Approach to Heritage from a Tourism Perspective

8.2.1 Moving Beyond the Disconnected Approach to Heritage and Tourists

Early studies on heritagization highlight the relationship between heritage and territory (Di Méo 1994). Heritage attachment is based on rootedness (Debarbieux 2012). Heritagization has its basis in the notion of identity, which is mediated first and foremost by territory. This territorialised and localist approach forms the foundation of the study of pro-heritage social movements, defined as mobilisations of non-profit associations and protest activity usually with local roots (Fabre 2010; Glevarec and Saez 2002). The politicisation of heritage is therefore generally considered to be a local matter, involving inhabitants of an area, whereas tourism development is seen as a form of dispossession at a local level in historic centres, for example (Garcia-Hernandez et al. 2017).

However, heritage is not a purely endogenous and strictly localised construct. Heritagization is often the result of modes of action involving flows. When heritagization is linked to local development issues by tourism, the methods used to select and enhance heritage are defined by stakeholders in the local area on the basis of differentiation, in order to make the destination attractive and unique. Furthermore, the tourist gaze (Urry 1990), which offers an "external" perspective, has often played a significant role in the identification, definition and protection of heritage. Thus the Grand Tour was a driving force in bringing a new heritage gaze to bear on antiquities. This anteriority of tourism in the chain can even be seen in iconic examples of heritagization such as the restoration work carried out in Venice in the late nineteenth century (Davis and Marvin 2004), and in Old Québec. Tourism does not always come along and "consume" an existing heritage, but produces heritage realities: it is a driver for heritagization (Gravari-Barbas 2018).

It is necessary to look beyond the heritage-tourism opposition in order to undertake an alternative analysis of this relationship (Lazzarotti 2011). The transition from heritage dominated by existence value, i.e. being its own sole justification (Prigent 2001), to a heritage which must generate the resources required for its upkeep and is therefore dominated by the economics of use value (Greffe 2003), places cultural tourism at the centre of the heritage agenda. Heritage is no longer a "stock" in opposition to a group of tourism mobilities, but becomes fluid, and based on the multiplicity and circulation of images, concepts, and practices. It is the heritage-rhizome, whose typical user and promoter is the cultural tourist (Greffe 2011, 2014).

This research places flows at the heart of the heritage process by inverting the relationship between heritage and tourism and recognising the production of heritage by people and social groups with no local connection to the heritage in question. The consubstantiality of heritage and territory (Di Meo 1994), is therefore challenged (Gravari-Barbas 1996, 2012). Thus, if tourism is increasingly being analysed in terms of a heritage-creation machine (Gravari-Barbas 2018), tourists are being viewed fundamentally in their role as heritage opinion leaders. There is little in the way of academic research, and few institutional developments, which rethink the relationship between heritage and distant places through the lens of emotional attachment, "concernment" and engagement. The aim here is to explore the possibility of moving beyond the relational disconnect between heritage and tourists.

8.2.2 A Relational Approach to Heritage via Tourism

Institutional and traditional approaches to heritage in the social sciences often focus on heritage policies rather than experiences, thus reflecting the decontextualisation of monuments from their locality (Fabre 2010). By contrast, several studies take a relational approach to heritage with the aim of defining the connections between heritage and individuals from the joint perspective of emotions and personal meaning. This relational approach has been implemented in the Global South in particular to demonstrate the disconnect between official heritage constructions and heritage experience (Harrison 2012). It has also legitimised localised conceptions of heritage in the form of relationships of affection operating in the gaps in official heritage regulations (Tornatore 2006).

This relational approach can be extended to tourism, which in certain forms is the expression of a close relationship with a distant heritage, as exemplified by memorial tourism and diaspora tourism. The close relationship between tourists and distant heritage sites is based on an identification with something far away connected to migration journeys (diaspora tourism or roots tourism) or with historical family connections to conflicts or disasters elsewhere (memory tourism or dark tourism).

The expression "roots tourism" refers to travel motivated by the idea of a real or imagined return to the location of one's family origins (Marie-Blanche Fourcade 2010). This diaspora tourism is encouraged by some states such as India (Goreau-Ponceaud 2015) and Mauritius, which have developed heritage activity around the arrival of Indian labourers at the Aapravasi Ghat immigration depot, a UNESCO World Heritage Site (Lowe Swift 2007), and also by private initiatives which may take the form of collective return of visitors to heritage sites, such as Jewish tourism on Rhodes (Sintès 2010). The identity aspect of the trip may be broader in scope and refer to communities of origin extending beyond established family ties, such as the creation of Little Italies in the United States (Conforti 1996; Debarbieux 2012), and African-American tourism in Philadelphia (Grant 2005) and on the Atlantic coast. In Benin, the engagement of African-American and Afro-Caribbean tourists has played a role in heritagizing the traces of slavery and structuring tourism (Araujo 2010). This diaspora tourism is based on and contributes to the production of heritage which provides a mechanism for identifying with a distant location.

In a similar vein, memorial sites and sites of suffering can be experienced by some tourists as personal identity and memorial reference points, either for their own history of a traumatic experience (veterans or victims) (Sather-Wagstaff 2016) or, in cross-generational terms, for family members and descendants preserving a social memory (Winter 2009). A trip is therefore an act of shared belonging, as is demonstrated by the practice of visiting battle fields which are organised along national lines (Jacquot et al. 2018).

The reasons underpinning these long-distance relationships with a heritage constructed and fostered by tourism are not purely biographical and genealogical. Looking beyond UNESCO tangible World Heritage Sites (Convention 1972), tourist flows can inform the production of transnational heritage collectives based on attachments and practices shared by tourists in an intangible heritage context. The implementation of the Convention of 2003 relating to intangible heritage contains the germ of a disconnect between heritage and local communities. Intangible heritage is based on the principle of recognition by communities (Maguet 2011), but the notion of "community" is not defined by the Convention, and the appendices leave the definition open, notably in terms of territoriality. Locality is a possible but not a necessary condition of the definition of community, as is shown by certain transnational inclusions in Intangible Cultural Heritage (ICH), such as falconry or the tango. The Faro Convention also offers an open definition of the notion of a heritage community, without predicating local roots in its formation. Heritage attachment potentially takes priority over geographical proximity in this conception. Some forms of ICH such as salsa, flamenco, and the tango (Canova and Chatelain 2015; Matteucci 2014) generate transnational tourism mobility by exponents towards the areas of origin of a practice. Travel is experienced as a means of reinforcing mastery of this practice and of belonging to a community of fellow practitioners (Cominelli et al. to be published), as in the case of les Compagnons du Devoir, the French journeymen's trade guild, which is listed as Intangible Cultural Heritage by UNESCO.

8.2.3   Motives for Attachment

Tourist attachments to heritage are formed for a variety of reasons: migration journeys, participation in events, and transnational communities of practice. These attachments also produce heritage and contribute to its preservation. What is the basis for this recognition of and attachment to a distant heritage? Several possible reasons can be advanced.

Firstly, the rhetoric of universalism and the heritage of humanity operates a shift in scale, moving away from the local by highlighting a shared ownership by all of humanity. This argument underpins the World Heritage Convention of 1972; its preamble refers to a "world heritage" whose exceptional value transcends local and national characteristics and whose deterioration would constitute "a harmful impoverishment of the heritage of all the nations of the world".[1] This Universalist argument informs a rational reading of heritage attachment via the concept of existence value which forms part of the economic analysis of heritage value (Vecco 2007). Existence value is the value attached to the very fact that a heritage element continues to exist, even in the absence of interest or personal use in the past, present or future. The World Heritage mechanism presupposes a universalisation of the exis-

---

[1] Universalist ideas refer to an ideal of peace between peoples which emerges from the League of Nations (Anatole-Gabriel 2016), but can also be viewed from a more critical perspective as legitimising forms of domination, ranging from a so-called "universal" museum to forms of interference in heritage.

tence value attributed to heritage assets. This opens up the possibility of decoupling existence value from local rootedness by extending this value existence to heritage seekers. Françoise Benhamou describes (2010) the "collective involvement" in World Heritage assets of a proportion of non-visitors. However, the theoretical existence of this existence value is not incompatible with concrete mechanisms allowing individuals to see value in the simple fact that a heritage site exists, such as tourism.

An alternative view, which is complementary rather than conflicting, explores heritage subjectivities in a tourism context by considering tourists' relationships with heritage. Looking beyond diaspora and memory tourism, or transnational sharing of an activity with its roots in intangible heritage, the study of tourists' relationship with heritage can be viewed more broadly by drawing on research exploring heritage subjectivities outside the framework of institutional approaches and dominant institutional narratives defined as "authorized heritage discourse" by Laurajane Smith (2006).

Local communities' relationship with heritage is called into question more frequently than that of tourists. Despite the rift produced by heritagization (Fabre 2010), local communities nonetheless forge relationships with heritage monuments which are a part of their everyday surroundings. These relationships are based on heritage "poaching", on attachments which are not acknowledged but can become apparent when heritage crimes, such as the fire at the Château de Lunéville, occur (Pecqueux 2013).

Relationships with heritage which operate outside the institutional framework can also be identified among tourists in times of crisis. In a study of donations made to the royal park at Versailles after the storms of 1999, Dassié (2006, 2009) shows that a proportion of donations came from abroad, and analysis of the covering letters points to two conclusions. Firstly, donations were often motivated by a past tourist experience recalled in these letters. In addition to the historic narrative associated with Versailles, there is also a private narrative based on the memory of a tourist experience which forges an emotionally-charged personal connection when a visit was made with a friend or relative. These donations were then presented as sponsorship of a tree, which is specifically identified, thus encouraging a further visit to see one's own tree and demonstrating a new personalized connection with a national historic monument which is also inscribed on the World Heritage list. In short, attachment is not only a prerequisite, but perhaps also the consequence of tourism mobilities.

When we move from an institutional reading to a subjective and relational reading of heritage, the ties between heritage and locality become looser, thus revealing the possibility of long-distance attachments even when there is no prior biographical connection. But can these relationships and attachments to heritage translate into tourist action in a heritage context?

8.3   What Is the Nature of Tourist "Concernment" in Heritage

Research focusing on social activism in the heritage space often suggests that mobilisations in support of heritage are rooted in the local community (Fabre 2013; Veschambre 2008). Is it possible to conceive of tourist action based on a relationship of attachment to a distant heritage? Both a moral and political reading of the connections between tourists and heritage are required in order to unpack the links between heritage attachment, "concernment" and engagement. In other words, how does the existence value conferred on heritage lead to types of engagement, and what form do they take?

8.3.1   "Concernment" and Its Motives

The issue of engagement and mobilising tourism for the benefit of heritage presents analogies with international political mobilisations and humanitarian activity (Zunigo 2007). When addressing the issue of local environmental action, Philippe Brunet (2008) developed the concept of *concernement* (concerned involvement or "concernment"). He defined this neologism as "directed behaviour which expresses itself in behaviour which is relatively active" – a relationship between the subject and object of "concernment" which is determined by the effect of situations on individuals, possibly resulting in forms of engagement (Gendron et al. 2007; Faburel and Tribout 2011). A theory of action therefore emerges from the connection between these two terms – a transition from "concernment" to engagement.

Boltanski's research (2007) on humanitarian engagement at a distance offers a model for the study of forms of tourist engagement relating to "concernment". Boltanski subscribes to a pragmatic school of sociology which focuses on how individuals justify their actions and the registers in which they assess, justify, and judge – in other words, the critical capabilities of individuals (Boltanski and Thévenot 1991). He explores the connection between values and moral feelings in the face of suffering, and the political action which may be prompted by the sight of suffering at a distance when no immediate action can be taken. This "distance" has two meanings: physical distance and the need for mediation via words and images, but also the fact that one is not directly connected, i.e. on the outside. It is therefore not a given that the sight of suffering will translate into political action, and there is a tension between the specificity of situations and recourse to types of generalisation. The intermediary role of the media is crucial as it must both establish the credibility of the theatricalisation of this suffering and offer "ways of engaging". This "concernment" manifests itself in different ways and is at the root of several registers of action stemming from the way in which people are affected: an investigation aimed at demonstrating a wrong (the "denunciation topic"), an appeal to the emotions experienced in respect of the wrong (the "emotional topic"), or sublimation when confronted with the sight of suffering (the "aesthetic topic") (Boltanski 1999).

The transposition of humanitarian solidarity to heritage issues may seem far-fetched, or even immoral. However, this is not about placing endangered heritage on a par with human suffering. This was one of the criticisms raised by donations for Notre-Dame cathedral in the context of rising social deprivation in France, with donors being accused of valuing heritage more highly than individuals in their hierarchy of priorities. The objective is to identify patterns of action with similar characteristics via remote media activity around heritage presented as endangered, giving rise to several possible regimes of action ranging from indignation to compassion, and belonging to different "topics".

This pattern can be tested empirically by looking at responses of transnational opinion to types of threat to heritage publicised in the media, and by examining the role of tourism, both in the formation of transnational public opinion on social media, and more actively via donations and engagement in situ.

8.3.2   Is Transnational Public Opinion Informed by Tourism?

UNESCO World Heritage campaigns are based on the hypothesis of extended heritage communities and on the fact that World Heritage Sites are protected by huge collectives (such as the World Heritage Centre's "People protecting places" campaign) and rely on this attachment for sponsorship.

The World Heritage Centre also relied for several years on interconnected international World Heritage communities to set up vigilance systems on social media. Thus in 2009, Francesco Bandarin, Director of the World Heritage Centre at that time, and Stephen Kaufer, founder and CEO of TripAdvisor, formed a partnership with the aim of preserving World Heritage Sites via TripAdvisor users. Francesco Bandarin, referred to the *engagement* of TripAdvisor members: "*we can, together, raise awareness of World Heritage as well as receive member feedback about sites. […] This certainly helps us flag site issues and provides useful information on how World Heritage travellers engage with the sites and their communities.*" CEO Steve Kaufer went even further: "*We're calling on the world's largest travel community to help preserve the places around the world that we all love. […] In support of UNESCO's World Heritage Centre, we will give not only dollars but also the collective wisdom and support of TripAdvisor's millions of travellers, and their trusted insights. We're eager to build global awareness about World Heritage Sites, and about sustainable and responsible travel.*"[2] In 2010, World Heritage Sites accounted for a significant proportion of comments, which can be analysed to create World Heritage Site rankings based on 3 TripAdvisor members' lists: the most recom-

---

[2] https://news.un.org/en/story/2009/10/318722-unesco-partners-tripadvisor-help-preserve-world-heritage-sites

mended sites, the best preserved sites according to comments, and the sites giving the most cause for concern according to travellers. This partnership also aimed to enhance the connection between tourism and World Heritage management by empowering tourists themselves through awareness raising and a surveillance role. The notion of "wisdom" highlights the popular capability for subjective assessments by tourists – a minor revolution in a world heritage system based on scientific expertise. But according to the Tourism Director of the World Heritage Centre, the experiment was inconclusive, and has since been abandoned.

However, looking beyond its uses, and criticism from heritage stakeholders, we can pursue this line of enquiry. TripAdvisor produces reviews of tourist products (hotels, restaurants, tours) and also micro-narratives about "attractions" which express experiences and tourist views extending beyond mere opinion (Compagnone 2017; Jacquot et al. 2018). In this respect, comments mean we can explore tourism evaluation, its values, and its possible relationship with vigilance, in order to highlight potential registers of "concernment" expressed about sites visited. In other words, when tourists describe their experiences, are they also sharing a judgement or concern about the state of heritage? Are they expressing, via social media, types of concern which mean that they are sharing existence value?

8.3.3   Venice and the Nature of Tourist "Concernment"

As we are reminded by the philosopher Massimo Cacciari (Yagoubi 2010) "Tourism was invented in Venice". Furthermore, Venice is an iconic example of transnational public opinion constructed by tourism mobility, reflected in the development of committees and international non-profit associations – notably during the floods of 1966 – and the creation of Save Venice committees. However, this construction of transnational public opinion began well before the floods. Venice plays a key role in debates on doctrines of heritage restoration, notably with the publication of *The Stones of Venice*, by Ruskin (2003), and the various refurbishment and restoration projects debated beyond the city and Italy itself from the nineteenth century onwards. William Morris, one of the founders of the Society for the Preservation of Ancient Buildings (SPAB), used the international section of SPAB to criticise the frequent restoration work carried out on St Mark's, and notably on its mediaeval mosaics (Donovan 2008). He lambasted cultural vandalism and Italian interventions, and launched petitions. An article in the *New York Times* in 1879 justified a type of interventionism in the form of international public opinion by stating that Venice belonged to the whole world (Davis and Marvin 2004). These debates notwithstanding, restoration and reconstruction work incorporated the tourist gaze, for example in the rebuilding of the Campanile which collapsed in 1902, by favouring a design similar to that of the original monument, with patinated bricks and a lift to allow tourist to reach the top more easily (Davis and Marvin 2004). In short, for over a century heritage conservation has taken place under the gaze of international public opinion, incorporating the tourist gaze, and fundraising for targeted projects has been taking place for several decades.

Does this expert international public opinion have any parallels or similarities with the experiences of ordinary tourists in Venice? What forms of "concernment" can be identified via the comments posted on TripAdvisor? Venice has received 1.03 million comments (from the creation of the platform until April 2019), across all categories and sites. By focusing just on the "attractions" receiving the highest number of comments (Grand Canal – 34,942 comments, St Mark's Square – 30,334, St Mark's Basilica – 23,599, etc.), is it possible to identify degrees of "concernment"? Comments on TripAdvisor were harvested via Web scraping, and sorted by language.[3] Analysis was carried out with lexical analysis tools using Iramuteq software (which can produce textual statistics and categorise types of discourse). Here, we will examine comments written in English, the dominant language on major TripAdvisor sites relating to Venice.

St Mark's is an iconic tourist experience venue. Comments focus on urban planning and architecture (with the dominant lexical field being beauty), but also on its atmosphere and musical entertainment. The grandeur of the site is highlighted in comments, stressing its global dimension. We divided the comments into 20-word segments and this new corpus (comprising all segments) was classified so that the content appeared in 6 classes: the impressive nature ("amazing") and beauty of the place (17.1% of the segments); the central position of the square, from an urban planning and tourism perspective (19.6%); the presentation of the architecture of the square (11.5%); the experience of overcrowding and recommendations on how to avoid crowds or cope with flooding (19.8%); free and fee-paying activities on the square, from the Caffè Florian to music (24%); and lastly, criticism of selfie stick and pigeon seed sellers (8%). Critical comments focus more on the tourist experience than heritage: hawkers, and crowds, notably from cruise ships, etc. Tidal phenomena (*aqua alta*) – whose frequency and severity have increased since the 1960s, triggering the declaration of a global emergency to save Venice after the appeal launched by UNESCO Director General René de Maheu – are fundamentally described as something to be tolerated or an inconvenience. If comments about St Mark's Square with a low rating (between 1 and 3) are extracted, overcrowding is the main source of disappointment, and many people posting comments describe the pleasurable experience of strolling in other parts of the city. Signs of maintenance work (scaffolding) also feature in comments either deploring their visual impact or criticising the advertising with which they are covered. In a similar vein, the restoration work on the Rialto Bridge in 2015 and 2016 was reflected on TripAdvisor in a number of comments complaining about not being able to enjoy the site or criticising the advertising covering it during the building works.

TripAdvisor therefore expresses a partial vision of issues in Venice: overcrowding, the growth of the cruise market and the omnipresence, and illegality in some

---

[3] This data collection work was carried out by researchers at the Leonardo da Vinci Engineering School (ESILV): Gael Chareyron and Jérôme da Rugna (Cousin et al. 2014).

cases, of certain commercial activities are viewed through the lens of the tourist experience. By contrast, some visitors express disappointment at the high visibility of heritage restoration work. "Concernment" is therefore generally subjective and stems from personal experience, based on the topic of sentiment.

How do tourists make the transition from "concernment" to engagement? And what are the potential mechanisms for tourist engagement?

8.4   From "Concernment" to Engagement

Popular fora in which tourists express their views are not usually concerned with the state of heritage. However, tourists are asked, by a variety of mechanisms, to play a role in safeguarding heritage. How do these mechanisms operate?

8.4.1   A Multiplicity of Tourist Engagement Mechanisms

Tourists can engage with World Heritage Sites in a wide variety of ways, and these can be differentiated. First and foremost, this engagement can be individual and specific, based on private approaches, or an institutionalised collective format via non-profit associations, international organisations or site managers. Engagement can be generic, or site-specific. Lastly, a multiplicity of methods and mechanisms for engagement exists based on the classification developed by Buonincontri et al. (2017): physical actions designed to mitigate the impact of tourism on the site (recycling, green mobility, etc.) or to help with maintenance; persuasive action and advocacy to convince people to adopt the cause and encourage others to come out in support of the site; a civic or legal form; and financial actions via donations or, in an inverse scenario, a boycott of products and services which have a negative impact on the site. These types of engagement can be carried out in situ or remotely.

These options are instantiated via mechanisms aimed at promoting tourist engagement in heritage site management. Mechanisms operate on different scales, with impetus from international stakeholders, notably the World Heritage Centre, but also in the form of private stakeholder or site management initiatives. Tourists are approached in different ways: as sources of funding, volunteer labour in situ (on practical projects, for example), or as vigilant representatives of international public heritage opinion.

How this compares with the engagement of local communities is also an area for debate: do these modes of tourist action differ from those of local inhabitants – are they supportive or supplementary? Or conversely is tourist engagement a sign of a change in the status of the tourist and a progressive putting down of roots at the site in the form of repeated visits or a second home?

8.4.2 Financial Contributions to Safeguarding Heritage

Tourists contribute financially to heritage sites first and foremost unintentionally, as consumers. Xavier Greffe (2003, 2014) describes the crisis in economic models for heritage which require it to be productive in order to be self-financing via visitor consumption (admission charges and heritage services). Promoting enhanced heritage status (inscription as a World Heritage Site, for example) creates a willingness on the part of visitors to pay more; in other words the price of admission and services can be raised.

These indirect contributions by tourists to heritage funding in the past have facilitated global projects spanning all sites. Even before the establishment of the World Heritage policy, UNESCO was considering the idea of a cultural tourism passport. This plan, put forward in 1950 by the International Tourism Alliance and enthusiastically received by UNESCO delegates at the conference in Paris in 1949 and then in Florence in 1950, proposed the introduction of a museum and monument safeguarding programme funded by imposing a tax on tourists entering a country in exchange for access to certain museums and monuments in that country.

In 1964, there were fresh discussions around the creation of an "international card" based on the model of a similar card introduced by the Council of Europe to facilitate cultural exchanges in Europe. Ultimately, this card was never introduced as the same difficulties arose around the issue of compensation in signatory countries, but it demonstrates the involvement of tourism in conservation issues (and carries the seed of the possibility of extending cultural citizenship to tourists).

8.4.3 Transnational Patronage

However, the idea of tourist engagement presupposes voluntary contributions in the form of donations which various heritage preservation committees and associations channel to different World Heritage Sites (Drouin 2011). These donations may take the form of significant contributions from personalities, or crowdfunding stimulated by digital campaigns.

Venice pioneered these committees with its international campaigns in the British and North American press in the nineteenth century (Davis and Marvin 2004). Natural catastrophes affecting heritage assets such as the snow storm in Versailles in 1951 (Pasquier 2015) or the floods in Florence and Venice in 1966 resulted in national and international appeals for donations.

The example of Versailles is particularly revealing. After an appeal for donations in 1951, management at the site, having identified the link between visitor enthusiasm and visitor involvement in safeguarding the site, developed a policy to improve visitor facilities and the quality of the visitor experience. More recently, the American Friends of Versailles has been founded. Its members represent a small subset of the substantial number of American visitors who are one of the largest groups to visit the palace, thus demonstrating a desire to get involved in supporting French heritage. The keen interest shown by Americans "is not only translated into visitor numbers to this architectural gem, but also into hard cash".[4] In 2004, funding from the American Friends of Versailles paid for the reconstruction of the Bosquet des Trois Fontaines, designed by André Le Nôtre in 1677. This was not merely a case of involvement in an ongoing project. The American Friends of Versailles chose the site on which to focus. This bosquet, which had been left untended, was not an urgent priority for the Palace. It represents to a great extent the desire of the foundation to take full responsibility for an aspect of heritage at Versailles in order to raise its own profile (Monier 2018). The association then turned its attention to the restoration of the Pavillon Frais in the Petit Trianon (inaugurated in 2013), and more recently to the ceiling of the Salle des Gardes de la Reine. For its part, the Association des Amis Européens de Versailles became involved in the restoration of Marie-Antoinette's bath chamber, which was inaugurated in 2011.

The situation at Versailles is not unique. Several monuments and museums capitalise on emotional attachments which often translate into donations. This is the case, for example, with the US-based association American Friends of the Louvre, a museum second only to the Metropolitan Museum of Art in terms of American visitor numbers. Several other American associations operate in the heritage space: the Versailles Foundation, created in 1970, the French Heritage Society (formerly Friends of Vieilles Maisons Françaises), the Kress Foundation, and the Mississippi Commission for International Cultural Exchange[5] (Monnier 2018). More generally, a large number of heritage projects are carried out using funds from international donors. The non-profit platform LoveItaly! offers international "donor angels"[6] the opportunity to fund the restoration and preservation of Italian heritage.

This external patronage managed by national and international committees and associations, whose donors' enthusiasm is fostered by tourism, is supplemented by crowdfunding promoted in situ to visitors by site managers. Thus the Louvre pursues its "Tous mécènes!" (Everyone is a patron!) campaign to channel visitor donations for the Winged Victory of Samothrace, for example, (with average donations of 50 euros and a total of one million euros raised), or to acquire the Book of Hours of Francis 1st. This crowdfunding brings certain benefits (visibility of the donor's name, tax benefits), but also helps to reconcile tourists to the fact that iconic works undergoing restoration are not on display. In Venice after the flooding in 2019, micro-donation facilities (4 euros by bank card at terminals) were introduced at various cultural sites, addressing visitors in different languages and repeating the responsible tourism slogan displayed throughout the city: Enjoy-Respect.

---

[4] Stéphane Lepoittevin, De riches Américains font revivre Versailles, *Le Parisien*, 21 avril 2004.

[5] Roxana Azimi, Stéphanie Le Bars, La cathédrale Notre-Dame de Paris, une passion américaine, Le Monde, 31 mai 2019.

[6] https://loveitaly.org/donors/

8.4.4 Voluntary Engagement of Tourists In Situ

In addition to these public and private mechanisms for channelling donations towards heritage projects by capitalising on the tourist experience, there are also forms of intervention in situ by tourists themselves, via volunteering projects. Volunteering can take several forms: reconstruction, restoration, preservation, and enhancement of heritage.

Tourists are contributing to the reconstruction of sites on the Cinque Terre coastline, a UNESCO World Heritage Site. The volunteer project run by Lega Ambiente, an environmental protection association, invites international students to work in the vineyards for ten days to rebuild terraces damaged by the fatal floods of 2011, or to clear paths. Three Americans who had visited Vernazza as tourists before settling there, set up *Save Vernazza,* a non-profit association with a mission to rebuild the village (Biagioli 2013). It signed an agreement with the tour operator Busabout[7] to encourage young people visiting Europe for three months to spend part of their trip working in an area with local residents. These young tourists pay to work in the vineyards as part of an initiative which combines voluntourism and heritage activity. The rebuilding work therefore brings together tourists who had visited Cinque Terre, or who are combining a visit with voluntary work.

Masson-Labonté (2011) analyses the restoration and revitalisation of Perillos, a village in the Pyrénées-Orientales region in southern France, which had been abandoned since the 1970s. The project is being carried out by the non-profit association Terre de pierre, which has been coordinating restoration since 2006, bringing together voluntourists and drawing on local expertise, techniques and materials. Tourists also contribute on a voluntary basis by raising the profile of tourism. English-speaking volunteers who travel to the Terracotta Warriors Museum in China help with signage in the museum, teach English to museum staff and conduct tours in English (Cochrane and Tapper 2006: 105). This form of "serious leisure" can be analysed as a means of identity-building via heritage activity (Orr 2006).

These initiatives can come from the non-profit sector or be more institutional in nature. The aim of the World Heritage Volunteer (WHV) programme created by the Coordinating Committee for International Voluntary Service (CCSVI) and the World Heritage Centre in 2008, "is to transcend borders and territories to bring young volunteers of the world together around a world heritage protection project".

A twofold relationship exists between heritage volunteering and tourism: tourism fosters volunteering, which can then be analysed as a form of tourism. Thus, several researchers (McIntosh and Zahra 2007) analyse these practices as alternative forms of tourism, from the perspective of volunteering practices and local impacts. These volunteering initiatives are in fact a form of niche tourism in terms of the number of people involved and their probable impact on heritage. Several associations, such as Rempart, banish the word "tourism" from their advertising, preferring the word "holiday" instead. The association's website uses the tagline:

---

[7] http://www.busabout.com/save-vernazza

"A REMPART project is an original way to have a holiday and make lifelong memories!" A survey of volunteers in Coucy (France) and Bizerte (Tunisia) carried by M. Obritin (2015) shows that although volunteers do not define themselves as tourists, they do explore the area for part of their trip. Furthermore, their choice of project is partly determined by exploration opportunities, and volunteers from France, for example, are more drawn to southern regions than volunteers from abroad, thus reflecting patterns of domestic tourism. On these restoration projects in rural areas, volunteer trips contribute to local "micro tourism" (Masson-Labonté 2011).

8.5 Conclusion

In conclusion, it would appear that tourism – via the various registers of activity discussed ("concernment", attachment, engagement) – plays a role in amplifying how people position themselves in the world through their emotions, commitment and actions. By expanding the scale of how we exist and live in the world, tourism is also a factor in attachment and engagement. If we set aside personal stories which foster a sense of attachment to more modest heritage sites, the venues which attract the highest levels of support (and donations) are the heritage big-hitters. The examples mentioned in this article (Venice, Versailles, Notre-Dame, the Louvre, and Cinque Terre) confirm that the engagement and generosity of tourists is proportionate to footfall. Very few studies on footfall in tourist destinations explore the issue of the bonds of attachment experienced by tourists. This would undoubtedly be a fruitful topic for future research.

Further research is also required in those porous regions which might allow us to approach issues relating to heritage tourism engagement via its subtext.[8] When the various expressions of "concernment" for a remote heritage are subjected to scrutiny, the vested interests underlying altruism are almost systematically exposed. The intention here is not to repeat this criticism, but to identify the ambiguity inherent in examining forms of tourists' moral engagement with heritage. Doubt lingers around the benefits which accrue from heritage engagement, leading to ostentation in discourse and mechanisms. There are varying degrees of benefit: a symbolic reward in the form of a plaque celebrating a patron's donation; privileged access to heritage spaces; a personal commitment masquerading as altruism; and even a blurring of the boundaries between tourist and resident in the case of second-home owners. Venice preservation committees reflect this ambiguity (Davis and Marvin 2004), and fundraising campaigns aimed at North American patrons offer benefits in kind: preferential deals at partner hotels, a special week in Venice with a number of private events at the city's monuments (the Regatta Week Gala), the promise of

---

[8] The heritage motivations of tourists are far from monolithic. B. McKercher and Hillary DuCros (2003: 55), point out that "many shades of cultural tourist exist", and that "the purposeful cultural tourist is not just motivated to travel for deep cultural experience".

opportunities to meet "real Venetians" descended from Venetian nobility, and more general guarantees of experiences which are off the beaten track. Save Venice, with a few exceptions, does not erect plaques for donors, contrary to usual patronage practice. However, the desire to make donors' contributions visible places the emphasis on spectacular projects to the detriment of preventive conservation, as is highlighted by UNESCO.

Lastly these forms of tourist "concernment" and engagement raise the issue of belonging in relation to these sites. The distinction between tourist and resident can once again be queried. It becomes even more complex in the contemporary context of multi-territoriality and multiple belonging (Stock 2006), and in the light of the complex motivations and motives for heritage tourist travel. However, these types of engagement also forge new links with sites.

References

Anatole-Gabriel, I. (2016). *La fabrique du patrimoine de l'humanité, éditions de la Maison des Sciences de l'Homme*. Publications de la Sorbonne.

Anderson, B. (1991). *Imagined communities, reflections on the origin and spread of nationalism* (p. 224). London: Verso.

Araujo. (2010). Welcome the diaspora slave trade heritage tourism and the public memory of slavery. *Ethnologies, 32*(2), 145–178.

Benhamou, F. (2010). L'inscription au patrimoine mondial de l'humanité: La force d'un langage à l'appui d'une promesse de développement. *Tiers-Monde, 202*(2), 113.

Biagioli, G. (2013). *La problématique habitants-touristes à Cinque Terre*. In M. Gravari-Barbas & S. Jacquot (Eds.), Actes du 4e séminaire de la Chaire UNESCO « Culture, Tourisme, Développement ». Touristes et habitants dans les sites du patrimoine mondial, UNESCO.

Boltanski, L. (1999). *Distant suffering: Morality, media and politics*. Cambridge: Cambridge University Press.

Boltanski, L. (2007, 1993). *La souffrance à distance*. Gallimard, Folio essais.

Boltanski, L., & Thévenot, L. (1991). *De la justification: les économies de la grandeur*. Paris: Gallimard, nrf Essais.

Brunet, R. (2008, octobre–décembre). De l'usage raisonné de la notion de « concernement: mobilisations locales à propos de l'industrie nucléaire. *Natures Sciences Sociétés, 16*(4), 317–325.

Buonincontri, P., Marasco, A., Ramkissoon, H. (2017). Visitors' experience, place attachment and sustainable behaviour at cultural heritage sites: A conceptual framework. *Sustainability*.

Canova, N., & Chatelain, M. (2015). Émergence et structuration d'un tourisme dansant. *Étude comparée de deux plateformes de la danse, Cuba et l'Andalousie, Géographie et Cultures, 96*, 109–130.

Conforti, J. (1996). Ghettos as tourism attractions. *Annals of Tourism Research, 23*(4), 830–842.

Cochrane, J., & Tapper, R. (2006). Tourism's contribution to World Heritage Site management. In A. Leask & A. Fyall (Eds.), *Managing world heritage sites*. Routledge.

Cominelli F., Condevaux A., & Jacquot S. (2020). Intangible cultural heritage and tourism: Research perspectives (33-48). In Gravari-Barbas M. (Ed.), *A research agenda for heritage tourism*. Elgar.

Compagnone, M. R. (2017). Le Storytelling dans les commentaires de TripAdvisor. In M. Bourdaa & M. Mattioda (Éds.), *Fragments d'un discours narratif: le storytelling dans tous ses états*. Synergies Italie (Vol. 13, pp. 81–91).

Convention. (1972). Convention Concerning the Protection of the World Cultural and Natural Heritage, UNESCO. https://whc.unesco.org/en/conventiontext/

Cousin, S., Chareyron, G., Da-Rugna, J., & Sébastien, J. (2014). Étudier TripAdvisor. Ou comment Trip-patouiller les cartes de nos vacances. EspacesTemps.net, Dans l'air, 29.08.2014, http://www.espace-stemps.net/articles/etudier-tripadvisor-ou-comment-trip-patouiller-les-cartes-de-nos-vacances/

Dassié, V. (2006). *une émotion patrimoniale contemporaine, le parc de Versailles dans la tempête, Ministère de la Culture, Mission à l'ethnologie* (199 p).

Dassié, V. (2009). Réinventer son patrimoine : du vent et des larmes pour le parc du château de Versailles. *Livraisons de l'histoire de l'architecture, 17,* 27–40.

Davis, R. C., & Marvin, G. (2004). *Venice, the tourist maze: A cultural critique of the world's most touristed city.* Berkeley: University of California Press.

Debarbieux, B. (2012) *Tourism, imaginaries and identities: Reversing the point of view.* Via No 1. https://journals.openedition.org/viatourism/1197

Debray, R. (1999). Le monument ou la transmission comme tragédie, Introduction générale. In L'abus monumental, *Actes des Entretiens du Patrimoine* (pp. 11–33). Fayard.

Di Méo, G. (1994). Patrimoine et territoire, une parenté conceptuelle. *Espaces et Sociétés,* 15–34.

Donovan, A. E. (2008). *William Morris and the Society for the protection of ancient buildings.* London: Routledge.

Drouin, M. (2011). Les associations de patrimoine et le tourisme. *Téoros, 30*(2), 59–61. https://doi.org/10.7202/1012242ar.

Fabre, D. (2010). Introduction – Habiter les monuments. In Daniel Fabre & Anna Iuso (dir), *Les monuments sont habités.* Editionsde la Maison des sciences de l'Homme.

Fabre, D. (2013). Émotions patrimoniales, sous la direction de Daniel Fabre, Paris, Éditions de la Maison des sciences de l'homme, coll. « Ethnologie de la France », cahier n° 27.

Faburel, G., & Tribout, S. (2011). Les quartiers durables sont-ils durables ? De la technologie écologique aux modes de vie. *Cosmopolitiques, 19*

Fourcade, M.-B. (2010). Tourisme des racines, *Téoros* 29(1) [Online] http://journals.openedition.org/teoros/483.

García-Hernández, M., De la Calle-Vaquero, M., & Yubero, C. (2017). Cultural heritage and urban tourism: Historic city centres under pressure. *Sustainability, 9,* 1346.

Gendron, C., Vaillancourt, J.G., Claeys-Mekdade, C., & Rajotte, A. (2007). *Environnement et sciences sociales* (432p). Laval: Presses Universitaires Laval.

Glevarec, H., & Saez G. (2002). *Le patrimoine saisi par les associations.* Ministère de la Culture – DEPS.

Goreau-Ponceaud, A. (2015). Les pratiques touristiques au sein de la diaspora indienne: entre institutionnalisation et désirs d'appartenance. In Sacareau, Taunay, Peyvel (dir.), *La mondialisation du tourisme. Les nouvelles frontières d'une pratique.* Presses universitaires de Rennes.

Grant, E. (2005). Race and tourism in America's first city. *Journal of Urban History, 31*(6), 850–871.

Gravari-Barbas, M. (1996). Le "sang" et le "sol". Le patrimoine, facteur d'appartenance à un territoire urbain. *Géographie et Cultures, 20,* 55–67.

Gravari-Barbas, M. (2012). Tourisme et patrimoine, le temps des synergies ? In Chérif Khaznadar (Ed.), Le patrimoine, mais quel patrimoine ? Internationale de l'imaginaire, No 27, Ed. Babel (pp. 375–399).

Gravari-Barbas, M. (2018). Tourism as a heritage-producing machine. *Tourism Management Perspectives, 26,* 5–8.

Greffe, X. (2003). *La valorisation économique du patrimoine.* La documentation française.

Greffe, X. (2011). *L'économie politique du patrimoine culturel, de la médaille au rhizome,* compte rendu de communication. Paris: ICOMOS.

Greffe, X. (2014). *La trace et le rhizome – Les mises en scène du patrimoine culturel* (270 p.). Presses de l'Université du Québec.

Harrison, R. (2012). *Heritage, critical approaches.* London: Routledge.

Jacquot, S. (2010). Monumentalités, destructions, dispositifs de remémoration en Arménie, de l'extraterritorial à Erevan. Dans Monumentalité urbaine, L'Harmattan.

Jacquot, S., Chareyron, G., & Cousin, S. (2018). Le tourisme de mémoire au prisme du « big data ». Cartographier les circulations touristiques pour observer les pratiques mémorielles, Mondes du Tourisme.

Lazzarotti, O. (2011). *Patrimoine et tourisme. Histoires, lieux, acteurs, enjeux*. Paris: Belin.

Lowe Swift, C. (2007). Privileging the diaspora in Mauritius: Making world heritage for a multi-cultural nation. *Diaspora A Journal of Transnational Studies, 16*(3), 287–322.

Maguet, F. (2011). L'image des communautés dans l'espace public. In C. Bortolotto (Ed.), *Le patrimoine culturel immatériel: Enjeux d'une nouvelle catégorie* (pp. 47–73). Éditions de la Maison des sciences de l'homme.

Masson-Labonté, A. (2011). La restauration du village de Périllos par l'association Terre de pierres : un exemple de micro-tourisme durable. *Téoros, 30*(2), 82–93. https://doi.org/10.7202/1012245ar.

Matteucci, X. (2014). Forms of body usage in tourists' experiences of flamenco. *Annals of Tourism Research, 46*, 29–43.

McIntosh, A. J., & Zahra, A. (2007). A cultural encounter through volunteer tourism: Towards the ideals of sustainable tourism? *Journal of Sustainable Tourism, 15*(5), 541–556.

McKercher, B., & DuCRos, H. (2003). Testing a cultural tourism typology. *International Journal of Tourism Research, 5*, 45–58.

Monier, A. (2018, April). The role of social capital in transnational elite philanthropy: the example of the American Friends groups of French cultural institutions. *Socio-Economic Review, 16*(2), 387–410. https://doi.org/10.1093/ser/mwx042.

Obritin, M. (2015). *Les chantiers de bénévoles pour la restauration du patrimoine: une nouvelle pratique touristique pour la sauvegarde des monuments?* Mémoire de Master Tourisme, IREST, Université Paris 1 Panthéon Sorbonne.

Orr, N. (2006). Museum Volunteering: Heritage as 'Serious Leisure'. *International Journal of Heritage Studies, 12*(2), 194–210.

Pasquier, E. (2015). André Cornu et la sauvegarde de Versailles. *Bulletin du Centre de recherche du château de Versailles* [online], https://journals.openedition.org/crcv/13234.

Pecqueux, T. (2013). Morale et politique dans le monument historique, L'incendie du château de Lunéville. In Fabre Daniel (Ed.), *Les émotions patrimoniales*. Editions de la Maison des Sciences de l'Homme.

Prigent, L. (2001). *Valeur d'usage et valeur d'existence d'un patrimoine. Une application de la méthode d'évaluation contingente au Mont-Saint-Michel*. thèse de doctorat de l'Université de Bretagne Occidentales, Sciences économiques (dir. M. Boncoeur).

Ruskin, J. (2003). *The stones of Venice*. Da Capo Press.

Sather-Wagstaff, J. (2016). *Heritage that hurts, tourists in the Memoryscapes of September 11* (236 p.). London: Routledge.

Sintès, P. (2010). Retrouver Rhodes, *Téoros, 29*(1) (online) http://journals.openedition.org/teoros/523.

Smith, L. (2006). *Uses of heritage*. New York: Routledge.

Stock, M. (2006). L'hypothèse de l'habiter poly-topique. Pratiquer les lieux géographiques dans les sociétés à individus mobiles. *EspacesTemps.net*. (online) https://www.espacestemps.net/articles/hypothese-habiter-polytopique/

Thiesse, A.-M. (1999). *la création des identités nationales* (385 p.). Editions du Seuil.

Tornatore, J.-L. (2006). Les formes d'engagement dans l'activité patrimoniale. De quelques manières de s'accommoder au passé. In D. Meyer, Vincent et Walter, J. (dir.). Formes de l'engagement et espace public, Questions de communication, série actes 3 (pp. 515–538). Nancy: Presses universitaires de Nancy.

Urry, J. (1990). Tourist gaze: Leisure and travel in contemporary societies (Theory, culture & society), Sage.

Vecco, M. (2007). *L'économie du patrimoine monumental*.

Veschambre, V. (2008). *Traces et mémoires urbaines, enjeux sociaux de la patrimonialisation et de la destruction*. Rennes: PUR.

Winter. (2009). Tourism, social memory and the Great War. *Annals of Tourism Research, 36*(4), 607–626.

Yagoubi, A. (2010). Le mythe de Venise. Interview avec Massimo Cacciari. *Sociétés, 109*(3), 41–53.

Zunigo, X. (2007). « Visiter les pauvres ». Sur les ambiguïtés d'une pratique humanitaire et caritative à Calcutta. *Actes de la recherche en sciences sociales, 5*(170), 102–109.

Maria Gravari-Barbas is a professor at the Université Paris-Panthéon Sorbonne (France). She is director of EIREST (Equipe Interdisciplinaire de REcherches Sur le Tourisme), a multidisciplinary research team dedicated to tourism studies, with main focus cultural heritage, development, and urban-tourism evolutions. She is editor-in-chief of the scientific journal *Via. Tourism Research*.

Sébastien Jacquot is a lecturer in geography at Université Paris-Panthéon Sorbonne (France) and member of the research team EIREST (Equipe Interdisciplinaire de REcherches Sur le Tourisme), a multidisciplinary research team dedicated to tourism studies, with main focus cultural heritage, development, and urban-tourism evolutions.

Chapter 9
Discussing Overtourism: Recognizing Residents' Needs in Tourism Management in Ticino, Switzerland

Mosè Cometta

9.1 Introduction

The term *overtourism* has been widely used by the press in recent years. This has led to several researchers also starting to deal with the phenomenon. Despite this, the notion of overtourism is still relatively vague and not well defined (Koens et al. 2018), leading some researchers to question its usefulness (Jóhannesson and Lund 2019). This chapter proposes to address an aspect that is important in the understanding of anti-tourism anger: spatial justice (Dufaux et al. 2009; Hadjimichalis 2011; Lévy et al. 2018; Soja 2010) and broader residents' needs.

Unlike the more classic cases of overtourism studies, we will not focus on a big city or a world destination, but on a semi-peripheral European region. In this case, therefore, it will not be a question of observing the inhabitant's opposition to a constant tourist pressure (Capocchi et al. 2019), but rather the reaction to two punctual tourism peaks. Despite these particularities, this case study shows some aspects common to the phenomena of overtourism – such as the opposition between the freedom of movement of tourists and the interests of residents (Perkumienė and Pranskūnienė 2019) or the perception by residents of the rudeness of tourists: a problem that can potentially become more radical (Tolkach et al. 2017) with the transition to a poly-topic lifestyle (Stock 2006) and the increase in global mobility (Urry 2007). The temporal span between the two tourist peaks analysed (1981 and 2017) will allow to highlight the evolution of tourism management in the region.

This analysis will allow to underline some aspects of anti-tourism phenomena that often have been associated to the notion of overtourism but that should be

This work was supported by the Swiss National Science Foundation under Grant POLAP1-172054/1.

M. Cometta (✉)
University of Turin, Turin, Italy

framed in a different way. In the conclusion, I will discuss this concept in order to assess some of its limits, exploiting the particularities of my case study.

Methodology

A series of annual reports from the *Ente Ticinese del Turismo* (ETT, Ticino's Tourism Organisation) from 1980 to 2013 were analysed. This permitted to observe the evolution of rationality in the management of tourism. 40 newspaper articles of *Corriere del Ticino* (CdT) – one of the major newspaper in Ticino – from 1981 and 29 online articles of different newspaper from 2017 were studied. This allowed for a comparison of the vision of the ETT with cases of controversy around a perceived excess of tourists. Citations were translated into English. Data was collected and analysed in 2018. Critical analysis (Foucault 2015; Hajer 2003) and content analysis (Mucchielli 1996) perspectives were mobilised to gain a grasp on the motivations that lead to the debate and the controversies. As previously shown by Kohlbacher (2006) and Wodak and Reisigl (2016), qualitative and critical discursive analyses will bring together both problem-oriented and theory-guided approaches, thereby granting sufficient flexibility and liability.

9.2   A Brief History of Ticino

The modern history of Ticino is marked by the colonization by the Swiss-German cantons and their disputes with the Italian regional powers. For centuries, its territory was divided into eight districts under the command of a different bailiff. The reason for this colonization lies not in the richness of the land but in its position: Ticino is in fact a strategic transit point between the north and south of the Alps, being one of the most direct ways to reach Milan (Fig. 9.1).

Its mountainous territory, an economy marked by subsistence agriculture, administrative divisions and strong emigration have made Ticino an underdeveloped and economically fragile region (Ceschi 1998). The parochial and rural mentality of the population (Diener et al. 2006), divided by diversified local customs and traditions, contributed to the fragility of the cantonal authority, which was imposed at the beginning of the nineteenth century (Ghiringhelli 1998).

After the Second World War, the arrival of Swiss and Italian capital completely changed the living conditions of the population. In a few decades, the urban transition has reduced the primary sector, while the tertiary sector has exploded. From 1947 to 1970, the number of buildings almost doubled (Caccia 1984). However, the authorities had many difficulties in governing, directing and coordinating this development, which therefore remained largely irrational and unplanned. The different attempts to give more powers to the central authority clashed with the parochial mentality of the population. One of the few examples of successful centralisation is

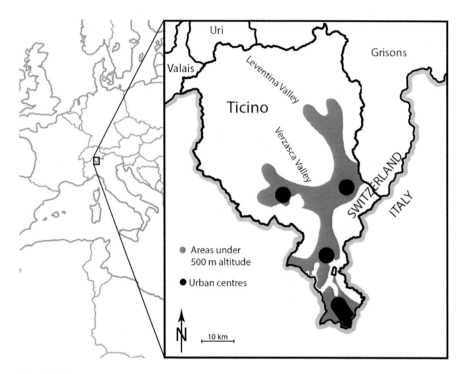

Fig. 9.1 The geographical position of Ticino, its main centres and plains

the creation of the ETT – a public organisation with the aim of promoting tourism in the canton.

The cantonal territory is divided into mountain valleys and a few plains. The advent of urban society has further strengthened the socio-economic disparities between these two areas. The Alpine valleys have always been a land of emigration – to the point that some researchers claim that abandonment is the true essence of those territories (Rossi et al. 1979, p. 27) – but with the urban development of the plains this phenomenon has intensified to the point of seriously worrying the authorities. In fact, to date, 4/5 of the population and 90% of the jobs are located in the urban plains, which, however, represent only 14.5% of the cantonal territory (RCT 2009, pp. 36, 42). These observations on Ticino's socio-territorial balance are important: in this chapter, we will observe how the territorial question – how to favour a certain understanding of spatial justice – is of great importance in the management of tourism.

9.3 The Keynesian Paradigm of the 1980s and Response to Overtourism

9.3.1 The Keynesian Paradigm of the 1980s

In the 1980s, the greatest concern of the ETT was to accompany the urban transition of the canton, using tourism as a tool for development. In order to achieve this result, however, it was necessary for the population to perceive tourism no longer as a submission to the foreign colonizer, but as a modern service in which to valorise its collective identity. A then ETT minister and president stated with concern that "for many parents whose children enter the labour market, tourism is still synonymous with servitude and humiliation" (Cotti 1983). For this understanding to change, however, a general reform of the tourism system was necessary. The actors involved had to integrate better into the local community – e.g. by promoting the use of Italian, the official language of the canton, to the detriment of German (Respini 1985; Solari 1983, 1987), the language of two thirds of the 1980s tourists (USTAT 2006), so as not to become a German-speaking oasis – and aim for a less quantitative and more qualitative tourism (Cotti 1983; Solari 1981, 1982).

Modernising the sector, removing the clichés that characterised Ticino as a "Mediterranean Switzerland" and its inhabitants as an ever-smiling, non-serious and slack-hearted population, would therefore have brought important support to the urban transition that Ticino society was experiencing. This struggle for authenticity, against stereotypes at first (Respini 1984, 1985) but also against the society of the spectacle (Solari 1986), characterized ETT's discourses in the 1980s.

The question of spatial justice was at the very heart of the ETT tourism concept in the 1980s. Driven by a Keynesian vision, they hoped to divert part of the economic growth of the sector to the peripheral valleys (Cotti 1980, 1983). The basic idea was that the territorial disparities between the different regions had to be eliminated. In the view of decision-makers, the urban transition must not create too many inequalities – further excluding the peripheral valleys – so as to ensure a certain cohesion of Ticino society. The greater the socio-territorial disparities, the more difficult it is to govern society. The public management of tourism positioned itself as a strategic sector fundamental for the development of Ticino society (Cotti 1980, 1981, 1982). Tourism was seen as a vector of modernity (Respini 1984, 1986; Solari 1986).

9.3.2 Keynesian Response to Overtourism

The Gotthard road tunnel was inaugurated on 5 September 1980. At that time, it was the longest tunnel in the world with a length of almost 17 km. This work symbolically marks the connection between Ticino and the rest of Switzerland and its inclusion in the continental urban network. Thanks to this infrastructure, the canton became more easily accessible by private traffic from the north. During the spring and summer of 1981 there was a significant increase in the number of tourists. This increased the concerns of the residents. The increase in traffic generated several traffic jams, especially in the Leventina valley, which leads south from the Gotthard (CdT 1981a, g, i, m).

The management of this situation created some tensions between policemen and tourists. The director of a local tourist organisation complained in the newspapers about the poor preparation of the agents: "as traffic increased, professional and behavioural shortcomings became apparent" (CdT 1981j). In turn, the Director of the ETT turned to the media, but to defend the work of the agents: for him "it is better to lose than to find tourists who believe that everything is allowed south of the Gotthard" (CdT 1981f). Other problems concerned the rudeness of some guests, due in part to overcrowding of hotels and camping, and a general lack of respect for local laws and traditions – e.g. young people bathing naked in rivers (CdT 1981d), or campers putting their tents on private land without permission (CdT 1981b, h). The ETT has repeatedly taken a stand in front of this situation, defending the authorities and clearly attempting to distinguish between tourists – respectful and generators of opportunities and wealth – and illegal campers – disrespectful and costly for the community. It was also briefly publicly debated whether transit tourists brought wealth or cost to the community (CdT 1981c, l).

The ETT leaders publicly stated that "tourism is not just economy, it must not compromise our identity" (CdT 1981e) and they committed themselves to the population to avoid quantitative excesses in favour of an improvement in the quality of tourists, at the same time asking for patience in the management of the phenomenon (CdT 1981k). The Keynesian position is therefore clear: tourism must serve a purpose external to the sector – the general improvement of the quality of life. In order to achieve this objective, it is therefore important to control tourism and prevent it from clashing with the interests of residents. The needs of the population – especially the economic needs of peripheral areas – are therefore at the heart of the concerns of tourism managers in the Keynesian paradigm.

9.4   The Neoliberal Paradigm of the 2010s and Response to Overtourism

The end of the 1980s was marked by numerous changes for tourism in Ticino. On the one hand, there was a major crisis in hotel bednights (Fig 9.2) -which did not, however, prevent a general growth in the sector, driven by non-hotel structures-, on the other hand, the end of the mandate of ETT Director of Marco Solari, a man of profound humanist culture, as well as the entry into cantonal government of a representative of the most extreme wing of the neoliberal current from 1995 to 2007.

Overnight stays at Ticino's hotels (milions)

Source: Ticino Turismo, Relazione annuale 2008

Fig. 9.2 The crisis in the hotel sector

9.4.1   The Neoliberal Paradigm

All this radically transformed the way of thinking about tourism management and the task of the ETT. The new management focuses almost exclusively on the hotel sector. Its main mission becomes the increase of tourist stays. Any reference to broader society issues disappears. The perspective therefore becomes essentially internal: the objective of the tourism management is to merely increase the number of tourists, and no longer to contribute to the balanced development of society. On the contrary, where the interests of society and tourism clash, the ETT defends its sector – e.g. by asserting the need to loosen legal constraints for new tourism buildings (Stinca 2000), limiting the right of opposition on the part of residents (ETT 1994). "It does not seem difficult to me to understand that the [tourism] relaunch passes through the renewal of the offer. This requires investment in facilities such as new golf courses, aqualand, new or renovated hotels and so on. We are not asking the state for money. We are only asking for more streamlined, less complex and time-consuming procedures, suitable for modern times" (Valli 1996, p. 1). A clear change in the perspective of the ETT can be observed: it positions itself no longer as a state actor that promote development policies, but rather as the representative of a private sector battling both with the state and with residents to expand the economic freedom of hoteliers. This can also be seen in the territorial disposition of the local tourist agencies: if during the Keynesian period they covered the whole cantonal territory, showing a particular proximity to local peculiarities, in the neoliberal phase they are grouped around the four main urban centres, privileging economic efficiency over territorial representativeness (Fig. 9.3).

This means that when faced with conflicts between the interests of residents and tourists, the ETT will no longer defend the population of Ticino. For the new

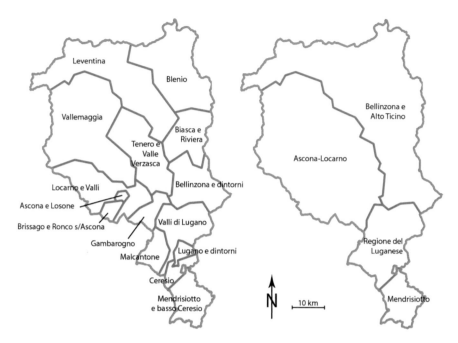

Fig. 9.3 The centralisation process of local tourist agencies between 1972 and 2014

direction, it is necessary that "the degree of acceptance of tourism (with its advantages, but also inevitable small and bearable disadvantages) by all Ticino people increases" (Foglia 1995, p. 3). It is the population that has to give up its desires in order to maintain its attractiveness for tourists and not damage the hotel sector. The interest of the institution is guided by a practical concern: "for too long there have been rumours of the inability of Ticino people to welcome guests with kindness" (Valli 1996, p. 1). In short, there is a need to "inform and sensitize the population" (Cantarelli 1998, p. 1) so that it will be friendlier to visitors.

9.4.2 Neoliberal Response to Overtourism

The year 2017 marks a symbolically important moment for Ticino. A video entitled *The Maldives of Milan* posted on YouTube by an Italian boy and describing the beauty of Verzasca valley (Fig. 9.4) becomes viral: for the first time Ticino tourism is in the midst of a veritable storm (Han 2017) triggered by new technologies. "In one day the video, published by Capedit, has collected over a million views" (TN 2017c). The video discourse was simple: to highlight the aesthetic beauty of the valley and make it known to Internet users (TN 2017a). This started a massive arrival of Italian one-day visitors during the second half of July. The sudden increase

Fig. 9.4 A view of the main location of the "Maldives of Milan"

in traffic in this peripheral valley has generated several problems – e.g. wild parking, traffic jams and parking scarcity for residents.

Some inhabitants have publicly complained in the media. The problems are the same as in 1981: the traffic, the rudeness of some of the tourists and the doubts as to whether the revenue generated by this wave of visitors exceeded the costs for the community. Traffic was the main issue. Verzasca "in the last few days is already having difficulty in managing the influx of visitors" (laRegione 2017a), to the point that "those who were there say that they feared a traffic blackout so great was the chaos along the road that leads to the different pools of the valley" (TN 2017b). "The first weekend after the publication of the video, on 10 July, saw an almost unmanageable influx of new Italian tourists. Unmanageable especially with regard to road traffic" (CdT 2017).

Rudeness is another important issue in the eyes of the residents interviewed. Some of them say that "these new tourists come, they dirty, they don't consume and they leave" (CdT 2017), "they sleep in their cars, wander half-naked along the roads and turn the valley into an open-air toilet" (TN 2017b).

In general, the discourses reveal the discomfort with Italian tourists (CdT 2017; laRegione 2017b; TN 2017b, c). This can be partly explained by the peripherality of the valley, its relative poverty, and by the difficulties linked to a cantonal labour market strongly influenced by the phenomenon of cross-border workers (USTAT 2017) – Italian employees are hired by companies that pay lower wages, thereby rendering working conditions more precarious. The grudge against the Italians, and the wider malaise in front of this situation of exceptional crowding, are however diminished by the institutions. The cause of the tensions should be attributed, from their economic and managerial point of view of the new ETT, only to "the lack of receptivity of the existing structures, and not to the new Italian tourist" (CdT 2017). The underlying argument is that the inhabitants should stop expressing their opposition in a polemical way, and accept the inconveniences to favour the tourism sector (TN 2017d). Institutions were thus refusing to describe what is happening as a *tourism invasion* (laRegione 2017b). Positioning themselves strongly in defence of tourists and against the polemical voices of the residents.

9.5   What Major Differences?

A first important difference between the articles that appeared in 1981 and those of 2017 is that in the second case the polemical tones are emphasized. This is partly due to the emotional and polemical shift in mass media, but also corresponds to a greater social malaise. Another important difference is the position of the institutions.

In the 1980s, they tried to differentiate between tourists and abusive campers, thereby diluting popular criticism. Yet, the institutions' definition of the tourist included respect for the local culture and population. This means that the interests of the population were the a priori from which the institutions departed to manage tourism in a paternalistic and Keynesian way. In 1981, therefore, the ETT leaders understood the problems of the population, publicly supporting the need to limit tourism on several occasions. By proposing a qualitative separation of the phenomenon, then, the authorities have established a discursive framing in which tourism was seen as a positive phenomenon, while the problems were linked to something different from tourism itself – namely abusive tourism, lack of respect and speculation. It is a virtuous circle in which protecting the interests of citizens means reducing criticism against tourism – and thus protecting this sector as well. The desire for a territorial but also social equality, therefore, was fully in line with this perspective: resolving the problems and inequalities affecting the population could at the same time improve the quality of life of residents, thus making tourism more accepted. The sector, by obeying these political and cultural objectives, could therefore guarantee itself long-term economic development, since it avoided any opposition to citizenship.

However, the hotel crisis, changes in the direction of the institution and the new neoliberal governance paradigm have disrupted this way of thinking. In a much more sectoral framework, tourism management has now to deal only with tourism. Disagreements with the population are no longer part of the internal planning of the sector, but rather of an external area which is no longer the responsibility of the institution.

This means completely abandoning any direct claim to the general development of society. Spatial justice disappears from tourism discourses. "Over the last three decades of the twentieth century, progressive forms of regionalism aimed at reducing spatial inequalities almost disappeared. They were replaced by a neoliberal or, perhaps more accurately, neoconservative regionalism that was essentially entrepreneurial and dominated by intensified pressures to compete for a place in the global economy rather that dealing directly with issues of poverty and uneven development" (Soja 2010, p. 65).

Clearly, this new understanding of tourism does not aim at a virtuous integration of the interests of the population with those of the sector. Rather, it favours the clash between these two perspectives and a wider incommunicability, as seen in the 2017 case. To tourism managers who are used to considering only the internal and economic issues of the sector, the complaints of the population appear incomprehensible and bothersome. To the population annoyed by the excess of tourists, the arguments of the leaders seem aggressive and disrespectful. In the medium to long term, this creates major imbalances. A clash of interests can be dealt with by arbitrage – as in the Keynesian perspective – or by the law of the strongest. The prevailing interest is imposed on minor ones: this means that the arguments of the resident population are silenced, ignored and dismissed as a non-constructive and polemical. In the long term, this means that the most fragile part of the population, the one most sensitive to the excesses of tourism, will no longer feel represented by the institutions. In turn, this paves the way for a far-reaching conflict between the sector's managers and the population.

This is clearly visible in the example of 2017: while some of the population complains on a political-emotional discursive level, the managers of the sector respond on an economic-administrative plan. Their arguments insist on the fact that more tourist infrastructure is needed, that the polemics of the protestors are not constructive and therefore should not be considered. This does not open up any possibility of dialogue: there is no offer of listening and understanding the arguments of the population.

9.6   Discussing Overtourism

With the advent of an urban world – or, as someone call it, a planetary urbanisation (Arboleda 2015; Brenner 2018; Merrifield 2013; Schmid and Brenner 2011) – and the general increase in mobility (Urry 2007), the number of tourists seem to multiply. The massification of tourism responds to its function of recharging the energy of the workforce, thus playing a key role for the stability of the capitalist system (Horkheimer and Adorno 2002). We are therefore witnessing the development of a society in which tourism plays not only an economic but also a fundamentally cultural and political role.

Harvey (2008, 2010, 2011) argues that the continuous processes of construction, transformation and expansion of urban areas are an exhaust valve for the economic contradictions of the capitalist system. For this, he employs the term *spatial fix*. Since tourism constitutes a fundamental element in recharging the energies of the workforce, allowing the system to continuously extract value from people, we could then call it a *cultural fix* to excessive existential efforts that capitalism impose.

With the growth in tourist flows, cases of resistance and opposition are also on the increase, especially in tourism hotspots (Colomb and Novy 2017). This phenomenon is not really new (Jóhannesson and Lund 2019, p. 92) as it has accompanied the massification of tourism since the second half of the twentieth century. Already in the 1970s, some researchers were observing the "golden hordes" that invaded the peripheries in search of pleasure and entertainment (Turner and Ash 1975). What seems new, however, is the intensity of these protests and their extensive ramification (Milano 2017). Often these movements advocate for an anti-tourist approach among institutions – what has been called trexit (Seraphin et al. 2018).

In this perspective, however, anti-tourist phenomena acquire a deeper meaning. In other words, they are not simply reactions to quantitative excesses in the number of tourists. The examples from Ticino show well how even isolated and punctual occasions are enough to trigger quarrels. The peculiarity of the Ticino examples, compared to case studies in tourist hotspots, is that they show how the anti-tourist phenomenon is common even in areas that do not normally suffer a particularly strong pressure by tourism fluxes. The discursive asynchrony between the claims of the population and the answers of the authorities makes it clear that this is not a merely quantitative issue. If this were the case, residents would be happy with the pragmatism of the institutions – which believed that an improvement in infrastructure was enough to solve the problems. Thus, the number of tourists itself is not a problem – or rather, not the main problem. To think that a certain quantity of tourists immediately (within a few days) trigger such controversial reactions would be to fall into a social determinism that is far too simplistic. On the contrary, we have to consider that the increase in tourists brings out tensions that are already latent. And so, the fact that tourism can be understood as the *cultural fix* of capitalism acquires all its meaning. My hypothesis is that anti-tourism reactions stage dissatisfaction with the whole neoliberal exploitation system.

Capitalism imposes the fragmentation of traditional social ties and an increasingly widespread paradigm of mobility (both spatial, social and cultural) on an individual scale. The cost of this pervasiveness of the market is, in psychological terms, important. Mass tourism is a complex phenomenon. From the tourists' point of view, it has the function of recharging their energy. From the residents' point of view, on the other hand, it can be seen as an invasion of their own living space, as yet another aesthetic commodification of a dimension of their lives. Moreover, a clear distinction between tourists and residents is not self-evident and it is based on a very problematic ontological substantivism (Jóhannesson and Lund 2019) – where to place migration and temporary displacements? The very conception of freedom of movement is at stake here (Ortar et al. 2018). The same person can therefore take advantage of the positive aspects of tourism and feel aversion to it as a social structure. It is not tourism that is at stake here, but what it represents in any specific case. The anger against excessive tourism is actually the consequence of the feeling of having been abandoned by the institutions. It is the result of the social exclusion that a purely economic management of the tourism sector creates.

So, talking about overtourism is problematic to say the least. Some scholars employ this concept to highlight the negative externalities of the tourism phenomenon (Goodwin 2017; Papathanassis 2017), especially for the most fragile resident groups – unable to withstand the pressures of tourism actors in the competition for space (Martín Martín et al. 2018). Environmental pressure are also underlined (Hampton and Hampton 2008; Wall 2019). But the term overtourism seems to indicate that the problem lies in the quantity, in the excess of tourism, and not in what tourism more generally represents. Appropriately tackling the phenomenon, saving the sector from anti-tourist excesses (Seraphin et al. 2018), implies not focusing only on the number of tourists, but broadly abandoning the neoliberal paradigm of tourism management. Adequate management cannot be limited to effective branding strategies (Seraphin et al. 2019). It must instead promote the integration of environmental and social interests in decision-making. Leaving behind a purely economic conception of tourism means rethinking globally the democratic nature of the institutions in an inclusive way (Mouffe 2005, 2013), in a particular version of the residents' right to the city (Harvey 2008; Lefebvre 1968; Purcell 2002).

For all these reasons, talking about overtourism when referring to anti-tourist reactions by residents risks distorting the problem, focusing attention on quantity and not on the underlying issues of social and political exclusion. This shows well that the overtourism approach, even if with good intentions and some interesting insights, is actually the result of a too narrow and internal understanding of the sector. In order to overcome these limits, it is necessary to think of tourism as a means of social analysis, in its broadest ramifications. Tourism studies should move from the analysis of tourism to the study of society *through* tourism.

References

Arboleda, M. (2015). Financialization, totality and planetary urbanization in the Chilean Andes. *Geoforum, 67*, 4–13.

Brenner, N. (2018). Debating planetary urbanization: For an engaged pluralism. *Environment and Planning, 36*(3), 570–590.

Caccia, F. (1984). Costruzioni fuori dalle zone edificabili. *Rivista Tecnica, 10*, 54–56.

Cantarelli, G. L. (1998). Considerazioni sulla stagione 1998 *Relazioni pubbliche e informazione*: Ente Ticinese per il Turismo.

Capocchi, A., Vallone, C., Pierotti, M., & Amaduzzi, A. (2019). Overtourism: A literature review to assess implications and future perspectives. *Sustainability, 11*, 1–18.

CdT. (1981a, 21.04.1981). Al Ceneri nodo del traffico: coda da Cadenazzo a Taverne! *Corriere del Ticino*, p. 11.

CdT. (1981b, 28.07.1981). I campeggiatori abusivi preoccupano la polizia. *Corriere del Ticino*, p. 9.

CdT. (1981c, 07.08.1981). I turisti in transito spendono... *Corriere del Ticino*, p. 9.

CdT. (1981d, 17.08.1981). Il Breggia e la casta Susanna. *Corriere del Ticino*, p. 11.

CdT. (1981e, 23.12.1981). Il turismo in Ticino non è solo economia. Non deve compromettere la nostra identità. *Corriere del Ticino*, p. 9.

CdT. (1981f, 12.08.1981). La Stradale sotto accusa? Due inviti a sdrammatizzare. *Corriere del Ticino*, p. 10.

CdT. (1981g, 04.07.1981). Leventina e Riviera puntano ora sul turismo di transito. *Corriere del Ticino*, p. 11.

CdT. (1981h, 11.07.1981). Locarno dichiara guerra ai campeggiatori abusivi. *Corriere del Ticino*, p. 11.

CdT. (1981i, 31.07.1981). Lunghe colonne nel rientro ieri da Bellinzona a Biasca. *Corriere del Ticino*, p. 9.

CdT. (1981j, 03.08.1981). Polstrada non all'altezza dice il presidente ETL. *Corriere del Ticino*, p. 9.

CdT. (1981k, 23.04.1981). Qualità nell'offerta turistica e pazienza se nella massa c'è anche il maleducato... *Corriere del Ticino*, p. 9.

CdT. (1981l, 19.08.1981). Turisti taccagni? Rispondono i negozianti di centro-città. *Corriere del Ticino*, p. 7.

CdT. (1981m, 27.07.1981). Un altro collaudo eccezionale per la galleria del S. Gottardo. *Corriere del Ticino*, p. 6.

CdT. (2017, 26.07.2017). Val Verzasca: l'invasione non piace a tutti. *Corriere del Ticino*. Retrieved from https://www.cdt.ch/ticino/locarno/180072/val-verzasca-l-invasione-non-piace-a-tutti

Ceschi, R. (1998). Il territorio e gli abitanti. In R. Ceschi (Ed.), *Storia del Cantone Ticino* (Vol. I, pp. 15–32). Bellinzona: Stato del Cantone Ticino.

Colomb, C., & Novy, J. (2017). *Protest and resistance in the tourist city*. London: Routledge.

Cotti, F. (1980, 25.06.1980). *Relazione del Presidente all'Assemblea*.

Cotti, F. (1981, 02.06.1981). *Relazione del Presidente all'Assemblea*.

Cotti, F. (1982, 05.07.1982). *Relazione del Presidente all'Assemblea*.

Cotti, F. (1983, 10.06.1983). *Relazione del Presidente all'Assemblea*.

Diener, R., Herzog, J., Meili, M., de Meuron, P., & Schmid, C. (2006). *Switzerland. An urban portrait*. Basel: Birkhäuser.

Dufaux, F., Gervais-Lambony, P., Lehman-Frisch, S., & Moreau, S. (2009). n°01. Avis de naissance. *Justice Spatiale/Spatial Justice, 1*(1), 1–2 (online) https://www.jssj.org/issue/septembre-2009-edito/.

ETT. (1994). Relazione Annuale *Commento generale*: Ente Ticinese per il Turismo.

Foglia, E. (1995). Considerazioni sulla stagione 1995 *Commento generale*: Ente Ticinese per il Turismo.

Foucault, M. (2015). *La volonté de savoir Œuvres* (Vol. II, pp. 617–738). Paris: Gallimard.

Ghiringhelli, A. (1998). La costruzione del Cantone (1803–1830). In R. Ceschi (Ed.), *Storia del Cantone Ticino* (Vol. I, pp. 33–62). Bellinzona: Stato del Cantone Ticino.

Goodwin, H. (2017). The challenge of overtourism. *Responsible Tourism Partnership, Working Paper*, 1–19.

Hadjimichalis, C. (2011). Uneven geographical development and socio-spatial justice and solidarity: European regions after the 2009 financial crisis. *European Urban and Regional Studies, 18*(3), 254–274.

Hajer, M. A. (2003). Discourse analysis. In *The politics of environmental discourse: Ecological modernization and the policy process*. Oxford: Oxford Scholarship Online.

Hampton, M., & Hampton, J. (2008). Is the beach party over? Tourism and the environment in small islands: A case study of Gili Trawangan, Lombok, Indonesia. In M. Hitchcock, V. King, & M. Parnwell (Eds.), *Tourism in Southeast Asia: Challenges and new directions* (pp. 286–308). Copenhagen: Nias Press.

Han, B.-C. (2017). *In the swarm: Digital prospects*. Cambridge: MIT Press.

Harvey, D. (2008). The right to the city. *New Left Review, 53*, 23–40.

Harvey, D. (2010). *Justice, nature and the geography of difference*. Oxford: Blackwell.

Harvey, D. (2011). The urban roots of financial crises: Reclaiming the city for anti-capitalist struggle. *Socialist Register, 48*, 1–35.

Horkheimer, M., & Adorno, T. W. (2002). *Dialectic of enlightenment*. Stanford: Stanford University Press.

Jóhannesson, G. T., & Lund, K. A. (2019). Beyond overtourism: Studying the entanglements of society and tourism in Iceland. In C. Milano, J. Cheer, & M. Novelli (Eds.), *Overtourism: Excesses, discontents and measures in travel and tourism* (pp. 91–106). Boston: Cabi.

Koens, K., Postma, A., & Papp, B. (2018). Is overtourism overused? Understanding the impact of tourism in a city context. *Sustainability, 10*, 1–15.

Kohlbacher, F. (2006). The use of qualitative content analysis in case study research. *Forum: Qualitative Social Research, 7*(1).

laRegione. (2017a, 19.07.2017). "Pazzesco": le Maldive sono in Ticino. *laRegione*. Retrieved from https://www.laregione.ch/culture/societa/1219474/-pazzesco%2D%2Dle-maldive-sono-in-ticino

laRegione. (2017b, 29.07.2017). Verzasca o Maldive, "non chiamate la invasione". *laRegione*. Retrieved from https://www.laregione.ch/cantone/locarnese/1220078/verzasca-o-maldive%2D%2D-non-chiamatela-invasione-

Lefebvre, H. (1968). *Le droit à la ville*. Paris: Anthropos.

Lévy, J., Fauchille, J.-N., & Póvoas, A. (2018). *Théorie de la justice spatiale*. Paris: Odile Jacob.

Martín Martín, J. M., Guaita Martínez, J. M., & Salinas Fernández, J. A. (2018). An analysis of the factors behind the citizen's attitude of rejection towards tourism in a context of overtourism and economic dependence on this activity. *Sustainability, 10*, 1–18.

Merrifield, A. (2013). The urban question under planetary urbanization. *International Journal of Urban and Regional Research, 37*(3), 909–922.

Milano, C. (2017). Overtourism y turismofobia. Tendencias globales y contextos locales. *Pasos. Revista de Turismo y Patrimonio Cultural, 16*(3), 551–564.

Mouffe, C. (2005). *The return of the political*. London: Verso.

Mouffe, C. (2013). *Agonistics. Thinking the world politically*. London: Verso.

Mucchielli, A. (Ed.). (1996). *Dictionnaire des méthodes qualitatives en sciences humaines et sociales*. Paris: Armand Colin.

Ortar, N., Salzbrunn, M., & Stock, M. (2018). *Migrations, circulations, mobilités*. Aix-en-Provence: Presses Universitaires de Provence.

Papathanassis, A. (2017). Over-tourism and anti-tourist sentiment: An exploratory analysis and discussion. *"Ovidius" University Annals, Economic Sciences Series, XVII*(2), 288–293.

Perkumienė, D., & Pranskūnienė, R. (2019). Overtourism: Between the right to travel and residents' rights. *Sustainability, 11*, 1–17.

Purcell, M. (2002). Excavating Lefebvre: The right to the city and its urban politics of the inhabitant. *GeoJournal, 58*(2-3), 99–108.

RCT. (2009). *Revisione del Piano direttore cantonale: Rapporto esplicativo 2009*.

Respini, R. (1984). *Relazione del Presidente all'Assemblea*.

Respini, R. (1985, 17.06.1985). *Relazione del Presidente all'Assemblea*.

Respini, R. (1986, 27.06.1986). *Relazione del Presidente all'Assemblea*.

Rossi, A., Consolascio, E., & Bosshard, M. (1979). *Costruzione del territorio e spazio urbano nel Cantone Ticino* (Vol. I. La costruzione del territorio nel Cantone Ticino). Lugano: Fondazione Ticino Nostro.

Schmid, C., & Brenner, N. (2011). Planetary urbanization. In M. Gandy (Ed.), *Urban constellations* (pp. 10–13). Berlin: Jovis Verlag.

Seraphin, H., Sheeran, P., & Pilato, M. (2018). Over-tourism and the fall of Venice as a destination. *Journal of Destination Marketing & Management, 9*, 374–376.

Seraphin, H., Zaman, M., Olver, S., Bourliataux-Lajoinie, S., & Dosquet, F. (2019). Destination branding and overtourism. *Journal of Hospitality and Tourism Management, 38*, 1–4.

Soja, E. (2010). *Seeking spatial justice*. London: University of Minnesota Press.

Solari, M. (1981, 02.06.1981). *Osservazioni del Direttore all'Assemblea.*

Solari, M. (1982, 05.07.1982). *Relazione del Direttore all'Assemblea.*

Solari, M. (1983, 16.12.1983). *Relazione del Direttore all'Assemblea.*

Solari, M. (1986, 09.12.1986). *Relazione del Direttore all'Assemblea.*

Solari, M. (1987, 22.12.1987). *Relazione del Direttore all'Assemblea.*

Stinca, G. (2000). Relazione Annuale *Commento generale*: Ente Ticinese per il Turismo.

Stock, M. (2006). L'hypothèse de l'habiter poly-topique: Pratiquer les lieux géographiques dans les sociétés à individus mobiles. *EspacesTemps.net* (online) https://www.espacestemps.net/articles/hypothese-habiter-polytopique/.

Ticino Turismo. (2008). Relazione Annuale 2008 *Osservatorio e commento alle statistiche*: Ente Ticinese per il Turismo.

TN. (2017a, 01.09.2017). Con le Maldive di Milano ho valorizzato il territorio. *TicinoNews.* Retrieved from http://www.ticinonews.ch/ticino/404919/con-le-maldive-di-milano-ho-valorizzato-il-territorio

TN. (2017b, 17.07.2017). La Verzasca come Rimini. *TicinoNews.* Retrieved from http://www.ticinonews.ch/ticino/395146/la-verzasca-come-rimini

TN. (2017c, 11.07.2017). "Le Maldive di Milano", ma è la Val Verzasca. *TicinoNews.* Retrieved from http://www.ticinonews.ch/ticino/393834/le-maldive-di-milano-ma-e-la-val-verzasca

TN. (2017d, 19.07.2017). Verzasca: "Servono bus navetta, non forconi". *TicinoNews.* Retrieved from http://www.ticinonews.ch/ticino/395633/verzasca-servono-bus-navetta-non-forconi

Tolkach, D., Pratt, S., & Zeng, C. Y. H. (2017). Ethics of Chinese & Western tourists in Hong Kong. *Annals of Tourism Research, 63*, 83–96.

Turner, L., & Ash, J. (1975). *The golden hordes: International tourism and the pleasure periphery.* London: Constable.

Urry, J. (2007). *Mobilities.* Cambridge: Polity Press.

USTAT. (2006). *Arrivi nel settore alberghiero, secondo il paese di domicilio degli ospiti, in Ticino, dal 1980 al 1999.* Retrieved from https://www3.ti.ch/DFE/DR/USTAT/allegati/tabella/T_100301_04C.xls

USTAT. (2017). *Lavoro e reddito. Panoramica del tema.* Retrieved from https://www3.ti.ch/DFE/DR/USTAT/allegati/prodima/3403_lavoro_e_reddito.pdf

Valli, S. (1996). Considerazioni sulla stagione 1996 *Note introduttive*: Ente Ticinese per il Turismo.

Wall, G. (2019). Perspectives on the environment and overtourism. In R. Dodds & R. Butler (Eds.), *Overtourism: Issues, realities and solutions* (pp. 27–45). Berlin: De Gruyter.

Wodak, R., & Reisigl, M. (2016). The discourse-historical approach. In R. Wodak & M. Meyer (Eds.), *Methods of critical discourse studies*. London: Sage.

Mosè Cometta is a visiting researcher at the University of Turin (Italy). He holds a PhD in Geography from the Institute of Geography and Sustainability, University of Lausanne. His research focuses on the construction of identity and the political tensions related to it.

Chapter 10
Rematerializing Tourism Studies: Toward a Political Economy of Tourist Space

Clément Marie dit Chirot

10.1 Introduction

Almost two decades have passed since British geographer Peter Jackson called for "rematerializing social and cultural geography" (Jackson 2000). The proposal was all the more important because geography, like other social sciences, was showing a growing interest in the question of identities, cultures and representations, sometimes to the detriment of a reflection on the forms of social and economic domination that permeate contemporary societies. This observation should undoubtedly be reconsidered today in the light of the evolution of geography research topics and approaches in recent years, particularly in France. Obviously, geography has been affected by the materialistic approaches that certain social sciences are experiencing, the most visible manifestation of which is the renewed interest in Marxist-inspired radical geography in the English-speaking world.[1] However, the changes are not uniform across the different research fields. While the return of materialistic theories is more visible in some areas of research, as is the case in urban studies, this movement has not had the same resonance in the field of tourism studies, where several authors have pointed out the influence of the "cultural turn" (Cousin 2010; Bianchi 2009; Gibson 2009; Hiernaux 2008; Milne and Ateljevic 2001). As a

This research was funded by the Pays de la Loire region under the *Angers TourismLab* program.

[1] In France, this return to materialistic approaches in geography is addressed in a series of recent publications such as the thematic issue of the journal *Carnets de géographes* devoted to "géographies critiques" (2012), and the collective work *Espaces et rapports de domination* coordinated by A. Clerval, A. Fleury, J. Rebotier and S. Weber (2015).

C. Marie dit Chirot (✉)
UMR CNRS 6590 ESO – University of Angers, Angers, France
e-mail: clement.marieditchirot@univ-angers.fr

M. Stock (ed.), *Progress in French Tourism Geographies*, Geographies of
Tourism and Global Change, https://doi.org/10.1007/978-3-030-52136-3_10

reaction to the economic focus of the first studies on tourism, tourism research seems to have adopted the opposite attitude in the past two decades, namely by focusing on the analysis of tourist practices and representations. Along with this renewed focus on cultural dimensions, the paradigms developed in previous periods are also being questioned. The attention paid to socio-economic inequalities inherent in the world of tourism too often led researchers to describe Manichean oppositions between dominant and dominated, particularly in the study of relations between tourists and host communities.

This theoretical shift has undoubtedly contributed to the reshaping of tourism research by allowing new issues to emerge and taking into account elements hitherto neglected by analysis, the first of which are tourists themselves, their practices and their representations. In doing so, however, tourism research has moved away from questions that are no less essential to understanding tourism, namely the structural inequalities and the macrosocial power relations inherent in the world of tourism in capitalist societies. One of the current challenges in tourism research could be to reshape the framework for a materialistic interpretation of tourism while avoiding the pitfalls of the critical approaches that have long dominated this field of research, particularly in geography. In order to clarify the meaning of such a project, this chapter will begin by describing the issues in light of the debates that have been prevalent in tourism studies for nearly thirty years. This perspective will make it possible to suggest avenues of research in order to promote the materialistic interpretation of tourism based on the theoretical system developed by Henri Lefebvre in *La production de l'espace* (1974).

10.2   The Materialist Approach to Tourism in Light of Certain Contemporary Debates

10.2.1   Materialism and Tourism Research: A Missed Opportunity?

Advocating for a materialistic approach to tourism may seem paradoxical when many authors have pointed out that economic reductionism has for so long confined tourism research to blind alleys. Notwithstanding the diverse academic contexts, a review of the scientific literature on tourism supports the observation, shared by many researchers, that "the economist perspective has dominated the understanding of tourism as a research topic" (Doquet 2010). In France, this tropism for the economic dimension of tourism goes hand in hand with the belated interest of social sciences for a subject considered not very serious (Knafou et al. 1997, p. 195), "a mobility perceived as frivolous" (Gravari-Barbas and Jacquot 2012) and therefore not worthy of scientific attention apart from its economic aspects. The economic focus of the first scientific studies on tourism could also be seen as an effect of the historical context in which tourism studies developed. Bertrand Réau and Franck

Poupeau observed that, when tourism research began in the 1960s, "research that makes tourism its main object of study is done in the context of land use planning and contractual research in full expansion" (2007, p. 6). The authors describe an "interdependence between researchers and the tourism sector: public institutions transpose methods and analysis frameworks from the private sector; tourism professionals are inspired, in return, by the analyses proposed by academics" (*ibid.* p. 9). This definitely has an effect on the approaches and issues developed around tourism. Tourism research consisted mainly in designing typologies of tourist resorts, measuring flows, counting tourists and their spending (*ibid.* p. 6). The tourists themselves were largely excluded from the analysis or seen "under the globalizing angle of demand" (Ceriani-Sebregondi et al. 2008), the dominant approach being mostly limited to "understanding tourism from the perspective of businesses and the merchant sector" (*ibid.*).

These contextual elements shed light on the economic bias that has long prevailed in the scientific study of tourism. The economic focus in question here, however, actually reflects an alignment with the concerns of professionals in the sector rather than a real theoretical or epistemological positioning based on "materialistic" assumptions justifying the focus on the economic aspects of tourism. And for good reason, for though the theoretical orientations most likely to adopt such an approach, particularly within the Marxist tradition, experienced a strong revival within the social sciences during the 1960s and 1970s, Marxist-inspired researchers were generally reluctant to spend time studying tourism. As the geographer Daniel Hiernaux points out, "the critical currents of Marxism – triumphant in the 1960s – continually repudiated and neglected tourism in favour of the preferred themes of the social sciences" (2008, p. 177).[2] In anthropology, Jean Michaud made a similar observation, stating that "the analysts aligned with Marx did not recognize tourism as an activity deserving any special attention" (2001, p. 24).[3] When Marxist-inspired researchers finally took an interest in tourism in the 1970s, their point of view was generally limited to denouncing tourism and pointing out its harmful social and environmental effects. At the opposite end of the scientific and political discourse promoting tourism as a factor for economic development, the proponents of this approach adopted a critical vision centred on the problem of the "impact" of tourism, which geographer Georges Cazes helped develop in the French context. This approach was particularly prevalent in the studies on developing countries, where international tourism was growing rapidly during that period (Britton 1982, 1991). While not always explicitly claimed as a conceptual framework, Marxist analysis often appears in the background as an ideological marker for militant researchers close to Third World movements (Sacareau et al. 2015, p. 17). Certain conceptual tools of structuralism and Marxism, such as the dependency and unequal exchange theories, were nevertheless used "to question tourism as a form of the asymmetrical relationship between Centre and Periphery" (Michaud, *op.cit.* p. 25). The attention paid to social

---

[2] Personal translation.

[3] For a similar finding in the English-speaking context, see Gibson (2009).

inequalities and domination was mainly focused on North/South relations, between the "wealthy societies of developed countries" (Cazes 1992, p. 5) and those of developing countries transformed into "pleasure peripheries" (Turner and Ash 1975).

Despite its influence, the impact theory soon revealed its shortcomings. In addition to sometimes involving caricatural visions of tourism, wherein the most radical followers of impact theory went so far as to consider tourism as a "perverse development" (Michaud 2001, p. 16), this approach tends to confine tourism studies to "the traditional dichotomy between positive and negative effects" whose limits Georges Cazes pointed out in the early 1990s, already indicating the need for epistemological renewal (Cazes 1992, p. 5). This paradigm dominant during the 1970s and 1980s was gradually undermined by criticism from different fields of the social sciences. The shortcomings most commonly alluded to include its tendency to view tourism as a reality external to the societies in which it develops and on which it has a positive or negative impact, at the risk of presenting tourist societies as passive in the face of an exogenous phenomenon. It is true that, by looking at tourism through a macrosociological lens, impact theories often failed to take into account the internal dynamics of tourist societies and local social relations and interactions. These shortcomings, as well as a number of "slippery" theorizations of tourism's economic dimensions, (Gibson 2009, p. 528), undoubtedly contributed to what Jean Michaud perceived as "an erosion of the analysis of host societies in their response to tourism from the very field of tourism research" in the period that followed (2001, p. 23). This erosion promoted a fundamental questioning of the scientific approach to tourism in an intellectual context marked by the influence of the "cultural turn".

10.2.2 New Approaches Thanks to the Cultural Turn

The 1990s and 2000s marked a turning point for tourism research. While the term "epistemological turn" (Roux 2009, p. 595) was sometimes used in the French context to describe this change, an evolution was also noted in the English-speaking world where several authors went so far as to refer to a "critical turn" in tourism studies (Ateljevic et al. 2007). Although it is not always possible to identify a specific turning point, John Urry's *The Tourist Gaze* seems to be a paradigm shift in the way social sciences viewed tourism. Faced with what he considered a "productivist bias" in previous tourism research (Urry 1990), the British sociologist opted for a radical change of perspective by making the "tourist gaze" a focus of the analysis, transposing a number of Michel Foucault's insights to the study of tourism. Inspired by the Foucauldian thinking on the relationship between power and knowledge, Urry emphasized the importance of discourses and perceptions, especially visual ones, in the functioning of power systems in tourist situations. The focus of the analysis shifted from the material aspects of tourism to its subjective and discursive dimensions, as the author sought to portray the complex workings of the tourism experience and the different forms of power exercised through it. Tourist discourses and representations have now been closely examined, and questions are being asked about the actors that produce them. Who are they? What are their goals? How do these representations, incorporated by tourists, participate in the different power systems?

The shift was carried out at several levels, the first and most obvious of which consisted in making tourists and their representations a focal point of tourism analysis. In this respect, sociologist Dean MacCannell went so far as to consider *The Tourist Gaze* the first serious account of the tourist subject, or subjectivity, in a field of research hitherto exclusively centred on production issues (2001, p. 24). More generally, this shift seems to correspond to a collective realization of the importance of issues long neglected by tourism research. In France, several important papers contributed to this change of approach and confirmed the predominant place now given to tourist practices and representations, to which the sociologist Rachid Amirou (1995) devoted a notable study. In geography, this evolution was embodied by the work of the Mobilité, Itinéraires, Territoires (MIT) team, led by Rémy Knafou, whose members helped develop a geographical approach to tourism by refocusing on tourism practices (Knafou et al. 1997; Ceriani-Sebregondi et al. 2008). Beyond the internal dynamics of the field, the evolution of tourism studies since the 1990s is part of a more global movement within the social sciences marked by the "return of the subject" (Réau and Poupeau 2007, p. 6) and by the cultural turn, which several authors explicitly cite as an influence (Urry, cited by Franklin 2001, p. 117; Sacareau et al. 2015).

10.2.3   New Interpretations of Power

The second theoretical shift has to do with the way in which tourism research now addresses power issues. Unlike the structural Marxist approaches in which forms of social domination were sometimes analysed using reductionist oppositions, contemporary studies provide a more flexible vision of power relations by pointing out their ambivalent and unstable nature in the context of tourist interactions. Again, the view taken by John Urry in *The Tourist Gaze* foreshadowed the paradigm shift that was coming. If power relations are now understood in their discursive dimension and no longer just from the economic angle, it is also a matter of breaking with the totalizing conceptions of power that have long dominated tourism research, like the divide between "hosts" and "guests" present in much of the scientific literature. Faced with the risk of essentialization and disregard of the agency of host communities, research in this perspective seeks to deconstruct the conceptual categories in play. This process involves reflection on how power is exercised over the tourists themselves, helping to discipline their bodies and shape their gaze. In other cases, the reflection is based on the microsociological analysis of the relations between the tourist and the host society, considered more capable of describing the complexity of tourist interactions. In the French literature, Sébastien Roux's (2011) paper on sex tourism in Thailand is emblematic in this respect, in that, in contrast to representations equating tourist prostitution to a form of exploitation based on class, race or gender, the author points out the ambiguity of the power relations and the room for manoeuvre available to the various actors involved in prostitution transactions. While this interpretation of power is sometimes clearly invoked (Simoni 2008), it is present more implicitly, and to varying degrees, in a growing body of current research, particularly in the English-speaking world. Although a systematic review of the theoretical references remains to be done, several authors point out the influence of post-structuralist theories in contemporary tourism studies (McGuckin 2005; Bianchi 2009). Bertrand Réau's examination of the most commonly cited theoretical references in the journal *Annals of Tourism Research* confirms that theoretical models from the social sciences are unequally cited in tourism studies. The prevalence of references to Erwing Goffman and Michel Foucault, or to authors influenced by them, contrasts, for example, with the almost total absence of other important figures in the social sciences (Réau 2015).

10.2.4 New Focal Points, New Blind Spots

Although this observation must be examined in the light of the various scientific contexts, it appears that the focus of tourism studies has undergone several major shifts in the last three decades or so. Broadly speaking, these developments shifted tourism studies away from a focus on receiving societies to a focus on tourists, from the economic dimensions of tourism to its cultural aspects, and from a macrosocial perspective to an approach more attentive to individuals and to the relationships between the actors. These theoretical shifts have undeniably enriched the analysis of tourism. However, criticism of earlier interpretations sometimes seems to have led to new blind spots and omissions that are also detrimental to understanding tourism. While the most visible advances at the conceptual level concern the study of tourism practices, new theoretical models are less evident in research on receiving societies. Despite attempts to decompartmentalize the study of tourism and to merge the analysis of tourism production and consumption, it seems that there has been a split between research fields that are "partially superimposed" (Michaud 2001, p. 27), but nevertheless distinct in terms of issues and conceptual tools. In this situation, some tourism researchers have attempted "to bring the theoretical framework of the anthropological sociological study of tourism back to what is most original about it: the tourist" (*ibid.* p. 23). In some cases, the productivist bias that long marked tourism research has given way to another form of radicalism, namely the predominance given to the cultural aspects of tourism. To the extent that choosing one theory also means ignoring others, it is true that "a focus on consumption means that other things are ignored and a different kind of partial truth emerges that creates the same single-minded blindness as did the putative predecessors who allegedly ignored consumption in favour of the work world of production" (McGuckin 2005, p. 68).

A similar observation could be made with regard to the approach to power relations inherent in tourism. Although challenging certain reductionist theories in the structural Marxist interpretation of tourism made it possible to add layers of complexity to the analysis, this approach sometimes turned the theoretical perspective too far in the opposite direction. As David Dumoulin and Magali Demanget point out in the introduction to a thematic issue of *Cahiers des Amériques latines* on the relationship between tourism and local societies, tourism research runs the risk of "shifting from the archetype of passivity leading to cultural destruction, to total resistance and total strategy, hence ignoring the unequal structural constraints" (2010, p. 17). Although the macrosociological vision of tourism tended to ignore the individual and the relationships between the actors, research marked by the influence of the cultural turn, on the contrary, tends to ignore the role of structures and instead focuses on microsociological logics, or even on "microscopic elements" (Hiernaux 2008, p. 183) of tourism. This trend has been described by Raoul Bianchi based on recent developments in the field in the English-speaking context:

> The preoccupation with the discursive, symbolic and cultural realms of tourism has for the most part been undertaken at the expense of any sustained analysis of the structures of relations of power associated with globalization and neo-liberal capitalism. In turn, the political orientation of the "critical turn" appears largely confined to questions of culture, discourses and representation within the confines of a globalizing free market system, which remains largely external to critical scrutiny (…). Power is thus envisaged as contingent, and permeates the "micro-practices" of everyday life. (…) tourist can often become the "target of power" themselves. (…) The point is not that such "micro-practices" (…) are insignificant, but that they often appear to be decoupled from the workings of capitalist economics and wider configurations of institutional power. (Bianchi 2009, p. 491)

One of the current challenges in tourism research could therefore be to provide a materialistic interpretation of tourism by developing theoretical tools that can shed light on the forms of social domination inherent in tourism, while avoiding the reductionism that has long marked critical approaches to tourism. This is the focus of the second part of the chapter. This reflection emerged in the framework of an empirical research that was conducted in the Mexican context, and will be based on the conceptual contribution of Henri Lefebvre to the analysis of the spatial dimension of tourism.

10.3   For a Revival of the Materialistic Approach to Tourism. What Theoretical Perspectives?

10.3.1   Questioning the Spatial Dimension of Tourism Based on Conflicts

Among the many avenues that the materialistic approach to tourism can take, we will describe the one used for a Phd thesis on conflicts related to the development of tourism in several Mexican regions (Marie dit Chirot 2014). More specifically, the approach is based on the analysis of tourist processes marked by intense struggles for space, in terms of local resistance to a tourist resort project, land tensions related to tourist urbanization (Marie dit Chirot 2015), and the emergence of tourist dynamics in the state of Chiapas, a region already plagued by social and political conflict (Marie dit Chirot 2011). The research aimed to examine the increase in these local conflicts in a society characterized by the prevalence of tourism,[4] but also by severe social inequalities and violent social relations. This stance is aligned with a social geography approach and considers conflict analysis as a preferred entry point for the study of social and spatial dynamics.

Faced with the recurring conflicts, it was quickly necessary to obtain the theoretical tools needed to grasp, beyond the singularities specific to each of the processes studied, the relations between tourist development and conflicts for space. In each case, the introduction of tourism was accompanied by an increase in tensions over the control of space, producing new conflicts or reactivating older divisions between local actors or social groups (Marie dit Chirot 2015). Land issues often play a major role in triggering the conflicts. This dimension illustrates the central place of land in social relations in Mexico, where agrarian reform in the twentieth century introduced specific forms of land ownership. However, the land dimension of conflicts rarely accounts for the complexity of the processes analysed. Though legal ownership of land is involved in the construction of groups, it operates in the same way as other political or ideological factors. Moreover, the tensions observed do not concern just the appropriation of the physical space, but more broadly involve access to the material and symbolic profits generated by tourism in the locations under dispute. This issue is particularly present in Chiapas, where some of the most violent conflicts do not concern land ownership, but the control of access points to tourist sites.

One of the theoretical aims of the research was therefore to examine the social contradictions that emerged in the different study areas during tourism development. This approach is similar to the "pragmatist materialism" advocated by the geographer Irene Pereira, for whom the role and contours of social structures are never given *a priori*, but must be systematically constructed from empirical observations (2015, p. 112). The analysis reveals regularities in the configurations studied. While many divisions often coexist, they are not all equally important in the overall functioning of local societies. Although conflicts related to work are sometimes present, the fiercest confrontations crystallize around social issues that are more directly related to space: access to housing, land tensions, control of access points to tourist locations, etc. In the various fields of investigation, these issues were often exacerbated by the development of tourism to the point where they appeared to be the main opposition structuring political and social life at the local level.

This problem calls for reflection on the way in which tourism modifies the value of places. By encouraging the emergence of new forms of centrality in previously

---

[4] Mexico is the number one tourist destination in Latin America with approximately 39 million international visitors per year, plus many more national tourists (although this is difficult to quantify). Tourism is also a strategic activity for the national economy and ranks third after oil revenues and *remesas*, remittances sent home by Mexican emigrants.

undervalued areas, tourism increases competition among actors and social groups for control of the places where the activity is concentrated. This concurs with the findings of the researchers of the MIT team, according to whom "the history of tourism in the world is largely a question of how to give value to places that had little or no value (…). Tourists change sand, snow, ruins and beet fields into gold" (Team MIT 2002, pp. 249–250). However, despite the many examples, this aspect does not seem to be the subject of in-depth theoretical reflection within tourism studies, unlike other fields of research where the question of conflicts occupies a more central place.[5] Given the scarcity of conceptual tools developed from tourism research, the conflicts observed during the investigation were examined based on a theoretical corpus *a priori* external to tourism research and dealing more broadly with the spatial dimension of social relations. Among the extensive theoretical output on the role of space in the dynamics of societies, reflection on tourist conflicts finds a special resonance in the Marxist philosopher Henri Lefebvre's seminal work, *The Production of Space* (1991 [1974]).

10.3.2   The Tourist Space and Its Contradictions: The Theoretical Contribution of Henri Lefebvre

One of the fundamental theories developed by Henri Lefebvre in *The Production of Space* consisted in reintroducing space into the Marxian tradition. This approach contrasted with the orthodox conceptions of historical materialism, which ignored space when analysing social relations in capitalist societies. Though the spatial dimension was present in Marx's work, in particular in the third volume of *Capital* through the theory of ground rent, it gradually disappeared from analysis in favour of the capital-labour opposition, considered by many Marxists as the main antagonism structuring capitalist society. Lefebvre advocated a return to the "trinity formula" initially proposed by Marx: "There were *three*, not *two*, elements in the capitalist mode of production. (…) Earth (…) capital (…), and labour (…) – three factors whose interrelationships still needed to be identified and clearly set forth." (1991 [1974], p. 325). This introduces a new complexity into the analysis of capitalist societies. Social dynamics are no longer played out solely around a central antagonism, however important it may be, but through a tangle of social contradictions whose intensity and articulation vary according to historical and societal contexts. The theoretical system developed by Lefebvre also makes it possible to differentiate social relationships in terms of their relationship with space. The philosopher thus distinguishes contradictions *in* space, i.e. the social relations for which space serves as a framework or support, from contradictions *of* space, antagonisms for which

---

[5] One example of this is in urban studies, where the study of conflicts has for many years given rise to a great deal of theoretical work, particularly on the question of the "right to the city" and "urban social movements".

space is the direct issue, foremost of which are contradictions related to land ownership. The contradictory nature of space lies in its finite aspect, in its status as a
limited and non-reproducible resource. Contradictions *of* space are particularly
strong when it becomes a scarce resource:

> Those commodities which were formerly abundant (…), which had no value (…) have now
> become rare, and so acquired value. (…) Consequently they come to have not only a use
> value but also an exchange value. (…) Natural space, at least under certain socio-economic
> conditions, becomes a scarce commodity. Inversely, scarcity becomes spatial – and local.
> Everything thus affected by scarcity has a close relationship with the Earth: the resources of
> the land, those beneath the earth (…) and those above it (…). (Lefebvre 1991 [1974], p. 329)

Beyond the question of land ownership, the concept of "contradictory space" developed by Lefebvre thus covers all the social contradictions that emerge when social
groups oppose each other for the material or symbolic appropriation of a portion of
space. Behind these contradictions, Lefebvre identifies a series of structuring oppositions: oppositions between abundance and scarcity of space, use value and
exchange value, periphery and centre, appropriation and property (Fig. 10.1).

Although tourism is not the main focus of his theoretical work, it is significant
that this part of Henri Lefebvre's work is marked by references to tourism, as when
the author states that "the space of leisure is the very epitome of contradictory
space". This theoretical intuition must be taken seriously by tourism research and
may well shed light on a large number of local struggles for the appropriation of
space in tourist locations. Basically, isn't the scarcity of space the very foundation
of any process of tourism development? The local space must be rare, or at least
singular, enough to arouse the interest of tourists. Displaying the real or supposed
features of a place becomes a way to woo the tourist desire and imaginary in a context of strong competition across regions and territories. Isn't the purpose of the
different forms of tourism labelling and certification, such as the World Heritage of
Humanity awarded by UNESCO, to generate scarcity and value for a strictly limited
space? The ideal dimension of the relationship with the tourist space intersects here
with its most material dimension when the forms of scarcity influencing representations are reproduced at the level of the physical space in which the tourist practices
and representations occur.

Fig. 10.1 The
contradictions of space
according to the theoretical
model developed by
H. Lefebvre. (Created by:
C. Marie dit Chirot 2014)

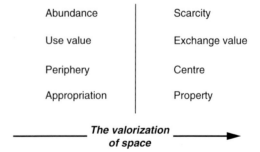

Abundance	Scarcity
Use value	Exchange value
Periphery	Centre
Appropriation	Property

The valorization of space ⟶

10.3.3   Towards a Political Economy of Tourist Space

Henri Lefebvre's theoretical contribution thus opens a certain number of perspectives likely to revive the critical, or even radical, approach to tourism. This approach involves developing an interpretation framework that focuses on the spatial dimension of inequalities and social power relations. This type of project could help develop of a totalizing approach to tourism that examines the way localized conflicts correlate to the structural contradictions of capitalism. In other words, the approach involves returning to historical materialism rather than abandoning it, and developing theoretical alternatives to the reductionist models contained in the structural Marxist approaches that have long dominated the geographical study of tourism. A first step could consist in investigating the localized conflicts about space in many tourist locations, by asking questions such as: are the conflicts encountered in tourist societies specific in any way? Does tourism exacerbate all social contradictions equally or some more than others? The study of tourism thus contributes to a more global understanding of inequalities and conflicts in contemporary societies and of the recompositions of capitalism, a major effect of tourism development worldwide. These changes involve the role of space in the dynamics of social relations, since, as Henri Lefebvre suggested, "the new shortages are not comparable to the scarcities of earlier times, for the notable reason that the relationship to space has changed" (1991, p. 330). According to this hypothesis formulated almost four decades before the subprime crisis, the economic transformations brought about in part by the development of the leisure sector – and more generally worldwide urbanization – are generating a renewed focus on the social question of contradictions that became less important with the development of industrial capitalism:

> Real property is no longer a secondary form of circulation, no longer the auxiliary and backward branch of industrial and financial capitalism that it once was. Instead it has a leading role (…). Capitalism has taken possession of the land and *mobilized* it to the point where this sector is fast becoming *central*. (…) Capital has thus rushed into the production of space in preference to the classical forms of production. (…) The mobilization of space becomes frenetic (p. 335–336).

This statement is similar to David Harvey's concept of "accumulation by dispossession" whose consequences are evident in many tourist spaces and characterize the new forms of rentier capitalism in the neoliberal era (Harvey 2010). Although the labour question remains undeniably central in the domination processes within the tourism economy, the class relations inherent in a tourist city are perhaps not strictly identical to those observed within an industrial city, which brings up questions about the recent increase in conflicts like those caused by the arrival of *Airbnb* in a growing number of urban spaces. Even though it was only until recently that gentrification studies have started to pay attention to tourism (Gravari-Barbas and Guinand 2017; Cocola-Gant 2018; Yrigoy 2019; Morell 2019), recent researches have shown that tourism development is now one of the most powerful driving forces of the phenomenon at the global level. As suggested by several authors, the rise of holiday rental websites and the emergence of a "platform capitalism" might represent the beginning of a new cycle in the gentrification process, reinforcing the necessity to actualize the conceptual frameworks that are commonly used to analyze gentrification in the light of tourism new dynamics (Aalbers 2019). Such a transformation invite us to revisit more specifically Neil Smith's rent gap theory (1979; 1987) as the potential profits allowed by holiday rentals – a far cry from those provided by other economic activities – lead to a drastic shortage of housing supply in many touristified urban spaces (Mermet 2017; Morell 2019), producing "a form of collective displacement never seen in classical gentrification, that is to say, to a substitution of residential life by tourism" (Cocola-Gant 2016). This phenomenon is not limited to Global North cities and is of special importance in southern societies where the weaker presence of urban middle-class tends to limit its contribution to gentrification and emphasize, at the same time, the tourists role as gentrifying elites. This example, just as much as the different kinds of land grabbing processes observed in rural regions where tourism development calls into question the presence of traditional agricultural activities, illustrates how a materialistic approach can provide a better understanding of the spatial dimension of tourism. The theoretical tools bequeathed by Henri Lefebvre will probably be valuable in laying the foundations of a "political economy of space" (Lefebvre 1991) and, more specifically, of tourist space.

References

Aalbers, M. B. (2019). Introduction to the forum: From third to fifth-wave gentrification. *Tijdschrift voor Economische en Sociale Geografie, 110*(1), 1–11.

Amirou, R. (1995). *Imaginaire touristique et sociabilités du voyage* (281 p). Paris: PUF.

Ateljevic, I., Pritchard, A., & Morgan, N. (2007). *The critical turn in tourism studies. Innovative research methodologies* (428 p). Oxford: Elsevier.

Bianchi, R. (2009). The "critical turn" in tourism studies: A radical critique. *Tourism Geographies, 11*(4), 484–504.

Britton, S. (1982). The political economy of tourism in the third world. *Annals of Tourism Research, 9*(3), 331–358.

Britton, S. (1991). Tourism, capital and place: Towards a critical geography of tourism. *Environment and Planning: Society and Space, 9*(4), 451–478.

Cazes, G. (1992). *Tourisme et tiers-monde, un bilan controversé* (Vol. 207). Paris: L'Harmattan.

Ceriani-Sebregondi, G., Chapuis, A., Gay, J.-C., Knafou, R., Stock, M., & Violier, P. (2008). Quel serait l'objet d'une "science du tourisme" ? *Téoros, 27*(1), en ligne. https://teoros.revues.org/1629.

Clerval, A., Fleury, A., Rebotier, J., & Weber, S. (2015). *Espace et rapports de domination* (400 p). Rennes: P.U.R..

Cocola-Gant, A. (2016). Holiday rentals: The new gentrification battlefront. *Sociological Research Online, 21*(3).

Cocola-Gant, A. (2018). Tourism gentrification. In Lees & Phillips (Eds.), *Handbook in gentrification studies* (pp. 281–293). Cheltenham/Northampton: Edward Elgar Publishing.

Cousin, S. (2010). L'enquête à l'épreuve du tourisme. *Espacestemps.net* (online). http://www.espacestemps.net/articles/le-tourisme-a-epreuve-de-enquete/.

Demanget, M., & Dumoulin, D. (2010). Introduction au dossier thématique « Tourisme patrimonial et sociétés locales en Amérique latine ». *Cahiers des Amériques latines, 65*, 19–25.

Doquet, A. (2010). "La force de l'impact. Paradigme théorique et réalités de terrain", *EspacesTemps.net* (online) https://www.espacestemps.net/articles/force-impact/.

Franklin, A. (2001). The tourist gaze and beyond: An interview with John Urry. *Tourist Studies, 1*(2), 115–131.

Gibson, C. (2009). Geographies of tourism: Critical research on capitalism and local livelihoods. *Progress in Human Geography, 33*(4), 527–534.

Gravari-Barbas, M., & Guinand, S. (2017). *Tourism and gentrifiaction in contemporary metropolises.* New York: Routledge.

Gravari-Barbas, M., & Jacquot, S. (2012). Les géographes et les métiers du tourisme. *Echogéo, 19*, en ligne.

Harvey, D. (2010). *Le nouvel impérialisme* (204 p). Paris: Les prairies ordinaires.

Hiernaux, D. (2008). El giro cultural y las nuevas interpretaciones geográficas del turismo. *Espaço e Tempo, 23*, 177–187.

Jackson, P. (2000). Rematerializing social and cultural geography. *Social & Cultural Geography, 1*(1), 9–14.

Knafou, R., Bruston, M., Deprest, F., Duhamel, P., Gay, J.-C., & Sacareau, I. (1997). Une approche géographique du tourisme. *L'espace géographique, 26*(3), 193–204.

Lefebvre, H. (1991) [1974]. *The production of space* (454 p). Oxford: Blackwell.

Maccannell, D. (2001). Tourist agency. *Tourist Studies, I*(1), 23–37.

Marie dit Chirot, C. (2011). De la confrontation sociale à l'attrait touristique, et réciproquement. Genèse et enjeux du tourisme politique dans l'État du Chiapas. *Espacestemps.net*, mis en ligne le 24 octobre 2011.

Marie dit Chirot, C. (2014). *Pour un morceau de terre. Enjeux sociaux et politique de la valorization touristique de l'espace au Mexique* (357 p). Phd thesis, Université de Caen-Normandie.

Marie dit Chirot, C. (2015). Relaciones de propiedad y conflictos por la apropiación del espacio turístico. Análisis comparativo entre Huatulco (Oaxaca) y Playa del Carmen (Quintana Roo) en México. In G. Marín Guardado (Ed.), *Sin tierras no hay paraiso.Turismo, organizaciones agrarias y apropiación territorial en México* (pp. 251–273). El Sauzal (Islas Canarias): PASOS Edita.

Mcguckin, E. (2005). Travelling paradigms: Marxism, poststructuralism and the uses of theory. *Anthropologica, 47*(1), 67–79.

Mermet, A.-C. (2017). Airbnb and tourism gentrification. Critical insights from the exploratory analysis of the "Airbnb syndrome" in Reykjavik. In M. Gravari-Barbas & S. Guinand (Eds.), *Tourism and gentrifiaction in contemporary metropolises* (pp. 52–74). New York: Routledge.

Michaud, J. (2001). Anthropologie, tourisme et sociétés locales au fil des textes. *Anthropologie et sociétés, 25*(2), 15–33.

Milne, S., & Ateljevic, I. (2001). Tourism, economic development and the global-local nexus: Theory embracing complexity. *Tourism Geographies, 4*(3), 369–393.

MIT (Équipe). (2002). *Tourisme I. Lieux communs* (319 p). Paris: Belin.

Morell, M. (2019). Turismo y diferencial de renta: no hay vacaciones para la lucha de clase. In Cañada & Murray (Eds.), *Turistificacion global. Perspectivas criticas en turismo* (pp. 309–323). Barcelona: Icaria.

Pereira, I. (2015). La structuration de l'espace par les rapports sociaux. In A. Clerval, A. Fleury, J. Rebotier, & S. Weber (Eds.), *Espace et rapports de domination* (pp. 111–120). Rennes: P.U.R.

Reau, B. (2015). Les "Tourism Studies": Excursions épistémologiques ou séjours interdisciplinaires? *Espacestemps.net*, en ligne. http://www.espacestemps.net/articles/les-tourism-studies/

Réau, B., & Poupeau, F. (2007), "L'enchantement du monde touristique", Actes de la recherche en sciences sociales, n°170, pp.4–13.

Roux, S. (2009). De quelques dynamiques contemporaines en anthropologie du tourisme francophone. *Cahiers d'études africaines, 193–194*, 595–602.

Roux, S. (2011). *No money, no honey. Économies intimes du tourisme sexuel en Thaïlande* (276 p). Paris: La Découverte.

Sacareau, I., Taunay, B., & Peyvel, E. (2015). La mondialisation du tourisme. In *Les nouvelles frontières d'une pratique* (266 p). Rennes: P.U.R.

Simoni, V. (2008). Shifting power. The (de) stabilization of asymmetries in the realm of tourism in Cuba. *Tsansta: Review of the Swiss Anthropological Society, 13*(2008), 11–19.

Smith, N. (1979). Toward a theory of gentrification: A back to the city movement by capital, not people. *Journal of the American Planning Association, 45*(4), 538–548.

Smith, N. (1987). Gentrification and the rent gap. *Annals of the Association of American Geographers, 77*(3), 462–465.

Turner, L., & Ash, J. (1975). *The golden hordes: International tourism and the pleasure periphery* (319 p). Londres: Constable & Co.

Urry, J. (1990). *The tourist gaze* (p. 183). Londres: Sage.

Yrigoy, I. (2019). Rent gap reloaded: Airbnb and the shift from residential to touristic rental housing in the Palma Old Quarter in Mallorca, Spain. *Urban Studies, 56*(13), 2709–2726.

Clément Marie dit Chirot is a social geographer at the faculty of Tourism & Culture (ESTHUA) with University of Angers (France) and member of the laboratory *Espaces et Sociétés* (UMR CNRS 6590). His work explores the political economy of tourism and its spatial dimension in Mexico, especially through the analysis of urban dynamics, public policies and land property issues. He is also a member of the editorial team of the Mexican scientific journal *Analéctica*.

Chapter 11
Tourism as Urban Phenomenon and the Crux of "Urban Tourism"

Vincent Coëffé and Mathis Stock

11.1 Introduction

This significance of tourism for the contemporary urban world is mainly approached under the heading of "urban tourism", more recently as "new urban tourism" (Novy 2010; Füller and Michel 2014). "Urban tourism" is indeed a term widely used in order to designate the practice of tourism in cities, with contributions and textbooks describing and explaining the phenomenon since at least the 1980's (Law 1994). Yet, it is not unproblematic to speak of "urban tourism", because – as in "rural tourism" or "mountain tourism" – it implies a specific form of tourism based on the geographical framing as specific milieus. As Ashworth and Page (2011, 2) state, "adding the adjective urban to the noun tourism locates an activity in a spatial context but does not in itself define or delimit that activity". In the case of urban tourism, it seems even more problematic since tourism is genuinely an urban activity because the involved actors are urbanites. Apart from the localising attribute in cities, could there be a "non-urban" tourism? In fact, we could read the history of tourism as urban history as well as central element of the ongoing "planetary urbanisation" (Lefebvre 2003). Since the beginning of the nineteenth century, tourists were leaving their urban residential places to learn urban culture across Europe, especially in Italy. They also have been imposing their urban worldview on landscape, nature, culture, leading to the emergence of national parks and seaside and mountain resorts. Tourism has been transforming formerly rural places into urban places,

V. Coëffé (✉)
UMR 6590 CNRS ESO-Angers, University of Angers, Angers, France
e-mail: vincent.coeffe@univ-angers.fr

M. Stock
Institute of Geography and Sustainability, University of Lausanne, Lausanne, Switzerland
e-mail: mathis.stock@unil.ch

where norms are based on urban civility, and the geographical imagination informed by urban imaginations of nature, authenticity, play.[1]

These questions are crucial because of tourism as incompressible element of the contemporary urban condition and urban processes (Stock 2019). Tourism does not only occur in cities, but has triggered urbanisation processes since its beginnings in the early nineteenth century, which have led to a specific territorial form that cannot be subsumed under the concept of "city" (Stock and Lucas 2012). Indeed, tourist resorts as specific kinds of urban places have been developing, where architectural, behavioural, economic and cultural elements of the urban can be recognized. Places like seaside or mountain resorts (we can think of Aspen, Zermatt, Deauville) develop a specific degree of "urbanness" or "urbanity" where a lack of regional centrality and density is combined with monumental architecture, presence of very diverse metropolitan (temporary) inhabitants and metropolitan-like services, and a price structure of urban rent comparable to metropolises (Equipe MIT 2002).

Yet, urban theory is commonly being understood as an interpretive framework constructed in order to gather the general features of cities (Scott and Storper 2014). As an ever-changing process of developing an ever more adequate formal language on the phenomenon of urbanisation and city-formation, urban theory supposes a different problem for tourism as a cultural practice. Yet, if regarded only as theory on the specific territorial form of cities, urban theory fails to adapt to the multiple processes of urbanisation, which also produce urban places of a different quality (Brenner and Schmid 2014). This is especially true for the multiple urbanisation processes triggered through tourism, e.g. resorts, spots, tourist agglomerations, etc.

This chapter aims at questioning the complex ways tourism and the urban are linked, and the ways urban theory respond to it. By mobilising Lefebvre's (2003) notion of the "urban", the link between several territorial forms, not only cities, comes into focus and the question of "urban tourism" could be expanded from the specific problem of the city towards more general urbanisation processes. Indeed, the notion of "transfer of urbanity" from the metropolises and cities to the resorts (Stock and Lucas 2012), but also other tourist places such as national parks or surf spots. This is consistent with Lefebvre's (2001) urban theory, where the urban revolution of the industrial city redistributes urbanity on other scales: "The leisure industry is coupled with the construction industry in order to extend cities and urbanisation to the seaside and the mountain areas" (Lefebvre 2001, p.152, authors' translation).[2]

---

[1] A congress on "Urban Worlds of Tourism" (*Les mondes urbains du tourisme*), held in January 13th–14th 2005 in Paris, showed the difficulty to bring together specialists of the urban who still consider tourism as too frivolous a dimension of the city, and therefore for scientific investigation, and the specialists of tourism, who consider the urban dimension only through "urban tourism", as if there was a "non-urban tourism". See Duhamel Ph., Knafou R. (2007b) for the publication of the main papers.

[2] « L'industrie des loisirs se conjugue avec celle de la construction pour **prolonger les villes** et l'urbanisation **le long des côtes et dans les régions montagneuses** » (Lefebvre 2001, p.152) ».

First, the pervasiveness of tourism in the contemporary urban world is a problem for urban studies. Contemporary urban places – be it cities, metropolises, city-regions or resorts – are today co-constituted by the presence of tourists. There is virtually no place left without the presence of touristic imaginations, practices, humans. It fosters a new quality of the urban through a reconfiguration of the economic, the political, the social as well as the symbolic dimensions and more or less controlled spatial rearrangement (such as urbanism). It also raises the question of the "right to the city" and the "right to centrality" (Lefebvre 1968) because tourists are temporary *inhabitants* of the contemporary cities and resorts. They develop specific absence/presence patterns and develop a mode of dwelling based on recreation; which precisely leads to the emergence of a new urban quality.

Moreover, urbanization processes are tourism-driven since its inception in the beginning of the nineteenth century and do not lead exclusively to the territorial form "city", but to spots, resorts, sites, enclaves etc. We can interpret the major part of the urbanization of mountains and seaside throughout the last 200 years as tourism-driven, for example in Florida, the European Alps, the Mediterranean Sea, but also the South-East of England, the Atlantic Coast and the Pacific Islands and Thai, Bali etc. From the sole perspective of the built environment, there has been a huge change through the transformation from non-built to built space (Soane 1993); but also through the growth of services, labour markets and diversity of residents, the quality of places have been transformed from rural and fishing places into urban places (even already urbanised places such as cities have been transformed – due partially to the deindustrialization – from manufacturing cities into tourist cities, which also changed their urban quality).

Within this chapter, tourism is defined as a system of places, actors and practices maintained in order to allow people for inhabiting *places of otherness* for the purpose of recreation (Knafou and Stock 2003). Tourism is here relatively narrowly delineated as evolving in a sphere defined by mobility (dis-placement) and recreation of individual actors, and is therefore different from other definitions, where "visitors" are addressed for multiple purposes such as conferences, business, pilgrimage and so on. For example, congresses, although an important structuring element of cities or other forms of temporary presence of "inhabitants" in the present mobility age, are excluded here. This is not to say that those elements are not significant in the contemporary urban economies based on mobility and co-presence.[3] Nor it is to say that there can be maintained a strict delimitation between tourist practices and other kinds of practices carried out by mobile individuals within the context of "de-differentiation" between social spheres (Urry 1995). However, the research interest focuses here on the specific ways the "tourist gaze", i.e. the touristic relationship to the world expressed in specific practices has effects on urbanization processes.

We identify three central problems urban studies face when approaching tourism. First, tourism does not only occur *in* cities, but triggers the development of a

---

[3] See the notion of « presential economy » (Davezies 2008).

variety of urban places. When approaching tourism issues, urban studies need to focus on tourism-informed urban places. Second, tourism produces a specific urban culture, which triggers the emergence of urban places and urban issues within tourist places. Third, tourism has been seen as element of urban flight to "peripheral" non-urban places. Yet, urban civilization informs tourism and, through the transfer of urbanity, is a powerful agent of urbanization in the seperipheries.

11.2   The Urban Foundations of Tourism

The expression "urban tourism", by focussing on tourism *in* cities shadows the question of the urban dimensions *of* tourism, and the extension of urban studies to specific tourist places. In our view, the very expression "urban tourism" is more an obstacle than a solution to the adequate approach of the different linkages between the urban dimensions of tourism, and the growing touristic dimensions of urbanisation processes. Is there a theory of the urban or at least a set of concepts at hand, which would allow for the investigation of the different ways tourism co-constitutes contemporary urban places? How urban studies are to integrate tourism in its theories, not mere as an economic sector, but as a "gaze" (Urry 1990) or a specific relationship to the world which qualifies urban places in a specific way as "destination" and acknowledges specific values to urban places, which in turn has economic, political and social consequences?

The term "urbanity" offers the possibility to go beyond the historical model of the city. French urban studies rely heavily on the concept "*urbanité*" (urbanity or urbanness) in order to address the urban dimensions of places, cultures and economies. Widely used since Lefebvre (2003) as a central element of urban theory in order to describe a specific urban quality of places, it is scarcely used in English. Yet, it has become recently to attention (Lévy 2014; Brenner and Schmid 2014) within a new debate in urban studies around the adequacy of the city as founding element of the urban (Scott and Storper 2014) and a "decentering perspectives on the urban" (Schmid 2018). A "new epistemology of the urban" (Brenner and Schmid 2015) would allow to go beyond the city-centred perspective and to recognize new urban forms and urbanisation processes. Tourism is related to these alternative urbanisation processes because it can be seen as a situation, where urban cultures are produced and reproduced, but also new forms of urbanity created: significant relationship to the urban and multiple encodings, imaginaries, interpretations of the urban are in the focus. How tourist practices express this urban way of life? How those urban practices produce urban qualities of places?

First, co-presence and civility are central element of urbanity because the specific distance management between bodies is a significant urban problem (Simmel 1903), which emerges also in tourist situations. For instance, the beach raises the question of nudity because of the exposure of the nude body to the sight of others. It is a problem raised since the beginnings of tourism, as shown by Corbin (1988) for the British seaside from 1780 to 1840, by Granger (2017) for French beaches from 1925 to 1940, or by Metusela and Waitt (2012) for the beaches of Illawarra on the east coast of Australia from the early nineteenth century to the early twentieth century. The emergence of nudity on beaches can be interpreted within the theoretical framework of Elias' (1939) process of civilization as the invention of new civilities through a specific control of emotions and affects in the Western world. It implies the definition of the adequate distance between bodies and thus the regulation of the "intimate distance", which avoids the intervention in the intimacy of the individuals. This is a fundamental principle in the existence of the public space in Western societies (Lévy 1999). In other words, the nude body on the beach strengthened the "civil inattention" (Goffman 1959), invented as an urban principle in the metropolis. The practice of feminine topless, emphasizes the way to produce civility in a tourist situation: this body exposure can be accepted through western public beaches as long as the tourist gaze doesn't produce a focused attention (Kaufmann 2000). The beach, developed initially as non-urban place, as a virgin place embodying the wilderness (see below), is therefore urbanised by tourists through urban civility, and transformed into a urban place.[4]

Second, urban norms and values can be connected to tourism as specific "habitus". Rather than a "class habitus" (Bourdieu 1994) or a "national habitus" (Elias 1997), it seems to be an *urban* habitus. It is constituted of the patterns of mobility and places, where spatial competences and spatial capital are engaged. As a result, anonymity in most situations of interaction is the rule and the acceptance of the other in public space. For tourists, that means they are no outsiders in tourist places, but legitimate persons in places developed for them. This is strongly related to the question of identification with other inhabitants, the diversification of social roles and the emergence of the individual within the metropolis are the matrix of practices. Tourist practices embody those elements because of the association with a place of otherness. Managing otherness necessitates specific competences learned through a process of socialization: "learning to be a tourist" (Löfgren 1999) is a key element of urbanization. Concerning the interactions with humans for example, the "resident" is the "Other" of the tourist, but the tourist is also the "Other" of the "resident", and the tourist can be the "Other" of the other tourists within the "society of tourists". This "urbanization of consciousness" (Harvey 1985) where the differences between individuals are acknowledged and accepted, but not fought seems crucial. It differs from the insider/outsider model Elias and Scotson (1994) thought of, insofar as the tourist remains a legitimate outsider in a "other place". Those features apply to the tourist in its manifold manifestations. For instance, the resort complex, where the otherness is managed trough urban form: instead of the tourist inhabiting close to the residents, the tourist inhabits an enclave, designed for tourists. This "enclavic space" (Edensor 2000) has also as a quality to avoid tourists to be in presence of otherness such as local food, local language etc. Approached as

---

[4] See also Orvar Löfgren's (1999) account of the practice of the Scandinavian beach in the nineteenth century as an « emotional space » based on urban middle-class norms.

indispensable technology for the management of otherness (Équipe MIT 2002), it allows also for appropriation of new urban competences.

Third, imaginations of nature are crucial in tourism, and lead to an urbanization of nature, *via* the production of discourse and imaginaries bounded in urban cultures of nature. As John Muir expressed it while creating the National Parks in the U.S.: "Thousands of tired, nerve-shaken, over-civilized people are beginning to find out that going to the mountains is going home, that wildness is a necessity, and that mountain parks and reservations are useful not only as fountains of timber and irrigating rivers, but as fountains of life" (cited in Runte (1979).[5] It stresses upon an urban imagination of nature as value for civilization. Moreover, not only through the co-presence of urbanites, but also the built environment – for instance Yellowstone's museums, hotels, campsites, access roads, etc. – national parks are urbanized, even if the densities of individuals are low. From there, nowadays' ecotourism can be seen as the similar pattern of imagining specific quality of nature.

The beach as one of the most significant tourism environments can be seen as an especially interesting case of urbanization of nature. Urbain (1994) has shown that it is not a fate if the tourist practices associated with the beach are classified as "natural tourism", but rooted in the dichotomy that exists in Western societies between nature and culture. The beach is a dreamed and fantasized object by urban culture, as much as a complex of bio-physical elements *per se*. Löfgren (1999) calls the globalisation of this imagination the "global beach". Constructed as a primitive, vacant stage associated with the paradise on earth, especially if it is "tropical", the beach is actually a paradoxical object: its visible naturalness appears from a rigorous work of artificialization of the elements. It becomes an urbanized nature through a work of purification of all the objects, which "soil" it. For example, the process of "dressing" is made through the dissolution of all the miasmas (Corbin 1988). At night, a wide spectrum of pollution is cleansed accordingly: household waste, seaweeds, the most unrefined elements left by the ocean, etc., as shows a case study of the Waikiki Beach (Coëffé 2014). There is a paradoxical return towards a "natural" nature by a subtlety invented by urbanites, where nature is staged as virgin thanks to its transformation as an artefact. This "heterotopia" (Foucault 1984), i.e. a "other place" is produced as a model of an ideal nature conceived from a "tourist gaze", invented and maintained by urbanites.

To sum up, we can develop a relational view on the urban by focussing on the ways people *inhabit* urban places by developing specific relationships with identities, civilization, practices, imaginations. It plays out in tourist practices specifically, and produces urban places through the co-presence of tourists, and their application of urban cultures.

---

[5] John Muir, "The Wild Parks and Forest Reservations of the West," *Atlantic Monthly* 81 (January 1898) in *Runte*, A. (1979) *National Parks*: the *American Experience*, Lincoln: University of Nebraska Press

11.3   Tourist Places as Urban Places

The city is not the sole territorial form of urbanity anymore, as numerous contributions have shown since Lefebvre (2003). Whereas urban theories now acknowledge this thesis (see Amin and Thrift 2002), urban studies dealing with tourism insisted mostly on cities. Yet, there is an interesting point in approaching tourist places in general as urban places, allowing for a better understanding of their geographical qualities.

11.3.1   The Urbaness of Tourist Resorts

The recent contributions of Judd and Fainstein (1999), Judd (2003) and Hoffman et al. (2003) illustrate how the problem of tourists and visitors *in* cities are raised, i.e. as "places to play" (Judd and Fainstein 1999). Judd and Fainstein (1999) present a three-fold typology of tourist cities: resort cities, tourist-historic cities and converted cities. Especially the identification of "resort cities" as a category seems to bear more questions than answers. On the one hand, resorts are of the highest importance in the spatial organization of contemporary societies, but cannot be approached as cities, due to the different urban quality (centrality, mass, heterogeneity, public space, etc.). On the other hand, in Europe, many of the original resorts have been developing into cities – Cannes, Baden-Baden, Montreux are cases in point – and as such, as tourist cities, we can approach them here. An alternative taxonomy – if needed – could be one on tourist places following different forms of urbanity (see Table 11.1).

The following criteria can help us to construct a more consistent framework of tourist places (see Table 11.1). First, the presence or absence of bed spaces distinguishes the *tourist site* from tourist places with accommodation capacity. Secondly, the criterion of the presence of a permanent population permits to distinguish the

Table 11.1 The different types of tourist places

	Presence or absence of accommodation	Presence or absence of local population	Variety of urban functions
Tourist sight (*site*)	–	–	–
Tourist (*comptoir*)	+	–	–
Tourist resort (*station*)	+	+	–
Tourist city (*ville*)	+	+	+

Source: modified after Knafou et al. (1997) and Stock (2001)

"*tourist post*"[6] from *tourist resorts* and *tourist cities*. Finally, the predominance of the tourist activity *versus* the variety of urban and touristic functions distinguishes two kinds of tourist places with permanent population, the *tourist resort* from the *tourist city*.

Resorts as relatively small and non-central places are different from cities, which are multi-layered complex central places. Resorts only can develop towards cities (such as Brighton), but cease then to be resorts *stricto sensu*, because of the development of central functions. Moreover, the dynamics are underestimated: all tourist cities are converted, if not perverted – in its original sense of complete substitution of activities by tourism – or diverted cities, i.e. the inscription of tourism within the city (see Équipe MIT 2002 for the development of this idea).

In order to grasp similarities and differences between tourist places, Lefebvre's (2003) proposal of the "urban" as a distinct concept of that of the "city" could be useful. Following H. Lefevbre, the concept of urbanity permits to grasp the different modes of existent of the urban places, where cities are distinguished by a specific degree of urbanity. Indeed, the multifold linkages between the urban and the touristic have not yet been addressed with sufficient accuracy: the touristic dimensions of the urban and the urban dimensions of tourist places could be questioned in this respect: all the tourist places are without no doubt urban places, but not cities.

This leads to the idea that tourist places could be framed as urban places. The metropolis-like services and the temporary centrality of tourist places permit to sustain this idea. Moreover, the serendipity – unforeseen encounters – occurring in tourist places pleads towards a reframing of the problem. Temporary densities in resorts might be high, equalising that of cities, and generating all sorts of traditional urban problems such as congestion, sewage and waste. It is because of the seasonal peaks that those densities are important. A two-fold interrogation is to be developed: how tourism produces specific qualities of urbanity, for instance in resorts? How a "touristic urbanity" as a specific modality of the urban, very different from suburban, central and the countryside can be reconstructed?[7]

11.3.2   Towards an Analytical Framework for the Urban Dimensions of Tourist Places

Four interrelated concepts could help to analyse touristically-informed urban places: centrality, density, diversity, public space. First, the issue of centrality is defined here as "the polarization capacity of space and attractiveness of a place or an area

---

[6] The term "*comptoir*" is derived from the trading post, established by colonial organizations, such as the East India Company. It means an access-controlled area, delineated for colonial purposes with little local linkages. The "tourist post" refers to such places as holiday clubs and resort hotels since the 1950s, the European bathing establishments of the 1850s, and tourist developments such as Beaver Creek in the U.S. and Les Arcs 1800 in France.

[7] See Lévy (2014) on different degrees of urbanness or urbanity.

that gathers actors, functions and objects of society" (Dematteis 2013, 162). It high-lights the effective importance of a place within a network of places for a specific human activity. Yet, this classical notion in geography is relevant also for non-commercial and non-daily activities. Especially, global centralities have come into the focus with the process of globalisation (Sassen 2002): global centralities of London, New York, Hong Kong or Cayman Islands for the finance industry, global centrality of Bayreuth for Wagner operas, of Tehahoupoo in Tahiti for surfing, etc. can be conceived. These are rather nodes in a "space of flows" (Castells 2001) than a command function over areas. In contrast with the global cities, these "globalised localities" (Albrow 1996) in tourism are rather small, albeit globally recognized tourist places, with visitors from all over the world: Chamonix, Zermatt, Davos, St. Tropez are such places, with small population size and global recognition. Therefore the "symbolic centrality" (Monnet 2000) is an important dimension to take into account. It allows for a shift for urban studies from *global cities* to *global urban places*, because of the global centrality of specific tourist places (Stock 2017). The question is then how to differentiate the degree of centrality for different types of tourist places, and how those centralities contribute to the urbanity of places.

It is interesting to relate this symbolic centrality to the symbolic capital Harvey (2001) addresses. Harvey (2001: 405) conceives of a "collective symbolic capital which attaches to names and places like Paris, Athens, New York, Rio de Janeiro, Berlin and Rome is of great import and gives such places great economic advantages relative to, say, Baltimore, Liverpool, Essen, Lille, Glasgow. The problem for these latter places is to raise their quotient of symbolic capital and to increase their mark of distinction to better ground their claims to the uniqueness that yields monopoly rent". As the enumeration shows, the content of the symbolic element is – at least at the time of Harvey's writing – a touristic content. Identifying the touristic symbols attached to urban places allows for understanding the advantages of places within a global field. This "touristic capital" of places (Darbellay et al. 2011; see Stock et al. in Chap. 12) would help to identify the touristic qualities as recognized by different actors, be it tourists or political or economic actors.

Second, the coupling of diversity/density – a classic element of urban theory since at least Wirth (1938) – of social realities allows for the measure of concentration and heterogeneity. Since the urban is a way to manage the distance between all the dimensions of a society, by prevailing the "copresence" over mobility or tele-communication (Lévy 1999), it implies the proximity between heterogeneous both material and immaterial objects. In this context, the co-presence of tourists and residents can spread the diversity towards the cultural dimensions. Urbanity emerges then from the co-presence of different nationalities embodying different norms and values as well as from different projects of place practices of co-present individuals (tourism, leisure, work, congress, incentive, residents, etc).

Third, the quality of public space is a central element, which discriminates the different places within the urban continuum. It is defined as space, which allows anyone to circulate freely, without being considered as an intruder (Hannerz 1980; Joseph 1998; Atkinson 2003). It is essential for tourism for public space is accessible as long as it allows the "visitor", including the stranger, to circulate through, without being totally lost (Coëffé 2010). For example, signage is a big issue for the tourists who lose their familiar landmarks: this is a fundamental element allowing tourists to *take place* and revealing their mobility skills. Beyond the legal properties as accessible, public space is also a "sensitive space" (Joseph 1998), where individuals observe and are observed while anonymity is guaranteed. It leads to "civil inattention" as we say above (Goffman 1959). In other words, weak links between the city-dwellers can be analysed as a way to produce more urbanity.

These first distinctions are to be used to appreciate the different urban dimensions of tourist places. Although tourism creates mono-functional spaces, the urban quality is distinct from industrial space. Interestingly, tourism transfers the urban from the cities to vacant or rural places, thanks to one of its main principle: mobility is a way to extend the urban by its both material (accommodation, transportation, etc.) and immaterial (values, norms, etc.) networks. As Lefebvre (1968) states: "Urbanites carry the urban with them although they do not bring urbanity".[8] Although this assertion could be discussed, an analysis of the degree of urbanity of different kinds of urban places seems to be the issue. The territorial form of the city as sole element of the urban is therefore to be integrated into a model of urbanity, where the different degrees are to be recognized by the researcher. This implies to focus for instance on tourism-produced qualities of urbanity.

Tourism constitutes a genuinely urban problem, and thus, produces urban places with specific qualities. With this framework in mind, we can raise the question how touristic dimensions contribute to define urban places. The production of tourist-informed urban places is not uniform, but very differentiated. How can we construct differentiated modalities of the touristically informed urban places, different types where tourism is present?

11.4 Tourism-Induced Processes of Urbanization

The expression of "urban tourism" shadows also a processual view on tourism and the development of urban places, where processes of urbanization and de-urbanization take place. Henri Lefebvre (2003) coins the term "urbanization" in a unique way, by articulating industrial revolution and urbanization. Notably, he designed a "historical axis of urbanization", between 0% and 100% where the classical city is destroyed by industrialization, and generalized to other levels of organization. This processual concept allows for unpacking how urban connections emerge and disappear as their valuations/de-valuations, updated by the practices, the investments, the *spatial fix* of monetary capital, the imaginary and the narratives of urbanization as the urbanity increase. It means intensification and diversification of social realities, whether it concerns the framework of the people, economic

---

[8] The French original reads: "Les urbains transportent l'urbain avec eux, même s'ils n'apportent pas l'urbanité" (Lefebvre 1968, p. 120).

activities, information, presence of "things" etc. According to our definition of urbanity, we define urbanization as the intensification and complexification of urban life. Tourism practices contribute to redefine the quality of a place as urban by adding new economic activities and political rules, but also new ways of inhabiting the place through lifestyle elements such as clothing, chosen instruments, ways to move etc. As such, urbanisation through tourism contributes to the ongoing "planetary urbanisation" (Lefebvre 2003; Brenner and Schmid 2014).

How, *via* touristification and reproduction of tourism, do urbanization processes emerge? How urban places develop new urban functions and new centralities through tourism? Scientific literature already underlines the relationship between urbanization process and tourism (Mullins 1991; Gladstone 1998; Equipe MIT 2002). In order to understand these processes linking the urban and the "touristic", the expression "double urban revolution of tourism" (Stock and Lucas 2012) has been coined in order to address the transformative effects of tourism on cities and on tourist resorts since the nineteenth century. As element of the transfer of urbanity from the city to other areas, tourism contributes to the ongoing planetary urbanisation. We distinguish here three different processes of urbanization through tourism: (1) the invention of seaside and mountain resorts during the nineteenth century, (2) the increase of urbanity of already established resorts, and, (3) the touristification of city centres. They have in common the quality of the place changes with the urbanization process as inhabited places, where different place attributes are developed.

11.4.1 The Emergence of Resorts as Urbanization Process

Historically, the first tourists of the eighteenth century, associated with the British elite, were urbanites and developed an "urban taste" when visiting the famous cultural cities in Europe, searching for the "gaze" of civilization (Towner 1985). Resorts were created, accommodated with urban amenities like the Grand Hotels (Walton 1983; Bruston and Duhamel 2000). This accommodation, by their monumentality and services provided, mimicked the metropolises and turned the resort into an urban place. The example of the Scarborough Grand Hotel, built in the 1870's is striking by its 12 floors, 4 towers, 365 rooms. Moreover, it allows tourists to undertake intense sociability, along the promenades or the assembly rooms. Whereas these places were at first made for the elites, the middle and working class managed to integrate this world, bringing social diversity. For example, the transformation of Brighton from an aristocratic to a working-class resort from 1840 to 1930 is a point in case (Urry 1990; Shields 1991; Stock 2001). In fact, these two social classes "needed" each other, the otherness arousing the interest of being here, in a conspicuous way for the elites.

We conjecture touristification corresponds to a specific type of urbanization, such as the increase of monumentality, interdependencies with other places of the urban system, but also because of the presence of tourists, whose presence increases the diversity of the place and proposes new patterns of interpretation of nature. The urbanization of resorts can be described as mono-functional urbanity, which emerges due to the almost exclusive practices of tourists, with urban amenities in a non-city environment. Architectural form and urban form highlight the urbanity of the premises by the monumentality and traffic problems. It is a seasonal urbanity where inhabited space of the resorts is *more* urban when tourists are there, and *less* urban when tourists are absent. As "tourist centres", they develop a specific touristic centrality as emergence of urban nodes giving a specific modality to the urbanization process.

11.4.2 Increased Urbanisation of Tourist Resorts: An Emergence of Centrality?

In tourism studies, the development of resorts is routinely addressed as life-cycle (Butler 1980) or as economic restructuring (Agarwal 2002). However, resorts also change in their urban quality over time (see Chap. https://doi. org/10.1007/978-3-030-52136-3_1212). Especially, it would be interesting to ask the question of emergence of centrality in places Christaller (1964) qualified as "peripheral" places without centrality. Battisti and Pagnini (1979) set out an interesting idea in their work on the development of tourist places: "when the flows of tourists to a peripheral region are increased, the holiday resort becomes fashionable and turns into a 'place for everybody'. At this stage, it is going to become a *real central place*, both in structure and if compared with the other peripheral tourist places, which will necessarily arise at a certain distance: it is there the 'elite' will move looking for peace and nature" (p. 85, our emphasis). Although the general tourism vision is somewhat naive – elite seeks tranquillity and nature –, the idea that tourist places become central places is interesting and could help to understand the centralization processes, and thus the urbanization processes. It allows for the formulation of a hypothesis: tourist resorts - formerly non-integrated because of their orientation towards a tourist population - become central places by their insertion in the regional system of cities. The process lies in diversification of urban functions that integrate to a relatively greater extent the urban functions of daily life at the expense of the non-daily life of tourists. Thus, urban services to individuals develop in places previously dedicated only to tourists, for instance by the emergence of commercial, residential and administrative functions.

It follows the assumption of the transformation of the spatial form of tourist resorts, i.e. that they cease to be tourist resorts and change into "resorts of diverse urban functions" or "tourist city" (see Équipe MIT 2002, 2011). Thus, the static distinction between tourist resort and tourist town can be articulated in a dynamic model. We propose the following hypothesis: resorts – non-central places – develop urbanity by becoming central places through the development of a regional centrality. At the same time, urban life is also changing: from urbanity only turned towards the temporary presence of tourist, to a more diversified urbanity, with diverse (multi-purpose) urban functions of different types of temporary inhabitants as well as local and regional ones, for whom it is their daily life surroundings. The former tourist resorts Brighton (UK), Eastbourne (UK), La Baule (France), Garmisch-Partenkirchen (Germany), etc. are examples of places that have acquired a certain regional centrality since their touristification.

One of the consequences is the recognition that there are processes of urbanization, i.e. creation and accumulation of urbanity that occur *without* agglomeration dynamics. Metropolitan areas, in the sense of accumulation of population and buildings, are indeed one of the geographical processes, which is the most observed and usually interpreted as the dominant form of urbanization (see for example Soja 1996). Nevertheless, we can dissociate agglomeration and urbanization, by noticing processes of agglomeration without emergence of urbanity and the process of urbanization without emergence of agglomeration. The industrial "cities" of the nineteenth century, the residential suburbs based on housing estates show signs of agglomeration, without the creation of a very high degree of urbanity. However, the resorts can be construed as cases of urbanization without agglomeration processes: despite 150 years of development of urbanity, Zermatt (5500 residents), Davos (10,000), Aspen (6000), have not developed large agglomerations (yet processes of urbanization by "second homes" occur). Other "formerly constituted" tourist resorts, such as Biarritz (France) and Crans-Montana (Switzerland) have developed an acute *diversity* of urban functions and thus agglomeration dynamics. The most spectacular examples are Miami Beach (Florida), Las Vegas (Nevada), Brighton & Hove (England) and Nice (France), but also smaller cities such as Santa Cruz (California), Garmisch-Partenkirchen (Bavarian Alps). We can conjecture the development from tourist nodes towards larger urban ensembles as "resort regions" (Soane 1993) or "tourist metropolises" in some cases like Azur Coast (Stock et al. 2017).

11.4.3 Touristification and Urbanization of Cities

If tourism creates in some cases *ex-nihilo* places like resorts, it has also invested urban places that have already existed formerly without tourism: cities. These places were visited by tourists interested in urban places associated with a prestigious past but in some cases affected by a decline in politic and/or economic dimensions. Some of these cities have remained touristic places and have even been visited by an increased number of tourists. Venice embodies these dynamic so that it can be analysed as a "touristified city" (Equipe MIT 2002), a place where tourism has become the main engine of urbanization, especially in the historic centre, which gathers most of the eight million tourists per year (plus 39 million "visitors" from cruises mostly). However, in this process, residents have decreased from 174,000 in 1951 to 56,000 in 2015, a dynamic which is not only due to "mass tourism" since it had already occurred during the nineteenth century – according to Stendhal, Venice gathered 180,000 inhabitants in 1790 but 30,000 in 1850 (see Équipe MIT 2005).

On the one hand, Venice has become dependent of a mono-economic function but on the other hand has tourism allowed it to remain a global centrality (Coëffé 2017). At a finer scale, we can even talk about urban "hyper-place" (Lussault 2017) when referring to San Marco Piazza, a place where the globalization intensity is high.

These "hyper-central" places can be found in other urban contexts like metropolises invested by tourism without becoming "touristified cities". Indeed, in the metropolises, tourism is only a part of the diversity (economic, cultural, etc.) although it is more or less spread over the whole urban space. In some metropolises, tourism can be particularly intense in few urban fragments, which can be named "Central Tourists District" (Duhamel and Knafou 2007a). At Paris, the space along the Seine which deploys the most prestigious monuments, embodies this configuration, whereas the tourist practices can invest other places like Montmartre, Etoile, etc. The tourist space goes even beyond "Paris intra-muros", reaching and urbanizing (increasing the degree of urbanity) some suburbs like Saint-Denis ("Basilique Saint-Denis", "Stade de France", etc.).

New York can be reconstructed as a global city thanks to many dimensions (economic, politic, symbolic, etc.) including the presence of tourists coming from all over the world. Times Square can be seen as a "hyper-place" where the degree of urbanity is maximum because of the density, diversity and intensity of the interactions between the different components of the society not only through the presence of residents, business travellers, etc., but also and even mostly through the presence of tourists: according to Lussault (2017), 50 millions of persons per year come to Times Square to enjoy its unceasing movements and activities; yet, the estimated figure might be too low if compared with Tokyo and its estimated 500 millions tourists - including also Tokyoites in this figure! - in 2018 (Tokyo Metropolitan Government, 2019). Its very high level of centrality is produced by its global attractiveness: individuals, imaginaries, objects, etc. are co-present and in the same time connected to different scales. In taking place at Times Square, an icon of New-York as a global city, each individual can experience both the "globalness" ("The World is here") and the "localness" (the perception of a place with space limits, a place which allows a direct contact with otherness, the emergence of gathering and the public skills associated with).

11.5   Conclusion

This chapter aims at contributing to question the complex relationship between the urban and the touristic dimensions of human societies by analysing some of its constituents. Routinely thought as "urban tourism", where only the city as territorial form is addressed, this relationship is in fact more complex than it seems to be at first glance. First, because there is a wider scope of urban places where tourism produces urbanity; second, because of urban cultures that inform the production of tourist spaces; third, because of the urbanization processes triggered through tourism. These elements are seen as components to solve the epistemological obstacle of "urban tourism". Thinking systematically "through" tourism to approach contemporary urban places, and thinking systematically the tourist places, practices, norms, corporealities, and cultures as *urban* issues is one of the solutions sketched out here.

This is relevant for urban studies, especially in the light of the recently shaped debate on the urban and different forms of urbanisation processes (Brenner and Schmid 2014, 2015; Schmid 2018). Especially the now well-established world cities network research suffers from a restricted view on global urban places, where tourism is not seen as an interesting element. For instance, Derudders and Witlox' (2005) contribution to the study of world city network, by studying airline data bases on flights between cities, is based on the 315 cities of the most important cities, gathered by Taylor et al. (2002). Yet, there are global tourist places such as Zermatt, Chamonix or Davos with a relatively greater global centrality than agglomerations such as Denver, highlighted as one of the nodes in the world cities roster. And the only tourist-oriented city appearing in the data set – Palma de Mallorca – is dismissed as non-conform to the problem: "nobody would argue that (Palma de Mallorca) is a major world city" (Derudders and Witlox 2005: 2378). This is but one example of the urge of reconceptualising the urban dimensions of tourism issues, where the concept of global centrality of tourist places (be it spots, resorts, cities, etc.) could be useful (see also Chap. 13 in this book).

Indeed, the focus on cities as sole territorial form instead of a focus on urban places in general is a major obstacle for thinking the urban/tourism nexus adequately. A surf spot such as Tehahoupoo in Tahiti could be analysed as a global urban place, because of its global centrality, produced through the "surf system" and linked to the "tourism system", especially because the tourist gaze as producer of urban places is a major element of urbanization processes. In metropolises, the tourist gaze also triggers global centralities, symbolic capital of place, diversity in cities within the globalization processes. Through tourist practices these urban places complexify their urbanity. Thinking through tourism allows for a contribution to the major contemporary issue of the ongoing "planetary urbanisation".

It is also relevant for tourism studies, where the urban dimensions are underestimated. Even National parks can be framed, within this approach, as urban places because of the urban imaginations of nature they carry with them and the urban park management they entail. By thinking tourism genuinely as urban, there is a renewed understanding of the relationship to nature at stake. Especially, the traditional binary between wilderness and tourist practice seen as antithetical and paradox can be understood as urban practice of an urban place. Moreover, resort development can be seen not only as "life-cycle" or "restructuring", but also as urbanisation and de-urbanisation processes. This would allow for an analysis of resort development not only as tourism development, but as emergence (and destruction) of centrality, public space, diversity of economic activities and mobilities (see also Chap. 12 in this book). From the perspective of urban theory, multiple tourism problems can be tackled, spanning from urban culture to spatial arrangements of global tourist places. The multiple manifestations of urbanity can be seen as both informing tourism and being informed by tourism. A renewed articulation between tourism theory and urban theory is to be developed further.

References

Agarwal, S. (2002). Restructuring seaside tourism: the resort lifecyle. *Annals of Tourism Research, 29*(1), 25–55.

Albrow, M. (1996). *The global age*. Cambridge: Polity.

Amin, A., & Thrift, N. (2002). *Cities: Reimagining the urban*. Cambridge: Polity Press.

Ashworth, G., & Page, S. (2011). Urban tourism research: Recent progress and current paradoxes. *Tourism Management, 32*, 1–15.

Atkinson, R. (2003). Domestication by Cappucino or a revenge on urban space? Control and empowerment in the management of public spaces. *Urban Studies, 40*(9), 1829–1843.

Battisti, M. P., & Pagnini, G. (1979). Considerations about the peripheral places of tourism. In J. Matznetter (Ed.), *Tourism and borders. Proceedings of the IGU working group: Geography of tourism and recreation*. Frankfurt: University of Frankfurt Press.

Bourdieu, P. (1994). *Raisons pratiques. Sur la théorie de l'action*. Paris: Seuil.

Brenner, N., & Schmid, C. (2014). The 'urban age' in question. *International Journal of Urban and Regional Research, 38*(3), 731–755.

Brenner, N., & Schmid, C. (2015). Toward a new epistemology of the urban. *City, 19*(2–3), 151–182.

Bruston, M., & Duhamel, P. (2000). Les grands hôtels témoins de l'histoire du tourisme. Le Splendid et Royal Hôtel à Saint-Gervais-les-Bains (Haute-Savoie). *Mappemonde, 59*, 5–9.

Butler, R. W. (1980). The concept of a tourist area cycle of evolution: Implications for management of resources. *Canadian Geographer, 24*(1), 5–12.

Castells, M. (2001). *The rise of the network society*. London: Wiley.

Christaller, W. (1964). Some considerations of tourism location in Europe: The peripheral regions underdevelopped countries recreation areas. *Papers of the Regional Science Association, 12*, 95–105. https://doi.org/10.1007/BF01941243.

Coëffé, V. (2010). Le tourisme, fabrique d'urbanité. Matériaux pour une théorie de l'urbain. *Mondes du tourisme, 2*, 57–69. https://doi.org/10.4000/tourisme.277.

Coëffé, V. (2014). *Hawaï. La fabrique d'un espace touristique*. Rennes: Presses Universitaires de Rennes.

Coëffé, V. (2017). Lieux de qualité et qualité des lieux touristiques dans un Monde de l'urbain généralisé, in Coëffé, V. (dir.). *Le tourisme. De nouvelles manières d'habiter le Monde* (pp. 287–333). Paris: Ellipses.

Corbin, A., (1994). *The lure of the sea*. Berkeley: University of California Press (1st French edition 1988).

Darbellay, F., Clivaz, C., & Stock, M. (2011). Approche interdisciplinaire du développement des stations touristiques. Le capital touristique comme concept opératoire. *Mondes du tourisme, 4*, 36–48.

Davezies, L. (2008). *La République et ses territoires : la circulation invisible des richesses*. Paris: Seuil.

Dematteis, G. (2013). Centralité, in Lévy, J., Lussault, M. (dir.), *Dictionnaire de la géographie et de l'espace des sociétés* (pp. 162–164). Paris: Belin.

Derudder, B., & Witlox, F. (2005). An appraisal of the use of airline data in assessing the world city network: A research note on data. *Urban Studies, 42*, 2371–2388.

Duhamel, Ph. & Knafou, R. (2007a). Le fonctionnement de la centralité touristique de Paris, in Saint-Julien, Th., Legoix R. (dir.), *La Métropole parisienne. Centralités, inégalités, proximités*. Paris: Belin.

Duhamel, P., & Knafou, R. (Eds.). (2007b). *Mondes urbains du tourisme*. Paris: Belin.

Edensor, T. (2000). Staging Tourism. Tourists as Performers. *Annals of Tourism Research, 27*(2), 322–344.

Elias, N. (1994 [1939]). The civilizing process. Oxford: Basil Blackwell.

Elias, N. (1997). *The Germans. Power struggles and the development of habitus in the nineteenth and twentieth centuries*. New York: Columbia University Press.

Elias, N., & Scotson, J. (1994). *The established and the outsiders*. London: Sage.

Équipe, M. I. T. (2002). *Tourismes 1. Lieux communs*. Paris: Belin.

Équipe, M. I. T. (2005). *Tourismes 2. Moments de lieux*. Paris: Belin.

Équipe, M. I. T. (2011). *Tourismes 3. La révolution durable*. Paris: Belin.

Foucault, M. (1984). Des espaces autres. *Architecture, Mouvement, Continuité*, n° 5, octobre, pp. 46–49.

Füller, H., & Michel, B. (2014). 'Stop Being a Tourist!' New Dynamics of Urban Tourism in Berlin-Kreuzberg. *International Journal of Urban and Regional Research, 38*(4), 1304–1318.

Gladstone, L. D. (1998). Tourism urbanization in the United States. Urban Affairs Review, vol. 34, n°1, p. 3–27.

Goffman, E. (1959). *The presentation of self in everyday life*. New York: Doubleday Anchor.

Granger, C. (2017). *La saison des apparences. Naissance des corps d'été*. Paris: Anamosa.

Hannerz, U. (1980). *Exploring the city*. New York: Columbia University Press.

Harvey, D. (1985). Consciousness and the urban experience. In *Studies in the history and theory of capitalist urbanization* (Vol. 1). London: Blackwell.

Harvey, D. (2001). *Spaces of capital. Towards a critical geography*. London: Routledge.

Hoffman, L., Fainstein, S., & Judd, D. (Eds.). (2003). *Cities and visitors. Regulating people, markets and city space*. Oxford: Blackwell.

Joseph, I. (1998). La ville sans qualité. La Tour d'Aigues: Éditions de l'Aube.

Judd, D. (Ed.). (2003). *The infrastructure of play. Building the tourist city*. Armonk: Sharpe.

Judd, D., & Fainstein, S. (Eds.). (1999). *The tourist city*. New Haven: Yale University Press.

Kaufmann, J.-C. (2000). Corps de femmes, regards d'hommes. In *Sociologie des seins nus*. Paris: Nathan.

Knafou, R., & Stock, M. (2003). Tourisme. In J. Lévy & M. Lussault (Eds.), *Dictionnaire de la géographie et de l'espace des sociétés* (pp. 931–934). Paris: Belin.

Knafou, R., Bruston, M., Deprest, F., Duhamel, P., Gay, J.-Ch., & Sacareau, I. (1997). Une approche géographique du tourisme. *L'Espace Géographique, 26*(3), 193–204.

Law, M. (1994). *Urban tourism: Attracting visitors to large cities*. London: Mansell Publishing.

Lefebvre, H. (1968). *Le droit à la ville*. Paris: Anthropos.

Lefebvre, H. (2001). *Du rural à l'urbain*. Paris: La Découverte

Lefebvre, H. (2003 [1970]). The urban revolution, University of Minnesota Press.

Lévy, J. (1999). *Le tournant géographique*. Paris: Belin.

Lévy, J. (2014). Science + space + society: Urbanity and the risk of methodological communalism in social sciences of space. *Geographica Helvetica, 69*(2), 99–114. https://doi.org/10.5194/gh-69-99-2014.

Löfgren, O. (1999). *On holiday. A history of vacationing*. Berkeley: University of California Press.

Lussault, M. (2017). *Hyper-lieux. Les nouvelles geographies de la mondialisation*. Paris: Seuil.

Metusela, C., & Waitt, G. (2012). *Tourism and Australian beach cultures. Revealing bodies*. Bristol: Channel View Publications.

Monnet, J. (2000). Les dimensions symboliques de la centralité. *Cahiers de Géographie du Québec, 44*(123), 399–418.

Mullins, P. (1991). Tourism urbanization. *International Journal of Urban and Regional Research, 15*(3), 326–342.

Novy, J. (2010). What's new about new urban tourism? And what do recent changes in travel imply for the 'tourist city' Berlin? In J. Richter (Ed.), *The tourist city Berlin. Tourism and architecture*. Berlin: Braun.

Runte, A. (1979). *National Parks: the American experience*. Lincoln: University of Nebraska Press.

Sassen, S. (2002). Locating cities on global circuits. *Environment and Urbanization, 14*(1), 13–30.

Schmid, C. (2018). Journeys through planetary urbanization: Decentering perspectives on the urban. *Environment and Planning D: Society and Space, 36*(3), 591–610. https://doi.org/10.1177/0263775818765476.

Scott, A., & Storper, M. (2014). The nature of cities: The scope and limits of urban theory. *International Journal of Urban and Regional Research*. https://doi.org/10.1111/1468-2427.12134.

Shields, R. (1991). *Places on the margin*. London: Routledge.

Simmel, G., (2002 [1903]). The metropolis and mental life. In Bridge G. and Watson S. (Eds.), *The Blackwell City Reader*. Oxford: Wiley-Blackwell, pp. 11–19.

Soane, J. V. H. (1993). *Fashionable resort regions: Their evolution and transformation. With particular reference to Bournemouth, Nice, Los Angeles and Wiesbaden*. Wallingford: CAB International.

Soja, E. (1996). *Postmetropolis*. London: Blackwell.

Stock, M. (2001). Brighton and Hove, station touristique ou ville touristique ? *Géocarrefour-Revue Géographique de Lyon, 76*(2), 127–131.

Stock, M. (2017). Le concept de centralité à l'épreuve du tourisme. Réflexions critiques. In: Bernard, N. & Duhamel, Ph. (Eds.), *Tourisme et périphéries. La centralité des lieux en question*. Rennes: Presses Universitaires de Rennes.

Stock, M. (2019). Inhabiting the city as tourist. Issues for urban and tourism theory. In T. Frisch, C. Sommer, L. Stoltenberg, & N. Stors (Eds.), *Tourism and everyday life in the contemporary city* (pp. 42–66). London: Routledge.

Stock, M., & Lucas, L. (2012). La double révolution urbaine du tourisme. *Espaces et Sociétés, 151* (4), 15–30. https://doi.org/10.3917/esp.151.0015.

Stock, M., Coëffé, V., Violier, P. (2017). *Les enjeux contemporains du tourisme. Une approche géographique*. Rennes: PUR.

Taylor, P. J., Catalano, G., & Walker, D. R. F. (2002). Measurement of the world city network. *Urban Studies, 39*(13), 2367–2376.

Towner, J. (1985). The grand tour. A key phase in the history of tourism. *Annals of Tourism Research, 12*, 297–333.

Urbain, J.-D. (1994). *Sur la plage. Mœurs et coutumes balnéaires (XIXe siècle-XXe siècle)*. Paris: Payot et Rivages.

Urry, J. (1990). *The tourist gaze. Leisure and travel in contemporary societies* (200 p). London: Sage.

Urry, J. (1995). *Consuming places*. London: Sage.

Walton, K. J. (1983). *The English seaside resort. A social history 1750–1914* (p. 265). Leicester: Leicester University Press.

Wirth, L. (1938). Urbanism as a way of life. *The American Journal of Sociology, 44*(1), 1–24.

Vincent Coëffé is a lecturer in geography at the faculty of Tourism & Culture with University of Angers (France) and member of the laboratory "Espaces et Sociétés" (UMR CNRS 6590). His work focuses on tourism urbanity, through the issues associated with the public space. His research integrates two fields more particularly: the corporeality of the tourists' practices and heritage development.

Mathis Stock is a professor with the Institute of Geography and Sustainability at Lausanne University (Switzerland), where he leads the research group "Cultures and Natures of Tourism". His research deals with the urbanising force of tourism, the controversies around tourism in cities, and mobility and multilocality approached from the perspective of practice theory. He dialogues with social theory and develops a theory of dwelling, posited at the heart of theoretical geography. He is editor-in-chief of the scientific journal *Mondes du tourisme*.

Chapter 12
Rethinking Resort Development Through the Concept of "Touristic Capital" of Place

Mathis Stock, Christophe Clivaz, Olivier Crevoisier, and Leïla Kebir

12.1 Introduction

Resort development is one of the most widely researched subject matters within tourism studies. It has been subject to numerous empirical studies since geography started covering the topic in the 1930s. Several theoretical models have also been presented (see Pearce 1987; Williams and Shaw 2004). The problem of resort development raises questions with regard to the process of a geographical place's touristification, i.e. transforming a place into a destination, as well as with regard to other processes that affect a constituted tourist resort. Empirical observation shows that tourist resorts undergo very differentiated trajectories, during which decline and restructuring are the rule (Williams and Shaw 1997; Agarwal 2002; Butler 2006); some resorts are, however, able to maintain a tourism activity over a long period of time (Equipe MIT 2011). It also raises the question of proper qualification of tourist resorts, which have been described as a specific territorial form of geographical places whose mono-activity and smaller size and shape distinguish them, for example, from cities (Equipe MIT 2002). Yet, urbanisation processes leads to an identification as "resort cities" (Judd and Fainstein1999).

A first version of this text has been published as working paper in the Working paper series MAPS of University of Neuchâtel (https://www.unine.ch/files/live/sites/maps/files/shared/documents/wp/WP_5_2014_MS_et_al%20(2).pdf)

M. Stock (✉) · C. Clivaz · L. Kebir
Institute of Geography and Sustainability, University of Lausanne, Lausanne, Switzerland
e-mail: mathis.stock@unil.ch; christophe.clivaz@unil.ch; leila.kebir@unil.ch

O. Crevoisier
University of Neuchâtel, Neuchâtel, Switzerland
e-mail: olivier.crevoisier@unil.ch

The fundamental question is therefore: How do some resorts maintain tourism for a long period, whereas others evolve into places where tourism is no longer dominant, and still others totally relinquish tourism as an economic and a cultural activity? Tourist resorts have very differentiated trajectories and it is worth asking how these different trajectories can be described and explained. This requires a historical contextualisation, since some tourist resorts, such as Chamonix and Zermatt, have existed for more than 150 years, whereas others were only developed in the 1950s (Benidorm), and still others are being created (Equipe MIT 2011). Moreover, certain resorts having stopped being resorts and have been transformed into cities, such as Brighton & Hove, Cannes, Atlantic City and Montreux, although they are still to some extent dependent on the tourism trade, while tourism totally stopped being an economic driver of the local system in previous resorts such as Malo-les-Bains and Tamaris (France).

The question raised does not solely address the rise and decline of tourism *in* a given location, but also the evolution *of* the territorial form of resorts. Research has shown that resorts undergo an urbanisation process during which their initial features change radically (Mullins 1991; Stock 2001; Equipe MIT 2002, 2011). Consequently, research that focuses only on the tourism activity in resorts and neglects their possible conversion into other territorial forms fails to answer the question raised above. Furthermore, since resorts are not isolated, they have been linked to the globalisation of tourism since 1800. Tourists, investors, politics, etc. construct, reconstruct and acknowledge the differences between tourist resorts and create a spatial hierarchy of resorts (Chadefaud 1988; Clivaz et al. 2011; Darbellay et al. 2011).

In order to answer some of the questions raised above, we provide a conceptual work on the touristic capital of resorts in a tourism field in order to describe and explain the evolution of tourist resorts. This article aims at a theoretical exploration of the concept of resorts' touristic capital. The touristic capital concept describes the competitive advantages that a local territorial system accumulates and the engagement of those actors in the global tourism field with such advantages. We suggest that the touristic capital concept refers the capital of a geographical place, such as a resort, in which multiple actors engage to maintain its touristic quality, or to enhance as well as maintain its relative position in the competitive tourist field. These advantages are relative to the capital of other resorts and also relative to multiple actors' judgements. Since tourists, markets, institutions, etc. are globalised, these advantages are played out in the global tourism field, i.e. a constellation expressing the power relationships between resorts. In order to maintain resorts' touristic qualities, these interdependencies need to shift the locus of power from a merely local system to the relationship between resorts as they occur in the global tourism field.

We will address the questions raised by suggesting the following steps: Firstly, a critical review is provided of existent models to show the strengths and limits of existing resort development explanations. Secondly, we will present a conceptual framework linking touristic places and their internal dynamics with the more global tourism field. This allows us to construct the touristic capital concept by identifying its relational character as an element of resorts in a global tourism field. Thirdly, we will examine the implications of this concept. The conclusion links touristic capital to the different empirically identified trajectories.

12.2   Resort Development: A Critical Review of Three Approaches

Research on the evolution, transformation and restructuring of tourist resorts has flourished since the 1970s. Since Butler's (1980, 2006) study, this change has been framed as either a tourism area life-cycle with several stages, or as the restructuring of tourist resorts (Williams and Shaw 1997; Agarwal 2012), but there are also more historically driven attempts in order to understand how resorts undergo changes in their place identity (Corbett 2001; Equipe MIT 2011).

12.2.1   Strengths and Limitations of the Life-Cycle Approach

Within a geographical approach to tourism, research on the development of tourist places is an important and well documented task. One of the best known is Butler's (1980) tourism area life-cycle model in which tourism is framed as a business cycle. This model is related to Christaller's (1955) attempt to understand tourist resorts as peripheral places where the social diffusion from elite to working-class people affects the resort development by turning an exceptional place into an ordinary place. In turn, Plog's (1974) model of the different tourists psychological characteristics that have affected the more elite or mass-tourism character of places is related to that of Christaller. Each of these models focuses on different aspects of a similar problem; we could call this the Christaller-Plog-Butler model. Besides the existing criticisms (see Butler 2006), *three* critical points have to be highlighted:

Firstly, the life-cycle model fails to acknowledge that tourist resorts undergo a transformation of place quality or territorial form during their development (Equipe MIT 2002). It is crucial to not only analyse tourism *in* a place, but also the changing qualities *of* a tourist place (Stock 2001). There may be an empirical measure of the decrease in tourism's relative importance *in* a place, but this does not necessarily mean that a *place* declines. There are various forms of transformation: from resorts to smaller villages, or from resorts to bigger urban nodes (Equipe MIT 2002). Brighton is a case in point: The decrease in importance of the tourist trade has gone hand in hand with the development of a huge diversity of urban functions. Currently, Brighton is a regional metropolis, not a tourist resort (Stock 2001).

Therefore, one problem of the above model is its sole focus on tourism activity, neglecting the overall socioeconomic dimensions of tourist places. The latter are also places for day trippers, for work and consumption for the local and regional population, as well as central places for different urban services (hospitals, schools, administrations, transport hubs, the service industry, etc.). To understand the development of tourist places, we have to develop an approach that understands the change in urban functions and place practices, and does not only focus on the touristic dimensions of places.[1] In short, the life-cycle idea does not acknowledge tourist resorts' multiple trajectories during which seaside resorts become cities, cities become tourist places, resort complexes become urban places and seaside resorts develop into residence communities (Equipe MIT 2011). Empirically, there are numerous examples of the incremental – not exponential – development of resorts and the multiple crises affecting them. Specifically, crises due to a lack of tourists are more probable than crises due to an overload of tourists (Equipe MIT 2002).

Furthermore, the focus on the local scale has led to the neglect of the specific global tourism regime within which the development of tourist places, such as seaside resorts and mountain centres, occurs. Consequently, we link the development of single resorts and the development of the entire global system of attractions (MacCannell 2001) to form a global tourism field (Clivaz et al. 2011). Not only should individual resorts be examined, but the interdependencies of resorts should also be examined. This leads to several questions: How should we conceive of the development of tourist resorts within global tourism? How do tourist resorts engage in cooperation and competition with other resorts? How do the interdependencies between tourist resorts occur? How do tourists, investors, politics, etc. construct, reconstruct and acknowledge the differences between tourist resorts? How is the hierarchy between resorts constructed?

Finally, contemporary models lack a time element. For instance, in Butler's model, time is not specified and is a black box. The advantage is that the model is less complex, providing an abstraction that allows very different kinds of resort development to be examined. Yet, for a thorough understanding of resort development processes, it is important to know how long a resort will develop: 5 years, 10 years, 50 years, 200 years? An investigation into the processes resorts undergo in relation to the time frame is therefore needed. Is it a rapid development? How can the different rhythms of resort development be distinguished? Are there breaks and bifurcations in the development? Related to the question of the time element, the question is: At what moment does a resort emergence? The historicity of place is important, because the moment of touristification is decisive to understand the development conditions. Places developed in the 1850s (Atlantic City), or in the 1970s (Cancun), experience very different socio-economic conditions when coming into being and developing. Therefore, both the time frame and the historical context need to be addressed.

---

[1] There is now a literature on the changing qualities of tourist resorts, especially as places for new forms of migration and multi-local dwelling, e.g. in Perlik (2011) and Martin et al. (2012).

12.2.2   The Restructuring Approach

The second approach seeks to analyse the political and economic conditions of resorts' economic transformations. The literature on restructuring has benefitted from insights from economy, geography and sociology. Restructuring means a change towards a "significantly different order and configuration of social, economic and political life" (Soja 1989, 159). The restructuring thesis has been widely used in urban geography and economic geography, but has also been utilised as a framework for the analysis of tourist resorts (Williams and Shaw 1997). Agarwal maintains that "contrary to the relative simplicity of the resort lifecycle, the restructuring thesis is an imprecise and complex body of theory which consists of a set of theoretical propositions about the widespread economic and social changes taking place in society and which involve deep changes in the geography of production and consumption" (Agarwal 2002, 27). This framework identifies the changing features of the capitalist economy from Fordist to post-Fordist production and consumption patterns.

The problem raised has specifically been that of resort decline – understandable within the British context - and the restructuring of tourism within a resort. Such resorts, which were highly prominent in the British tourist culture until the 1950s, have since exited the market, with resorts in the Mediterranean and South-East Asia replacing them. Research has proposed the following causes of their decline: firstly, the collapse of the domestic market due to the accessibility of alternative destinations (Cooper 1997); secondly, the social change in the clientele, i.e. the erosion of high and average income tourists frequenting these resorts (Demetriadi 1997) and the parallel increase in the numbers of visitors who are not high spenders (Cooper 1997). Moreover, this development may also be explained as a *cultural change*: Similar to the nineteenth century shift in focus from the beach's therapeutic, medical function to its pleasure and leisure function, a progressive shift in interest has occurred from the sea to the sun (Urry 1990), triggered by technological elements that change the accessibility of other places and alters the terms on which the competition between destinations is based (Urry 1997; Cooper 1997; Soane 1993; Demetriadi 1997; Agarwal 1997).

Although the analysis of the reasons for tourist resorts' decline has clearly explored interesting research questions, it remains contradictory. *The extent to which* the forces at work are endogenous/exogenous, cultural or economic, institutional or infrastructural remains unknown. In particular, the existing research has very little to say about the role of the different types of actors – whether they are tourists, political decision-makers, land owners, developers, local entrepreneurs, traders, citizens, etc. – involved in the process of tourist development in general and in the maintenance or decline of tourist activities in particular. The question of *how* they are negotiated between the different types of actors needs to be examined.

Furthermore, the existing research does not explore spatial restructuring in terms of the transformation of resorts' territorial forms. Instead of studying a resort's changing qualities, research has studied the changing quality of tourism within a resort. Therefore, there is no clear understanding of the consequences of this decline process for the quality of places. What kind of places are they now? Are they still tourist resorts, or have they been transformed into *something else*? These kinds of questions remain unanswered.

12.2.3   The Transformation of Place Qualities

A third approach focuses on the transformations of tourist resorts' place quality. This approach comprises the idea that resorts have been invented, constructed and reproduced as resorts over time. The transformation does not only affect the local economy, culture and society, but also the place quality. The historian Soane (1993) proposes an interesting approach. He identifies the changing place qualities as from resorts towards resort regions, as occurred in Brighton, Los Angeles and Nice. Soane understands resort regions as the scale of former local resorts changing into a regional scale of an agglomeration of resorts. The Côte d'Azur example is particularly significant – formerly separate resorts underwent expansion and achieved the urbanisation of the seashore. Currently, the whole Côte d'Azur – from Menton to Toulon – is urbanised and offers tourism services. Soane (1993) calls this a resort region, while Equipe MIT (2002, 2011) calls it tourist conurbation. Other examples are Florida, which, between St. Augustine and Key West, has tourist-centred places along the coast and the Sunshine Coast in Australia, which is centred around Brisbane, where tourism-centred urbanization processes have been observed (Mullins 1991).

An important insight that this research identified is the need for a proper distinction between different place qualities in order to reconstruct the transformation of resorts into different territorial forms. Distinguishing between a tourist city, tourist resort, tourist enclave and a tourist site, Equipe MIT (2002) proposes a model of tourist place development in which changing place qualities are the core issues. The identified trajectories include from tourist resort to city, from tourist site to tourist resort, from tourist enclave to tourist resort where tourism is ever present. But there are also processes towards urban places without tourism, such as from resort to suburb, or from resort to recreational community. In these cases, tourism no longer informs the place quality, but other features do. The touristic elements have often been transformed into residential qualities.

12.2.4   Conclusion

Resorts cannot be analysed as isolated places, as they are related to a system of places where cooperation and competition occur. Their relative position in a hierarchy of resorts, which the emergence of ever new tourist resorts, practices and products challenges, is dependent on the global resort system. The emergence of new tourist gazes and practices had huge effects on the classic mountain destinations, for example, the decisive invention of the Mediterranean Sea as a summer vacation place from the 1920s onward; previously the winter season had been preferred and hotels closed in the summer season (Equipe MIT 2005). It also triggered the decline of British seaside resorts (Williams and Shaw 1997). The emergence of Alpine skiing in the beginning of the twentieth century triggered the emergence of new resorts especially designed for skiing, which challenged the older fashionable summer resorts that did not open during the winter, which one of the protagonists describes in the book *Skiing* (Lunn 1913).

It also raises the question of where crises originate. Is there only one crisis, as suggested in the Christaller-Plog-Butler model, with too many tourists (from lower social classes) that affect the carrying capacity? Evidence shows there are multiple crises: urbanism-driven, ecological, economic and political crises (Agarwal 1997). A historically-driven approach suggests all tourist resorts seem affected by crises at one moment in their history, but respond differently to them. The differential capacity to cope with crises might be one of the key problems when trying to identify the mechanisms of tourist resorts' transformation. It also leads to the question: Where do bifurcations (i.e. the change in the trajectory, or the transformations of resorts) originate? Do they originate from the practices of tourists who invent ever new practices and modify their spatial preferences? Do they originate from entrepreneurs who propose new goods and services to tourists, such as the emergence of winter holidays in the mountains in St Moritz in the 1860's? Do they originate from public policy? In fact, throughout history, we observe different sources of resort transformation: New practices invent new tourist places, such as North Americans living in Paris going on summer vacations to the Mediterranean sea (Löfgren 1999), public policy regarding the French development of Languedoc-Roussillon and La Plagne, while private economic operators were decisive in the development of ski areas in the U.S. (Beaver Creek) and in the development of resort complexes (*Club Méditerranée* in various locations). In both cases, practices that already existed elsewhere were mimicked and transferred. Resort development does not, therefore, rely on a single trajectory, but is dependent on a great number of interwoven practices. In order to understand the differentiated effects of the economic, political, geographical and sociological dimensions, we build a framework of resorts' touristic capital.

12.3 Towards a Conceptualisation of "Touristic Capital" of Resorts in a Global Tourism Field

Capital is a polysemic concept in social sciences, rooted in political economy, but now widely used in different disciplinary contexts. Individuals (Bourdieu 1984; Putnam 2000), firms, institutions, states (Bourdieu 2012) and geographical places (Harvey 2001) deploy capital in keeping with their different uses in sociology, geography, economy, regional science, etc. We explore the possibility of assigning a specific capital to tourist resorts.

12.3.1 Capital as a Concept Developed in Several Disciplines

Capital is one of the most famous political economy concepts. Marx had a technical and social vision of capital as a capitalists-owned production means. Capital allows capitalists to control the production and circulation process, turning money into commodities and commodities into possibly more money. Capital is accumulated quantitatively and the entire system is oriented towards maintaining the profit rate. In respect of space, Marx considered relocation one of the most important means of maintaining the profit rate. Harvey popularised this idea with his spatial fix concept (2001). The spatial fix of economic capital is therefore the transformation of money into a localized built environment. Harvey also gave the term spatial fix a second meaning: Analogous to a technological fix, it means a spatial strategy of displacing capital to overcome the contradictions of capitalism, such as local over-accumulation.

From an economic point of view, actors not only have to find ways to maintain the profit rate locally, but large international tourism companies, like tour operators, also constantly re-allocate their activities around the world to maintain their profit rate. Therefore, for tourism resorts, the dynamics of economic capital is not based on relocation, but needs another understanding. The central economic process consists of the qualitative reorganisation of various objects – such as the landscape, hotels, reputation, infrastructure, etc. – through the local institutions (or, sometimes, in spite of them) in order to maintain a sufficient level of economic value creation locally. Here, sufficient means that monetary income allows the reproduction of the local system in a competitive global tourism field.

In this perspective, capital is both a set of objects – the natural and built environment, a place's symbolic reputation – and the local capabilities to manage and reorganise them in order to turn them into a monetary income. In this case, capital does not refer to capitalists' ownership, as in neoclassic and Marxian traditions, but to a set of local objects, institutions and capabilities that interact dynamically and more or less coherently. This is linked to current institutional economics in which capital is the set of all of a society's innovation and production capabilities. For instance, knowledge embedded in people, in a landscape that no-one owns, or in local tales is part of a society's capital if it is, in one way or another, included or potentially included in economic circuits. Consequently, Camagni and Capello (2013) define territorial capital as "the set of local assets, – natural, human, artificial, organizational, relational and cognitive – that constitute the competitive potential of a given territory." (p. 1387).

Bourdieu extended the capital concept within sociology – in the sense of social, cultural and symbolic capital, besides economic capital – as a disposition of individuals who, as agents, engage in a specific field. Bourdieu made a significant contribution by defining a specific field of interest within which capital occurs (Bourdieu 1992). This specification is especially useful to understand that tourist resorts compete in the tourism field, but not, for instance, in the steel production or higher education fields. Bourdieu also considers nation-states and institutions, such as universities, as disposing of and engaging in specific social fields with their different kinds of capital (Bourdieu 2012). This allows capital to be conceived on a collective level and not only on an individual level. Valuating individual or collective attributes as capital depends on a capacity to capture a significant portion of the material and immaterial resources – the trophies or gains at stake in the field (in the case of tourism, e.g., market shares or prestige) – for the capital holders, in order to enhance their position in this specific competitive field.

A third concept – spatial capital – is currently being developed as a capital *of* space within geography. Framed as the advantages of a given area, Harvey (2001, p. 405) describes this capital as "collective symbolic capital which attaches to names and places like Paris, Athens, New York, Rio de Janeiro, Berlin and Rome is of great import and gives such places great economic advantages relative to, say, Baltimore, Liverpool, Essen, Lille, Glasgow. The problem for these latter places is to raise their quotient of symbolic capital and to increase their mark of distinction to better ground their claims to the uniqueness that yields monopoly rent". Urban capital is therefore a collective symbolic capital that different kinds of actors recognize as a certain marker of meaning. It is interesting to note that Harvey approaches the collective symbolic capital as only other-directed, i.e. towards *investors*. Nevertheless, there is no indication of the specific field in which this symbolic capital occurs. In its attempt to understand how tourist places maintain their tourism trade over a long period, Equipe MIT (2011, p. 222) mentions a "capital of a space". It stresses, "the spatial fix of the invested economic capital and the urban capital are a token of durability, especially because of the evolution potential towards other forms of activities" (Equipe MIT 2011, p. 235). The authors acknowledge infrastructures and urbanness as capital that can be transformed into multiple activities when tourism declines. Capital of space is regarded as a resilient element that prevents a place from collapsing.

We can build on these contributions to define the touristic capital as a collective capital linked to geographical places. Touristic capital can be defined as an ensemble of physical, economic, social, political, urban and symbolic characteristics that permits a place – and the actors living in it, developing it, or exploiting it - to position itself in a tourism field and, in comparison to other tourist places, to gain advantages. This concept aims at understanding the differential capacity of tourist places to maintain (or to lose) touristic quality – relative to the modification of the tourism field – over a certain period of time. Touristic capital is therefore conceived as both a potential for further development and an actual advantages acquired through a long-term construction process.

12.3.2   The Concept of a Touristic Capital of Resorts in a Global Tourism Field

Touristic capital is understood as a place's set of characteristics accumulated over time and engaged as advantages *vis-à-vis* the institutions, practices, markets of competing tourist places, which can be described as forming a *tourism field*. These characteristics can be of *spatial* (the location, qualities of space, degree of urbanness, etc.), *socio-cultural* (the knowledge, know-how, competences, attitude towards tourism, stratification of local society, etc.), *political* (the governance/political steering capacity, inter-policy coordination, coherence and robustness of institutional designs and rules, conflictuality of decision processes, etc.), *economic* (the financing capacity), *environmental* (the state of the environments, landscape and biophysical resources) quality. Here, we take into consideration six different dimensions referring to the resource and governance, urban and reputational, monetary and knowledge dimensions of resorts' touristic capital (see Clivaz et al. 2011; Darbellay et al. 2011; see Figs. 12.1 and 12.2).

In order to build a dynamic representation of touristic capital, we first consider that touristic capital – on a national and a global scale – allows for the adaptation of local resources to the global conditions of the tourism field's competitiveness, institutions and symbols. The touristic capital and the global tourism field shape each other and are in dynamic interaction (see Figs. 12.1 and 12.3).

The first loop represents the development of resorts as the valorisation of items within a tourism growth regime in which use value and monetary value are constantly developed as tourism valorisation. *Monetary flows*, which are measured in terms of incomes and investments – the black arrows in Fig. 12.1 – drive these

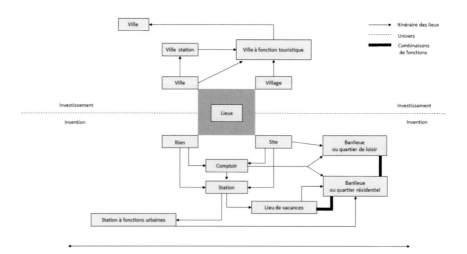

Source: Equipe MIT (2002)

Fig. 12.1 The model of changing place qualities (Source: Equipe MIT (2002))

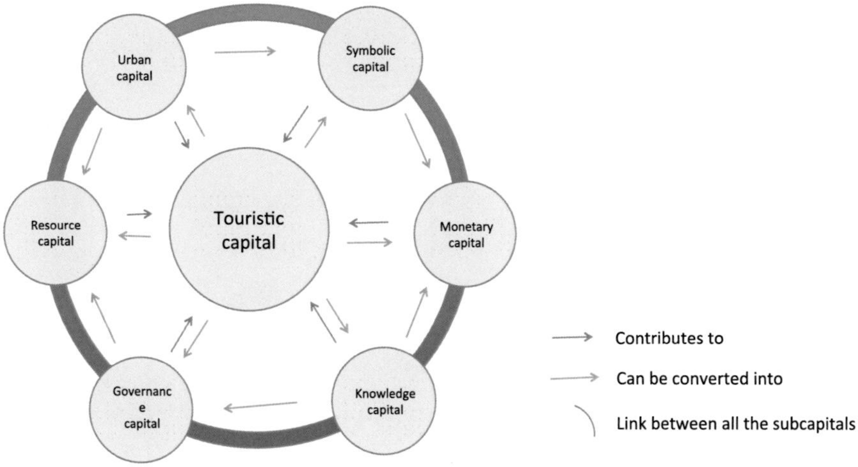

Source: own elaboration

Fig. 12.2 The dimensions of touristic capital (Source: Own elaboration)

accumulation processes. Local players, who will/will not invest and develop their position in the tourist field, capture the inward monetary flows originating from tour operators and/or tourists expenditures. For instance, entry fees, accommodation, catering, etc. allow monetary flows. Conversely, enjoying public goods or experiences, like walking in the mountains, on public beaches, etc. does not allow the capture of monetary expenditures. In tourism, compared to other fields of activities, there is usually relatively less overlap between what tourists practise and what they pay for. This means that some of the local players catch the income flows directly, while others depend on the redistributive, secondary flows. This also explains why tourism resorts cannot be regarded as simple agglomerations of market-related companies. Touristic capital contributes to the local capability to build a converging representation of what happens in the field and then directing the more or less collective actions to renew the common resources. This also presumes that there are collective rules and institutions that share the monetary costs and benefits.

The *tourism field* consists of a configuration of actors and norms whose actions have the same interest and the same intentionality – a touristic engagement with the world, i.e. a tourist gaze – in order to fabricate, commercialise and consume material and immaterial tourist goods and services, but also to elaborate the norms and laws concerning transport and hospitality services, the food/drink quality, landscape preservation, etc. Therefore, we conceptualise the diversity of actors as an interdependent configuration (i.e., mutually dependent in an asymmetric power relationship) within the same logic of interest – tourism. A multi-scalar network of people, places, institutions and firms, whose actors have different kinds of *advantages* with which they engage while enacting processes, represents this configuration. These advantages are therefore the elements of the touristic capital of resorts engaged in

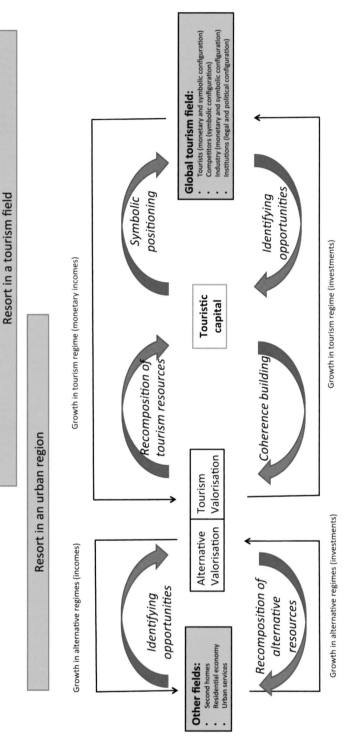

Fig. 12.3 Touristic capital in the tourism field (Source: Own elaboration)

the touristic field. The global field of tourism should not be regarded as a passive selection of innovations that tourism players propose. Value creation, especially in experiential activities, requires customers' active involvement, as well as that of many other players like journalists, guide writers, tour operators, etc. These players play a role in the construction of various places and practices' meanings. Therefore, a market should not be regarded as the meeting of largely independent supplies and demands, but rather as a global stage (Jeannerat 2013) where producers invest various resources to build this stage and where customers engage in experiences (Pine and Gilmore 1999; Lorentzen 2009; Lorentzen and Jeannerat 2013). Moreover, spectators and critics – journalists, experts, tour operators, lawmakers, and international governmental and non-governmental organisations – scrutinize, comment, legitimize or stigmatize the play presented on the stage.

From an economic view, the market exerts quantitative and qualitative competitive pressures on places. In terms of prices, the problem is particularly acute in high cost countries, because actors cannot escape the local labour, land, or real estate costs, while having to provide basic services like accommodation and food. In qualitative terms, the local players, who take their resources and competences into consideration, eventually develop a representation of the field's evolutions and *identify the opportunities* they provide for a resort. This qualitative, symbolic competition creates the conditions for supply side differentiation and improvement of the understanding of customer aspirations. The innovation process in a place can be regarded as a re-invention process of the local objects (the landscape, buildings, cultural traditions, local competences, etc.) in order to build new tourism resources that will be more aligned with the evolving clientele. This process need not just be seen as an imposed constrain, but also as an active process of changing the global conditions of the tourism field. For instance, Alpine skiing was developed in only a few places before becoming a world standard. This *symbolic positioning* is especially significant regarding the price and symbolic positioning of a resort in the global tourism field.

Drawing on the identification of opportunities, local actors *rearrange tourism resources* by selecting adequate objects pertaining to the global tourism field. This process is dependent on the quality of the touristic capital in terms of governance and knowledge. In turn, this process contributes to the definition of tourist capital through the valorisation of specific items within a tourism regime. For instance, the transformation of snow into a tourism object in some resorts in the Alps at the start of the twentieth century extended the traditional summer season to the winter. In turn, this process strengthens the touristic capital of a resort. However, coherence building is crucial to valorise objects as tourism attractions. *Coherence building* refers to the local political and private actors' capacity to valorise objects within tourism, especially by providing infrastructure. Coherence building thus refers to the political dimensions of touristic capital, for which governance and local institutional arrangements are crucial. Consequently, coherence building leads to tourism valorisation, which in turn strengthens touristic capital.

As resorts develop, they accumulate or valorise items (infrastructure, flats, buildings, etc.) that other actors – not necessarily related to tourism (local residents, workers, etc.) – can use. As such, resorts are confronted with the urban growth accumulation system, which consists of the residential economy, either through the creation or the development of new uses for existing items. Signals that a developing or a pre-existing urban region provides, trigger this accumulation system. The articulation between the resort accumulation system and the urban growth system can be a source of tension, as they can compete for existing resources (e.g., the transformation of hotels into apartments and tourists' appropriation of a city's popular neighbourhoods). Urbanisation can also be a source of complementarities and support the resort development, for instance, by allowing the building of certain infrastructures (a concert hall, a public transportation system, etc.) with a minimal demand-level requirement. The mobilisation of touristic capital allows the *recomposition of resources*, due to the *alternative valorisation* of objects previously valorised as tourism resources. By *identifying opportunities* in other fields, the valorisation process and monetary incomes are triggered for resources that have ceased to be part of the tourism growth regime.

A second loop can therefore be described because resorts are not only embedded in a global tourism field, but also in an urban region and are present in other fields besides tourism. From a processual point of view, accessibility and urbanisation characteristics change over time and allow new kinds of linkages to an urban region. Specifically, the transformation of resorts into places for leisure or into residences for an urban region's inhabitants is crucial (Equipe MIT 2002). As a consequence, elements like the landscape, events, the availability of personal services, reputation, infrastructure, etc. can also be valorised in other economic activities, as they contribute to urbanness in general. This loop develops on the basis of previously built and accumulated tourism resources, but is valorised in different types of activities, some related to tourism, while others are totally unrelated. For instance, a (business, academic, etc.) congress is the valorisation of infrastructure in a global congress field, but through the presence of temporary mobile individuals related to tourism. Another alternative valorisation is the transformation of obsolete tourism accommodation into forms of housing stock for residential use. The urban region therefore constitutes the adequate horizon of action within which the touristic capital of a place is engaged.

12.4   Implications of the Concept

Capital is understood here as accumulated resources and the capacity to mobilise these resources. Touristic capital is a situated construction of diverse actors at a certain place at a moment in time. The concept of capital is linked to the capacity, disposition and mobilisation of highly diverse elements (whether physical objects, formal or informal rules, the symbolic dimensions of nature, etc.) within a tourism field.

Firstly, touristic capital is conceived as fundamentally relational and relative. Resorts possess capital under the condition that its constituting elements have *value* for other actors in the relevant configuration, here the touristic field. For resorts, touristic capital is the capacity to produce tourist goods and services with value for the global economic and symbolic market, which tourists, tour operators, hotel owners, travel agencies, etc. recognize as value. According to Bourdieu (1984), this refers fundamentally to symbolic capital, because the different actors involved need to share similar cognitive frames. It is interesting to note that touristic capital is co-constituted through interaction between the multiple actors, who encode the signification of a place (local decision makers, producers and diffusers of marketing strategies regarding tourist goods and services), and those who decode this symbolic realm (tourists, guidebooks, travel agencies, etc.). Therefore, the local society does not entirely control the touristic capital, due to the multiplicity of actors involved in its valuation in the tourism field. Furthermore, touristic capital is partly symbolic and can therefore be interpreted in multiple ways.

Secondly, tourist capital evolves over time, as does the touristic field. On the one hand, there is an accumulation process of touristic capital, which symbolic, cognitive, resource and urban elements trigger. Touristic capital is the result of a reciprocal reinforcement of the different elements in the sense of positive retroactions in the local system. This capital is therefore more than the sum of its parts, but is the relationship of these parts' potential synergies. However, touristic capital can also be destroyed, for instance, through the loss of reputation, a lack of resources, political instability, etc. On the other hand, the touristic field also evolves as ever new resorts enter the field and old established resorts exit it (Antonescu and Stock 2014). The acceleration of tourism's globalisation goes hand in hand with integrating new resorts into the touristic field, therefore establishing new patterns of competition.

Finally, touristic capital can be transformed into forms of economic activity other than tourism. For instance, via urbanisation, an in-depth restructuring is triggered through the conversion of touristic capital into economic or resource capital. The spatial fix of economic capital through real estate investment (hotels, second homes, resort complexes) is one of the salient examples of the fungible nature of touristic capital leading to urban capital. Other examples of the fungible nature of tourist capital refer, for instance, to the change in objectives (from tourism to other forms of economic development) within a growth coalition (Logan and Molotch 1987) as a form of political capital conversion. Resource capital (water, sand, infrastructures, etc.) might also transform into activities other than tourism, for example, hydro-electricity, manufacturing, commercial zones, residences, etc.

The touristic capital concept allows the following hypothesis to be formulated regarding the transformation of tourist resorts: Resorts' variable capacity to *accumulate* (i.e. *capitalise on*) competitive tourist advantages, which enable them to sustain the *relay* (as in a relay race) between different forms of tourism over the course of time, or to *convert* these advantages (i.e. this *capital*) in the context of active restructuring strategies, can explain change in the course of their trajectories. Conceptualising the touristic capital as an advantage within a network of places also necessitates the empirical reconstruction of the global tourism field. It is therefore an attempt to better understand how the network of tourist places emerges and how the relative importance of tourist resorts has continued to change throughout history. The touristic capital concept captures this relativity, especially through its insistence on the symbolic dimensions. This symbolic capital reflects the value of a resort in the global tourist field.

However, tourist resorts do not only change in the tourism field, they also participate in other fields. This is especially apparent when local tourism experiences a crisis and connecting to other fields besides tourism becomes necessary. For instance, many resorts have developed congress centres to capitalise on their accommodation capacity, which tourists may fill. To enter the congress field, such resorts use their advantages that, relative to those of metropolises, have proved to be appealing over the last 70 years: their landscapes, small-size settlements and recreation activities combined with adequate infrastructures (congress centre, hotels, knowledge in catering, etc.). This seems to be particularly clear within metamorphosis trajectories (Clivaz et al. 2011) during which places lose symbolic capital in the tourist field, but try to convert this symbolic capital into advantages in other fields. Another example refers to the real estate field in which tourist places are either positioned as permanent or secondary residences of finance centres, international corporations, or international associations. These places become interesting as real estate investments, not as tourist place.

12.5 Conclusion

Tourism development over the last 200 years has been a dynamic process. The transformation of tourist resorts is linked to the multiple processes of reconfiguration of the economic, social, geographical and cultural contexts. Specifically, despite the remarkable persistence of some attractions and places, that which is recognized as a tourist attraction is regularly revised (Equipe MIT 2011). With the globalisation of tourism, the ever expanding tourism field is subject to ever new places entering it, while other places exit it. Newcomers modify the web of interdependencies and, therefore, the touristic capital of each tourist place. The concept of resorts' touristic capital in a global tourism field may help us better understand several important problems.

Firstly, the accumulation and engaging of touristic capital could be the key element to understanding why resorts have continued to develop tourism activities for more than 150 years despite various crises and reconfigurations of the tourist gaze. Governance and institutional resource capital, urban and reputation capital as well as monetary and knowledge capital are engaged in only one sector, namely tourism; no attempt is undertaken to diversify the economy. The only diversification processes refer to tourism where the scope and the depth of the activities change over time. Zermatt is a case in point (Roy et al. 2012; Guex 2016; Sauthier 2016): Huge crises, such as those at the end of the *Belle Époque* tourism (1870–1914), did not affect the local tourist activity. The invention of Alpine skiing was used as an opportunity to change the business model from only Alpinism towards a summer *and* winter resort. Since 1960, Zermatt has had a higher winter than summer clientele, and offered about 2 million bed nights and around 20,000 beds in 2010. It has become a highly diversified, global mass-tourism resort, serving as a recreation place for a huge diversity of people, including alpinists, visitors, skiers as well as the wealthy and the middle-class of more than 100 nationalities.

Secondly, the collapse of tourist resorts may be explained by an incapacity, due to political struggles and diverging monetary and knowledge capital, to transform the accumulated touristic capital into a renewed tourism sector after a tourism crisis. Finhaut (Wallis) is a case in point (Sauthier et al. 2012; Guex 2016; Sauthier 2016): Contrary to Zermatt, the crisis at the end of the *Belle Époque* brought tourism to an end. In 1912, Finhaut – in the canton of Wallis in Switzerland – was the second most important tourist resort after Zermatt, but thereafter struggled to recover after the loss of its English clientele. Low urban capital – tourism had not changed the village structure into a more developed urban node – did not allow for utilising the touristic infrastructures for other purposes. The reputational capital was rapidly destroyed and could not be rebuilt. Several attempts were made to reconnect with tourism through supposedly radioactive water cures and skiing, but these activities competed with other resources, such as hydro-electricity exploitation. Today, Finhaut is a village with 300 inhabitants who work in the nearby cities; only one tourist site (the barrage d'Emosson) remains and the remaining hotels have been transformed into apartments.

Thirdly, the fungible nature of the various capital elements leading to other kinds of capital and an urbanisation process, in which the tourism valorisation of objects gives way to alternative valorisations, may explain the metamorphosis of resorts into highly diversified resort regions (Soane 1993). Montreux is a case in point (Guex et al. 2012; Guex 2016; Sauthier 2016): The end of the *Belle Époque* tourism in 1914 brought a brutal decrease in the number of tourists. The 1912 peak of a bed capacity of 7500 – probably one of the largest in the world at that time – collapsed to only 3000 within 10 years, of which only 2500 were left in 2010. During the rise of tourism from 1850 to 1910, the population of Montreux increased from 3000 to 20,000. All the introduced urban amenities (electricity, telephone, telegraph, banks, etc.) triggered an important urbanisation process. This reconfiguration of the local system made use of the tourist infrastructure, transforming it into residences as well as into congress and convention spaces. Several attempts were made to reconnect with tourism (the Montreux Jazz festival, the heritage, Chillon castle, wine tourism, etc.). A new urban regime, in which hotel managers do not play a central role, is now in place. Montreux is currently a highly diversified city within the Lemanic metropolis, with tourism still playing a role, but as just one among many other activities. Montreux can therefore be interpreted as a successful restructuring rather than a decline.

In sum, we contend that the variable capacity of resorts to *accumulate*, i.e. *capitalise on* the competitive tourist advantages that enable them to sustain the *relay* between different forms of tourism over the course of time, or to *convert* these advantages in the context of active restructuring strategies, can explain the variable character of tourist resorts' trajectories.

Through this analysis, the three distinctive characteristics of our approach emerge. Firstly, the crucial importance of considering the territorial form in order to avoid analysing the tourism in a place instead of the local territorial system. The transformation of the place quality is an issue for resort development. Resorts do not remain resorts, but evolve into different territorial forms, which have to be taken into account if we are to understand how tourism activity can be maintained or transformed over time. The urban quality, i.e. the accumulation of an urban capital in terms of diversity, density and centrality, seems to be crucial for resilience to crises. Secondly, the uneven capacity for dealing with crises is only partially dependent on strategies and equally dependent on a resort's position within a global network of tourist places. Each new innovation over the past 200 years has put tourist resources at risk of depreciation, due to changing images and practices. The promotion of the Mediterranean Sea as a major summer destination triggered the obsolescence of British seaside resorts as well as the stagnation of Alpine mountain resorts. Tourist cultures and tourist gazes constantly modify the global network of tourist places. The growing number of new wealthy and middle-class tourists who can access tourism practices in all major metropolises allows certain selected resorts to diversify their clientele and to respond to the risk of obsolescence. This response is related to the local society's knowledge and governance capacity.

Thirdly, tourist resources are a very complex problem if they have to be produced and reproduced over time. These practices regard geographical places with a certain tourist gaze and produce ever new potential resources as monetary interactions, but local operators mobilise and construct knowledge, invent, make use of and enforce regulations in order to derive monetary capital from tourism resources. However, local operators also have the problem of regulating their secondary resources, such as water, soil, urbanism and public space, which tourists use but do not pay for. Conflicts about the ownership and the management of resources have been identified as a crucial element in responses to crises.

The interpretation of the different resort trajectories as uneven and engaging differently constituted touristic capital as well as the conversion of this capital into other forms of capital seems an important step for a more thorough analysis and explanation of what happens to tourist resorts over a long period.

References

Agarwal, S. (1997). The public sector: Planning for renewal? In G. Shaw & A. Williams (Eds.), *The rise and fall of British coastal resorts: Cultural and economies perspectives* (pp. 137–158). London: Cassell.

Agarwal, S. (2002). Restructuring seaside tourism the resort lifecyle. *Annals of Tourism Research, 29*(1), 25–55.

Agarwal, S. (2012). Relational spatiality and resort restructuring. *Annals of Tourism Research, 39*(1), 134–154.

Antonescu, A., & Stock, M. (2014). Reconstructing the Globalization of Tourism: A Geohistorical Perspective. *Annals of Tourism Research, 45*, 77–88. https://doi.org/10.1016/j.annals.2013.12.001.

Bourdieu, P. (1984). Quelques propriétés des champs. In *Questions de sociologie* (pp. 113–120). Paris: Minuit.

Bourdieu, P. (1992). La logique des champs. In *Réponses. Pour une anthropologie reflexive* (pp. 71–90). Paris: Seuil.

Bourdieu, P. (2012). *Sur l'Etat : cours au Collège de France (1989–1992)*. Paris: Seuil.

Butler, R. (1980). The concept of the tourist area cycle of evolution: Implications for management of resources. *Canadian Geographer, 24,* 5–12.

Butler, R. (Ed.). (2006). *The tourism area life cycle. Conceptual and theoretical issues.* Clevedon: Channel View Publications.

Camagni, R., & Cappello, R. (2013). Regional competitiveness and territorial capital: A conceptual approach and empirical evidence from the European Union. *Regional Studies, 47*(9), 1383–1402.

Chadefaud M. (1988). *Aux origines du tourisme dans les pays de l'Adour : du mythe à l'espace : un essai de géographie historique.* University of Pau: University Press.

Christaller, W. (1955). Beiträge zu einer Geographie des Fremdenverkehrs. *Erdkunde, 9*(1), 1–19.

Clivaz, C., Nahrath, S., & Stock, M. (2011). Le développement des stations touristiques dans le champ touristique mondial. In P. Duhamel, B. Kadri, & P. Violier (Eds.), *Tourisme et mondialisation.* Paris: ETE.

Cooper, C. (1997). Parameters and indicators of the decline of the British seaside resort. In G. Shaw & A. Williams (Eds.), *The rise and fall of British coastal resorts: Cultural and economies perspectives* (pp. 79–101). London: Cassell.

Corbett, T. (2001). *The making of American resorts (Saratoga Springs, Ballston Spa, Lake George).* Piscataway: Rutgers University Press.

Darbellay, F., Clivaz, C., Nahrath, S., & Stock, M. (2011). Approche interdisciplinaire du développement des stations touristiques: le capital touristique comme concept opératoire. *Mondes du Tourisme, 4 ,* 36–48. https://doi.org/10.4000/tourisme.543.

Demetriadi, J. (1997). The golden years. English seaside resorts 1950–1974. In G. Shaw & A. Williams (Eds.), *The rise and fall of British coastal resorts: Cultural and economies perspectives* (pp. 49–75). London: Cassell.

Equipe, M. I. T. (2002). *Tourisme 1. Lieux communs.* Paris: Belin.

Equipe, M. I. T. (2005). *Tourismes 2. Moments de lieux.* Paris: Belin.

Equipe, M. I. T. (2011). *Tourismes 3. La révolution durable.* Paris: Belin.

Guex, D. (2016). *Tourisme, mobilités et développement regional dans les Alpes Suisses. Montreux, Finhaut, et Zermatt du 19ème siècle à nos jours.* Neuchâtel: Alphil.

Guex, D., Roy, J., Sauthier, G. (2012). *La trajectoire historique du développement touristique de Montreux entre 1850 et 2010.* Working Paper de l'IUKB (2).

Harvey, D. (2001). *Spaces of capital: Towards a critical geography.* Edinburgh: University Press.

Jeannerat, H. (2013). Staging experience, valuing authenticity: Towards a market perspective on territorial development. *European Urban and Regional Studies, 20*(4), 370–384.

Judd, D,. & Fainstein, S., (dir.), (1999). The Tourist City, New Haven, Yale University Press.

Löfgren, O. (1999). *On holiday: A history of vacationing.* Berkeley: University of California Press.

Logan, J. R., & Molotch, H. L. (1987). *Urban fortunes. The political economy of place.* Berkeley: UC Press.

Lorentzen, A. (2009). Cities in the experience economy. *European Planning Studies, 17*(6), 829–845.

Lorentzen, A., & Jeannerat, H. (2013). Urban and regional studies in the experience economy: What kind of turn? *European Urban and Regional Studies, 20*(4), 363–369.

Lunn, A. (1913). *Skiing.* London: Nash.

MacCannell, D. (2001). Tourist agency. *Tourist Studies, 1*(1), 23–37.

Martin, N., Bourdeau, P., & Daller, J.-F. (Eds.). (2012). *Les migrations d'agrément. Du tourisme à l'habiter.* Paris: L'Harmattan.

Mullins, P. (1991). Tourism urbanization. *International Journal of Urban and Regional Research, 15*(3), 326–342.

Pearce, D. (1987). *Tourism today. A geographical analysis.* London: Longman.

Perlik, M. (2011). Alpine gentrification: The mountain village as a metropolitan neighbourhood, *Revue de géographie alpine, 99*(1), online: URL: http://rga.revues.org/1370; https://doi. org/10.4000/rga.1370

Pine, B. J., & Gilmore, J. H. (1999). *The experience economy: Work is Theatre & every Business a stage.* Boston: Harvard Business School Press.

Plog, S. C. (1974). Why destination areas rise and fall in popularity? *Cornell Hotel and Restaurant Administration Quaterly, 14*(4), 55–58.

Putnam, H. (2000). *Bowling alone. America's declining social capital.* New York: Simon & Schuster.

Roy, J., Guex, D., Sauthier, G. (2012). *La trajectoire historique du développement touristique de Zermatt entre 1850 et 2010.* Working Paper de l'IUKB (3) – 2012.

Sauthier, G. (2016). *Pouvoir local et tourisme: jeux politiques à Finhaut, Montreux et Zermatt de 1850 à nos jours.* Neuchâtel: Alphil.

Sauthier, G., Guex, D., Roy, J. (2012). *La trajectoire historique du développement touristique de Finhaut entre 1860 et 2010.* Working Paper de l'IUKB (1) – 2012.

Shaw, G., & Williams, A. (1997). The private sector: Tourism entrepreneurship – A constraint or a resource? In G. Shaw & A. Williams (Eds.), *The rise and fall of British coastal resorts: Cultural and economic perspectives* (pp. 117–136). London: Cassell.

Soane, J. (1993). *Fashionable resort regions: Their evolution and transformation with particular reference to Bournemouth, Nice, Los Angeles and Wiesbaden.* Wallingford: CAB International.

Soja, E. (1989). *Postmodern geographies : The reassertion of space in critical social theory.* London: Verso.

Stock, M. (2001). Brighton & Hove, station touristique ou ville touristique? *Revue Géographique de Lyon-Géocarrefour, 76*(2), 127–131.

Urry, J. (1990). *The tourist gaze.* London: Sage.

Urry, J. (1997). Cultural change and the seaside resort. In G. Shaw & A. Williams (Eds.), *The rise and fall of British coastal resorts: Cultural and economies perspectives* (pp. 102–113). London: Cassell.

Williams, A., & Shaw, G. (1997). Riding the big dipper. The rise and decline of the British seaside resort in the twentieth century. In G. Shaw & A. Williams (Eds.), *The rise and fall of British coastal resorts: Cultural and economies perspectives* (pp. 1–18). London: Cassell.

Williams, A., & Shaw, G. (2004). *Tourism and tourism spaces.* London: Sage.

Mathis Stock is a professor with the Institute of Geography and Sustainability at Lausanne University (Switzerland), where he leads the research group "Cultures and Natures of Tourism". His research deals with the urbanising force of tourism, the controversies around tourism in cities, and mobility and multilocality approached from the perspective of practice theory. He dialogues with social theory and develops a theory of dwelling, posited at the heart of theoretical geography. He is editor-in-chief of the scientific journal *Mondes du tourisme.*

Christophe Clivaz is a political scientist and holds a PhD in public administration. He is an associate professor at the Institute of Geography and Sustainability at the University of Lausanne (Switzerland). His teaching (within the framework of the Master in Tourism Studies and the Certificate of Advanced Studies "Tourism, Innovation and Sustainability") as well as his research work focuses on issues of governance of tourist places (in particular mountain resorts and natural parks), on the comparative analysis of tourism policies and on the challenges posed by climate change to the tourism sector.

Olivier Crevoisier is an economist with interest in regional science and is a professor with University of Neuchâtel (Switzerland). His research deals with innovative milieus and visitor economies.

Leïla Kebir is an economist with interest in regional science. She is a professor with the Institute of Geography and Sustainability at Lausanne University (**Switzerland**).

Chapter 13
The Contemporary Expansion of Tourism as Third "Tourism Revolution"?

Philippe Violier

13.1 Introduction

Tourism as mobile mode of inhabiting the world has significantly changed over time. Invented in England at the end of the seventeenth century (Boyer 1996; Tissot 2000), it was initially a practice undertaken only by a small number of people and reserved for aristocrats and rentiers. A first change then occurred in the mid-nineteenth century resulting in a major increase in numbers due to the invention of the tourist guide, the adoption of railways for recreational purposes and the invention of tourist resorts (Equipe MIT 2005) and of tour operators (Tissot 2000). This expansion peaked in Europe in 1914, the outbreak of First World War (*Belle Epoque*) and the end of the so-called Gilded Age in the USA. The 1930s in the US and the 1950s–1960s in Europe then saw the beginning of mass tourism whereas there was much greater access to tourism in a context of strong economic growth throughout the Western World. Social evolution and the relative dissemination of wealth generates pressures which stimulate innovation and which in turn favour the consumption of tourism because "when a new productive system materializes, social change is, therefore, a prerequisite" (Dockès 1990, 44). The shift to mass tourism was made possible by technical and organizational changes such as the invention of low-cost hotels, particularly establishments belonging to Pueblos group created in the Balearic Islands, or the standardization of organized tours. To sum up, each step in the socio-technical system produces a reconfiguration of the tourist system.

Therefore, we work with the hypothesis of "tourism revolutions", i.e. a fundamental change of the entire tourism system. Tourism is here defined as a system,

P. Violier (✉)
Angers University, Faculty ESTHUA, Espaces et Sociétés Lab (UMR CNRS 6590), Angers, France
e-mail: philippe.violier@univ-angers.fr

© The Editor(s) (if applicable) and The Author(s), under exclusive license to
Springer Nature Switzerland AG 2021
M. Stock (ed.), *Progress in French Tourism Geographies*, Geographies of
Tourism and Global Change, https://doi.org/10.1007/978-3-030-52136-3_13

that is a set of interrelated elements (Knafou and Stock 2013), which constitute a social practice before being an economic reality: "Tourism is neither an activity nor a practice, nor an actor, nor a space, nor an institution: it is the whole as a system. And this system includes: tourists, places, territories and tourist networks, markets, practices, laws, values and a range of other social institutions" (Knafou and Stock 2013, 1018–1020). The constitution of a relatively autonomous economic system is the result of tourists wishing to use intermediaries to achieve their tourism projects. This emergence of tourism has been called "tourism revolution" by Boyer (1996). Analogous to the "industrial revolution", the "tourism revolution" is defined as invention of a new social practice characterised as a system whose finality is the recreation of individuals outside of their quotidian space-time. Equipe MIT (2011) built on that idea to propose the reconstruction of the history of tourism as "three revolutions". The current tourism system is seen as the "third tourism revolution" because of the expansion as individualised mass tourism on the global scale. This third tourism revolution comes after the invention of tourism around 1800 as first revolution and the mass tourism with its long emergence from the 1870s until the 1970s as second tourism revolution.

The following questions are asked: What are the characteristics of the current tourism system? What are the changes that occurred from the "traditional" mass tourism? The chapter will examine the following characteristics of this third revolution: (1) access to tourism for non-Western societies which make up the bulk of those tourists involved in this emerging phenomenon, while at the same time the collapse of the Soviet bloc confirmed the preference for the capitalist tourism model and led to the disappearance of the Communist-era tourism model; (2) the diversification of activities with an increasing demand for personalization in the West, and which is also gaining popularity on the fringes of emerging societies, partly driven by innovations in the techno-digital sector and the renewal of Fordist tourism among the middle classes in emerging societies; (3) tourism development for the whole world through processes of diversification, including the invention of new activities and its intensification by emerging societies.

13.2 More Tourists Than Ever in an Increasingly Tourist-Oriented World

The dynamics of tourism are characterized by strong growth in the number of people traveling and a level of spatial expansion such that the whole world has now become a touristified space. This has an effect in both directions as most societies both welcome tourists and undertake tourism themselves. This evolution is the culmination of three processes. Firstly, in developed countries tourism has become a normal activity. Secondly, the advent of the industrial revolution in so-called emerging countries has introduced tourism to societies that were hitherto totally excluded from it. And thirdly, barriers to destinations which restricted visitors are now being progressively removed.

13.2.1   The Tourism Explosion in Developed Countries

The shift in the social diffusion of tourism which began in the mid-twentieth century is now continuing in developed countries. In all liberal, anciently tourist-orientated countries, flows continued to grow despite the turn down in rates of economic growth seen following the so-called "Glorious Thirties" period, and despite the slowdowns and financial slumps due either to reductions in purchasing power or political events such as terrorist attacks or health crises such as the SARS outbreak. In France, for example, Gilles Caire (2015) showed that tourism activities had become an essential element for people's happiness and self-esteem. This has remained the case despite the difficulties, especially as economic changes resulting in job losses and unemployment mainly affect the least qualified members of society who already travel less than the rest of the population.

The dynamic has been reinforced by the disappearance of the communist economic and political model identified by Jacques Lévy (2008) as an interruption of the process of globalization. In communist countries the collapse of the Soviet Union spelled the end of a centrally-planned tourist system which limited both domestic and international mobility. In these states, people's mobility was strictly controlled both for those exiting the country, a privilege reserved for elite members of the unique ruling-party, and to allow the limited entry of foreigners keen to discover these countries. These latter countries were held back by strict travel rules such as the need to make a visa application several months in advance, the obligation to declare each day's accommodation, the constraints of having a daily currency exchange rate fixed by the authorities at a comparatively high level, especially in relation to the opportunities for actually spending the money. The internal market was also controlled and most travel was organized by an authorized company and then only to intended establishments. Political collapse resulted in a relaxation of the rules relating to freedom of movement and led to the transition to a capitalist economy, including in the tourism sector. As a consequence, the inhabitants of the former USSR and its so-called satellite countries have joined the universal system.[1]

---

[1] Some authors include Russia in the list of emerging countries (in the acronym BRICS, the R stands for Russia) which we will deal with in the next point. This approach is questionable and represents probably an overgeneralization. This is because the USSR was at the time the second largest economy in the world in addition to having a permanent seat on the UN Security Council and its political collapse did not permanently and radically impinge on its economic power beyond the structural weaknesses which remain, such as its over-reliance on the energy and mining sectors. The transitional confusion suggested that Russia ought to be downgraded, but Putin's rise to power and his voluntarist policy has shown that it is a force to be reckoned with in a multi-polar world.

However, distance continues to restrict the extent of flows and globalization remains a regionalization factor in the sense that most tourist trips are made within a specific region of the world and transcontinental tourist trip are still a minority, as shown in Table 13.1. We note that arrivals from a state on the same continent still represent more than 60% of all visitors. Morocco is an exception since flows from Africa represent only 3.7% of visitors, but the conventional continental breakdown does not actually correspond to geopolitical, social and economic reality. Morocco, on the fringes of Europe, welcomes lots of visitors from this continent who represent nearly 88% of all visitors, a large part of whom are Moroccans living abroad.

To these international tourists, we have to add what is called "domestic tourism" in order to give an adequate representation of the current significance of tourism in developed countries. This domestic tourism is, like its international counterpart, difficult to assess because the UNWTO takes a global approach to non-migrant mobility and aggregates travel for all purposes (business, pilgrimages, visits to relatives and friends, etc.). However, we are not in a position to assess whether the share of relatives and friends is greater in domestic tourism than in international tourism. In any case, in all the countries of the world of large surface area the proportion of those who do not leave the country is greater than the proportion of those who cross borders. In France about 75% of people are tourists at least once a year and only 25% of them leave the hexagon, which includes individuals who frequent the overseas departments and regions and overseas territories.

Table 13.1 Arrival numbers of non-resident travelers from the same continent after UNWTO

Destination country	Total number of international tourists arriving in millions	International tourists arriving from the same continent in millions	International tourists arriving from the same continent shown as a percentage
USA	75.6	46	61
Brazil	6.6	4.5	68.7
France	82.6	64.5	78.1
Spain	75.3	66.4	88.2
Italy	52.4	44.8	85.6
South Africa	10	7.5	74.6
Morocco (as a whole)	10.3	0.4	3.7
Morocco (Europe)	10.3	3.9	38
Morocco (Moroccans Resident Abroad)	10.3	5.2	50
Japan	24	20.7	85.9
Thailand	32.6	22.6	69.2
Australia	8.3	5.2	62.4
New-Zealand	3.5	2.4	69

Source: UNWTO (2018)

13.2.2 Access to Tourism for Non-Western Societies

In the last forty years, the increasing number of people traveling around the world is due to the access to tourism for non-Western societies, whereas up until the 1980s tourism remained a Western privilege. This change has not affected every country but is widely observed. Economic reform is accompanied, generally, by tourism reform. Tourist activities, hitherto reserved for a limited elite have spread to the middle classes, as Peyvel (2015) shows concerning Vietnam. The involvement in tourism of emerging countries has been progressively increasing since the end of the twentieth century. In the 1960s and 1970s Japan and other countries in its zone of influence, Taiwan, South Korea and Singapore, had already joined the industrial revolution but the figures involved were relatively small, particularly due to the significance of Confucian ethics. According to the values approved by this ideology, respect for authority means one should not take paid holidays if your boss does not, although holidays were already much more limited than in Western Europe. On the contrary, from the 1980s onwards all emerging countries had joined the tourism revolution and especially the densely-populated continental states such as Brazil or China, which therefore affected global flows.

China is a case in point. The extension of the tourism system based on free enterprise was accordingly favored when economic reforms (introduced by Deng Xiaoping in China starting in 1979) began to affect the population's mobility from 1986 onwards. Although the overall trend is clear, there is a statistical bias. The statistics, when referring to the term "tourist", include very heterogeneous forms of mobility and particularly within the country itself. On the other hand, the political system which recognizes the newly reintegrated territories such as Hong-Kong and Macao, and which controls the borders, leads to an overestimation of the flow of Chinese tourists because they include people crossing from the Mainland into the two former colonies and vice versa. As such, out of the 141.8 millions arrival recorded by China, 81 million came from Hong Kong and 23.5 million from Macao (according to the UNWTO 2018). This entry by China into the club of tourist nations has however turned tourism in East and South-East Asia upside down because of the distance effect which favors countries in close proximity. For many countries which have seen a significant tourism expansion, China has become by far the largest tourist target-market, especially Thailand (Violier and Taunay 2020).

This extension of the tourist system was first rolled out in a relatively divided capitalist world on the scale of continents or regions of the world: Chinese tourists traveled with Chinese companies and Europeans were escorted by European TOs. But from 2015 onwards we saw an interpenetration which foreshadows the emergence of global leaders. As such, the holdings of the major hotel groups now reveal investments from around the world, from Europe, North America, China and the Middle East. The Club Méditerranée company, an emblematic symbol of the social diffusion of tourism in France, is now owned by Fosun, a Chinese company. However, this dynamic is not continuous as seen by the contract drawn up between the group Pierre et Vacances Center-Parc with the Chinese group HNA Group, looking to create a joint venture theoretically based on the Center-Parc model in China, and which was then the cancelled by the French group due to the level of indebtedness of their Chinese partner which was deemed to be excessive.

13.2.3 The Difficult Assessment of the Increase in Visitor Economies on a Global Scale

As a consequence of these changes, a widespread process of tourism diffusion is in progress around the world. Various methods can be used to measure it. The first approach exploits the data produced by the UNWTO. The international organization collects statistics compiled by each country and the UNWTO data allow us to produce a map which quantifies border crossings by individuals in the context of non-migratory mobility (Fig. 13.1). The comparison between the map of 1985 and that of 2015 provides confirmation that the East Asia region of the world is where the phenomenon of economic emergence and tourism is the most significant, both because of its continued growth and due to the huge population concerned.[2]

However, the data used here suffer from a range of limitations which distort the appreciation of the tourism phenomenon on a global scale, beyond the limitation of border crossings which we have already identified. First, the UNWTO has produced a generalized definition of tourism which is very broad. On the one hand, various different mobility-types are considered by the institution as being tourist-related. As such, business trips which depend wholly on the sphere of companies, and therefore work-related constraints, are included. Pilgrimages are similarly considered, even though a necessary program of rituals applies and individuals are unable to choose and visit sites which are imposed on them. We notice in particular that Saudi Arabia still does not issue tourist visas and that its international visitor numbers are mainly focused on the Hadj. In addition to that, trips to further the purposes of education or training are included. The organization has even introduced a category for "other reasons" which clearly shows that it is a flexible definition that leaves the context open to various erroneous interpretations. On the other hand, a trip is considered to be tourism-related when it falls within a very flexible range of nights away, from just a single night to up to an entire year. Even in the most economically advanced countries, which offer the greatest number of days off or holidays, the total never exceeds 40 days. Secondly, this definition by the UNWTO is open to interpretation by countries and several calculation methods are used (Stock et al. 2017). Finally, UNWTO enacts the two-fold dichotomy tourism/migration of international mobility. This distinction appears simplistic regarding the complex set of mobility practices and leads to interpretative problems.

---

[2]This is without including, as we have noted, those counting methods which in China accentuate the phenomenon.

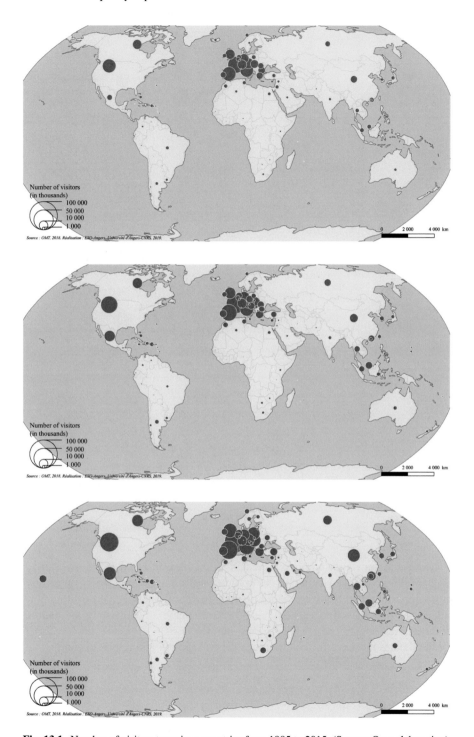

Fig. 13.1 Number of visitors to various countries from 1985 to 2015. (Source: Own elaboration)

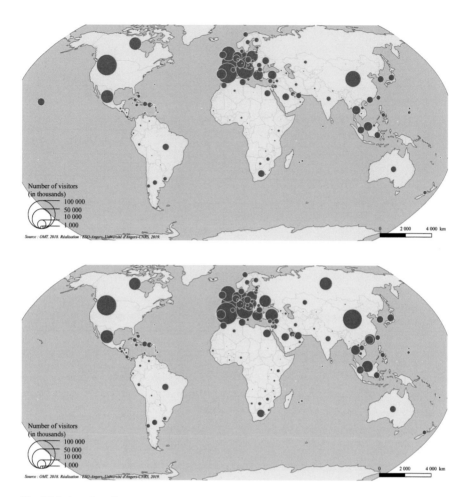

Fig. 13.1 (continued)

Moreover, the visitor-numbers provided on the basis of UNWTO statistics only concern people crossing international borders, while domestic tourism is generally more important. Although in small countries, the number of people traveling outside its borders may well exceed that of those moving around within the nation, domestic tourism is generally the greater part of tourism. However, the territorial mesh of states makes it difficult to gauge the real growth of tourism. In continental

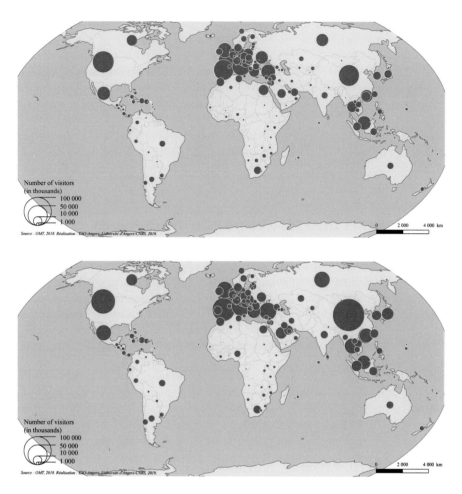

Fig. 13.1 (continued)

nations there are many state subdivisions (the various provinces in China or states in the USA) that may have a greater population than many countries in the world. Inhabitants of these continental states travel considerable distances – for instance 5.000 km from New York to Los Angeles – without being considered so-called international tourists, whereas in Europe a distance of 5.000 km would bear the attribute of international tourism.

A geography of tourism unburdened by institutional statistics is at stake. Alternative approaches are possible in order to build an image of global tourism which favours the scale of elementary sites, instead of relying on the extremely heterogeneous mesh of states. One of these prefers a historical approach by looking at the tourism development of sites and is based on the analysis of tourist guides (Antonescu and Stock 2014; Antonescu 2016). A second looks at the appearance of place names in scientific and other journals (Equipe MIT 2011; Gay and Decroly 2018). A third uses tour operator catalogs (Violier 2011; Taunay and Violier 2015; Violier and Taunay 2020). The latter option will be discussed further in Sect. 13.3.4. of this chapter.

13.3 The Shift from Mass Tourism to Individualized Mass Tourism

The affirmation of an individualized mass-tourism system is also characterized by the tension between the persistence of mass tourism in the sense of a broad social access of people across all social classes, and a dynamic of customized tourist practices, where bundles of activities are personalized and individualized (Cuvelier 1998). This tension is between an ever broader access to tourism and the diversification of practices. Although tourism has become a widespread practice in advanced industrial countries, and which deserves to be called mass tourism in the sense of mass consumption and is accessible to the greatest number of people, it has also evolved.

13.3.1 Diversification of Activities

Although tourism remains a discriminating social practice in the sense that there is still a fringe of excluded individuals, it is nevertheless widely practiced in advanced industrial countries. This is especially relevant if we consider that in France among the 35–40% of people who do not take vacations in a given year, for half of them it is a choice and not a constraint, albeit also an economic one. Authors who lament that tourism is not fully generalized often fail to specify that those having not gone away on holiday do not provide economic reasons (Khiati and Gitton 2016) to explain their actions. For 50% of these people there is effectively the problem of economic exclusion, but the others invoke various reasons. Some are structural, like the preference for discovering their home region, while others are conjunctural (expecting a new child, building a new home etc.) (Khiati and Gitton 2016).

Yet, activities have become more diverse and highly individualized. Firstly, tourism requires a mastery of the techniques in order to access modes of transport, accommodation, tourist places etc. Even adopting spatial technologies such as

Table 13.2 Tourism worlds and individual choice

Worlds as defined by Pascal Cuvelier (1998)	Geographical dimensions		Individual choice
	Distance	*Heterogeneity*	
Simple	Weak	Weak	Independence
Self-organized and individually tailored	Medium	Medium	Encounter with otherness as an exciting experience
Organized or flexible and individually tailored	High	High	
Fordist Standardized services	Very high	Very high	Rest

trains, planes, cars, etc. requires the use of knowledge. The capacities and skills acquired in fact lead to significant inequalities between individuals (Löfgren 1999; Equipe MIT 2002; Lucas 2014; Guibert 2016). Secondly, people's individual projects are also diversified by the effects of distinction (Bourdieu 1979; Urry 1990), where tourist places and tourist practices are valued for symbolic profits. The TO's discourse bear witness to this trend with an increase in the number of references to values such as sustainable development, romance, social responsibility or relationships with others. Some highlight the opportunity to meet local populations while others boast about being alone with images of deserted beaches.

Economist Pascal Cuvelier (1998) proposes a model of so-called "tourism worlds", which combines the complexity of the offer (ranging from standardized to flexible modes of organisation with the desire for autonomy or heteronomy of individuals. He concludes several "worlds" are juxtaposed in current tourist practices (Table 13.2). However, a geographical approach underlines the fact that the individual choices do not only take into account these two factors but also two of the key spatial dimensions, i.e. distance and heterogeneity of the world. Beyond that, very skilled individuals may opt for a fully-organized service as long as it corresponds to their wishes at the time: for example, a desire for rest and relaxation and therefore they want an inclusive package.

13.3.2   Diversification of Tourist Practices Supported by the Diffusion of the Techno-Digital System

In fact, the flexible mode of organization within the tourism industry did not replace a standardized mode but instead increased the scope of options. For the diversification of access modes to tourist places, the diffusion of digital technologies within the tourism production mode has been playing a key role, especially for the shift towards a personalized mass tourism. This can be interpreted as a new innovation cycle, where a set of innovations has accompanied the shift to personalized mass tourism and has made it possible, in the same way that the advent of mass tourism emerged due to a succession of technical and organizational innovations, such as economy hotels or mass tour operators.[3] The major technological revolution, which allowed for the switch to personalization came from the infusion of tourism by digital technology: every "tourism world" has been affected. The stakeholders involved in standardized mass tourism have been adopting the innovation to better control their costs. For instance, the tour operator Marmara operates differently according to the destination: on the one hand, it offers destinations of the southern and eastern Mediterranean areas, which combine medium-distance and a relative degree of "otherness". This kind of standardized holiday guarantees a certain required volume of customers in order to make a profit on the number of holidays sold and not because the unit cost is particularly low. To achieve this, Marmara mostly sells its holidays online, which allows them to control their operating costs. On the other hand, more distant destinations such as the islands in the Indian Ocean, the Caribbean or Southeast Asia, require higher access costs and expose people to greater levels of otherness which then limits the number of individuals likely to choose them. Marmara therefore uses more personalized and less online-marketing.

But digital technology not only allows for standardization, but also for personalization and disintermediation, which means putting people in direct contact with the local actors at their destination. This innovation is being led by TOs. The market has thus seen competition emerge in the form of VSBs operating solely on the internet and offering tailor-made solutions. The major companies in the sector have therefore been forced to adapt to this competition and this has not always been a successful transition. The use of digital technology and the search for economies of scale have forced firms to cut back the number of brands they use. A proliferation of web applications has made self-organized trips to destinations possible. Some provide access to sites and establishments while others give advice about the services available such as guided tours, visitor information, access to medical services, accommodation which accepts pets etc.

However, this addition of digital solutions has been used in certain experiments which have proved irrelevant and have been abandoned, such as dynamic packaging. This has been replaced with either a customized layout of preconceived blocks or, in destinations where the supply is concentrated such as in large cities, a choice between two categories of options, one for accommodation and the other for activities. This essentially changes the relationships between the various actors.

13.3.3 The Evolution of Intermediation

The choice of individuals to use intermediaries, or not, can be theorized according to the model presented in Fig. 13.2. This model is based on an analysis of activities, which compares two extreme situations, otherness on the one hand, and familiarity

---

[3] As reported by Miguel Segui Llinas (1998), the shift in the Balearic archipelago to mass tourism was accomplished by different economic actors using innovative strategies, for instance low cost hotels, increasing group size, lowering the qualifications, etc.

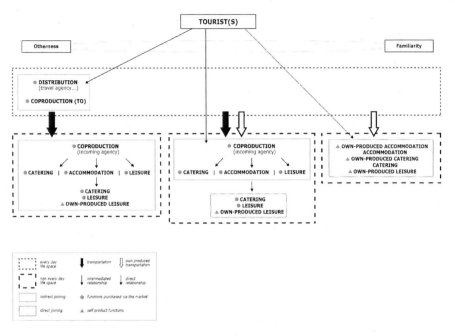

Fig. 13.2 A model of tourism intermediation. (Source: Own elaboration)

on the other. In one case, individuals are required to implement their tourism project with a strong objective sense of otherness, which is to say with horizons of otherness that can be defined (language, culture, ways of being, corporeal discomfort etc.) resulting from either the cultural or biophysical heterogeneity of the world. To counter this otherness, individuals look for "spatial technologies" (Stock 2008), such as an all-inclusive organized trip with the aim of discovery or a stay at a club hotel in the case of those looking for rest or the opportunity to play. The value chain (travel agent – tour-operator – carrier – host) works well. In the other case, in a situation of strong familiarity tourists enter into a direct or unmediated relationship with a variety of businesses. This is the case, in particular, for individuals who live in mainland France and who undertake their tourism activities there too. This case is the most common in French tourism: in 2017 only 19% of overnight stays induced by a private trip took place in a foreign country or one of the country's overseas territories.

However, it also occurs generally when non-residents have acquired an extensive skills-set due to frequent stays. In this case, a large proportion of the needs can be met by self-production by tourists, including finding food, transport and even accommodation. In between these two polar situations, an intermediate configuration can be defined which links the value chain for transport and accommodation functions to a constellation from which individuals select options according to their project. This preliminary approach consists of identifying the combinations of types of systems relating to the actors which are present.

13.3.4 The Spatial Concentration of Tourists

The analysis of tourism mobility shows that these inequalities have a nominal effect on the hierarchy of tourist places. They affect the options for access or comfort but destinations are only marginally impacted. To back up this assertion, we analysed tour operators' catalogues for specific destinations and compared the choice of destinations with the results obtained during interviews conducted with self-organized tourists. The results differ only slightly. While the catalogues push tourists towards all-inclusive tours, specific transport options and high-class hotels, the tourists prefer to use public transport and home-stay accommodation, yet both types of tourists practice the same destinations (Violier and Taunay 2020).

By analyzing the catalogues from various international companies, we developed a typology of tourist sites based on their global centrality, by which we mean the density of their connections to other places in the world.[4] This approach allows us to avoid two major methodological obstacles usually encountered in approaches on a global scale based on statistics provided by the World Tourism Organization. In fact, these statistics are (1) acquired through the use of a broad definition of tourism that confuses different types of mobility under the term "tourism" (such as business trips, VFR, pilgrimage, health, education, etc.), and (2) produced at the scale of individual countries or "territories", which is too large a scale for precise studies at the local level. Even if we use the latter statistics, the flows are at least measured at a regional administrative level and not directly at the tourist sites on a local level.[5] The analysis can be rendered more complex by including the levels of visitor numbers. Because of lack of data, we use here as proxy the frequency of citations of the toponyms of tourist places in the TO catalogs.

We identified three degrees of globalization or "global centralities" of places (see Fig. 13.3):

- *universal* global places: these are tourist places where people from every society in the world meet;
- places for *several worlds*: these are places where people from various worlds meet but not all nations are represented;
- places for a *single world*: these are where individuals from a limited number of worlds meet (one or two only);
- at last, we group in a fourth type of places, not mapped here, *outside the world*: those without any international tourists like North Korea, Iraq...

With this framework in mind, we can understand the following characteristics of global tourism. First, the *universal places* and the places of *several worlds* of the World fall into several categories:

---

[4] See also Stock (2017) on global centralities of tourist places within a global tourism field.

[5] For instance, a researcher looking at the statistics published by the Chinese government will find the number of travelers staying in Beijing, but nothing relating to those who took an excursion to the Great Wall which is of course a very popular option.

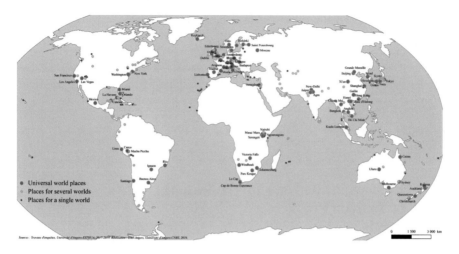

Fig. 13.3   Global centralities of tourist places. (Source: Own elaboration)

1. the metropolises of the world where the concentration of wealth has led to the concentration of monuments, museums and cultural establishments that all individuals in the different societies of the world want to visit;
2. the old metropolises that have lost their activity but are now animated by tourism such as Venice, Cusco, Xi'an...
3. incomplete metropolises, i.e. cities whose metropolitan functions are not fully developed but which are considered as metropolises in tourist relations, namely Las Vegas, Cancun, Orlando
4. the great sites, either biophysical such as Iguaçu, Victoria Falls, or built by men such as the Great Wall of China and Machu Pichu; the distinction between biophysical and historical is not simple as shown by the example of Uluru, which is considered cultural by the aborigines and natural, under the name of Ayers Rocks, by the others; we also note the absence of the pyramids of Egypt because of the prolonged stop of the visit of the country following the unrest that has been shaking the country since 2011.

The essential difference between the centrality of universal and several worlds is they are less frequented. Second, the places of only *one world*. This last category is in fact globally more made up of tourist places devoted to seaside rest. Seaside resorts are confined to the category of places for a single world because such practices, which around the world have developed on the margins and thus in places created *ex nihilo*, are systems related to relative proximity. Thus, the Americans favour the Caribbean Basin and the beaches of Florida and California, Asians generally prefer to head towards Thailand and Southeast Asia, whereas Europeans opt for the Mediterranean. Yet, the latter often travel to the Indian Ocean or the archipelagos off the West African coast for geographical reasons, because the Sahara is a southern obstacle in getting to seaside destinations. Only a few places are exceptions when the seaside development has reached an urbanity and diversification of urban functions that distinguish them from more ordinary seaside resorts. This is the case of Cancun or Nice.

We can conclude that personalization of activities does not bring about a geographical dispersion of individuals and social groups, but rather encourages the disparities between on the one hand the highly symbolic places where people from around the world meet, and, on the other, the less touristified peripheries. Global centralities of tourist destinations are linked to different tourism worlds constructed by market segmentation.

13.4 Homogenization and Diversification of Tourism Practices

The process of globalization has been fuelling a debate around the question of the standardization and homogenization of societies and individuals (Robertson 1992; Lévy 2008). The hypothesis formed is that densification of relations between places through communication and mobility lead to a reduction of the sense of otherness between societies and to standardization. Although we can acknowledge this process, it is nevertheless accompanied by a reverse process of diversification, or the emergence of new practices which in turn spread and enrich tourism, such as shopping for Asians (Duhamel 2018). In the same way, existing practices are diversifying as new objects are invented, such as the natural parks in the United States (Equipe MIT 2005). Which role tourism plays in this dialectical evolution? How tourist practices take part in homogenization and diversification of societies, and thus the globalization of tourism?

13.4.1 Homogenization

We contend the spread of tourism on a global scale is already a process of standardization, which has been accompanying the homogenization due to the industrial and capitalist revolution. At face value, it involves the generalization of *identical practices* despite of the heterogeneity of the world. For instance, Qianyan Sun shows (2013) that in Yunnan the Tiger Leaping Gorge was first visited and developed for tourism by Westerners, both as tourists and tourist-industry actors, which prompted the Chinese to take on these different roles. This shows that the spread of tourism is taking place by imitating the practices of Westerners taken as references both in the way of living the World through tourism and in the invention of the means that allow the implementation of these practices. The process of globalization by *imitation* of existent specific tourist practices can be observe, also apparent in the spread of specific practices like skiing, golfing, surfing etc.

More generally, similar "tourist modes of inhabiting" are observed, which we can interpret as universal ways of inhabiting the world rather than forms of homogenization (Taunay and Violier 2015). The dichotomy between the association of rest and stay on the one hand and discovery and touring on the other can be seen as a universal paradigm of tourist practices. This dichotomy plays out the following way. In the first case (rest and stay), individuals prefer to sleep at a tourist place chosen for the quality of its location and its infrastructure for a relatively long period, often for a week. This does not exclude secondary mobility, as an addition to the main reason for choosing the tourist place, and may include a tour of the surrounding areas. Our above comparison between the TO catalogs from different international companies reveals that this duality is systematically present. In the second case, a tour takes place via a network of tourist places, some of which are selected for their intrinsic visitor interest while others are chosen for their convenience, in particular to allow accommodation when distances become too great.

Finally, the activity of discovery also involves a universal dimension of relationships to the other. It has been observed that the Chinese will visit China's ethnic minorities, as Westerners have done before them (Taunay and Violier 2015). This is an issue of self-construction and apprehension of identity in the encounter with the other, even if it is difficult to achieve. Yet, tourists are characterized by their "omnivorous" tourist behaviour (Taunay and Violier 2015), which means their propensity to mix several activities in various combinations, even if a prevailing dominant tourist practice dictates the choice of site to be visited.

The analysis of the relationship between tourists and locals has been analysed as a transformation of cultural systems brought into contact, but acculturation, a concept forged to qualify the process, was then hijacked to be equated with acculturation, often vigorously imposed, even westernized, in the colonial and neo-colonial context that prevailed until the 1980s (Turner and Ash 1975; De Kadt 1979; Mathiesson and Wall 1982; Vasquez 1984; Crick 1989; Cazes 1992). These excesses have been pointed out (MacCannell 1976; Shaw and Williams 2002) and the encounter has been re-examined in a more dialogical approach highlighting the active role of the inhabitants in relation to the tourists (Picard 1992). In social psychology, the concept of interculturation emphasizes on the relational dimension of the encounter and the resulting exchanges (Clanet 1990; Guerraoui and Troadec 2000; Guerraoui 2009). This approach can be transposed to geography, as place appears to be an essential part of this interculturation. The beach of Kuta is praised in Indonesian tourist guides primarily because it allows people to see Westerners there and because this encounter tends to reduce the mystical fear of the sea (Pickel et al. 2018). Consequently, globalization can be interpreted not only as a means of homogenization but also of mutual learning.

13.4.2 Differentiation

This process of diffusion of tourism practices by homogenization is linked dialectically to a reverse process of differentiation which provides for an enrichment of tourism practices. The inclusion of previously excluded societies encourages the invention and dissemination of new practices. For instance, the creation of natural parks due to North American society can be interpreted as an entirely new tourist practice because it assembles a new quality of place, a new quality of people, new imaginaries to already existent practices (MIT 2005). In the context of emigration to the continent, the promotion of biophysical attractions was thought of as compensation for the division between the old continent with its rich cultural heritage and new countries, forcibly included in the Western world and emptied of their cultural references (MIT 2005). This invention was then distributed around the world, notably in Europe, where the twentieth century saw also the emergence of natural parks. In the process, it underwent a modification: conceived in a sparsely populated world, it has been transformed in the European context of a more densely and already urbanized space. The notion of "parks" in the United States in particular included historical memory sites and is therefore not reserved just for biophysical objects, as in the European context. In addition, its reception by the public is a central issue: North American parks stress the accommodation options, while in Europe, the closure and preservation prevail. This is one example of the diffusion of tourism accompanied by a process of differentiation. Many other examples can be identified, where the invention of new practices goes hand in hand with transformation in the dissemination processes, especially because of the differential appropriation of tourist practices by specific individuals and societies. They range from the invention, by US Americans in Europe in the 1920s, of the tradition of going to the Mediterranean Sea in *summer* instead of the winter, the invention of going to the mountains in winter instead of the summer in the 1870s in Switzerland, etc. (Equipe MIT 2005).

Contemporary Chinese tourist practices exemplify the dialectics between dissemination and differentiation seem to have two modalities. First, within the model of Elias and Dunning (1994), where leisure is seen as "de-routinizing" and a "relaxed control" of self-control and emotions, we can observe one of the places of relative relaxation of constraints which support tourism has been the beach for Western Societies.[6] Although in the Chinese world rest and relaxation is also seen as a tourist practice, it is valued unlike discovery in the sense of an opposite hierarchy between relaxation and discovery. In fact, the Chinese visit hot spas to relax. This activity takes place in establishments which take advantage of the hot natural springs located in low mountain areas. Bathing takes place either in the hotel rooms or in dedicated areas in close proximity to the accommodation and which are either

---

[6] The beach is effectively an invention which has included this space in the territory of society since the seventeenth century, first in the Netherlands and then in North-Western Europe, but was up until that point regarded as disgusting. See the work of Corbin (1988), Löfgren (1999), Equipe MIT (2005) for a thorough investigation of the changing signification of the beach for tourism.

Table 13.3 Different dominant activities at the seaside

Event	Dominant activity	Europe	China
Invention	Walking	17th to mid-19th centuries	1970/1980
Affectation 1	Sociability	1850	1990
Affectation 2	Games	1880	2010
Affectation 3	Rest	1920	?

covered or in the open air. People go there at the end of the day, at nightfall and, once outside, the sociability of the activity helps the relaxation. Stays are generally short, often for just one night, so people travel relatively short distances. The countryside is then, for the Chinese, the most effective destination for rest and relaxation. 70% of Chinese people travel to bucolic destinations to relax. In China, the beach is not nearly as popular as it is in Europe. In addition to that, the way people behave at the beach is different: having white skin is the clear priority and bodies are rarely exposed, especially those of the women (Coëffe et al. 2014). The use of the body for swimming or other nautical activities is less common and instead most people prefer to just sit or stand or walking around.

This comparison between the various seaside activities in different cultures reinforces the hypothesis of a gradual conquest of a new territory, i.e. the beach, by individuals in a society. It happens in phases (Table 13.3), where the beach is invested by ever new activities, where the body is more and more engaged. Informed by media reports and their own tourism experience (theirs around the World and those of westerners in China) of how westerners use the beach, the Chinese may pass through these different stages in a much shorter time than the two centuries required by Europeans.

Secondly, individuals who leave their world to undertake tourism activities transfer characteristics specific to their world to the places they visit. For instance, the Chinese tourists are specific in their systematic requirement for access to fashion boutiques during their practice of discovery in metropolises. The TO catalogues in particular highlight outlet villages which are shopping centres designed specifically for selling off end-of-series products. These are located on the outskirts of major cities, for instance in Austin (Texas), Barcelona (La Roca) or Paris (La Vallée Village located near the Disneyland Paris theme park). The Chinese distinguish themselves also at global tourist places, where individuals from societies round the world meet and interact, by transferring a different way of engaging with the place from their world. For example, the analysis of Chinese TOs' catalogues shows that on the Rio de Janeiro beaches – where people from all societies in the world gather – Chinese tourist prefer walking along the famous beaches of Copacabana and Ipanema, just as they do in Sanya on the island of Hainan, whereas Western tourists would practice the beach by swimming, beach volley etc. (Violier and Taunay 2020). This diversity in the way of behaving as a tourist depending on your society poses problems for the international companies which need to adapt their models to the societal realities. For instance, *Club Méditerranée* in China had to create karaoke rooms or fishing games to suit their Chinese guests. Yet, recent research carried out in China raises the question of the uniformity of the Chinese tourism world. The work by Christophe Guibert and Benjamin Taunay (2019) on the issue of the tourist body highlights the different ways of behaving at the beach in both Qintao, Shandong Province and Hainan Island. These approaches give rise to questions about whether several different Chinas exist.

13.5 Conclusion

Tourism is therefore an expanding system affected by a double-headed dynamic. On the one hand, the number of people on the move is increasing. Populations have been set in motion due to access to mass consumption, as well in anciently constituted tourist societies of the Global North as in developing countries of the Global South. On the other hand, the number of destinations has been increasing, and the tourism industry has been changing from a Fordist to a flexible accumulation model. Indeed, the standardization of tourism in the Global North facilitated social diffusion, yet is questioned by individuals and social groups in favour of more individualized practices. Therefore, several different models are available to individuals in the middle- and upper-classes in emerging countries. This diversification of tourist practices has been especially made possible due to the digitalisation of the tourism system. This expansion can be identified as third tourism revolution after the invention around 1800 and the mass tourism from the 1870s on.

From a geographical point of view, two interesting characteristics of the global tourism system can be analysed: first, the constitution of global centralities of destinations, where people from all over the world meet. They can be identified as universal global places, whereas places for *several worlds* and places for a *single world* construct other forms of centrality. However, the hierarchy of destinations has not been subject to significant change: the most popular tourist places around the world are still targeted by all the tourists, no matter which society they come from.

This diffusion of tourism around the world stimulates debate about the standardization of the world inevitably engendered by globalization in the sense that social norms including tourism are established and shared by all societies. However, we witness new forms of tourism that incorporates new practices as a result of contact with different cultures, or adjustments of existent tourist practices. Through the perspective of tourism, we gain therefore a specific understanding of globalization as a dialectical process of homogenization and global diversification.

References

Antonescu, A. (2016). La dynamique du champ mondial des lieux touristiques. *Constitution et analyse d'une base de données historique à partir d'un corpus de guides de voyages.* PhD dissertation, Lausanne University.

Antonescu, A., & Stock, M. (2014). Reconstructing the globalisation of tourism: A geo-historical perspective. *Annals of Tourism Research, 45*(1), 77–88. https://doi.org/10.1016/j.annals.2013.12.001.

Bourdieu, P. (1979). *La Distinction. Critique sociale du jugement*. Paris: Les Éditions de Minuit.

Boyer, M. (1996). *L'Invention du tourisme*. Paris: Gallimard.

Caire, G. (2015). Partir à tout prix. La résistance du désir de vacances des français. *Partance, 1*, 23–28.

Cazes, G. (1992). *Tourisme et tiers-monde. Un bilan controversé. Les nouvelles colonies de vacances*. Paris: L'Harmattan.

Clanet, C. (1990). *L'interculturel. Introduction aux approches interculturelles en éducation et en sciences humaines*. Toulouse: Presses Universitaires du Mirail.

Coëffé, V., Guibert, C., & Taunay, B. (2014). L'aire du bronze: jalons pour une analyse de la circulation et de l'appropriation du hâle (de Hawaï à Hainan). *L'Information géographique, 78*(1), 73–91.

Corbin A. (1988). *Le Territoire du vide : l'Occident et le désir du rivage, 1750–1840*. Paris: Flammarion.

Crick, M. (1989). Representation of international tourism in the social sciences: sun, sex, sights, savings and servility. *Annual Review of Anthropology, 18*, 307–344.

Cuvelier, P. (1998). Anciennes et nouvelles formes de tourisme: une approche socio-économique. *Tourismes et sociétés*. Paris: L'Harmattan.

De Kadt, E. (1979). *Tourism passport to Development? Perspectives on the social and cultural effects of tourism on developing countries*. New York: Oxford University Press.

Dockès, P. (1990). Formation et transferts des paradigmes socio-techniques. *Revue française d'économie, 5*(4), 29–82.

Duhamel, P. (2018). *Géographie du tourisme et des loisirs. Dynamiques, acteurs, territoires*. Malakoff: Armand Colin.

Elias, N., & Dunning, E. (1994). *Sport et civilisation: la violence maîtrisée*. Paris: Fayard.

Équipe, M. I. T. (2002). *Tourismes 1. Lieux communs*. Paris: Belin.

Équipe, M. I. T. (2005). *Tourismes 2. Moments de lieu*. Paris: Belin.

Équipe, M. I. T. (2011). *Tourismes 3. La révolution durable*. Paris: Belin.

Gay, J.-C., & Decroly, J.-M. (2018). Les logiques de la diffusion du tourisme dans le Monde: une approche géohistorique. *L'Espace géographique, 47*(2), 102–120.

Guerraoui, Z. (2009). De l'acculturation à l'interculturation: réflexions épistémologiques. *L'Autre, 10*(2), 195–200.

Guerraoui, Z., & Troadec, B. (2000). *Psychologie interculturelle*. Paris: Armand Colin.

Guibert, C. (2016). Les déterminants dispositionnels du "touriste pluriel". Expériences, socialisations et contextes. *Sociologies* (online), http://journals.openedition.org/sociologies/5688

Guibert, C., & Taunay, B. (2019). Usages sociaux et spatialités du bronzage en Chine. *EspacesTemps. net* [online] https://www.espacestemps.net/articles/usages-sociaux-et-spatialites-du-bronzage-en-chine/; https://doi.org/10.26151/espacestemps.net-9468-vg57

Khiati, A., & Gitton, F.-P. (2016). Moins d'un Français sur deux part au moins une semaine l'été. *Le 4 pages de la DGE*, 65. http://www.entreprises.gouv.fr/files/files/directions_services/etudes-et-statistiques/4p-DGE/2016-12-4p65-non-depart.pdf

Knafou, R., & Stock, M. (2013). Tourisme. In J. Lévy & M. Lussault (Eds.), *Dictionnaire de la géographie* (pp. 1018–1020). Paris: Belin.

Lévy, J. (Ed.). (2008). *L'invention du monde. Une géographie de la mondialisation*. Paris: Presses de Sciences Po.

Löfgren, O. (1999). *On holiday. A history of vacationing*. Berkeley: University of California Press.

Lucas, L. (2014). *Habiter touristique et agencement de l'espace urbain: le cas de Los Angeles. Recherche sur le concours des compétences des individus quant à leurs manières de faire avec les épreuves spatiales d'une métapole touristique*, PhD, Lausanne University.

MacCannell, D. (1976). *The Tourist. A New Theory of the Leisure Class*. Berkeley: University of California Press.

Mathiesson, A., & Wall, G. (1982). *Tourism, economic, physical and social impacts*. London/New York: Longman.

Peyvel, E. (2015). Devenir touriste dans un pays socialiste: le cas du tourisme domestique au Viêt Nam. In I. Sacareau, B. Taunay, & E. Peyvel (Eds.), *La mondialisation du tourisme. Les nouvelles frontières d'une pratique* (pp. 117–144). Rennes: Presses Universitaires de Rennes.

Picard, M. (1992). *Bali. Tourisme culturel et culture touristique*. Paris: L'Harmattan.

Pickel-Chevalier, S., Violier, P., & Parantika, A. (2018). Le tourisme, agent d'interculturation socio-spatial ? Le cas des pratiques touristiques littorales indonésiennes à Bali et à Java. *L'Espace géographique, 47*(2), 140–158. https://www.cairn.info/revue-espace-geographique-2018-2-page-140.htm.

Robertson, R. (1992). *Globalization. Social theory and global culture*. London: Sage.

Segui Llinas, M. (1998). *Les nouvelles Baléares. La rénovation d'un espace touristique mythique*. Paris: L'Harmattan.

Shaw, G., & Williams, A. (2002). *Critical issues in tourism. A geographical perspective*. Oxford/Malden: Blackwell Publishers.

Stock, M. (2008). Il mondo è mobile. In J. Lévy (Ed.), *L'invention du monde: une géographie de la mondialisation* (pp. 132–159). Paris: Presses de Sciences Po. https://www.cairn.info/l-invention-du-monde--9782724610413-page-132.htm.

Stock, M. (2017). Le concept de centralité à l'épreuve du tourisme. Réflexions critiques, in: Bernard N. & Duhamel Ph. (éd.), *Tourisme et périphéries. La centralité des lieux en question*. Rennes, Presses Universitaires de Rennes.

Stock, M., Coëffé, V., & Violier, P. (2017). *Les enjeux contemporains du tourisme. Une approche géographique*. Rennes: Presses Universitaires de Rennes.

Sun, Q. (2013). *Les pratiques touristiques en voyage auto-organisé en Chine*. Thèse de Géographie, Université d'Angers.

Taunay, B., & Violier, P. (2015). Un modèle chinois des pratiques touristiques? Analyse des spécificités et des invariants au niveau des pratiques et des lieux fréquentés par les touristes chinois et internationaux en Chine. In I. Sacareau, B. Taunay, & E. Peyvel (Eds.), *La mondialisation du tourisme. Les nouvelles frontières d'une pratique* (pp. 99–116). Rennes: Presses Universitaires de Rennes.

Tissot, L. (2000). *Naissance d'une industrie touristique. Les Anglais et la Suisse au XIXème siècle*. Paris: Payot.

Turner, L., & Ash, J. (1975). *The Golden Hordes. International Tourism and the Pleasure Periphery*. London: Constable.

UNWTO. (2018). *Yearbook*. Madrid: UNWTO.

Urry, J. (1990). *The Tourist Gaze*. London: Sage.

Vasquez, A. (1984). Les implications idéologiques du concept d'acculturation. *Cahiers de sociologie économique et culturelle, 1*, 83–121.

Violier, P. (2011). Les lieux du monde. *EspacesTemps.net*, Textuel, 22.08.2011.

Violier, P., & Taunay, B. (2020). *The tourist places of the world*. London: Wiley-ISTE.

Philippe Violier is a professor and dean of the Department of Tourism & Cultural Studies in Angers University (France). He was from 2010 to 2019 editor-in-chief of the scientific journal *Mondes du tourisme*. His work explores the relationship between actors in tourism space. Its latest research looks at globalisation of tourism and global centralities of tourist places, published in his book *The Tourist Places of the World* (Wiley-ISTE).

Correction to: Tourists and the City: Knowledge as a Challenge for Inhabiting

Léopold Lucas

Correction to:
Chapter 3 in: M. Stock (ed.), *Progress in French Tourism*
Geographies, **Geographies of Tourism and Global Change,**
https://doi.org/10.1007/978-3-030-52136-3_3

The chapter "Tourists and the City: Knowledge as a Challenge for Inhabiting" was previously published with incorrect affiliation. It has now been updated.

Léopold Lucas
Univ. Littoral Côte d'Opale, Univ. Lille, ULR 4477 - TVES - Territoires Villes
Environnement & Société, Dunkerque, France

The updated online version of this chapter can be found at
https://doi.org/10.1007/978-3-030-52136-3_3

Printed by Books on Demand, Germany